THE
YOUNG REBECCA

THE
YOUNG REBECCA

Writings of Rebecca West 1911–17

Selected and introduced by

Jane Marcus

INDIANA UNIVERSITY
Bloomington / Indianapolis

Manufactured in the United States of America

Library of Congress Cataloging-in-Publication Data
West, Rebecca, Dame
The young Rebecca: writings of Rebecca West,
1911-17 / selected and introduced by Jane Marcus.
p. cm.
Includes index.
Contents: The lamp of hatred—Battle-axe and scalping knife—A reed
of steel—A blast from the female vortex—Fleet Street
feminist—Miscellaneous slings and arrows.
ISBN 0-253-23101-9
I. Marcus, Jane. II. Title
(PR6045. E8A6 1989)
828'.91209—dc20

89-31300
CIP

1 2 3 4 5 93 92 91 90 89

for our mothers

in memory of Dame Rebecca's
Isabella Campbell MacKenzie Fairfield

and for mine
Ruth Healy Connor

Contents

Preface

I FIRST read Rebecca West's early feminist and socialist essays while studying the literature of the women's suffrage movement in Britain. Histories of the movement have largely ignored what she wrote on the subject and Dame Rebecca's journalistic writings from 1911 to 1917 have been buried in fading journals for too long. This selection, starting with articles written when she was eighteen, gives some indication of their brilliance and their permanent value. The quality of the writing equals the quality of the thinking. Her intellectual curiosity, her passionate responses to political and literary events, and her experience in the suffrage campaign brought forth a profusion of newspaper articles, clear, highly polished, often uproariously funny – but something more too. Hers was a journalism of the highest order. (She was, incidentally, the first woman reporter in the House of Lords, in 1924.) She was called by some a 'Bernard Shaw in petticoats', and he himself proclaimed a few years later 'Rebecca can handle a pen as brilliantly as ever I could, and much more savagely.'

All her life Rebecca West has written in praise of virtue and condemning wickedness. She finds moral relativism ridiculous, and says so in essays and her fiction. She was a propagandist of genius. Of the thousands of articles produced for and against the feminist movement in the first two decades of the century, Rebecca West's are among the finest. The essays collected here represent about half of what Rebecca West wrote in the six years from 1911 to 1917. Her Letters to the Editor alone would make a substantial book. And the uncollected essays from 1917 to the present would fill several large volumes.

Covering a wide variety of subjects from suffrage, national politics and trade unionism to domesticity, sex-antagonism and crime, and including many reviews of books and plays, she wrote then as a convinced socialist (notwithstanding her critical feelings about the emergent Labour Party) and a dedicated feminist, and consequently provoked a storm of correspondence. In this early work, beautifully written and always provocative, readers may judge for themselves the quality of Dame Rebecca's mind: they will be surprised to discover how much of what she wrote, even before the First World War, remains up-to-date, relevant to our own aspirations.

Without Dame Rebecca's help, encouragement and example this book would not have come to exist. Many people and libraries have helped as well. My special thanks to Jill Craigie, who first introduced me to Dame Rebecca, shared the early clipping books in her fine collection of Women's Suffrage Papers, gave me shelter and shared her abundant knowledge of the history of English feminism. Professor G. Evelyn Hutchinson, author of the bibliography of Rebecca West's writing, has been extremely helpful and has provided copies of essays and reviews from the Rebecca West Collection, Bienecke Library, Yale University. My thanks to David Erdman and his staff at the New York Public Library and my former student, Eileen Brookoff, for copies of the American articles. I am also grateful to participants in the Modern Language Association special session on Rebecca West, for sharing their knowledge of Rebecca West's work: Bonnie Zimmerman in particular, and Moira Ferguson, Elizabeth Janeway, Motley Deakin, and Marshall Best of Viking Press for encouraging us.

I am also indebted to the Fawcett Library, London, the British Library, Colindale and the Newberry Library, Chicago. My teacher, Samuel Hynes, first introduced me to Rebecca West's books and taught me how to find the works of 'lost' women writers in secondhand bookshops. A Research Fellowship from the National Endowment for the Humanities enabled me to do the research and writing for this book. My thanks to the staff of the Matematisk Institut, Aarhus Universitet, Aarhus, Denmark, which provided excellent facilities in which to work and an atmosphere in which feminism is the norm, not the exception. I am grateful to Virago Press, and to Ursula Owen in particular, for their enthusiastic editorial suggestions. Both Dame Rebecca and the editor thank Ursula Owen for her faith in the project and her ability to negotiate across the ocean.

The photographs were given to me by Dame Rebecca. Most of the essays are copyrighted in her name. We are grateful to the *Daily Telegraph* and to the owners of copyright for the *Daily News* and the *Daily Herald* for permission to reprint the articles from these newspapers. We have made every effort to find the owners of copyright for now defunct journals and apologise to any we may have missed.

JANE MARCUS, 1980

THE
YOUNG REBECCA

Part I

The Lamp of Hatred

Selected Articles from
The Freewoman and
The New Freewoman,
November 1911 – October 1913

Editor's Introduction

'A strong hatred,' Rebecca West wrote in *The Freewoman*, 'is the best lamp to bear in our hands as we go over the dark places of life, cutting away the dead things men tell us to revere.' What an ideal to oppose to the traditional lady with the lamp! But Rebecca West, though only nineteen, was a *woman* with a lamp. It was the feminine ideal of self-sacrifice that she was attacking as dangerous and reactionary, just as Ibsen had attacked it in his plays. Self-sacrifice was the most mortal of sins, a sin against life itself. She roused women to do battle with their own masochism, to weed out the natural slave, the victim in their souls. It was the dead souls of women she wanted to resurrect. As she herself put it, feminism was 'something more than a fight for the vote. It was a fight to grow in art, in science, in politics, in literature: it is a fight for a place in the sun.' A woman must no longer choose the role of the woman behind the great man, mother, sister, lover or wife to his genius. She must stop being the muse and become mistress of her own art, her own science, herself.

Like Olive Schreiner, Rebecca West claimed that sexual and political freedom were for strong women. At the age of eighteen she had already shown signs of this strength. She had, as she says, 'grown up in an air thick with conversation about literature, politics, music, painting'. Born Cicily Fairfield in 1892, she was the third daughter in the family. Her Anglo-Irish father was for a time a military man, then turned to journalism; her mother, coming from a musical family, had a superb gift as a pianist and struggled heroically against poverty to give her daughters a good education. Much of Rebecca West's early life was lived in London in virtual penury, but when she was ten the family returned to Edinburgh, their native city. She won a scholarship to George Watson's Ladies College in Edinburgh which she left at the age of sixteen. At seventeen, after studying at the Academy of Dramatic Art, she went on stage, but she herself admits she was not a success as an actress (one story has it that she was discovered reading a textbook on evolution during rehearsals!). It was during this period that she selected the pseudonym Rebecca West, after the character in Ibsen's *Rosmersholm* which she was once engaged to play by an optimistic manager.

Rebecca West had taken part in the agitation for women's rights from the age of fourteen when she was 'ragged and worried for wearing a Votes for Women Badge'. She had been a teenage dogsbody in the Pankhursts' organisation, the Women's Social and Political Union, and her first published piece had appeared, at the age of sixteen, in the form of a letter to the *Scotsman* on the subject of women's suffrage. In 1911, when she was just eighteen, she turned to employment on the staff of *The Freewoman*, which had just been founded. Years of passionate work and study were behind this talented debut. She had begun typing her poems and stories, alone in a room, with mumps, at the age of nine, and had been writing and reading ever since.

The Freewoman (later to become *The New Freewoman* and eventually the *Egoist*) holds an interesting place in the history of radical and feminist journalism. Financed by Harriet Weaver, and edited by Dora Marsden, the first number appeared on 23 November 1911. Years later, in 1926, Rebecca West recalled what it was like to work for the paper. 'Dora Marsden', she wrote in *Time and Tide*, another feminist weekly which she helped to found together with Lady Rhondda, Cicely Hamilton and Helen Archdale in 1920, 'left us a heritage in the unembarrassed honesty of our times.'

The paper was the creation of Dora Marsden, who was one of the most marvellous personalities that the nation has ever produced. She had, to begin with, the most exquisite beauty of person. She was hardly taller than a child, but she was not just a small woman; she was a perfectly proportioned fairy. She was the only person I have ever met who could so accurately have been described as flower-like that one could have put it down on her passport. And on many other planes she was remarkable. In her profession she had been more than ordinarily successful. Though she was still under thirty, she was head of a Training College for Teachers. She was one of the fighting suffragettes under Mrs Pankhurst, and in the course of her activities she had shown courage that even in that courageous company seemed magnificent. She had been to prison more than once, and had behaved with what would have been amazing heroism in any woman, but which was something transcendent in her case, since she was physically fragile and the victim of a tiresome form of ill-health.

She conceived the idea of starting *The Freewoman* because she was discontented with the limited scope of the suffragist movement. She felt that it was restricting itself too much to the one point of political enfranchisement and was not bothering about the wider issues of feminism. I think she was wrong in formulating this feeling as an accusation against the Pankhursts and suffragettes in general, because they were simply doing their job, and it was certainly a whole time job. But there was equally certainly a need for someone to stand aside and ponder on the profounder aspects of feminism. In this view she found a supporter in Mary Gawthorpe, a Yorkshire woman who had recently been invalided out of the suffrage movement on account of her injuries sustained at the hands of stewards who had thrown her out of a political meeting where she had been interrupting Mr Winston Churchill. Mary Gawthorpe was a merry militant saint who had travelled round the provinces, living in dreary lodgings, speaking several times a day at outdoor meetings, and suffering fools gladly (which I think she found the hardest job of all), when trying to convert the influential Babbits of our English zenith cities. Occasionally she had a rest in prison, which she always faced with a sparrow-like perkiness. She had wit and common sense and courage, and each to the point of genius.

These two came together and planned this paper, but Dora Marsden played the chief part of organising and controlling it throughout the whole of its life, for at the time Mary Gawthorpe was sick almost unto death.

Dora Marsden came to London with her devoted friend Grace Jardine, who was Martha to her Mary, and they found a publisher to finance them . . . I did not join them till later; in fact, I never wrote for *The Freewoman* till it had got such a bad name for its candour that I was forbidden to read it by my family, and thus I came to adopt my present pseudonym. The initial group consisted of Dora Marsden, Grace Jardine and a glorious red haired Bachelor of Science, who had been in and out of gaol for the cause, named Rona Robinson. They went at first for all the conventional feminist articles of faith. In their early numbers I fancy they represented as nearly as possible the same programme as the National Woman's Party. That programme has certainly been accepted by English women of the subsequent period with an extraordinary completeness. I think there are probably hardly any subscribers to the quiet orthodox woman's weekly of today, *Time and Tide*, who do not take it for granted that it is degrading to women, and injurious to the race to leave the financing of the mother and her children to the double-barrelled caprice of the father and the father's employer. They may differ regarding the specific remedies they proposed to end this state of affairs, but hardly any of them would defend it. I am convinced that this change of outlook is partly due to the strong lead given by *The Freewoman*. But the greatest service that the paper did its country was through its unblushingness. It parallelled the achievement of Miss Christabel Pankhurst, who did an infinite service to the world by her articles on venereal disease. The content of them was not too intelligent. It blamed the impurity of men for a state of affairs to which the impurity of women and the social system are also contributory causes. But it mentions venereal diseases loudly and clearly and repeatedly, and in the worst possible taste; so that England fainted with shock and on recovering listened quite calmly when the experts came forward and said that since the subject had at last been mentioned they might urge that the State could do this and that to prevent these diseases. Even so, *The Freewoman* mentioned sex loudly and clearly and repeatedly and in the worst possible taste; and likewise the content was not momentous. Those who laugh at Freud and Jung should turn back to those articles and see how utterly futile and blundering discussions on these points used to be even when they were conducted by earnest and intelligent people. But *The Freewoman* by its candour did an immense service to the world by shattering, as nothing else would, as not the mere cries of intention towards independence had ever done, the romantic conception of women. It pointed out that lots of women who were unmated and childless resented their condition. It pointed out that there were lots of women who were mated and who had children who found elements of dissatisfaction in their position. It even mentioned the existence of abnormalities of instinct. In fact it smashed the romantic pretence that women had as a birth-right the gift of perfect adaptation; that they were in a bland state of desireless contentment which, when they were beautiful, reminded the onlooker of goddesses, and when they were plain were more apt to remind them of cabbage. If this romantic conception had been true, there would have been no reason for the emancipation of women, since if they could be happy anywhere and anyhow, there was no need to alter their environment. It had to be admitted that women were vexed human beings who suffered intensely from male-adaptation to life, and that they were tortured and dangerous if they were not allowed to adapt themselves to life. That admission is the keystone of the modern Feminist movement.

Dora Marsden made her point with unique effectiveness, considering the length of the paper's life. Nevertheless the paper was coming to an end psychically when it came to an end physically. Its psychic death was due to the fact that Dora Marsden started on a train of thought which led her to metaphysics. She began to lose her enthusiasm for bringing women's industry on equal terms with men, because it struck her that industrialism destroyed more in life than it produced. She began to be sceptical of modern civilisation and this led her to preaching a kind of Tolstoyism which would have endeavoured to lead the world back to primitive agriculture. I waged war with her on this point in a correspondence that the curious might hunt down in the files. I signed myself therein Rachel East.

Described by one contributor as a 'technical trade journal on Womanhood', harassed by the censors, attacked by the press, banned by W. H. Smith's newsstands, *The Freewoman* had a brief happy life, bearing aloft the 'lamp of hatred', striking angry sparks off the flinty dogmatism of feminism and socialism. It was concerned to develop its own philosophy of free love and individualism, and from the start male writers as well as female were involved. It attempted to present a broader front than simply the vote in its feminism, and was often implicitly and sometimes explicitly critical of suffragette militant tactics.

By the time *The Freewoman* joined the other threepenny journals in 1911, the woman's suffrage cause alone produced several weekly journals; when the Woman's Freedom League broke with the WSPU, they edited *The Vote*, but it was scarcely competition for *Votes for Women*, the weekly paper of the WSPU, produced with great style and professional competence by Emmeline and Frederick Pethwick Lawrence, who contributed to the movement not only money and organisation, but a brilliant flair for propaganda. Christabel Pankhurst edited *The Suffragette* from exile in Paris after 1913, while her sister Sylvia edited the *Women's Dreadnought*, her paper for East End working women (later, when she supported the Communist Party, it became the *Workers' Dreadnought*).

Apart from Robert Blatchford's *Clarion*, and the *Daily Herald* whose editor was George Lansbury, the press, whatever their view of the women's movement, detested the militant tactics of the suffragettes. But though it would not be true to say that the press as a whole was against *votes* for women, some newspapers undoubtedly were. The anti-feminism in *The Times* reached its apogee in a violently misogynist attack on the whole sex by Dr Almroth Wright, a highly distinguished surgeon. *The Times* printed his article on its front page, throwing the full weight of its editorial powers to prevent women from getting the vote. Rebecca West's brilliant response to this article was both witty and scathing.

Though Rebecca West, as a feminist, regarded herself as living 'in a time of war', politically she too drifted away from the Pankhursts in 1912 when they initiated what she calls 'a programme of massive vandalism'. The divergence was not necessarily traceable to that development (though she didn't support their arson campaigns, which alienated them more than any other from most of the population). She considered the destruction of valuable property foolish rather than shocking; certainly she regarded it as less wicked than the attitude of political leaders who broke their pledges and ordered the forcible feeding of suffragettes at risk of life and health rather than accede to the demand for women's enfranchisement. Rebecca West left the WSPU partly because she was out of sympathy with Christabel's growing puritanism (Christabel wrote her famous book on venereal disease *The Great Scourge And How To End It* in 1913); she also disliked the constrictions implicit in concentration on a single purpose, working to win the vote. She recognised that the Pankhursts had a job to do and respected them for it, yet, for her part, she had also to feel free. Rebecca West was and is an artist, a creative thinker – and incidentally, unlike most daughters from the middle classes in those far off days, she had also to earn a living. And so she, and other 'New Women', so long announced in novels and plays, continued to write sane, witty prose in *The Freewoman* and then from 15 June 1913, for its successor, *The New Freewoman*.

The New Freewoman, in 1913, its single year of existence, published some of the frankest material on sexuality to appear for several decades. Dora Marsden herself published a series of articles suggesting a prostitutes' guild, to be run like a trade union, as well as a remarkable article on so called female 'frigidity'. But over the year, impatience with suffragette tactics and pressure from some of the male contributors (including Ezra Pound) to print poetry and translations, gradually took the paper further from feminist questions. On 15 December 1913, the issue announced that in future the paper would be called the *Egoist*. In June 1914 Dora Marsden resigned as editor, handing over to Harriet Shaw Weaver who later published James Joyce's *Portrait of the Artist as a Young Man* and extracts from *Ulysses* in its pages. (Rebecca West remembers Harriet Shaw Weaver as 'the Saint Bernard in human form who kept on and on rescuing James Joyce from the continuous alpine storm of misfortune which raged around him'. It seems odd now to her that the 'angel' of *The New Freewoman*'s philosophical anarchism and the champion of such a writer should become a member of the Communist Party.)

In the first five years of its publication, male writers including Ezra Pound and Ford Madox Ford, dominated the *Egoist*'s pages, and while its literary content increased, the feminist writing gradually diminished. For a while Rebecca West was literary editor, but she clashed with Pound, finding her judgements continually by-passed. 'The routine of the office was not impeccable,' she later wrote drily in *Time and Tide*. She saw that Ezra Pound, whom she had engaged for the paper, was determined to turn the *Egoist* into an *avant garde* paper with no special interest in feminism. She was also in poor health at this time. And so she severed her connections with the paper.

Rebecca West's articles in *The Freewoman* and *The New Freewoman* were serious and unsettling, no less for radicals than the rest of the population. She was a first-rate critic, whether reviewing books, criticising anti-suffragist philosophy, assaulting confused socialist thinking (albeit from the position of a socialist), or defending the cause of women. On reading Harold Owen, the anti-suffragist, who proposed marriage as a solution to the 'Woman Problem', Rebecca West tried to imagine what would happen 'if all we brazen hussies who are suffragettes and feminists became converted to Mr Owen's belief that every woman ought to throw up her economic independence and get some man to keep her! Think of us rushing about, trying with all that vitality we are at present misdirecting in clawing policemen and wrecking the home to attract men whom we knew did not value goodness in a woman! We *will* paint the town red!'

When the Marxist Belfort Bax argued that women were too privileged already and were never punished for criminal actions, she answered 'I publicly challenge him to prove the sincerity of that statement, to go forth in the disguise of a woman, smash a jeweller's plate-glass window and abstract a diamond necklace, assault a policeman, set fire to the National Liberal Club, and assassinate Sir Edward Carson. If he believes his own statement he will do it fearlessly. And I will pay the forty-shilling fine he pretends would be his "nominal punishment".'

She is now in some respects a solitary: certainly she claims to be free from any political ties. But in her writing of this period she was clear that the issues of feminism were inseparable from those of socialism. Reviewing a book on Indian women, she wrote in 1911 'There are two kinds of imperialists – imperialists and bloody imperialists.' She abhorred the author's advice that Indian women take up a 'genteel calling'. 'Now we in England know what this playing at wage-earning, this pathetic skulking on the outskirts of industry brought us to during the Victorian era. It brought women the most humiliating and the most hungry period of oppression they had ever endured. The feminist must take a bolder line. If she is going to enter the labour market she must take her capital with her – she must try from the first to capture the commanding forces of industry, from which she can dictate the conditions of her own labour.' She never fell into the trap of thinking that any woman in a position of authority assists the Cause. On the contrary, Rebecca West made clear that it is not a triumph to have a 'lady' on the London County Council. 'Now that she has proved our point of the equality of the sexes she must go; for the arguments of oppression are not less dangerous from the lips of women than they are from men.' She argued a common-sensical reason for women's election to Parliament. 'Indeed, unless there is something horribly perverse in the order of things, fifteen years spent in bearing and rearing children ought to be a better preparation for the business of governing one's fellow creature than an equal space of time spent in cross-examining scoundrels.' She attacked the 'public schoolboys who make up the House of Commons' and 'that most malignant libel spoken by the rich against the poor – that the average housewife of the lower and middle classes is an ignorant incompetent. This is one of the most cherished beliefs of the wholly undomesticated women of the aristocratic classes. It is of course, a device to cheat poor girls out of their education.' Sentimental cant about the quiet joys of the domestic sphere inspired her to retort: 'Domesticity is essentially drama, for drama is conflict, and the home compels conflict by its concentration of active personalities in a small area. The real objection to domesticity is that it is too exciting.'

Her articles were daring, and often joyously so – a counter to all those who felt then, as too often now, that feminism represents something gloomy and sour. They are good examples of a level of anarchist feminism in literary criticism. They demonstrated again and again her wide reading, her original and extraordinarily good judgement, her wit, and her astonishing grasp of the complexities of political and emotional life. When she was provocative, it was always to a purpose. She had a remarkable capacity to reach the core of the issue.

Her essays are those of a clever, vivacious, fiercely professional person – a woman whose keen-edged mind might, one would think, be reflected in disdain for feminine 'frivolities' and any conformity to fashion. In fact, when she visited America a decade after these essays were written, or did lecture tours in Britain, journalists hardly knew whether to fill their columns with her intelligent remarks or with elaborate descriptions of her looks, clothes, and personality. In 1925 the *Leeds Mercury* gave an account of Rebecca West (by then a famous name). 'It is hard to lay a finger on the exact centre of her charm. It may have lain in the reflective earnest gaze of those luminous eyes ... or in the sudden startlingly vivacious smile which seemed to dance like a live thing over her features when the humour of some experience or thought struck her afresh. But more than all, it was her vitality which fascinated. It didn't seem to matter what she said, every word of it was brimful of interest and delight. We felt that Rebecca West's life was a definite thing, every moment of which had some emotion to be felt, some experience to be lived through.' The *York Herald* said of her: 'Her work as a novelist has proved that she is not only an advanced type of womanhood, but also a psychologist, sociologist, and a philosopher of the first order.'

Often people turn their work into a substitute for living. No one could say that of Rebecca West. In her personal involvements, her passions and aestheticism, she conveys the impression of having scaled the depths and the heights. Her love affair with H. G. Wells is famously recorded, and she brought their child up alone in a world where people still spoke in hushed tones of 'fallen women'. She was married for thirty-eight years to Henry Maxwell Andrews, with whom she travelled widely, and nursed him in the last five years of his life. Her astounding output – travel books, fiction, history, biography, critical essays, reviews – suggests not merely an extraordinary fertility of imagination, but a formidable discipline in her work. She speaks several languages.

Vera Brittain, author of *Testament of Youth*, saw Rebecca West when she appeared on the London scene in her twenties as the embodiment of the feminist cause, the twentieth-century successor to Mary Wollstonecraft. Today, in her eighties, Rebecca West is working on her autobiography. In her suffragette days, feminists hoped that by achieving equality society would learn to accept feminine, life-giving values, to counter the world of aggression and cruelty: they saw no point in playing a game according to the rules laid down by men. Rebecca West's comments on men at the time were sometimes acid. 'Hair cutting is the sort of work a man should do. Women should be saved for more important jobs', or 'English women are handicapped by the fact that men have passed laws encouraging female morons.' 'I am an old fashioned feminist. I believe in the sex war. When those of our army whose voices are inclined to coo tell us that the day of sex antagonism is over and that henceforth we have only to advance hand in hand with the male, I do not believe it.' And perhaps most telling of all: 'The man who is really virile, who is a person of power, never fears any accession to power on the part of a woman. But all those who are not indulge in anti-feminism.' Things have not changed.

Rebecca West has always known that 'no great thing happens suddenly'. Today she makes it clear that she would still prefer men to make good mothers than that women turn themselves into good company directors and politicians. She no longer sees the solution in terms of dogma or simple ideologies. But in one essential respect she has not changed: she remains a feminist.

The Position of Women in Indian Life

The Position of Women in Indian Life by the Maharani of Baroda and S. M. Mitra

There are two kinds of imperialists – imperialists and bloody imperialists. The feminist who belongs to the first variety, and considers blood to be an incident in imperialism and not its aim and glory, has long wanted some sort of description of Indian womanhood and how its conditions have been affected by British rule. And this is what the title of the book written by the Maharani of Baroda and S. M. Mitra, *The Position of Women in Indian Life*, seems to promise.

However, it turns out to be an account of the various social organisations and activities of women in Great Britain, and a rough sketch of the path down which Indian feminism is going to progress – or rather toddle. For the Maharani's aims would not justify a quicker pace. She seems to regard the unseemly muddle into which women's affairs have fallen today in Europe as something for which Indian women should strive. In fact, she takes a step backward. She actually recommends women to take up 'genteel callings', such as enamelling, furniture carving, decorative needlework, illuminating. Her timid attitude towards the woman worker may be estimated from the following extract:

> The profession of domestic architect is in itself exceedingly interesting, and one which Indian women might, in part, very well take up. The oversight of the workmen would have to be left to men, nor could women very well climb the scaffolding to superintend the progress of the building; but the drawing of the plans and the details could easily be done by our women if they made it the subject of professional study. There is, however, no need for women to undertake the entire architecture of the house. There is ample room for their talent in designing portions of the interior – such as useful wall-cupboards, mouldings, friezes, ornamental designs for doors and windows, and the general decorative details of construction.

Now we in England know what this playing at wage-earning, this pathetic skulking on the outskirts of industry, brought us to during the Victorian era. It brought to women the most humiliating and the most hungry period of oppression they had ever endured. The feminist must take a bolder line. If she is going to enter the labour market she must take capital with her – she must try from the first to capture the commanding fortresses of industry, from which she can dictate the conditions of her own labour.

Moreover, the authors repeat over and over again that most malignant libel spoken by the rich against the poor – that the average housewife of the lower and middle classes is an ignorant incompetent. This is one of the most cherished beliefs of the wholly undomesticated women of the aristocratic classes. It is, of course, a device to cheat poor girls out of their education. 'Domestic science' is designed to elbow out of the school curriculum all subjects likely to develop the minds of the girl scholars, and thus leave them, irrespective of their individual gifts, fit for nothing but domestic service. The authors err, too, in attributing the over-supply of 'poorly paid governesses and half-educated girl-clerks' to 'a training . . . far too abstract, too intellectual'. It is obvious that this glut of worthless labour is partly due to the desire of parents to absorb their daughters into unprofitable domestic labour, partly to the lack of first-rate educational facilities, and partly to the fact that a woman knows that her labour capital – her education, her talent, her experience – is confiscated on her entrance into marriage.

The truth is, the authors' feminism is out of date. They apologise for woman, and nag at her for the inborn failings of human nature. They are too complaisant about her underpayment, blandly remarking, after a comment on the miserable wages of matrons, that 'salaries in England are not large. For instance, the Prime Minister of England gets a smaller salary than the Governor of an Indian Province.' And they are confused by the old-fashioned idea that it is the labour of women who are not wholly dependent on their own earnings which depresses the general level of women's salaries. As a matter of fact, we know that these make the finest trade-unionists. Surely the authors misinterpret the feminist opposition to regulative legislation of women's labour. It is not the regulative aspect of it that the women object to, but the fact that it is regulation framed according to the conception of woman held by the public-schoolboys who make up the House of Commons.

Yet the authors have an immense enthusiasm for the cause of feminism, and see it as a coming force in the movement towards the unity of India. The pity is that they have not seen beneath the surface of English life. They do not realise that in spite of that august institution, the International Council of Women, the average woman

worker is growing thin on 'no salary but ample opportunities for
Christian work'.

[This article signed Cicily Fairfield.]
The Freewoman, 30 November 1911

The Gospel According to
Mrs Humphry Ward

Barricaded from the fastidious craftsman behind the solid Totten-
ham-Court-Road workmanship of her mental furniture, Mrs
Humphry Ward has been able to preach her gospel unappreciated
by revolutionaries. This is a pity. Because Mrs Ward reveals to us the
psychology of the clergyman class – the class which throughout the
Victorian era peopled the Church and the universities to the exclusion of any other. With the single exception of the scientist group,
they have sent no message of inspiration to this generation. Yet the
excellent economic position which they enjoyed, which enabled
them to monopolise the higher education, made it inevitable that
they should leave their mark on England. To take only one instance
of their activities, they were responsible for the beginnings of modern
journalism – God forgive them! But, on the whole, they mean very
little to us – Matthew Arnold, Kingsley, Coventry Patmore, Anthony
Trollope. But it helps us to understand the House of Commons if we
can grasp their point of view: and that is most lucidly and naïvely
shown in the works of Mrs Humphry Ward.

Even her deficiencies are of value to the student. For instance, at
first sight it seems merely a very damning proof of the worthlessness
of Mrs Ward's writing that she should have written her two most
pretentious works, *Robert Elsmere* and *The Case of Richard Meynell*,
about a national movement which could not exist, but a movement
which she describes as sweeping over the country and turning the
hearts of Englishmen to flame. This modernist movement, which
aimed at regulating the Church of England's doctrine and ritual
according to the conclusions of historical research upon the life of
Christ, is alien from, not only the Englishman, but the human mind.
Jesus of Nazareth sits in a chamber of every man's brain, immovable,
immutable, however credited or discredited. The idea of Christ is the
only inheritance that the rich have not stolen from the poor. It is now

a great national interest (not a faith), and as such is treated with respect, and as securely protected from 'modernising' as the tragedy of *Hamlet*. And although Mrs Ward has been 'turning her trained intellect' (to quote her publisher) on the universe for nigh on sixty years, that has not struck her. She regards the Englishman as going to church with the same watchful eye of possible improvements as when he attends the sanitary committee of the borough council. She does not understand that the Englishman, having discovered something that, whether true or not, is glorious to the human soul, is not going to tamper with it. This misunderstanding is so typical of her class. For, see how in the House of Commons the respectable always try, by encouraging mean thrift, to rob the poor of their improvidence, which, uncomfortable as it is in its results, is nevertheless their one means of protest against their conditions.

A defect which Mrs Ward shares not only with her own class, but with the modern world, is her lack of honour. Honour, in the time of Elizabeth, was quite a lovely and sensible thing. It was a jolly sort of code, such as holds good between skippers on the high seas, a fine cheerful recognition of mutual responsibilities. It bound together those bands of pioneers as they trampled down dangers on the virgin shores of the New World in loneliness and thirst. It made literature beautiful with discussion of the debts of the soul. The difference between our outlook and theirs is very well illustrated by Thomas Middleton's imperial tragedy, *The Changeling*. Beatrice, a noble lady, is betrothed to a man she hates. She hires de Flores, a poor gentleman, to kill this man. That service done, de Flores demands that she should become his mistress. On her refusal, he holds the secret of their conspiracy over her head. Now, what struck the Elizabethan about this ghastly story was not the blood-guilt of Beatrice, nor the brutal lustfulness of de Flores, but the treachery of de Flores in blackmailing the lady, and the nice point as to exactly how far Beatrice had contracted these base obligations. We have travelled far from that now. For the Englishman became spoilt by too much prosperity, and began to worry about his soul and, as a Puritan, reverted to savagery. For henceforth he did not regulate his moral conduct according to honour, but according to his various taboos. So honour left us, to shine only in broken reflections from the work of our great artists.

Mrs Ward is not one of these. For an example of her complete lack of sense, let us turn to *Daphne*. There you see, set down without disgust, the wooing of an underbred American heiress, Daphne, by an able-bodied young Englishman, Roger Barnes, who is frankly in love with her money. Mrs Ward seems to think it quite a wholesome arrangement, even setting down in cold fact that Roger blamed his wife for extravagance. They live an uneventful and, one might say, animal life in England for some years, and then Daphne gets bored with Roger. She moves over to America and divorces him according to the kindly laws of that country, taking custody of their only child. With a fine sense of what is fitting, the child dies. Hence the father takes to drink and lives with a shop-girl. Had he been a workman who had lost his job, how disgusted and contemptuous Mrs Ward would have been! So, overcome by remorse, Daphne returns to England and offers to live with him again. Then comes the one gleam of horse-sense discernible in Mrs Ward's books. Roger prefers to die without the companionship of a woman he dislikes. Mrs Ward does not see it like that, however. It seems to her the most tragic note of all.

Now, what lesson does Mrs Ward learn from this rather trivial story? The chief lesson would be, one would think, that it is a bad thing that a man should eat if he does not work; and that it is a very vile thing that a man should earn his living by entering into a sexual relationship. But actually the only thing it suggests to Mrs Ward's trained intellect is that divorce is too easily granted in America. Unmoved and undismayed, she suggests that the rich woman and her parasite should have continued to live together until death corrupted their mean bodies. And why? Mrs Ward never answers that question. She never hears it, because she does not consider that personal relationships need the sanction of honour. To her, all things done in the name of the taboo of marriage seem beautiful.

It may strike one in reading *Daphne* that it shows a strange habit of mind to consider whisky and shop-girls as the only alternative to a happy married life. But Mrs Ward has a poor opinion of men, and a worse one of women, whom, with Zarathustra, she considers 'still cats and birds: or, at the best, cows'. Of course, Mrs Ward is largely in agreement with Nietzsche – not only in this, but in her firm belief in the Superman, whom she considers to be realised in the aristocratic classes of this country, her contempt for democratic art and her voluble prejudice against socialism. But Nietzsche's Superman is to have quite a good time, exulting in his eternal Bank Holiday, with the wide world on Hampstead Heath. But Mrs Ward's characters, judging from her ideal figure, Catherine Leyburn, would at their highest fail to enjoy the spiritual exhilaration of a meeting of the Poor Law Guardians.

Catherine Leyburn is revealed to us in her youth and in her late middle-age in the pages of *Robert Elsmere* and *The Case of Richard Meynell*. The distinguishing characteristic which differentiates her from, for instance, Isabel, in *The New Machiavelli*, is her physical abandonment. On every page her face works with emotion and is illuminated by a burning flush; once she has slowly succumbed to the turgid wooing of Robert Elsmere, she drenches him with tears and kisses. A spiritual upheaval is a picnic to her. Whensoever she approaches a deathbed, one has an uneasy suspicion that she is glad to 'be in at the death'. After many years of widowhood, whiled away by the perusal of the lives of bishops, she dies as easily as she has lived. What a life! Never once had she earned the bread she ate. She had spent her life in thinking beautiful thoughts, in being a benign and beautiful influence . . . Never will Woman be saved until she realises that it is a far, far better thing to keep a jolly public-house really well than to produce a cathedral full of beautiful thoughts. 'Here they talk of nothing else than love – its beauty, its holiness, its spirituality, its Devil knows what! . . . They think they have achieved the perfection of love because they have no bodies! – sheer imaginative debauchery!' It was of Hell that that was said. When people plead that 'Woman should stand aside from the ugly mêlée' of things as they are, and 'hold high the banner of the Ideal', which is the usual way of alluding to Catherine's life of loaferdom, they are instructing her in her damnation.

Mrs Ward's gospel is an easy one. If she was Mrs Mary A. Ward, of Port Matilda, Pa., USA, it would be expressed something like this: 'Girls! Make life a joy-ride! But don't talk back to the police!' This easy gospel will give its disciples the heritage one may see in the faces of so many 'sheltered women': a smooth brow, that has never known the sweat of labour; the lax mouth, flaccid for want of discipline; eyes that blink because they have never seen anything worth looking at; the fat body of the unexercised waster. And within, the petulance of those who practise idealism on the easiest methods: a pastime that develops the conceit of the artist, with none of the wisdom and chastening of art.

The Freewoman, 15 February 1912

Letter to the Editor of
The Freewoman
A Reply to Mr Hubert Wales

Madam,

This is most damping. In 'The Gospel of Mrs Humphry Ward' I write a positively eloquent paean on energy, and hurl my thunderbolts at the woman who will not think. And three weeks later Mr Hubert Wales startles me by accusing me of worshipping industrialism, and despising the contemplative life (in which he seems to include the practice of art and philosophy). I feel hurt.

Of course, I meant nothing of the sort! How could a feminist worship the industrial system? It makes the same demand from women as does the home – physical drudgery, combined with mental inertia.

When I wrote that sentence, 'Never will woman be saved until she realises that it is a far, far better thing to keep a jolly public-house really well than to produce a cathedral full of beautiful thoughts,' I was writing about the parasitic women of the upper and middle classes, whose 'beautiful thoughts' are the effortless pulp of Ella Wheeler Wilcox, not the fierce struggles towards the light of George Bernard Shaw. The Catherine Leyburns of England are about as fit for the stern intellectual discipline of the contemplative life as are the loafers on the Embankment.

I really advised the parasitic women to become publicans because it occurred to me that the various duties of that profession, such as wringing a licence out of a bench of insolent country gentlemen, paying the rent regularly on quarter-days and chucking out the drunkards on Saturday night, might foster the qualities of independence, thrift and firmness of character, so sadly lacking among upper-class women of today.

Rebecca West
The Freewoman, 14 March 1912

Taking on Mrs Humphry Ward in 1912 was brave and foolhardy for a young woman with literary aspirations, equivalent to a young man, expecting to launch his career with insults to Henry James. For she was the grand old woman of English letters and the formidable figurehead of the Tory anti-suffrage campaign. Rebecca West has herself described her as intellectually formidable. *She was the niece of Matthew Arnold and the daughter of Dr Thomas Arnold 'famed for his desperate attempts to make something of the male sex at Rugby'.* Mrs Ward's most famous coup against the cause of women was the publication in the magazine Nineteenth Century of an anti-suffrage petition signed by many of England's most prominent women, including Virginia Woolf's mother Julia Stephen, and Beatrice Webb (who later recanted). Delia Blanchflower, a novel written by Mrs Ward to expose the iniquities of the suffragettes probably did the Cause more good than harm. Dame Rebecca found the anti-suffragist's literary debasement mysterious, for she found her memoirs A Writer's Recollections admirable. Virginia Woolf agreed with Rebecca West's estimation of the novelist who dominated the female literary world of their youth; she found the novels encrusted with Victorian black beads, hanging like the 'mantles of our aunts' in the lumber-room of literature. Yet she too admired the memoirs and used them for the writing of her Oxford chapters in The Years. Her formidable presence must have seemed to those radical young women like a female equivalent of the statue in Don Giovanni, a matriarchal bulwark, against whom the 'freewomen' threw the manifesto of their paper, 'the revolt of women, philosophic anarchism and a general whip-round for ideas which would reform simultaneously life and art.' 'More, no doubt, we would have taken on,' says Rebecca West, 'had there been time.'

The Gospel According to Granville-Barker

Humanity is a little lost dog looking for a master. Men seek without cease some pilot passion to which they can surrender their heavy burden of freedom. The heroes worshipped by the people are those who have succeeded in this search. St Teresa was the slave of her religion, Paolo and Francesca stripped themselves of all worldly things for love, Joseph Chamberlain gave himself up to a flame-like passion for Tariff Reform. To be respectable one must abandon oneself to duty, that impulse to seek salvation by doing the things one doesn't want to do, which is so deeply rooted in all savages. But there has always been an unconsidered minority who wanted to keep the burden of their freedom, in order to indulge in the joy of thinking. They found a pure joy in solving an equation, and dreamed of the greater joy in solving the problems of life itself. They imagined victories of reason more splendid than any amorous conquest or the slaying of any wild beast. This was resented by the slaves of passion as cold and inhuman. In the Middle Ages the slaves burnt the thinkers in large numbers: and now they use 'intellectuals' as a term of acrid dislike and contempt. So that the thinkers have usually stood aloof and disguised their ecstasy. Hence, when a man arises who shamelessly revels in the joys of thinking, who flaunts it as Chesterton flaunts his love of beer, we ought to stand back and look at him.

Granville-Barker is this man. Thought bubbles from him like laughter from a healthy child. It is more than a religion to him – it is a sport. One can imagine the hostess at a country-house dinner party asking him, 'And do you hunt, Mr Barker?' He would reply, with the proud modesty of one who knows a trick worth two of that, 'No. I think.' Every one of the four plays that he has published is an eager and happily passionate discussion of some important discussion of some important problem of life. The smallest of them, *The Voysey Inheritance*, seems at first only the story of a young solicitor who finds that his father's flourishing family practice has been built up by the wholesale embezzlement of his clients' funds and the payment of princely dividends out of non-existent capital; and his struggles to right the accounts by further embezzlement that shall at least protect the poorer clients from utter destitution. But really it shows the difficulties of the honest man who tries to build a just commonwealth out of the swindling social system of today. Even in his one short story, *Georgiana*, which was written during convalescence after a severe illness, his delighted spirit hovers over the hard problem of an irregular relationship.

Of course Shaw, too, has this insatiable appetite for debate, this fierce refusal to leave things as they are. But there are two great characteristics that mark off Barker from Shaw. One is Barker's unconventionality. For all Shaw's audacious discussions, there is not one character in all his eighteen plays who infringes the conventions in practice. But Barker again and again draws sinners of the deepest dye with the most ardent sympathy. In that comprehensive survey of modern womanhood, *The Madras House*, the woman he values most is Miss Yates. She has the talent to become an excellent shop-assistant: she has a spark of genius which makes her refuse to accept the convention that if marriage is denied to her so is motherhood.

Shaw never brought anything so anarchic as an unmarried mother on to his stage. Although he cultivates the flower of argument so well, he does not like the fruit of action. But Barker, glad disciple of the joy of thinking, embraces logic like a lover, and shows all the consequences of the theories he advances. The other distinguishing characteristic of Barker is his humility. He has not forgotten God. He knows that any moment the skies above may open and a mailed hand descend to wreck the reasoned course of human life. He respects the mysterious fumblings of the human mind. There is an illuminating evidence of this in *The Madras House*, when Philip Madras, the head of the drapery firm, Miss Chancellor, the stern spinster guardian of the shop-girls' morals, and Miss Yates are met together to discuss the question of the latter's fall. She has told them how she brought a wedding-ring to wear when she saw the doctor:

Philip: Miss Yates, have you the wedding-ring with you?
Miss Yates: Yes, I have . . . it's not real gold.
Philip: Put it on.
   Miss Yates, having fished it out of a petticoat pocket, rather wonderingly does so, and Philip turns, maliciously humorous, to Miss Chancellor.
Philip: Now where are we, Miss Chancellor?
Miss Chancellor: I think we're mocking at a very sacred thing, Mr Madras.
Miss Yates: Yes . . . and I won't now.
   With a sudden access of emotion she slams the ring upon the table. Philip meditates for a moment on the fact that there are some things in life still inaccessible to his light-hearted logic.
Philip: True . . . true . . . I beg both your pardons.

Wild censors would not have dragged that apology out of Shaw. And it is just that spirit, that reverence towards Life, that makes Barker's thought so valuable.

Now, at present, the great result of the thirteen years of ecstatic contemplation of the earth that have passed since the writing of Barker's first play is a very vigorous hatred. He hates the sterility of life. All emotion, not only love, is a desire for procreation. When a little child hears a pleasant sound, it cries, 'Again! again!' But soon mere repetition fails to satisfy. The child imitates the sound, and that fails too. At last it achieves happiness in the creation of a new sound. Older children always sit down to paint or write after they have seen a picture or read a story that appeals to them, and attempt to create. So life ought to be a struggle of desire towards adventures whose nobility will fertilise the soul and lead to the conception of new, glorious things. To avoid the ordeal of emotion that leads to the conception is the impulse of death. Sterility is the deadly sin. Today so many of our activities are sterile. Our upper classes are impotent by reason of their soft living. Our lower classes have had their vitality sweated out of them by their filthy labours: they can only bear dead things. They say that the work that is the excuse for the rowdy bustling of the hideous city could, under a more efficient system of organisation, be adequately performed by a third of the existing firms. Parliament, built up by the lawyers, the fine flower of the intellectual classes of England, is a barren thing. Our art is an anaesthetic rather than an inspiration.

Every one of Barker's plays is a protest against some form of this sterility. *Ann Leete* is a cry against the fruitlessness of a highly bred class whose energies are diverted into political intrigue. *The Voysey Inheritance* is an indictment of the profitless muddle of the present economic conditions. *Waste* contains not only the picture of a woman who had so much of the fear of life that is the beginning of all evil that she could kill her unborn child; it is an accusation against the governing class which has lost the mysterious quality that makes one's actions bear fruit. 'A peasant . . . a dog might have it.' *The Madras House* is a judgement of womankind. He shows many types, and they are all spiritually sterile. The six Miss Huxtables, who exist in idle maidenhood on Denmark Hill, getting nothing from life, giving nothing to life. Old Mrs Madras, who refuses to cultivate the qualities of her humanity and womanhood, but ceaselessly demands from her husband the rights of submission and companionship she should only have expected during the brief hours of their love, that are really not much use to her now that she hates him. But the worst scoundrel of all is Jessica Madras, the married woman who, by virtue of being Philip's wife and the mother of one child, has secured the right to complete idleness for the rest of her life. Everything she touches turns to voluptuousness. She whiles away the boredom of her lazy life by delicately thrusting flirtation on hard-working men, well knowing that her ladyhood will protect her from any disagreeable complications. Even art she uses to smother God in her. When she comes in, sick with disgust at the squalid world of ugliness and suffering outside her four walls, she can sit down and forget it all in playing Beethoven. To her, whom the world excuses on the ground of her grace, her culture and her motherhood, Barker says: 'You consume much, but you produce nothing. You live by your sex. When you walk abroad you distract men's thoughts to petty sensuousness. You must either be shut up in a harem or you must be a free woman.' And he tells her how she must do it. 'There's a price to be paid for free womanhood, I think . . . and how many of you ladies are willing to pay it? Come out and be common women among us common men!'

That is the solution of the question. We accept it, and we are working towards it. But sometimes it seems rather a questionable ideal – to work among common men, to be sucked under into the same whirlpool of sterile activity. In *The Marrying of Ann Leete*, the earliest and most exquisite of all his plays, Barker showed us a fruitless family. There is Carnaby Leete, who has infected his whole family with the perverted passion of political intrigue; his daughter Sarah, who has flitted lovelessly from a husband in one political camp to a lover in the other, to serve her father's interest; his son George, who despises the game, but is too sick of soul to leave it; and the younger daughter Ann, who, at the very moment of her betrothal to her father's latest political ally, rebels. She means to find her place in the eternal purpose. She finds it by going 'back to the land'. She marries the gardener, thinking that in the simple life of the people, spent so innocently in 'sowing seeds and watching flowers grow and cutting away dead things', she will be able to live and feel fruitfully.

It is the easy solution that would appeal to a very young man. It is the solution that fascinates the child-like minds of Chesterton and Belloc. Perhaps Barker realises now that one finds oneself no nearer the essential things of life by going back to the peasantry than a civilised man would achieve freedom by joining a savage tribe. He would find the religious ceremonies of an African tribe more complex than those of the Church of England; he would find the etiquette of beads far stricter than any decree of fashion in Mayfair, and the marriage laws would be more irrational than those of Holy Church herself. And in the same way the peasant has to live up to more superstitions than the most over-civilised town-dweller. He is bound to the past, which is no guide to us. Perhaps if Barker returned to the manner of *Ann Leete*, in which he speaks with a vivid dramatic idiom he has since obscured by echoes of Shaw and the Fabian Society, he might suggest some other way to freedom. As it is, he has given us a strong hatred, the best lamp to bear in our hands as we go over the dark places of life, cutting away the dead things men tell us to revere.

The Freewoman, 7 March 1912

Rebecca West's father had once been known in London as the only man to equal Shaw in debate. She herself found much to admire in Shaw's work and often praised his skill in argument and his gift of tongues in an age which saw the debasement of the language. She once described his head as like that of a 'flirtatious Moses'. But she criticised some of his arguments and positions, though this was from the first a battle between equals. He admired her wit and style, and was flattered when she was called a 'Shaw in skirts'. The play he wrote for the suffragettes to use as a fund raiser, Press Cuttings, is a polemical farce in which all the characters, male and female, are presented as stereotypes. But though the women win the arguments, their stereotypes are also the more offensive and extreme. It is true that Shaw wrote to the papers to denounce forcible feeding and the Cat and Mouse Act, but his dialectical arguments for women's rights did less to advance the Cause than has generally been supposed.

On 15 September 1913, Rebecca West reviewed Shaw's Androcles and the Lion in The New Freewoman, lamenting the fact that 'we have no English drama' except for Granville-Barker's Marrying of Ann Leete, and mocking his stage-managing of Shaw's play. That Granville-Barker whose talents she compared to Chekhov's in The Cherry Orchard, should be stage-managing Shaw seemed to her ridiculous, especially when he had contrived to represent a forest by a washing line hung with purple, white and green kimonos. (The audience got the point, for these were the colours of the suffragette martyrs.)

Against the background of broken light and perverse images of beauty shone the religious faith of Mr Shaw, unintelligible to the average pagan dramatic critic by reason of its Christian bias. Androcles is an early Christian Kipps, a simple soul. He, the tamest thing among men, is not afraid of the wildest thing among beasts because he loves it. He is the truly religious man fearing not the fiercest passion that may rise out of his humanity because he loves life. He is the middle-class man who will not practise asceticism, and who has made all revolutions since the beginning of time; who goes off with his lion friend, crying, 'While we are together no slavery for me, no cage for him!' And there was genius in the picture of the martyrs so Christian that they talk no more of Christ than William Blake talked of God, which is a lesson in psychology to the Alice Meynell and Francis Thompson school of poets. There was, in the decision of Lavinia and Ferrovius, a splendid illumination on the duty of the soul. In her hour of martyrdom fear showed Lavinia that the stories and dreams of Christianity were but stories and dreams! Yet she chose to die for the passion she had poured into her worship of them, and for the great truth too great to be grasped by the little brain that lay behind them. And Ferrovius, finding that all his body was made for man, served man rather than the Christ for whose service he had not been made. It is the soul's duty to be loyal to its own desires. It must abandon itself to its master-passion.

The New Freewoman, 15 September 1913

Views and Vagabonds

Views and Vagabonds by Rose Macaulay

Miss Macaulay's new novel, *Views and Vagabonds,* has the initial disadvantage of a heroine who lets her father feed the baby on beer and red herring, keeps old and sticky paper-bags because it do seem a pity to waste paper-bags, and kills mice with the poker. And not only does Miss Macaulay gloss over nothing; she actually defends her heroine's right to amuse herself in all these ways.

Louie Robinson, a hand at the Enderby papermills, had the misfortune to be married by Benjie Bunter, a wealthy young man, who had come to the conclusion that only the workers had any right to exist, and consequently had set up a blacksmith's forge at Wattles, the Cambridgeshire village where she had her home. Louie thought he was marrying her for love. Her own love was not such as gave or invited demonstrations; she seems to have done little but gaze at him with dumb affection, except when he scalded his hand, when she sat on gazing but also fetched the Vaseline. But gradually she began to realise that his marriage was only an incident in his 'World for the Workers' campaign. 'I said, and I maintain, that we should all marry the hardest workers we know.' But as for affection . . . 'That is naturally one of the points I have taken into consideration. It would be ridiculous not to. In my opinion people ought not to marry without caring for each other.' A temperate frame of mind that disheartened Louie.

Then a baby came, and Louie felt that she had justified her position by providing a son for Benjie, whom he could train up as a worker in the way he should go. But then old Mr Robinson, 'knowing that babies like a bit of whatever we get', gave John a fatal taste of beer and red herring. Louie said little, certainly no word of blame against her father, but henceforward stood about the garden hugging a pet rabbit in her empty arms, a sad figure of colourless, speechless grief.

So for a change Benjie takes her up to London to stay with his people. And Louie is put under the magnifying-glass as a type: the representative working woman. All the Bunter family jostle round, calling their friends to look. They decide to educate her, and she follows them apathetically from the Academy to St Paul's, from the House of Commons to *Lohengrin*. Their attitude of interest in her class and their disregard of her personality shows her the more clearly the place she fills in her husband's life. So she leaves him, saying: 'You took me along with the forge and the rest . . . You can marry for a sort of game, but I can't, and that's 'ow it is.'

So they part company. Benjie goes off caravanning with his cousin Cecil, a Girton girl, to preach the gospel of garden cities, and Augustus John, and sweetness and light in the agricultural counties. And people talk scandal, which Louie hears, and nearly breaks her heart over. But she suffers in silence, until news comes that alters her attitude to Benjie. He isn't really a Bunter, but their adopted child; he is no longer an aristocrat with a self-conscious mission to the lower orders, but a peasant like herself. Furthermore, he has been burnt in a fire and needs her mothering. So she starts off at once to find him and bring him home.

It is a bad moment for Benjie. For he has just come to the conclusion that expounding the beauties of Augustus John to rustics isn't much use, and that indictments of the ugliness of their dwellings and the inadequacy of their religion aren't really in good taste. He adopts a new philosophy. 'If joy should fill the world, the Kingdom of Heaven would be come upon it in truth; so let each do his part in that fulfilling, and make and take joy while he could, and strive no more against life, which was surely good enough.' So he is just going off to seek his way of joy by caravanning round the country *without* a propaganda.

And then Louie turns up, demanding that he should return to 'a nice new-looking house, none of them old nasty whitewash-and-thatch things they had there before; they're all gone, and these are nice semis – yellow brick, you know, with pretty carved porticoes – ever so nice, they are.' So Benjie had to puzzle out a new aspect of his philosophy. 'Happiness counts. But whose? Yours or mine?' More out of moral bewilderment than any real love for humanity, he decides, 'yours'.

So Louie gets her yellow semi, ever so nice, and calls it Daisyville. And later on she also gets a new baby, and she calls it Stanley Wilfred, and feeds it with cake out of her mouth. And she won't let Benjie have tea in the garden in case them nasty sniggering Wilkinsons next door overlook the tea-table. And everything is very horrible and vulgar, as Miss Macaulay says Louie has every right to be.

Of course, Louie's troubles are most distressing. Probably she did look as 'if, giving up all solutions of immediate problems, she fell back on the wisdom of the age'. My tortoiseshell tabby looks like that sometimes. She has her troubles, too; only last week they drowned two of her kittens. But that doesn't make her a tragic or dignified figure. And neither is Louie. In fact, from her general character, her want of physical charm, her lack of response to other personalities, her apathy towards new sights and sounds, we may suspect anaemia. There are two ways of wanting love. There is the way of sending out the whole force of one's vitality to a fair fight – perhaps to win, perhaps to lose, but certainly to fight. And there is the way of waiting outside as though love were a soup-kitchen and a marriage-certificate the soup-ticket, in the tremulous attitude of one cringing for charity. Louie's way was the second.

Of course, the painting of weak personalities may be good art. In the present case it certainly is, for *Views and Vagabonds* is an exquisitely written book. But, unfortunately, Miss Macaulay uses Louie as a representative type of the poor – the inarticulate poor, she would probably call them. She appears to think that vitality decreases in direct ratio to social position, and that Louie with her weak grip on life is a typical peasant. If this were so it would be an excellent thing to form immediately an oligarchy with the proletariat in chains. But the proletariat isn't like that. Even the agricultural labourers have shown in their peasant revolts that they have courage and passion. In view of the fact (quoted quite shamelessly in a pamphlet which invites subscriptions to the Anti-Socialist Union) that 956,185 agricultural labourers earn from 9s 3d to 20s 9d a week, the modern movement towards the city is an evidence of their good sense. To appeal for love towards the poor on the ground of their occasional imbecility is treachery. Of course, they do this often in sketches in the Saturday *Westminster Gazette*, when Liberal ladies write in the style of Mr A. C. Benson breathless accounts of how on the way home from a Free Trade lecture they met a man quite bent with rheumatism, and another man who was a little drunk (but quite respectful) . . . No, they didn't say anything . . . but it was *so* impressive . . . deep, slumbering passions of the poor . . . their silent tragedies . . . Of course, Miss Macaulay, being a worthy artist, does not indulge in these spiritual picnics over the ailments and orgies of the poor. But she says we ought to forgive the poor their vulgarities, because of their weakness, not because of their strength.

And that, by the way, is a treachery women often commit in the name of feminism. They say that they too 'give up all solutions of immediate problems'. They allege that they 'fall back on the wisdom of the ages'. Which is a transparent trick. And they appeal for equal rights with men because of their weakness. In other words, they claim liberty because they are natural slaves.

The Freewoman, 21 March 1912

Woman Adrift

Woman Adrift by Harold Owen

Mr Harold Owen is a natural slave, having no conception of liberty nor any use for it. So, as a Freewoman, I review his anti-feminist thesis, Woman Adrift, with chivalrous reluctance, feeling that a steam-engine ought not to crush a butterfly.

Woman Adrift is a respectable piece of journalism, illuminated towards the end by some passages of meteoric brilliance, which starts out to prove that men are the salt of the earth, and women either their wives or refuse . . . 'Woman is wholly superfluous to the State save as a bearer of children and a nursing mother.' There is a kind of humour in the way these things work out. Just as Napoleon proved in his latter end that no man dare be a despot, so Mr Owen finishes by showing that all men are fools and a great many of them something worse.

It would be unchivalrous, and might tend to increase arrogance among women were I to describe Mr Owen's loose thinking and arbitrary judgement. So we will pass over his arguments in favour of his conclusions. Two examples will suffice to show how he arrives at these. He attempts to quash the argument that a woman ought to have a vote because she pays taxes by stating that in return for her taxes she is a 'citizeness' – which sounds like something odd out of a menagerie – and that anyway John Hampden was an MP. And in a chapter entitled 'Superfluous Woman', which ought to stand for all time as an example of the impudence sex-privilege may engender in the most insignificant male, he is obviously upset by the fact that two women really have attained to the first rank of scientific eminence. So this is how he turns it off: before these women can receive any credit, 'it will be necessary to prove that the collaborated discovery made by Madame Curie, and the original researches of Mrs Ayrton would not have been made by a man, if not thereabout, then very shortly after'.

I trust this pernicious principle will not be generally adopted. Particularly in the literary world. I shall be ruined if, when I complete my monograph on 'The Possibilities of Polygamy in the South-Eastern Suburbs of London', my publisher accepts it, but declines to pay me until I can prove that Mrs Humphry Ward would not have written it, if not thereabout, then very shortly after.

But when I said that this book proved the worthlessness of men, I was not arguing from the particular to the general. It is a fact that his conclusions result logically to the discredit of men. He begins by describing the average man as a 'big, powerful man, all brain and muscle, and not only the governing spirit in the home, but the breadwinner outside it': a combination of Jack Johnson, Mr Gladstone and Shakespeare; of such immense wage-earning powers that he can support all his unmarried female relatives as well as his children and wife (or wives, as the fine fellow may choose); of such delicate moral perceptions and universal experience that he is the wise arbiter of all these destinies.

And he leaves one wondering whether one can safely lend an umbrella to one's uncle.

To take up one of these conclusions by which Mr Owen damns his own sex, one should turn to Chapter XIII, in which he argues that women should not be enfranchised because the administrators of the law deal leniently with women criminals. In support of this assertion he brings forward a few cases in which women appear to have been treated gently on account of their sex, and one case in which a woman received a much lighter sentence than her male partner in guilt. It would be easy to prove that such is not the general rule by citing the opinion of greater legal authorities than Mr Owen. But that would spoil the fun. So let us concede him his point. This amounts to an admission that men prefer bad women. For in no other branch of industry but crime do women receive preferential treatment. And the tenderness of the administrators of the law does not extend to women when they are victims of crime: witness the overwhelming number of cases in which sympathetic judges sentence men to trivial terms of imprisonment, varying from a fortnight to three months, for the most barbarous crimes against women and girls. I present Mr Owen with the further evidence that the female officials of institutions governed by men are often remarkable for hardness and brutality, and that the circulating libraries are full of the biographies of courtesans and murderesses written by men for men.

Now, consider the appalling results of the recognition of this principle, if all we brazen hussies who are suffragettes and feminists became converted to Mr Owen's belief that every women ought to throw up her economic independence, and get some man to keep her! Think of us rushing about, trying with all that vitality we are at present misdirecting in clawing policemen and wrecking the home to attract men whom we knew did not value goodness in a woman! We *will* paint the town red. And it will be Mr Owen's fault.

Again, Mr Owen gives his sex away in the course of his remarks on Mill's *The Subjection of Women*. He quotes a passage in which Mill pleads that the higher education will increase domestic happiness by creating a community of interests between men and women, and he triumphantly points out that after fifty years of the higher education, women have begun to turn their backs on marriage. How naïve, how frank! If I belonged to a sex that was so transparently undesirable, that after only fifty years of the higher education women recoil from it in aversion, I should bury myself tidily in quicklime.

But why do women sometimes turn away from marriage in aversion? Mr Owen again obliges. It appears that men are hogs. This is not my own belief, it is Mr Owen's. In Chapter XII he sets forth with enthusiasm that men have no sense of decency in conduct, that they are even as beasts of the field, and that unimaginative debauchery – 'bodily unfaithfulness ... rather than spiritual unfaithfulness' – comes natural to them. 'If a wife is unfaithful to her husband, a bigger revolution takes place in her moral nature than may take place in the moral nature of her husband.' In other words, a man is always more of a hog than is a woman.

Ugh! Men aren't like this – brawny and immoral pigs, with their swelled heads up in the clouds and their feet firmly planted in the gutter! Some men are clean, wholesome beings that can stand on their merits as human beings, and can lay aside the armour of their sex-privileges with an easy mind! Yet . . . this book will stir up many doubts. Many a loving wife will lay aside *Woman Adrift* and wait in fear and trembling for her husband – to feel him for those enormous biceps, to look in his face for any signs of swinishness, to listen for those words of beneficent advice and confounded interference which Mr Owen regards as man's chief gift to woman. Thank God, she will be disappointed. Or a man-provoked sex war would be upon us.

It is interesting in this connection to contrast Mr Owen's stealthy attack on his own sex with the loyal and friendly attitude towards men shown in his quotations from *The Freewoman* (alluded to above).

And I think that this is an occasion to remind all men, as well as Mr Owen, that a time has come when their work must have some value beside the sex-privilege of the worker. I believe that the ordinary thing to do would be to compliment Mr Owen on his sincerity; but sincerity is an easy thing for one who labours in a vainglorious cause. Deprived of this merit the book has few others, for it is ill-informed and loosely reasoned. I say this in all kindness, because I believe Mr Owen might do better work if he did not waste his time pluming himself on being of the same sex as Shakespeare.

The Freewoman, 28 March 1912

The Matador of the Five Towns

The Matador of the Five Towns by Arnold Bennett, *The Charwoman's Daughter* by James Stephens

It is at present the custom of fools to decry Mr Arnold Bennett's work as 'photographic'. Now photography is an adult recreation, and Mr Bennett is the child among the authors of today. It takes the eyes of youth to see a tram-car lumbering down a high street as the unconquerable chariot of love traversing his kingdom. It takes the palate of infancy to retain such a gluttonous appetite for life. It takes a child to accept so seriously the mission of justifying God's ways to men.

In *The Matador of the Five Towns*, Mr Bennett plunges deeper and deeper into the sea of human affairs. He broods excitedly over the green immensity of the football field, that unimpressive arena whither the workers habitually repair to let loose over an insignificant game the passions inherited from forefathers to whom life was an unsettled and surprising adventure – passions suppressed or nagged to death by the prison-regulations of the industrial muddle. He picks up from the vast field one of the figures that is hired to play this game – one Jos Myatt, a piece of strong flesh, blatantly stupid, of no earthly value save for his strength of sinew. A fancy product of civilisation, an unbeautiful superfluity kept for sport, without the grace that excuses a miner's whippet; a creature without achievement, save for a collection of 'pots' gained as a racing-bicyclist – 'debased and vicious shapes, magnificently useless, grossly ugly, with their inscriptions lost in a mess of flourishes'. A creature now on the verge of senility, soon to become carrion: for at thirty-four a footballer is near the end of his career. Surely a being on whom we can satisfy the human appetite for despising people.

Then we follow Jos Myatt home to the pub he keeps, The Foaming

Quart, and suddenly find ourselves in the midst of a majestic crisis. That night he 'is obliged to sit in a mean chamber and wait silently while the woman of his choice encounters the supreme peril'. He broods gloomily over her torments, he is terrified in the face of this savage development of life. And at dawn his wife bears twin children. He exults, stupidly and silently. Then in the early morning, as he stands wrangling in the bar over an absurd wager, his wife dies. Could there be more grim a catastrophe – more terrible a testimony that the hearts of the gods are deceitful above all things and desperately wicked – than that the woman one loves should die by the fruit of that love? And Jos faces it magnificently. '"As God is my witness," he exclaimed solemnly, in a voice saturated with feeling, "as God is my witness," he repeated, "I'll ne'er touch a footba' again!"' For love of his dead wife he espouses senility. He buries his fame beside her even as Rossetti laid his poems in his wife's coffin. He behaves royally; and we perceive that royalty is bestowed on all of us by the splendid experiences Nature metes out to our common humanity. We may become Supermen and Superwomen as fast as we will, but we can never earn the right to despise anybody, except those voluntary paupers, those moral malingerers that refuse experience. This is a sad thought. How nice to be a Tory, and have half a nation to despise. How nice to be a male anti-feminist, and have half the world's population to despise. These are the *menus plaisirs* one must renounce in embracing theories of liberty.

Another remarkable book that deals with the royalty of commoners is James Stephens' *The Charwoman's Daughter*. This year I shall date the coming of spring from the day I read this book. And, indeed, it is like a wood being awakened by spring. As the buds leap out on the trees, so word by word unfolds its beauty: each lovely in itself and an essential note in the larger symphony of loveliness. It develops slowly with the sedate yet spendthrift elaboration of Nature herself, and every page brings the book to a ripe beauty that one can hardly bear to leave, just as one wants every April day to linger for ever. Nothing can express the delicate strength of his style: to read the quick, beating sentences is like holding a bird in one's hand.

Mr Stephens, in a passion of inquisitiveness, has run up the five flights of a Dublin tenement and burst into the attic – 'the first storey on the way down from heaven', as the French say – and invades the privacy of the perfect heroine. Now it is a strange thing that Mr Arnold Bennett, with all his faculty for seeing through brick walls, is never completely successful in portraying young women. Always his young women have the slightly vulgar air of a conjurer trying to make an impressive mystery out of a commonplace trick with a bowl of goldfish and a couple of rabbits. But there again is Mr Bennett's childishness: he has never got over his infantile admiration for the bland, magnificent creature in the draper's windows, whose superb dignity and unchangeable sweetness he does not attribute to the fact that she is made of wax. The best love-story in the collection of tales that follow *The Matador*, 'Jock-at-a-Venture', is enacted between an old local preacher and a strolling actress nearing forty, a motherly body, such as Mr Bennett can draw with genius. Never could he achieve such a miraculous heroine as Mary Makebelieve, the char-woman's daughter. She is too busy with the mysteries of life to waste time looking mysterious. To show what a whirl of delicious specula-tion occupied her, let us quote her reflections on the ponds in St Stephen's Green Park:

She knew every bird in the Park, those that had chickens, those that had had chickens, and those that had never had any chickens at all. These latter were usually drakes, and had reason on their side for an abstention that might otherwise have appeared remarkable; but they did not deserve the pity which Mary lavished on their childlessness, nor the extra pieces of bread with which she sought to recompense them . . . Some of the eels swam along very slowly, looking on this side and on that as if they were out of work or up from the country, and others whizzed by with incredible swiftness. Mary Makebelieve thought that the latter kind had just heard their babies crying; she wondered, when a little fish cried, could its mother see the tears when there was already so much water about, and then she thought that maybe they cried hard lumps of something that was easily visible.

So she lived a delightfully exciting life, wherein it was a thrilling adventure to go out for a day's charring, until she was courted by a policeman – a monument of physical force, a thing blown out by consciousness of masculinity into a horrible bladder! Let the apostles of virility take notice: 'She wished dumbly that the man would go away, but . . . to endanger the dignity of a big man was a thing which no woman could do without a pang . . . The memory of that would sting her miserably for weeks, as though she had insulted an elephant or a baby.' Could anything be more sweetly chivalrous than Mary? She meets the happier fate she deserves, for she is left walking out with a young man who discovers in a fight with the policeman that 'his courage exceeded his strength, as it always should – for how could we face the gods and demons of existence if our puny arms were not backed up by our invincible eyes?'

But it is Mary's mother that makes this book great. She is one of those lank black figures whirling lean arms in an ecstasy of irritability, her shrill voice mounting from peak to peak of enjoyable invective, that the Irish players sometimes showed us. She was also that pattern to all democrats – a real mother. To her Mary was the pet lamb of an enchanting flock, all of whom had a claim on her love when they needed it. Nor was she the Madonna type, clasping an unnaturally quiet infant who must be either drugged by soothing syrup or stuffed by some skilful taxidermist. She was an enthusiastic devotee of the whole rowdy business of motherhood. There is a delicious scene concerning that. Mary goes out to do a day's charring, leaving Mrs Makebelieve sadly ill. When she comes back,

Mrs Cafferty was sitting on her mother's bed, two small children and a cat were also on the bed, two slightly bigger children were under the bed, and two others were galloping furiously up and down the room . . . The pair of infants on the bed were playing the game of bump; they would stand upright, then spring high into the air and come crashing down on the bed, which then sprung them partly up again . . . Sometimes they fell on Mrs Makebelieve: always they bumped her.

Mary is naturally aghast. 'Are you better?' she asks. 'I am, honey,' Mrs Makebelieve blandly replies. 'Those children done me good.' Unaccountable beings, these mothers!

And Mrs Makebelieve had all the virtues. Even she was a Freewoman . . .

Her god was Freedom and her religion Love. Freedom! Even the last rags of it that remain to a regimented world! That was a passion with her. She must order her personal life without any ghostly or bodily supervision . . . And this last fringe of freedom was what nuns had sacrificed and all servants had bartered away. One must work, but one must never be a slave. These laws seemed to her equally imperative; the structure of the world swung upon them, and whoever violated these laws was a traitor to both God and man.

Art and propaganda have this much connection, that if a propaganda makes art impossible, it is clearly damned. That such a delicate and exquisite fairy-tale can be written about Freewomen is an answer to the argument that feminism will mar the beauty of life, and so wreck art. Our thanks to Mr Stephens for praying that the devil is not going to have all the best tunes.

The Freewoman, 4 April 1912

Men, Mind and Morals

Problems of Men, Mind and Morals by E. Belfort Bax, *The Solemnization of Jacklin* by Florence Farr

Problems of Men, Mind and Morals is further evidence of the fact which the Labour Party proved long ago – that when a socialist takes to being dull, he is much duller than anybody else. Tariff Reformers do amusing tricks with loaves, and Ulstermen call on the name of God most entertainingly; but there is no comic relief about socialists. Mr Bax solemnly debates over such sedative subjects as, 'Is one ethically justified in drinking alcohol?' in the most earnest manner. But at the same time his conclusions are most unorthodox – including, free love and the old-fashioned dogmatic atheism of the 'Hall of Science' type – so that the effect is as startling as though the members of a church debating society should leap to their feet and blaspheme. He dislikes Christ for the most conservative reasons; for his unruly conduct in disturbing the members of the capitalist classes who were 'lawfully engaged in earning their livelihood' in the temple, and for his impertinent precocity in ' "disputing" with his learned elders' at the age of twelve. Yet had Mr Bax hired a boy of twelve from the nearest council school to 'dispute' with him over his proof-reading, he might have learned that to write a sentence such as this: 'My own "lay" observation leads me to the conclusion that, while (1) there is a limit for every man beyond which he cannot continue imbibing alcohol without deleterious effects, (2) that this limit is subject to such wide individual variation that no hard-and-fast rule can be usefully formulated concerning it' – is to be not only commonplace, but also ungrammatical.

A certain interest attaches to his essay on 'Modern Feminism', as he is one of the few articulate anti-feminists among socialists. However, this interest is minimised by the fact that he seems to know little or nothing about feminism. He states that 'no feminist has the smallest intention of abandoning one of the privileges of women', and formulates certain demands which amount to the obligation of every woman to maintain herself, and equal treatment of men and women under the law. 'I can imagine,' he exclaims vividly, 'the sort of wry face the feminists would make at the bare suggestion of these equitable demands.' These remarks plainly point to the appalling fact that Mr Bax has the temerity to write upon public affairs without reading *The Freewoman*.

The other great plank in his platform is a startling theory that 'women at present constitute an almost boundlessly privileged section of the community. A woman may, in the present day, do practically what she likes without fear of anything happening to her beyond a nominal punishment.' Now this is not true, as Mr Bax knows. I publicly challenge him to prove the sincerity of that statement: to go forth in the disguise of a woman, smash a jeweller's plate-glass window and abstract a diamond necklace, assault a policeman, set fire to the National Liberal Club and assassinate Sir Edward Carson. If he believes his own statement he will do it fearlessly. And I will pay the forty-shilling fine he pretends would be his 'nominal punishment'. He need have no fear of the wry face of the feminist: I will pay it gladly, for this brief saturnalia would open a new and thrilling field of activity to women.

What lies behind all this nonsense is a consciousness of the leniency of the law towards female criminals. This leniency is due to the bad conditions of passenger transport before the opening of the Inner Circle of the Metropolitan Railway in 1884. Before that date young men living in the Temple were cut off from the social life of their class. A visit to Chelsea or Kensington meant either an expensive cab-drive or a long journey in a stuffy omnibus at an exorbitant fare. Naturally, the young legal gentlemen, deprived of the society of women of their own class, made the acquaintance of women of the lowest kind. One obvious effect of these associations was the notorious fact that, in the middle and end of the last century, a judge's wife was as likely as not unpresentable. But the most lasting result was the tenderness of the law towards female criminals. For when a disreputable woman entered a court of law, although she personally might be unknown to the legal gentlemen therein, her kind was not. Her vices had been convenient to them in the past; therefore they could hardly be expected to punish them in the present. Thus there was established a tradition of maudlin sympathy and good-fellowship with the female defendant.

That Mr Bax can adduce this squalid folly of his sex as an argument against the enfranchisement of women is only another proof of the slatternly moral sense bred in men by the possession of sex-privilege.

Mr Bax alludes in terms of disgust to the defence of Daisy Lord by feminists. 'To read the gush on that occasion, one might have thought that the murder of new-born children represented the highest ideal of motherhood.' Statements like this really do give a feminist a wry face.

The State kindly allowed Daisy Lord to be born fatherless in a workhouse ward, and then kicked her and her mother out into the cold and dirt. After having provided Daisy with an expensive education which seems to have been no earthly use to her, the State permitted her to enter a laundry. By neglecting to inspect that laundry or to interfere when the owner paid Daisy a pittance of from five to ten shillings a week, the State tacitly consented to Daisy being brought to such a state of physical and mental starvation that any kind of emotion – even illicit and imprudent love – was a thing not to be resisted. Then, when she was going to have a child, the State created such a strong feeling against her that the last drop of courage was squeezed out of a weakened body, and she dared not risk exposure by calling assistance during childbirth. So that, in a fit of delirium, she killed her baby.

Then Mr Bax wants the State to finish its beneficent ministrations to Daisy by hanging her. This is the limit.

The release of Daisy Lord was one of those hopeful signs that the State does sometimes try to do the gentlemanly thing. But Mr Bax does not want the State to be a gentleman. He wants the State to be an orderly collection of atheists living with docile she-atheists and obedient little atheists, whom they will take on Saturday afternoons to visit the tomb of Karl Marx and explain what a very much more genteel person than Christ he was. This has the smell of death about it.

A bracing change from Mr Bax's gloom is Miss Florence Farr's *The Solemnization of Jacklin*. It is true that it is very depressing for women workers to read that an unhappy couple struggling along on £900 a year can only afford scrambled eggs for lunch and roller-skating for recreation. But it is an invigorating novel, and contains a most charming semi-supernatural gentleman, the son of Eros by a wealthy American lady, who picturesquely goes to sleep among the Annunciation lilies or dallies at Fontainebleau talking pantheism and theosophy and anything else that comes handy to beautiful ladies.

'Solemnization,' Miss Farr explains, 'is the work of making her mind clear by first-hand experience.' Jacklin solemnizes herself by divorcing her husband, marrying a dissipated artist, having a baby and going back to her first husband. The main thesis seems to be that married couples ought to part for a time and try other partners, so that they will learn to appreciate each other better. This adds a new terror to life. Falling in love being the squandering of emotion that it is, an interpolated and impermanent love affair seems a heavy price to pay for the privilege of ending where one started.

But, at any rate, fantastic and obscure as the book may be, Miss Farr does try to get somewhere. She sees life as an ocean bounded by infinity, not as a drop of water to be examined under the microscope. Reading her book is like straying into the chapel of some vast cathedral after an hour in the corrugated-iron Little Bethel of Mr Bax's dogmatism.

The Freewoman, 25 April 1912

Correspondence between Mrs Hobson and Miss West

By calling housework 'rat-poison' in a May 1912 issue of The Free-woman, *Rebecca West brought the wrath of the household gods and goddesses upon her head. Mrs Hobson (whose book she had savaged) replied, egging Miss West on to further speculations on the repressive nature of reformers' schemes of domestic economy.*

... The Miss Wests of the world are mistaken in believing that because they themselves (having possibly suffered from an overdose of it) regard all work in the home as 'domestic slavery, to be shunned like rat-poison', that any large number of women would share their view. It is fortunate for the Miss Wests, as well as for the rest of us, that the majority would probably always choose of their own accord to do this kind of work (under improved conditions and with the help of labour-saving inventions) even after the fullest measure of freedom had been attained, and they would choose it for the sheer joy of it and the opportunities it gives to make and extend happiness.

Florence Edgar Hobson
The Freewoman, 28 May 1912

Rebecca West replied:

Madam, Mrs Hobson begs the pardon of Art for her impertinence in writing *A Modern Crusader* in drama form, on the ground that she thereby attracted my attention. This is flattering but embarrassing; because it was not the play that evoked that page and a half of mine. The play – I say it in no malicious spirit – hurt me so much that I tried to forget it as much as possible. It was the scheme for the home schools, which reached me through the legitimate channels of propaganda in the pages of the *Contemporary Review*, which drew my attention back to the play.

I find it impossible to argue with a person who holds the doctrine of original sin. Mrs Hobson is 'sure that better cottages and higher wages would not alone change the slattern and the muddler into the sort of woman who can manage the better homes and healthier cottages'. Well, I am quite certain that in most cases they would. This shows that Mrs Hobson believes that there are varieties of women separate and immutable – the slattern, the housewife, the muddler, the manager – as distinct from one another as the lion from the cockatoo. Untidiness and laziness, like all the 'beastliness' of the poor, are largely accidents of environment. A woman is a slattern for one of two reasons. She may have a strong inclination towards some other sphere of activity and an active loathing for domestic work, or she may be sickly and exhausted. That there is a direct ratio between a woman's physical exhaustion and her efficiency as a homekeeper is proved by the fact, so often observed by teachers and inspectors, that the larger a family is the less well cared for it is. Therefore, Mrs Hobson's plea that because communal kitchens and public crèches are a long way off we ought to teach domestic economy leaves me cold. I think that teaching domestic economy to starved women is as silly as teaching reading and writing to starved children. The education authorities have had to abandon the latter attempt. They have to feed the children. How much easier the task of teaching them has become, I need not tell Mrs Hobson. Similarly, if society feeds its women, it will find it hardly necessary to teach them domestic economy.

For domestic work is the most elementary form of labour. It is suitable for those with the intelligence of rabbits. All it requires is cleanliness, tidiness and quickness – not moral or intellectual qualities at all, but merely the outward and visible signs of health. If people are dirty, slovenly and slow, it is usually because they are ill-nourished and sickly. And that is what the poor as a whole are.

And this brings me to the accusation that I ignored the settlement side in my 'unfair summing-up of the home school scheme in the sentence, "Mrs Hobson would wish a mother to spend her days making baby-clothes and cooking the dinner."' That's not a summing-up of the home school scheme! That's a description of Mrs Hobson's attitude of mind. Moreover, so far as I can gather from *The Mission to Mothers*, the settlement side is to consist – besides visits from the lady-in-charge to the women's homes, which seems an impertinent habit on her part – of mild entertainments in the evening. Which does not disprove my remark.

But the real reason why I did not touch on the settlement side was that it seemed to me the most discreditable part of a well-meant scheme. I loathe these attempts to poke the sickly and exhausted poor into unspontaneous gambols. Surely everyone can see that a community must be sick unto death before its amusements have to be organised and imposed upon it. The whole of this home school scheme is an attempt to pay back the countryside in bad halfpence what the rich stole from it in good gold. Before the village life of England was wiped out in the latter half of the eighteenth century the villagers went out on the summer evenings and danced Laudnum Bunches and Constant Billy on the green till the moon came up. It is, of course, merely a matter of aesthetic perception whether you prefer them to sit docilely in a home school hall while the vicar's wife sings Tosti's 'Goodbye'. Because you won't get them to practise art now any more than domestic economy. They're tired and cross and hungry, and they won't play.

I take a keen interest in school hygiene, as it happens, and I cannot say that I am impressed by Mrs Hobson's remarks. I know that many teachers and inspectors feel that they are attacking the problem at the wrong end. But few of them are simple enough to suggest that the teaching of domestic economy is the right end. 'More money and better housing' is the commoner suggestion. I doubt exceedingly that in the given case – the cleansed child recontaminated by a filthy home – a graduate of the home school would do much good. If she could keep the child clean when rearing six children on twenty-two shillings a week, and living in a house the walls and wood of which are rotten with bugs and the water supply of which is down three flights of stairs – well, I can only conclude that there will be a class in miracles, conducted by the vicar.

There seems to be no other point to be answered except the last paragraph, wherein Mrs Hobson rebukes the 'Miss Wests of the world' – ye gods! what a picture this calls up – for regarding domestic work as 'rat-poison'. That simile has had a great success. It has been so widely quoted by a scandalised Press that I hope it will ultimately enter the language – one of those

> ... jewels five words long,
> That on the stretched forefinger of all time
> Sparkle for ever.

Mrs Hobson declares that the 'Miss Wests of the world' – what *is* this new species to which I have given my name? – 'are mistaken in believing that ... any large number of women would share their view' as to the hatefulness of domestic work. She implies that I found it hateful because I did too much of it, and approached it with ignorance and dislike, unmitigated by ideals and the intelligence to plan for leisure. That is not so. I never had more than the usual amount. I was certainly not ignorant (having been exposed to the ponderous pedagogy of a school of domestic economy); and I had no reason to dislike it any more than any other kind of work. I don't quite know what Mrs Hobson means by 'ideals'. I rather fancy she means conceit. Certainly I didn't pretend when I was frying potatoes that I was doing anything as important or useful as my friend who was studying science in the laboratories of the neighbouring university. So I surrender the claim to ideals. But as for *intelligence!* But – ah, well! it's no use saying that – Mrs Hobson wouldn't believe me.

Hatred of domestic work is a natural and admirable result of civilisation. I deny absolutely Mrs Hobson's declaration that 'the majority would probably always choose of their own accord to do this kind of work'. This is not true. The vast majority of women refuse domestic work. The working-class woman will turn her hand to anything rather than become a servant. The first thing a woman does when she gets a little money into her hands is to hire some other poor wretch to do her housework. The recent movement down the kitchen stairs – the last tumble of which is the King's College home science course – has no support among the women who are alive: the working women. For heaven's sake let us take this unpleasant job and give it over to the specialist to organise as a trade process.

I am not a materialist, so I cannot sympathise with Mrs Hobson's fear that the home – the relationship between a man and a woman and their children – will be broken up by the abolition of drudgery. I can only say that I love my mother none the less because we send our washing to a steam laundry.

In conclusion, I would like to point out the insensate extravagance of this down-the-kitchen-stairs movement. Mrs Hobson advocates the establishment of these home schools all over the country. She prudently declines to calculate the cost of the sites or building, and only commits herself to an estimate of the furnishing – £150. But she quite fearlessly declares that the *dead loss per annum* on each of the schools (which will accommodate only six pupils at a time) will amount to £271 4s. Think of it! Surely that £100,000 endowment fund of the King's College course should have satisfied these kitchen recruiting-sergeants. All over the country gifted girls, who might

have done their part in analysing food values or harnessing electricity
to the home, are breaking their hearts for lack of university opportunities; the need for school clinics grows more crying every day; poor
working women must walk the streets by night because there are no
municipal lodging-houses for them. And Mrs Hobson calmly allo-
cates thousands to the condescending instruction of poor defenceless
girls in the gentle art of sucking eggs!

Rebecca West
The Freewoman, 6 June 1912

Spinsters and Art

The Considine Luck by H. A. Hinkson, *The Spinster* by H. Wales,
The Trespasser by D. H. Lawrence

The baldness and badness of popular novels is as touching as the
ugliness of a cherished rag-doll. What overflowing tenderness must
be in the heart of the child who loves this monstrosity, we think. And
so with the people who read these novels – what tireless imaginations they must have, to perceive joy in these bare chronicles! We
superior persons are too feeble to go searching for beauty on our own
like that. We wait idly until Thomas Hardy comes back from wit-
nessing fierce wars between the flesh and the spirit, and Conrad sails
home from the strangest and most distant tropic. But the common
man picks up some artless work such as *The Considine Luck* by H. A.
Hinkson, and creates his own beauty. He takes the puppet heroine,
Grace Smith, and paints her wooden cheeks with the flush of his
sensuous dreams; he lights her eyes with the radiance he has seen in
unattainable women in pictures or at theatres, till Grace Smith is
more fair than his first love. In a sense he writes his own books.

I fancy that *The Considine Luck* is the sort of book that the Bishop
of Bristol referred to as 'wholesome literature', in his recent address
to the pupils of Colston Girls' School, advising the young ladies not
to adopt as a profession the writing of objectionable fiction. (Surely
his Lordship is mistaken in regarding this as an important opening for
women. Nobody ever tried to bribe me to write objectionable fiction.
And the people who tell you that they came to London five years ago
with three shillings and are now worth half a million, did it by
inventing new kinds of sausages and things like that, not by writing
objectionable fiction.) The only thing that distresses me about the

work is the startling promiscuity of the second heroine, Flo Dallas. A simple child of nature, reared on the Irish hills, she nourishes in her young bosom a pure passion for Sir Jasper, the hero, until one day her cousin, Hugh Venables, breaks the news to her.

'I suppose you have heard the news?'
'What news?' she inquired, with a throb of anxiety.
'That Sir Jasper is going to marry Grace Smith.'
'Marry her,' echoed Flo blankly.
'Yes, no doubt about it . . .' But Flo was not listening. She had sat down at the foot of the tree and, after making several brave attempts to control her emotion, she suddenly burst into tears.

I regret to say that when she got up again she was engaged to Hugh Venables. This is a form of treachery that constantly takes place in novels. For a lesser thing than this Winston Churchill was called a turncoat. And there is still some scandal talked about St Peter. The hero who suffers from unrequited love is allowed to go away and shoot big game in decent despair. But the heroine may transfer her alliegance with horrid facility.

Another lady of trying habits is Mr Hubert Wales' *The Spinster*. We have all of us had experience of the terribly confidential old lady in the crowded railway-carriage who will tell us about the operation her son has just undergone, and how it runs in the family. The Spinster was troubled with a similar unbridled candour. Although close on forty, and gifted with that training in deceit which an unattractive appearance imposes on women, she goes about confessing (with imbecile quiet dignity) the secret of her life to her sisters, her cousins and her aunts, the butcher, the baker and the candlestickmaker, and – finally – a coroner's jury. I abstain from revealing what the Spinster's secret really was, in view of the fact that Mrs Humphry Ward is a reader of *The Freewoman*.

All the same, *The Spinster* is a great work. This is the first production by Mr Hubert Wales that I have ever read. I was held from the very first page, whereon I read: 'There were reservoirs of love in her – of wife-love and of mother-love – accumulating reservoirs, which had never been tapped.' This is luscious imagery. 'The Tapping of the Spinster' would be an exquisite title for a poetical play. And the conception of fate as a Metropolitan Water Board regulating the flow of spiritual liquids is immense. I find Mr Wales difficult to place as an artist. Undoubtedly his style derives largely from Mr Frederick Harrison, though the breezy incident of the Spinster's mother throwing the new potatoes at the housemaid obviously shows the influence of Strindberg. In philosophy it would not be too much to say that Mr Wales stands shoulder to shoulder with Ella Wheeler Wilcox.

It is not unkind to say that the above two books need never have been written. Of course, one is glad that they have been written, just as one is glad that there are dog-shows at the Horticultural Show, even though one never goes near the place oneself. One likes to think of all those jolly little puppies; and similarly one is glad that Mr Wales feels up to his work, and quite certain that a lot of people will get ingenuous pleasure out of Mr Hinkson's book. But here is a book that is on a different plane, a book that was worth the writing, *The Trespasser* by D. H. Lawrence. Last year Mr Lawrence published *The White Peacock*, in which there was some imagination, but much more fancy, which had within therefore the seeds of both genius and decay. Mr Lawrence has conquered. This book is magic.

The first half of the book concerns itself with the week that Siegmund, a middle-aged and unsuccessful violinist and music-teacher, and Helena, his pupil, spend in the Isle of Wight. Except for the thought of his shrewish wife, avid for the fidelity of a husband she dislikes, and his family, which varies from lank unfriendly adolescence to warm and adorable infancy, they live in ecstasy. To begin with, one must consider the difficulty of staging ecstasy in the tameness of that landscape. Surely the extreme mildness of the nearer holiday resorts explains the insipidity of the Londoner. The northern wage-slave can go to Blackpool, whose vulgarity shouts magnificently to heaven like the strains of a hundred massed brass bands, or to that touching attempt at tropical beauty, the Isle of Man. The Glasgow artisan can sail down the Clyde till the land shivers into a thousand islands before the marvel of the ragged Arran peaks against the Atlantic. But the Londoner can go on no such excursions to learn that romance is real. He must go to Margate.

The Isle of Wight, that vast kitchen-garden dimpled with vicarages, is nearly as bad, but Mr Lawrence's vision can transmute it. 'The way home lay across country, through deep little lanes where the late foxgloves sat seriously, like sad hounds; over open downlands, rough with gorse and ling, and through pocketed hollows of bracken and trees.' The chalk is on fire with the sun.

All things, it seemed, were made of sunshine more or less soiled. The cliffs rose out of the shining waves like clouds of strong, fine texture, and rocks along the shore were the dapplings of a bright dawn. The coarseness was fused out of the world, so that the sunlight showed in the veins of the morning cliffs and the rocks. Yea, everything ran with sunshine as we are full of blood, and plants are tissued from green-gold, glistening sap. Substance and solidity were the shadows that the morning cast round itself to make itself tangible, as Helena herself was a shadow, cast by that fragment of sunshine, her soul, over its inefficiency.

The description of the ecstasy of love has been done before, often impertinently, in view of the supreme achievements of Shakespeare and Swinburne. But Mr Lawrence not only treats it with reality, he attains past it to the most godlike point of discontent; he perceives the failure of love. It is true that passion fuses these two into one. But it does not endure. They are torn apart temporarily by circumstance; they are divorced for ever, except for moments which are half-dreams, by temperamental differences. And these are conditions found in almost every union. That the highest experience in life is generally incomplete explains why the greatest geniuses, the men who are likest gods, have refused to become men of action and have been artists. Art is so much fuller of perfection than life. Has any man experienced anything so beautiful as 'Kubla Khan'?

The gulf between the lovers lies in the fact that Helena is a sentimentalist.

Siegmund ... might play with the delicious, warm surface of life, but always he recked of the relentless mass of cold beneath – the mass of life which has no sympathy with the individual, no cognisance of him. She loved the trifles and the toys, the mystery and the magic of things. She would not own life to be relentless. It was either beautiful, fantastic, or weird, or inscrutable, or else mean and vulgar, below consideration. He had to get a sense of the anemone and a sympathetic knowledge of its experience into his blood before he was satisfied. To Helena an anemone was one more pretty figure in her kaleidoscope.

She was all fancy and no imagination. On a still night by the sea in the glimmer of many stars she was capable of quoting:

> Die Luft ist kühl, und es dunkelt,
> Und ruhig fliesst der Rhein.

And by day she made her own bad poetry for herself.

The pink convolvuli were fairy horns or telephones from the day fairies to the night fairies. The rippling sunlight on the sea was the Rhine-maidens spreading their bright hair to the sun. That was her favourite form of thinking. The value of things was in the fancy they evoked. She did not care for people; they were vulgar, ugly, and stupid as a rule.

That was her sin. She despised life. Even her love was a cold-blooded theft. As a man complains in the book: 'These deep, interesting women don't want us; they want the flowers of the spirit they can gather of us. We, as natural men, are more or less degrading to them and to their love of us; therefore they destroy the natural man in us – that is, us altogether.' So she steals his passion to build herself more feeble, romantic dreams, and gives him nothing in return. So that when he goes back to his unfriendly home he has nothing between him and the stars, by whose light he sees life as miserable and as lonely as, as a matter of fact, it generally is if one is not a fanatic of some kind. So he falls through the vault of madness down to quiet suicide.

This latter part of the book is by far the finest, but one regrets Mr Lawrence's scornful attitude towards Siegmund's wife. The deserted wife is the most pathetic figure in the world, however contemptible she may be, for she has based her whole life on the false assumption that the love of man is a static rather than a rhythmic condition. Perhaps it has been necessary for the race that she should make that mistake. Since in all of us the devil's part wishes to play Napoleon and have power, it is probable that those not gifted with emotional fastidiousness should refuse to accept the responsibility of wifehood and motherhood without the bait of power over a man until death.

At any rate, Beatrice was nearer the heart of Siegmund than Helena, for Helena was the spinster through and through. Continually she was being revolted by some physical lustiness of Siegmund; the sight of his strong throat above his flannel shirt, his childish trick of whistling through his teeth, his great, bull-like strength.

She looked at him, and again shuddered with horror. Was that really Siegmund, that stooping, thick-shouldered, indifferent man? Was that the Siegmund who had seemed to radiate joy into his surroundings, the Siegmund whose coming had always changed the whole weather of her soul? . . . His radiance had gone, his aura had ceased. She saw him a stooping man, past the buoyancy of youth, walking and whistling rather stupidly – in short, something of the clothed animal on end, like the rest of men.

She used to withdraw to the sentimentalist's voluptuous chamber of self-torture to become a self-scourging moralist, and would distress his simplicity with her sobs. Continually she receded from him into the nook of some obscene fastidiousness, some icy distaste for life.

The fact was she was drunk with the spinster's ethereal conception of man. The spinster, looking out on the world through the drawn curtains of the boarding-school or the equally celibate, boarding-house, sees men as trees walking – large, dignified, almost majestic. Like Helena, she refuses to see their helplessness, their pathetic defeats in the strife against circumstance and temperament. Perpetually she conceives them as masters of the situation.

This spinster conception of man has had its ill effect on literature. Consider how many books are written by spinsters, how many more for spinsters. In all these men are drawn as strong gods. Even in Charlotte Brontë this is apparent. Her men are marred by a perpetual dignity. A married woman would not have believed in Mr Rochester for one minute; a man who had been taken in so flagrantly by a lunatic wife might have an appealing, wistful charm, but he would not have been in the least like that noble gorilla. It is all very well to say that Charlotte Brontë had experience of the weakness and crimes of men. They were evidenced in her father and her brother, and somehow one expects one's relatives to be incompetent and beastly. It is not until one meets a man on the grounds of, not duty, but attraction, that his faults strike one with surprise.

Out of that surprise there ought to come Art. We want novels written by women about men. Very few men have ever succeeded in creating men as they have succeeded in creating women. Some woman ought to write a novel about a man and the struggle of his soul with the universe, as moving and as pathetic as *Tess of the D'Urbervilles*. It would be a great thing for a woman to do as much for one man as Meredith did for all his women.

That is why the spinster question is really an urgent matter. Today there are hundreds and thousands of spinsters all over the country, produced for the most part by educational systems. Hence you have a large population deprived of the possibility of wifehood and motherhood. The only people to whom such a deprivation could be of any value are artists. But then again, a spinster is usually a sentimentalist, and therefore incapable of art.

So what is the good of all these spinsters?

The Freewoman, 11 July 1912

Letter to the Editor of *The Freewoman*

The relationship between celibacy or sexuality and the artist was a subject of deep concern to the readers of The Freewoman. *Rebecca West replied to their complaints on 1 August 1912:*

Madam, I once edited a woman's page (for a week), so I can give people advice as to how to use up odd scraps of macaroni, velveteen and biscuit-tins, and how to play the fool by painting drainpipes and milking-stools. But I refuse absolutely to give any advice to 'A Disappointed Reader', who appears to contemplate stepping down the primrose path in order to please the Editor of *The Freewoman* and myself. She ought to toss up.

To begin with, spinsterhood is not necessarily a feminine quality. It is simply the limitation of experience to one's own sex, and consequently the regard of the other sex from an idealist point of view. Walter Pater and A. C. Benson are typical spinsters: Miss May Sinclair, though an unmarried woman, is not. I thought my reference to 'the spinster, looking out on the world through the drawn curtains of the boarding-school or the equally celibate boarding-house' made it plain that spinsterhood implied a segregation from the opposite sex. Portia, for instance, accustomed to manage men and suitors from her girlhood, was not a spinster.

As a mother sacrifices everything to her children, and an artist sacrifices everything to her art. I never said that an artist ought to be a mother. Therefore I do not wince at the remark that 'instead of sending our girls to studios, conservatoires of music, or making them familiar with the masterpieces of literature, we should first see to it that they become mothers'. When Ruskin said that no one could paint until he had seen Venice, I wonder if people thought he disapproved of artists learning to draw. 'The artist declares itself at an age when at least most women are spinsters: roughly speaking, from four to eighteen years of age.' And if you starve it of intellectual and emotional experience, it will go away again. If, when the infant of five shows signs of poetic gifts, you shut her up in a prison cell, her epics will be of poor and monotonous quality. For want of emotional experience Jane Austen's imagination never developed virility. And, though of course her comic characters had human failings, her heroes (that is, the men she regarded from a sexual point of view) were 'strong gods'.

The reference to 'jeers at the spinster and the mother-in-law' makes one feel how splendidly right the people are, even in their vulgarity. The spinster is ridiculous because she is limited. (I write as a most typical spinster.) The mother-in-law is ridiculous, as any parent is who attempts to exercise authority over a grown-up child.

Some day I am going to review in these columns Miss Sinclair's book on the Brontës, but not just now. The remarks of X, the lady who is sure she would have loved Mr Rochester, do not impel me to hasten to the task. She interests me when she libels me, because it shows how low the profession of journalism has fallen in the popular mind.

She states, 'I have serious doubts as to whether your reviewer can have read these novels.' Now, I earn my living as a journalist. People actually pay me coin of the realm to write about literature. If I have not read the literature I write about, I obtain that money on false pretences. As I consider the profession of journalism to be at least as honourable as that of medicine, I resent the imputation of quackery.

The Freewoman, 1 August 1912

English Literature, 1880–1905

English Literature, 1880–1905 by J. M. Kennedy

Mr J. M. Kennedy is a bishop *manqué*. He writes in the solemn yet hiccupy style peculiar to bishops, with a 'however', or 'indeed', or 'of course' interrupting every sentence. 'The force of adulatory superlatives has long been weakened owing to the manner in which injudicious critics have scattered them over the ephemeral productions of modern novelists . . .' This must have been written in apron and gaiters. Perhaps Mr Kennedy is a bishop in some secret church of the Nietzscheans.

This history of modern English literature is irritating because Mr Kennedy writes as a critic rather than a scholar, and it is as a scholar that he is a distinguished writer. As a scholar he is enthusiastic and ravenous. With the thoughts of all dead masters of language living in his brain, he can see very clearly the relation of these modern artists to the past. The chapter on Walter Pater, although quite unsympathetic, is very remarkable for its intimate knowledge of every problem that Pater's mind touched. From this point of view the book is well worth reading, if only for the learning that flashes from his pages . . . We discover that 'romanticist' is simply a term used by Mr Kennedy towards those he dislikes. It would be much more vigorous to use some plain English term that we all understand, such as 'blighter'.

Hence the value of the book depends entirely on Mr Kennedy's standard of blighterhood. This standard is difficult to define, because of Mr Kennedy's inconsistency. As an example of this there is the contrast between his treatment of Oscar Wilde and of George Gissing. He misses the true tragedy of Wilde, the common enough tragedy of the clever young provincial who enters the deadly dull salons of London and, finding that the wit which was exacted from him as ordinary conversation by the more particular provinces is hailed as genius by the bored Londoners, forthwith abandons honest, artistic work. He misses the significance of *De Profundis* altogether, and discredits its doctrine for quite the wrong reason.

> There is a factor underlying . . . the book which has never been sufficiently taken into account, viz., that Wilde is here speaking as what Nietzsche would call an inferior man. He has been degraded, he is suffering, he is wretched, and in order to justify his degradation and sorrow and wretchedness, he endeavours to set them upon a philosophical foundation, and to use this new foundation in addition as the basis of a new theory of art and truth.

Of course *De Profundis* is the most convincing proof of the inconquerable quality of Wilde's soul. He was hard and shallow; he wrote of great things, but he wrote with a pen dipped in ink and not in blood. On him the blows of society could make no impression. *De Profundis* is his last and most successful joke; wherein, by the deft use of his imprisonment and the Christian code which he had infringed, he induced the world which had inflicted his imprisonment to feel perpetually in his debt.

Yet though Mr Kennedy discredits the doctrine of *De Profundis* because it is the work of an inferior man, later on he gives George Gissing the highest rank as an artist, far above Wells or Shaw. Now, if there ever was an 'inferior man', it was Gissing. Other men, such as Shaw, have been as poor as Gissing, but none of them have been so completely absorbed by poverty. In his depression he lost all sense of colour and all buoyancy of sight. This is proved by the lengthy nature study quoted by Mr Kennedy, in which Gissing takes an inventory of a sunset like a not too enthusiastic auctioneer. His books deal constantly with the theme of unrequited love, which is pathetic, but not dignified. A passion that fails to inspire passion in another is defeated in the main object of its being. If there is anything undignified about Christianity, it is not Christ's crucifixion, but his unrequited love for the world. How can Mr Kennedy consistently praise such a messenger of misery?

Of course, Gissing's novels are great in spite of his wretchedness, for there is very little in this theory that art cannot be conceived of sorrow, and that suffering may not be included in the basis of a new theory of art and truth. They say *Hamlet* was written after the death of Shakespeare's son; and certainly it delights in suffering. Such masterpieces as this and *Tess of the D'Urbervilles* leave one not, as Mr Kennedy declares, with a sense of the valuelessness of life because of sorrow, but with a sense of the value of everything in life, even sorrow.

Both Mr Shaw and Mr Wells come under Mr Kennedy's definition of blighterhood. He scolds at Shaw for writing of an ephemeral phase of humanity and not of the changeless nature of man, as the Greek dramatists did. To every sensitive mind it is obvious that the Greek dramatists looked on life from a very local point of view. The nature of man may not have changed since the days of Sophocles, but the conception of fate has. My humanity feels humiliated when I read of Oedipus gouging out his eyes because an impertinent fate, who is liker the malicious mother-in-law in a Criterion farce than anything else in modern art, has cheated him into marrying his mother and killing his father. No human being can see humanity absolute, unbound by chains of time and circumstance. Hence Shaw and the Greeks are right in choosing the ephemeral journalistic point of view.

The attack on Mr Wells is more loosely reasoned. It depends mainly on the assumption that: 'If there is any being who is at the diametrically opposite pole to an artist, it is a mechanic or anyone with a mind interested in mechanics,' which is disproved by the memory of Michelangelo and Leonardo da Vinci. Therefore, because Mr Wells has a scientific imagination, he cannot have an artistic imagination. Mr Kennedy also accuses him of timidity in his treatment of the novel. 'Like the Church of Rome, it is aristocratic in its nature: its message is flung to the world, and must be taken or left.' I like the idea of writing a novel at the public in the same haughty way in which one flings a clothes-brush out of the window at a serenading cat; but it will take some time to accustom me to an association between timidity and Mr H. G. Wells.

Moreover, he misses the really high purpose which the *Yellow Book* school fulfilled. These young men of artistic ambition came into the world to find that style was held in contempt. Dickens had dragged the English language through the mud, Browning had thrown bricks at it, Trollope was sitting on its chest and reading the lessons to it. The house of art was full of men who had magnificent messages, but nevertheless ate peas with their knives. This revolted Wilde, possibly because, coming from Ireland, he was accustomed to hear good, clean English; but in any case he and his followers set about imposing style on English literature. That was the purpose of their existence, and they fulfilled it. There was no new philosophy in the air, so they had no new gospel to preach. But they improved our manners. It is thanks to them that we are as fastidious about words as we are about personal cleanliness.

The atmosphere of the nineties, full of a calm beauty, perhaps more beautiful because undisturbed by any spiritual upheaval, was brought before us last week for a little time, when Miss Florence Farr gave her last recital to the psaltery. Miss Farr is the last of those subtle women of the nineties who veiled their loveliness with a becoming melancholy born of tragedies that were, one is sure, very enjoyable while they lasted. Content to be themselves works of art, they did not desire to project their beauty into eternity by becoming artists. Miss Farr's art of reciting to the psaltery is typical of her period. It is unimportant from every artistic point of view; yet nothing could be more exquisite than the speech of that lovely, level voice, in which the tears glimmer perpetually, like dewdrops in long grass.

Very significantly, this recreation of a past decade was preceded by a play by a woman of this generation, *Edge o' Dark* by Gwen John. It was a brutal thing, a horror of drink and adultery and murder played out in the black squalor of a Derbyshire cottage. Marred by a violence that was probably the sign of an artistic nervousness due to inexperience, it yet had a germ of tragic beauty. The woman, played by Miss Gladys Jones, who is too weary of men to care for vengeance against them and goes out to die, is a figure of pity and dignity. There is no doubt that this younger generation would find it much harder to deal with the violent subjects their hunger for a completer representation of life leads them to choose were it not for the tradition of beautiful technique imposed on them by the *Yellow Book* school.

I must confess that the passage in Mr Kennedy's book, which gives me the most tranquil pleasure is an entry in the index: 'Sex, The unimportance of, p. 224.' This is Napoleonic. One yearns to grovel, just a little. This clarion note re-echoes in the letter-press when Mr Kennedy exclaims: 'Even at the present day there are men, though their number may be relatively small, who would . . . willingly see the whole female sex at the bottom of the sea if they thought for a minute it would tend to interfere with their ambitious designs.' That thrills me. It is just how I feel about the male sex. I greet Mr Kennedy as a kindred spirit. There is just one weakness about our position. Owen Glendower once boasted: 'I can call spirits from the vasty deep.' To which Hotspur replied: 'Ay, so can I, and so can any man. But will they come?' That is our difficulty. Mr Kennedy and I may stand side by side on Southend pier from dawn to dusk calling our respective opposite sexes down to the vasty deep. But will they come?

The Freewoman, 25 July 1912

Strindberg: the English Gentleman (1)

The Confession of a Fool and *Plays* by August Strindberg

Writers on the subject of August Strindberg have hitherto omitted to mention that he could not write. His vain face, with the hot, angry eyes, the little lustful mouth, the rumpled forehead and sharp, peevish chin, proclaims that he had neither the strength nor the humour to become an artist. The following moving quotation conveys his literary atmosphere: 'In the course of the evening I recited Longfellow's "Excelsior" to her. Genuinely touched by this beautiful poem, I fixed my eyes on her, and as if she were hypnotised her face reflected every shade of feeling expressed on my own. She had the appearance of an ecstatic, a seer.' His economics are the crudities of the British Socialist Party, delivered with the languor of the Fabian Society. His religion has the wistful ingenuity of theological speculations carried on in bed by a tired child: he believes this earth to be a hell, in which we suffer for former sins, and from which we struggle to rise to salvation. One very blatant defect in his plays is the lifelessness of the minor characters, which contrasts with Ibsen's vivid realisation of his smallest parts. The engineer in *Little Eyolf* and little Hilda Wangel in *The Lady from the Sea* live as intensely as Rita Allmers or the Man from the Sea. In Strindberg's greatest play, *The Father*, besides himself and his wife, there is not one living character. Various puppets come on and give information with the accuracy and curtness of Bradshaw; even the little girl over which Strindberg and his wife quarrel till he goes mad speaks like an automaton. But, of course, Strindberg's plays are bad by necessity of his style: one cannot create great drama out of ugly phrases. He tries to paint the battles of emotion between nobility and sensuality, and one cannot paint strong emotions as ugly, because only weakness is ugly. Because he failed to realise this, his plays are unspeakably horrible. His confession is not beautiful and purifying, like the confession of Sir Aglovale de Galis. One feels humiliated and degraded as one would feel in some sordid chapel when the minister confessed to the congregation that he had long been a secret drinker.

It is necessary to insist on this because, although Strindberg must be studied in England, it would be disastrous if he became an artistic influence. That kind of brutality comes so easy to Teutons that it would spread quickly. It must be recognised that the value of his works is purely moral and not artistic.

Strindberg, who was neither a good nor a wise man, had a stroke of luck. He went mad. He lost the power of inhibition. Everything down to the pettiest suspicion that the dog had been given the leanest mutton chop, poured out of his lips. Men of his weakness and sensuality are usually, from their sheer brutishness, unable to express themselves. But Strindberg was mad and articulate. That is what makes him immortal.

The Confession of a Fool is the triumph of his articulateness. It is the story of his first marriage. At the age of twenty-six, when he was a poverty-stricken Court librarian, he met a middle-aged Baron of gross life and his Baroness, a beautiful and refined Madonna, who yearned for the stage. Gradually the Baroness and the young librarian become lovers. Finally, as the Baron has a liaison with a younger woman, he agrees to divorce her. For some months they live in an illicit relationship. Now that she is released from the restraint of her social position, she shows clearly that she is a woman of evil disposition; she has a taste for strong drink and light love. But, bestially infatuated by her physical charm, he is still her lover. He forces her to bear a child, whom he legitimatises by marrying her. After that he perceives her vices to be as the sands of the sea. She becomes a drunkard and an adulteress; she is dirty in her personal habits and financially dishonest. She loves the company of rakes and prostitutes, and develops the blackest perversities. But for ten years he not only submits to, but insists on, the embraces of this unpenalised member of the criminal classes; he makes her the mother of his children. They persist in this offensive marriage for ten years, after which time they consent to a divorce.

The main fact of life which he grasped in the clairvoyance granted him by this appalling experience is that love is a miracle. It is the only miracle that ever happened. It is the only successful alchemy, since it transfuses the untransfusable. That love makes two persons become one is the only pledge we have that the religious passion, the desire of the individual to become the universe, is not an illusion. The ecstasy of love is impermanent, like the ecstasy of art. It is only rarely that the sculptor feels at one with his marble or the poet becomes his poem. The ecstasy is so tremendous that life could not endure its permanence. Besides, differences of experience mould each soul so different from all others that each one knows itself an Ishmaelite and fears its brother. They may be united for a minute, but for eternity they are divorced by their differences of temperament. As Yeats says, far more forcibly than Strindberg could ever say anything, because he uses beautiful language:

I think that all deep passion is but a kiss
In the mid-battle, and a difficult peace
'Twixt oil and water, candles and dark night,
Hillside and hollow, the hot-footed moon,
And the cold, sliding, slippery-footed moon;
A brief forgiveness between opposites,
That have been hatreds for three times the age
Of this long 'stablished ground.

It would be difficult to credit it, but Strindberg actually rebels against the impermanence of love. He is perpetually crying out because after love has gone there comes hatred. It does not if the lovers turn to the contemplation of either of the two other impermanent good things of the earth – art and childhood; but it does if the lovers are sensual persons infatuated with the pleasure of sex.

Strindberg's style is so grossly material that the mind refuses to recognise the perception of a spiritual truth as the cause of his agony, and seeks for a material explanation. Europe has found that material explanation in his madness, and thereby has not enjoyed the value of his confessions. His lack of inhibition made him reveal his psychology with insane frankness. But his psychology was quite sane. It was that of the ordinary English gentleman.

To show how like an English gentleman Strindberg was, we may take a few examples of the effect of passion on him.

Taciturn, morose, not at all pretty, the Baroness left the conversation entirely to me, and since she made no replies, it soon degenerated into a monologue . . . All at once my eyes, travelling round the room, were arrested by a display of her ankles underneath the tablecloth. I beheld her finely shaped calf, clothed in a white stocking; a gaily embroidered garter belted that charming muscle, which turns a man's head because it stimulates his imagination and tempts him to the construction of the whole of the remaining form. . . . At the time I took it for an accident, but later on I learned that a woman is always conscious of being looked at when she exhibits more than her ankles.

Passages such as these require some fortitude in the reading and a constant reminder to oneself that Strindberg really is a European thinker. A little later on they have a quarrel on the gravest grounds, in which he lets loose a torrent of moral indignation on the poor little wretch's head.

All at once, with a word of apology, she put her two feet on the cushioned seat, pretending to be worn out with fatigue. Her languid glances, her tears had left me unmoved; I had kept my head, my strength of purpose, in spite of her fallacious logic. Now everything collapsed. I beheld her adorable boot, a tiny piece of her stocking.

One understands at last, looking downwards, what anti-suffragists mean by 'indirect influence'. There are two sixpenny periodicals, called the *Sketch* and the *Tatler*, which have a similar pre-occupation with women's ankles. They have photographs of actresses lifting their skirts in a determinedly provocative manner or matronly Spanish dancers paddling at Ostend. These periodicals are widely read by English gentlemen. One suddenly understands why. Since the publication of Sir Almroth Wright's letter, we have known that men were swine. Now we know that they are asses. Another anti-feminist publication, and no woman will ever think of loving a man again.

The Freewoman, 15 August 1912

Strindberg:
the English Gentleman (2)

Strindberg's theoretical anti-feminism is disappointing: it is simply the gospel preached at any anti-suffrage meeting put in more pretentious language. But his practical relations with women are intensely interesting. For he cherished all the ideals of an English gentleman: marriage and the family.

During all this time she led the life of a woman free from all duties as mother and wife. My health did not permit me to accompany her to the artistic circles which she frequented, and consequently she went alone. Sometimes she did not come home until early in the morning; very often she was intoxicated, and made sufficient noise to wake up the whole house. I could hear her stumbling into the night nursery where she slept.
What is a man to do in a case of this sort? Is he to denounce his own wife? Impossible! Divorce her? No! I looked upon the family as an organism, like an organism of a plant: a whole of which I was a part. I could not exist independently of it, without the mother; life seemed impossible to me even if I had had the custody of the children. My heart's blood, transmitted through my wife, flowed through the veins of their small bodies. The whole was like a system of arteries intimately connected and interdependent. If a single one were cut, my life would ebb away with the blood which trickled down and was sucked up by the sand.

This uncleanly respect for marriage is largely due to the sordid circumstances from which he sprang. He was the third child of a small tradesman and a barmaid, who reared eight children in three rooms on a starvation diet, and he was a living proof that 'the poor are useless, dangerous, and ought to be abolished'. He suffered from the vulgar fear of loneliness. The worker, his nervous system unhealthily stimulated by the clang of the factories or the buzz of the city, dreads silence. The crush and riot of Blackpool or Douglas is part of his holiday enjoyment. He makes friends feverishly with strangers in railway carriages and buses. This hunger for the closest possible personal relationships, this contempt for the proud soul's privilege of isolation, leads the poor into early marriages. It bound Strindberg to his wife: he huddled up beside that loathsome woman, hung with the filthy rags of sin, rather than endure his own society.

Moreover, his early privations had thwarted his temperamental desire to be a tyrant. No one would permit such a neurotic weakling to govern them. But with a small capital, the most impotent man, whom no sane person would put in charge of the ginger-beer stall at a village flower show, can tyrannise until death over a woman and her children. The unsuccessful bully can always become the father of a family.

Besides, the institution of marriage gives the licence which is the necessary corollary of law. It is obvious to the meanest mind that sexual relationships may be good or evil. A universal test which declares all relationships entered into under certain conditions to be good and all other relationships to be evil saves much mental effort. And those whose spiritual tendency is not towards virtue can acquire its reputation by conformity to these conditions. This would appeal to Strindberg.

While it is painful to reflect what base considerations may lead a man to cherish the ideals of an English gentleman, it is still more painful to consider to what a hideous crime they led him. Strindberg's marriage is as disgraceful as drunkenness. He chose a woman whom he knew to be a liar and coward, expert in every vice, and so unfit for pure passion that during her divorce she betrayed her lover with her former husband – an obscene crime that staggers the mind – and made her his wife. This was a damning confession of personal baseness. It argues a lack of physical fastidiousness in the man that he could bear to live in the same house as this woman. It argues spiritual rottenness in the man that he could desire to perform the miracle of love with this woman. To transfuse oneself with an ugly, sensual soul is a movement towards death and not towards life. Love becomes destruction and not creation. So it is not surprising that Strindberg's art is so purely autobiographical and non-creative. The true artist knows all the secrets of all women, from the Madonna to Faustine, and tells them with truth and reverence. Strindberg's works are a not obscene, but Ibscene, account of his cat-and-dog relations with three most unpleasant women.

But besides his offence against himself, he offended against the race. Possibly this poor woman, one of Nature's prostitutes, was meant to be the instrument of fate upon men, seeking out the hidden spot of rottenness in unworthy men who usurped authority, and dragging them down through lust and death to their rightful impotence. But Strindberg set her tyrant over posterity by making her a mother. If there is any red blood in the veins of the Eugenics Society, it will pay an annual visit to Stockholm in order to defile Strindberg's grave. He made this poor wretch the mother of five children, three of whom survived to transmit the poison of their parents' blood. Can one imagine a crime more brutal in its direct results, more universal in its ultimate consequences, than this? But Strindberg knew no penitence. The only thing possible for a moral man who found himself in Strindberg's position, and was fully conscious of his own neurasthenia and his wife's immorality, would be to hide from the children they had so outrageously brought into the world, and let others better and saner nurture them. But, being so like the English gentleman, Strindberg believed in the home. So their children were brought up to learn at their mother's knee the force of a drunken blow and from their father the frenzy of a madman. And when, after ten years, husband and wife discovered that their marriage was too disorderly to exist any longer, they fought for the custody of the children, quite undeterred by any sense of personal unworthiness. That unseemly episode is detailed in *The Link*, one of the three plays translated by Edwin Björkman.

Strindberg looked on the child with a sense of property. 'I doubted the legitimacy of my children; I was haunted by the suspicion that although they bore my name and were supported by my earnings' (thrifty even in despair) 'they were yet not my children. Nevertheless, I loved them, for they had come into my life as a pledge of my future existence. Deprived of the hope to live again in my children, I floated in mid-air, like a poor phantom, breathing through roots which were not my own.' It did not concern him that a worse fate than being a reincarnation of Strindberg could hardly befall a human being. The children must be useful to him: if they do not fulfil the purpose of gratifying his desire for physical immortality they should not exist.

This is a most candid admission that the cult of the family does not imply the worship of the child. The Puritans, who maintained the family in its most rigid form, disliked the child. The President of the Mothers' Union, when she gave evidence before the Divorce Law Commission, adopted a tone which should have brought upon her the attention of the NSPCC. It was nothing to her that children are brought up in homes devastated by a drunken mother or an adulterous husband. It was nothing to her that the children of a relationship between a separated wife and a man should grow up in an atmosphere darkened by suspicion and disrespect. It was nothing to her that the children of a marriage rendered hateful by incompatibility of temper should have their nerves shattered in their infancy. Certainly the ideals of English gentlemen and gentlewomen are not brilliantly sensible. But this desire to conserve the unhappy marriage is vicious.

Happiness is unsatisfying as an end in life. To the artist it can only be a passing phase. To grown men and women it is as incidental as the landscape seen from one's bedroom windows. But it is the necessary basis of marriage. The child needs happiness for its spirit just as it wants milk for its body. That is why every extension of the divorce law is a victory for the child. The happy marriage, which is the only proper nursery, is indissoluble. The unhappy marriage, which perpetually tells the child a bogey-man story about life, ought to be dissolved. Therefore suffragists who claim that women ought to get the vote because they are so often the underdogs in disgusting marriages, and sometimes get beaten by the brutes they have been wicked enough to choose as husbands, ought to be accounted enemies of Woman and the Race. To submit to unhappiness is the essence of the surrender of personality, which is sin. Submission to poverty is the unpardonable sin against the body. Submission to unhappiness is the unpardonable sin against the spirit.

The Confession of a Fool is one of the most moral books ever published. Madness opened the mouth of Strindberg, and he voiced the sentiments of the English gentleman with such appalling clarity that Sir Jesse Boot has resolved to protect our feminine delicacy, though we die of rage at his attempt. The book has been banned in the libraries. This is insufferable. This is a most useful book, that might make all the difference in the world to young men and women: it would help them to decide whether to accept or reject the present order of things. For it is the articulate and logical expression of the tendencies of the governing and middle classes. It is more representative than both Houses of Parliament. The anti-feminism is that of

Mr F. E. Smith; the sensual love of the family that of Mrs Humphry Ward; the concern for the outer husks of marriage and the contempt for the child that of Lord Halifax. Even the most appalling passage in the book is typical of the English gentleman. Strindberg sells his wedding-ring to raise the cost of a debauch and then rebukes his wife for her distress by saying:

> You committed an act fraught with tragic consequences for the whole family, for through it I am compelled to doubt the legitimacy of my children. You have dishonoured four people: your three children, of doubtful paternity, and your husband, whom your infidelity has made a common laughing-stock. What, on the other hand, are the consequences of my act?

This inability to recognise the obvious consequences of an anti-social act is quite a feature of English thought. I believe the phrase, 'the alleged injustice of a double standard of morality of men and women', occurred in a letter to the *Morning Post* rebuking the immorality of *The Freewoman*, signed by Earl Percy.

Everyone ought to read this book. It ought to be the occasion of a great spiritual revival. To those who, in the language of the evangelical, have forgotten God in obeying the law it will come as a terrible warning. Many of us, particularly women, have sufficient fastidiousness to abstain from immorality. It is harder to abstain from morality, to refuse the licence given us by law, to submit things to the sterner test of right and wrong. Strindberg was a good man: he believed in marriage, the home, the family. The horror of his sin sends one running back to the feet of God. Who is Sir Jesse Boot that he should stand between us and God?

The Freewoman, 22 August 1912

The Normal Social State

Madam,   I want to ask you a few questions – no, rather, I want to criticise you.

You believe, I have recently discovered, that everybody ought to possess a plot of ground on which they should produce their own food, and that that should be the main business of everybody's life. You wicked editor! This is very much too easy a way out. Your solution is uneconomic, and it is immoral. It is uneconomic because in a generation or two the nation would be starving. It is immoral because it would lead to slavery.

To begin with, the idea of producing all one's food from one patch of ground is preposterous. Is the Evesham market-gardener to stop producing the best plums in England and grow inferior potatoes? Is the Sleaford farmer to stop producing the best potatoes in England and grow inferior plums? You know quite well that every district has a separate 'talent' for producing different crops. Moreover, you really cannot do without cattle, for milk and butter are necessary even if you give up meat. You disapprove, I gather, of cattle being raised under cover and fed with farm produce; they must be allowed to graze. You believe this, in spite of the fact that you must know it takes three acres of grazing to raise one head of cattle, while it takes only one acre of tillage. May I point out that it has been found impossible to raise stock economically on small-holdings? In Ireland, of course, it has been attempted for centuries, with the result that the State you object to so much has now to step in with imported pedigree boars, asses and cattle, to improve the degenerate stock thus produced. Besides this aspect, I wish you joy in managing a small-holding of grazing and tillage combined, and keeping the land 'clean'.

I gather you object to all co-operation, for co-operation implies the State. Yet how are you going to break up rough land without the aid of machinery, which you cannot possibly own individually, the cost being enormous, though it would pay you to own it communally? Really adequate stockyards can only be built co-operatively. I cannot imagine that you will disapprove of the use of the machine in agricultural processes, though it is 'unnatural'. All agricultural processes are, strictly speaking, 'unnatural' and the Scottish peasantry who indulge in them in their 'purest' and most 'untainted' form are the most degraded of all peasantries (immorality and drunkenness being their customary amusements).

Moreover, do you think we all have a talent for agriculture? It needs as much temperament and laborious study as does the art of music. I can think of no department of agriculture (except parts of forestry, which, of course, being of purely commercial value, would be of no use to your ideal State – I beg your pardon, your ideal normal social life) which does not require skill and knowledge. Think, if you were in possession of a rough piece of land and had broken it up by spade-work (having scorned the co-operative steam cultivator), what would what was left of you do next? What 'cleaning' crop would you put in? Where would you put in lime and soot or nitrates? How would you put in green manure? Would you recognise the various pests as they appeared, and how would you treat them? And do you really believe that you would get the man or woman who was yearning to get back to the dear, old, immoral system where they had obeyed their primitive instincts (just as primitive as the agricultural instinct) by being sailor or actress or musician or doctor to give the attention that such problems demand? Not a bit of it!

That is why your system is uneconomic. It necessitates an inferior food supply, repudiates the necessary machinery for developing the soil, and gives the land over to inefficient farmers. Remember, land never marks time. It either goes forward under efficient farming or by lying fallow, or it goes back under inefficient farming. A nation of amateur agriculturists would kill England in half a century. The land would refuse to yield food.

The immorality of your system lies in its imposition of a certain way of life, which requires a very special kind of temperament, on all temperaments. Did you never meet men who could not bear to live more than a year in one place, who were tramps by nature? Very good and valuable men they often are. I suppose you have some object in forgetting artists and scientists. What good would a plot of ground be to W. H. Davies, or Lord Lister, or Freud? Surely they have enough 'property' in their heads. Do you think that you will get artists and scientists to produce art and science in the evenings when they have got the asparagus patch off their minds? You will get as much respectable craftsmanship as you like, and possibly some excellent recipes for herb tea. But you will get no great art or science. Much as you dislike civilisation, are you prepared to take the responsibility of killing science? Freud has begun (by studies engrossing the passion of a lifetime, not by a hobby carried on in the evenings) to solve the question of insanity. Does it seem to you more important that he should grow his own food? Bashford is getting on nicely with the cure for cancer; much better stop, grow cabbages, and let people die in agony. There is no reason to believe that agriculture will eradicate these evils. I know well a certain family which has lived on the land for many centuries; since 1780 every member of it has died of cancer. And to push things back to an extreme example of your theories, the inhabitants of many of the Pacific Islands who live in a manner that would (theoretically) delight you are periodically decimated by virulent forms of a disease commonly associated with the evils of Western civilisation. (Man was not quite mad when he turned to civilisation; he was aiming at happiness, and he was certainly going *somewhere* to find it. You are merely returning to a position he found untenable.)

Once you admit that artists and scientists do not need the kind of 'property' you advocate for all, it seems to me the whole system falls about your ears. If you agree not to enslave certain types to agriculture because their strength renders them valuable to life, you must give the other types who will find the agricultural life distasteful (not many, but quite sufficient to be considered) a chance to show their strength, or you are immoral!

I have assumed that you do not mean agriculturists to exchange produce, because that immediately necessitates the intervention of the State, which you repudiate. I suppose you know all about that: the necessity for co-operative markets and State market officials, etc. But, even accepting your view of the self-contained producer, I cannot imagine agriculture proceeding at all without State aid. If it had not been for research in State laboratories and State-distributed prophylactics the potato plant would have been wiped out time and again in both this country and America. How can you look on agriculture as such an amateurish affair?

I *cannot* understand your view of the land from an economic point of view.

Am I wrong in thinking that if your agricultural ideal goes your whole attack on socialism goes with it? Obviously land is the only form of property you can approve of, bearing in mind the attitude of your paper on usury and 'dead' property. It seems to me that the socialist method of recognising that we all possess 'living' property – the faculty of cultivating the land, it may be, or weaving beautiful cloth, or bringing up children, or curing illness – and rewarding us all alike is preferable to your method of dumping us all down on the land irrespective of our different souls. It is more spiritual. It is more compatible with free-will. It recognises that we are 'in reality only a collection of individuals, whose superficial likenesses dissolve into unlikenesses immediately they are traded upon'.

This is why you must justify your economic view of the land. Because your moral view depends entirely on your economic view. You think of the land as something that only has to be scratched affectionately to give a living; something no more exhausting than keeping a dog. I believe it to be nothing of the sort, but to be as absorbing and jealous as every kind of work must be. Ecstasy if you love it, hell if you don't. Please lay your reasons for your view before us!

Rachel East
The Freewoman, 5 September 1912

*One is reminded by Rebecca West's letter that our Edwardian sisters
and brothers too, like many radicals and feminists in the sixties and
seventies, went back to the land to grow organic cabbages and bake
their own bread: as she makes clear, as an ideology for everyone, she
regarded this as a distraction from making the social revolution.*

Marriage

Marriage by H. G. Wells

Mr Wells's mannerisms are more infuriating than ever in *Marriage*.
One knows at once that Marjorie is speaking in a crisis of wedded
chastity when she says at regular intervals, 'Oh, my dear! . . . Oh, my
dear!' or at moments of ecstasy, 'Oh, my *dear*! My *dear*!' For Mr
Wells's heroines who are loving under legal difficulties say 'My man!'
or 'Master!' Of course, he is the old maid among novelists; even the
sex obsession that lay clotted on *Ann Veronica* and *The New
Machicvelli* like cold white sauce was merely old maids' mania, the
reaction towards the flesh of a mind too long absorbed in airships and
colloids. The Cranford-like charm of his slow, spinsterish gossip
made *Kipps* the delightful book it was; but it palls when, page after
page and chapter after chapter, one is told how to furnish a house . . .
    And then there is Mr Wells's habit of spluttering at his enemies. He
splutters less in *Marriage* than in *The New Machiavelli*, but in the
hospital atmosphere of the latter, where a soul-sick man drugged
himself with the ether of sex, it seemed less offensive than in this
purer, brighter air. Altiora Bailey reappears as Aunt Plessington and
makes a speech that would be perfect but for its omission of the
phrase, 'the morass of destitution'. There is a devilishly realistic
picture of the English humorist whose parodies have drawn tears
from the sentient part of the nation for the last twenty years. It is
great fun, but at times it is ill-mannered. It offends one beyond
measure in the last impressive pages of the book. Trafford has withdrawn from busy, sterile London, where he sold his scientific genius
to buy pretty things for his wife, and now knows himself to be a
commercial prostitute, and has sought the clean snows of Labrador.
There, he thinks, he can clear his mind of the lies of civilisation and
begin to seek God. Sickness strips him of all fear and deceit, so that he
communes with God. Wonderingly he finds out what life is:

... Something trying to exist, which isn't substance, doesn't belong to space or time, something stifled and enclosed, struggling to get through. Just confused birth-cries, eyes that can hardly see, deaf ears, poor little thrusting hands. A thing altogether blind at first, a twitching and thrusting of protoplasm under the waters, and then the plants creeping up the beaches, the insects and reptiles on the margins of the rivers, beasts with a flicker of light in their eyes answering the sun. And at last, out of the long interplay of desire and fear, an ape, an ape that stared and wondered, and scratched queer pictures on a bone ...

In the midst of this ecstatic perception of life he stops to define Mr Pethick Lawrence.

A Gawdsaker? ... Oh, haven't you heard that before? He's the person who gets excited by any deliberate discussion and gets up wringing his hands and screaming, 'For Gawd's sake, let's *do* something *now!*' I think they used it first for Pethick Lawrence, the man who did so much to run the old militant suffragettes and burke the proper discussion of woman's future.

It is good, but not worth while interrupting a triumphant meditation over the disordered earth. It is really a matter of good manners.

This Trafford had fallen a victim to a parasitic woman; he had laid his very soul on the altar of Our Lady of Loot. An aeroplane accident dropped him on to the lawn of a Kentish vicarage, in which was staying Marjorie Pope, a beautiful girl of twenty. At that age, when the fine body should have been protected by a vitality that bared its teeth at weakness and ugliness in fierce fastidiousness, she was seriously thinking of marrying Will Magnet, the humorist, 'a fairish man of forty, pale, with a large protuberant, observant grey eye – I speak particularly of the left – and a face of quiet animation warily alert for the wit's opportunity'. But she was willing to do it, her life being governed by gluttony and laziness ...

After Oxbridge, unless she was prepared to face a very serious row indeed and go to teach in a school – and she didn't feel any call whatever to teach in a school; she had an invincible objection to work of any kind – she would probably have to return to Hartstone Square and share Daffy's room again and assist in the old, wearisome task of propitiating her father.... Marriage was escape from all that; it meant not only respectful parents, but a house of her very own, furniture of her choice – that was the real attraction to Marjorie – great freedom of movement, an authority, an importance.

For the sake of sideboards and prestige she was willing to give herself to a fool and transmit folly to her children ... And the really fine and encouraging thing about the book is that Mr Wells sees that Marjorie is a thorough scoundrel. The horror of it is that, confused by her clear eyes and copper hair, he accepts her scoundrelism as the normal condition of women.

Something, probably Trafford's clean physical vigour, overcame her natural carelessness of destiny, that cold sensuality that made her think of her body as a thing to barter for sideboards. So she eloped with him, and henceforth mastered his life and beggared it. She wanted 'things' – old Dutch clocks and wonderful dinner-dresses and Chippendale chairs. And she claimed them from him because she was his wife and the mother of his child.

There is something sinister about a figure such as the great Christ who hangs on the cross athwart the Catholic cathedral at Westminster. The blood about his brow, the distortion of his mouth, the tension of the body, the changeless attitude of pain, convey at last the sense of an eternal hunger. The lights of a thousand candles, all the incense of the pious, the daily worship of millions, have whetted him to the remorseless acceptance of the lives of men and the reason of nations. Not till the roof of the world falls in will that hunger cease from feeding on the hearts of men; and then, amid the dust of the universe, one can imagine a God impatiently making a new world of worshippers. Perhaps it is because of this harsh lien on the world's love and sympathy that blasphemy is the one crime that all men commit before they die.

And women have taken for themselves the right to claim worship, by virtue of the suffering through which they pass to bring men into the world – although a casual glance at the worshippers might show them that they had done it carelessly and without exclusiveness – and of the beauty of their lives. There is no end to their hunger. They send men they do not know into the snowy wastes to trap silver foxes, and set the men they do know working at barren, profitable commercial muddles to buy the pelts. For in particular they demand material, inessential things. And they get them; but also they get hatred and curses that are the inevitable offerings to divinity.

Trafford had a genius for scientific research. 'I want research,' he moaned when delirium overtook him in Labrador, 'and that still, silent room of mine again, that room, as quiet as a cell, and the toil that led to light. Oh! the coming of that light, the uprush of discovery, the solemn joy as the generalisation rises like a sun upon the facts – floods them with a common meaning. That is what I want. That is what I have always wanted . . .' Marjorie began her attack on his soul by disliking his work and putting a background of domestic dispeace to the splendid foreground of his laboratory.

He went home about half-past five and found a white-faced, red-eyed Marjorie, still dressed, wrapped in a travelling-rug, and crumpled and asleep in his study armchair beside the grey ashes of an extinct fire . . . 'Oh, where have you been?' she asked almost querulously. 'Where *have* you been?' 'But, my dear!' he said, as one might speak to a child, 'why aren't you in bed? It's just dawn.' 'Oh,' she said, 'I waited and waited. It seemed you *must* come. I read a book. And then I fell asleep.' And then, with a sob of feeble self-pity, 'And here I am!' She rubbed the back of her hand into one eye and shivered. 'I'm cold,' she said, 'and I want some tea.'

That repulsive desire for tea is a masterly touch. It reminds one of the disgust one felt as a healthy schoolgirl when one saw the school-mistresses drinking tea at lunch at half-past eleven. It brings home to one poignantly how disgusting the artificial physical weakness of women, born of loafing about the house with only a flabby mind for company, must be to an ordinary, vigorous man.

A little later he discovered that to furnish her house daintily with Bokhara hangings and brass-footed workboxes she has spent every penny of his income of six hundred and frittered away a thousand of his capital. She avoids discussion by having a baby in a sentimental and rather pretentious way. Although she knows that his work is being cut out of his life as one might cut a living man's heart out of his breast, and that its place is being taken by popular lectures to the scientifically-minded of Pinner and such parts, she continues to ruin him by buying post-impressionist pictures and hoarding up bills. Finally she breaks his spirit by having another baby.

So he drops research and takes up the manufacture of synthetic rubber. For nine years he runs this business and plays tedious games with rubber shares, while Marjorie lets herself go with the price of his perdition in a great, beautiful house filled with the creations of genius and silly, chattering people. 'Look at this room,' cries Trafford in despair, 'this litter of little satisfactions! Look at your pretty books there, a hundred minds you have pecked at, bright things of the spirit that attracted you as jewels attract a jackdaw. Look at the glass and silver, and that silk from China!' He suddenly rebels. He takes Marjorie away to the heights of Labrador where, between combats with lynxes and wolverines, sickness and famine, they brood on Life.

Marjorie, somewhat impertinently, uses her own worthlessness as the basis of a generalisation as to the worthlessness of all women.

What are we women – half-savages, half-pets, unemployed things of greed and desire – and suddenly we want all the rights and respects of souls! . . . I've begun to see what it is to be a woman . . . . We're the responsible sex. And we've forgotten it. We think we've done a wonder if we've borne men into the world and smiled a little, but indeed we've got to bear them all our lives . . . A woman has to be steadier than a man and more self-sacrificing than a man, because when she plunges she does more harm than a man . . . And what does she achieve if she does plunge? Nothing – nothing worth counting. Dresses and carpets and hangings and pretty arrangements, excitement and satisfaction and competitions and more excitements. We can't *do* things. We don't bring things off! And you, you Monster! You dream you want to stick your hand out of all that is and make something that isn't begin to be! That's the man!

Trafford confirms her suspicions.

You're a finer individual than me . . . You're more beautiful by far than I, a woman for my man. You've a keener appetite for things, a firmer grip on the substance of life. I love to see you do things, love to see you move, love to watch your hands; you've cleverer hands than mine by far . . . And yet – I'm a deeper and bigger thing than you. I reach up to something you don't reach up to . . . You're in life – and I'm a little out of it. I'm like one of those fish that begin to be amphibian. I go out into something where you don't follow – where you hardly begin to follow . . .

So they go home in a very good temper.

And Mr Wells agrees with them. That is the terrible thing, for there is no author who has a more religious faith; nor one who speaks his gospel with such a tongue of flame. His first sin lies in pretending that Marjorie, that fair, fleshy being who at forty would look rather like a cow – and the resemblance would have a spiritual significance – is the normal woman; and the second lies in his remedy, which Marjorie discovers in a period of spiritual turmoil brought on by debt. 'A woman gives herself to a man out of love, and remains clinging parasitically to him out of necessity. Was there no way of evading that necessity?' she meditates sentimentally. 'Suppose the community kept all its women, suppose all property in homes and furnishings and children vested in them . . . Then every woman would be a princess to the man she loved.' The cheek of it! The mind reels at the thought of the community being taxed to allow Marjorie, who could steal her lover's money and barter the brightness of his soul for brass-footed workboxes, to perpetuate her cow-like kind. I can see myself as the one rebel in this humourless State going forth night after night to break the windows of the barracks of Yoshiwara where Marjorie was kept in fat ease, and going to prison month after month until . . .

But '*all* women!' 'Suppose the community kept *all* its women . . .'

Heavens, I shall be inside too! I object to living under the same roof as Marjorie.

I wonder about the women who never come across any man who is worth loving (and next time Mr Wells travels in the tube he might look round and consider how hopelessly unlovable most of his male fellow-passengers are), who are not responsive to the lure of Dutch clocks and forget, as most people do, the colour of the dining-room wallpaper, who, being intelligent, can design a becoming dress in five minutes and need think no more about it. I wonder how they will spend their time. Bridge-parties, I suppose, and possibly State-facilitated euthanasia . . .

Let Mr Wells and any other man who loathes the daughter of the horse-leech reflect a minute: 'What would happen to Marjorie if she had to fend for herself?' That is a very important reason why women should be made to work. Under present conditions Marjorie is a handsomely subsidised young woman. For she is to many the typical wife and mother, since she has not her more sensitive sister's objection to the monotony and squalor of domestic drudgery that men have thrust on the wife and mother. But supposing she had to work. How long could she stand it? The weaker sort of Marjorie would be sucked down to prostitution and death, the stronger sort of Marjorie would develop qualities of decency and courage and ferocity. It is worth trying. Not only because men ought to be protected from the monstrous demands of Our Lady of Loot, but because women ought to have a chance of being sifted clean through the sieve of work.

The Freewoman, 19 September 1912

These articles quite naturally attracted the attention of H. G. Wells who promptly began to pursue the fiery young feminist. As a measure of her intellectual honesty, it must be pointed out that she continued to attack and criticise his writing despite the fact that they became lovers. Though she always championed the cause of unwed mothers her own experience does not lead her to recommend it for other women. We have seen evidence of her intellectual and political commitment to feminism, but Rebecca West's power as a writer springs too from deep emotional roots in female experience.

. . . And those who loved me gathered round me as I lay on the brink of death and dragged me back, tearing my flesh with the sharp teeth of their love. My mother sat by my bed and cried from the collarbone, sobs that scald the throat. My sisters moved reproachfully about the room, saying to me with their deep-set eyes, 'So you meant to leave us, after we have gone so loyally with you through all these years of poverty and tragedy.' And sometimes the man who loved me, in whose house I had done this thing, came and looked at me. And from his heavy, patient sweetness I saw that I had committed the sin that had been committed against me: seduction. For though my lover had left my body chaste he had seduced my soul: he mingled himself with me till he was more myself than I am and then left me. Well, wasn't that what I was doing when I shot myself? One never escapes from the body of one's mother. Wouldn't my death be a brutal destruction of my mother's substance? My sisters and I had made an interesting life out of our uneasy circumstances. Had I the right to run away and leave them short-handed and to discolour our masterpiece by violent memories?

The New Freewoman, 1 August 1913

H. G. Wells himself published his scheme for the 'Endowment of Motherhood' in the pages of The Freewoman, *where it was roundly criticised. Perhaps it was the spirit of competition with Rebecca West (or a peculiar form of wooing) which inspired him to write a witty piece of advice to the suffragettes, also in* The Freewoman, *called 'Mr Asquith Will Die'. H. G. Wells was wrong. Asquith did not die. Rebecca West dismissed Asquith as 'the chief of all flunkeys, undistinguished even in his crimes, a man who would make an excellent butler.' (See her* Clarion *essays in the next chapter.)*

So Simple

The Consumer in Revolt by Teresa Billington Greig, *Dreams, and Dream Life and Real Life* by Olive Schreiner, *The Naked Soul* by Louise Heilgers

The worst of being a feminist is that one has no evidence. Women are capable of all things yet, inconveniently, they will not be geniuses. This is brought home to one during the publishing season. Reading the advertisements of new books by men such as Wells or Conrad or Bennett is like planning a journey to the Isles of Greece on the map. The names of two women, Violet Hunt and May Sinclair, rouse in one something of the same excitement, but no certainty. In spite of their first-rate intelligences and sense of character they escape genius. It would be hard to say why women have refused to become great writers. Undoubtedly marriage eats like a cancer into the artistic development of women. A man must wait until he has reached maturity before he can sit down and write an important novel. Before that time he must earn his living and coerce the public's attention by doing unimportant work which disciplines his technique. But a woman during this period of immaturity either neglects literary work altogether or she plunges into important work at once, being protected by her man from the necessity of doing uncongenial work.

Another quality which keeps women from literary greatness is their timidity towards adventure and lack of faith in life. Accustomed to have in her hands the comfort of her husband and children, she feels less adventurous than brutal when she walks empty-handed out of her safe home and treads new paths. This fear of taking risks influences her in the choice of occupation. Women flinch at the risk of taking up an artistic career and gravitate towards safe professions like the Civil Service, not in any white passion of statecraft, but because it is notorious that the Government forgives all crimes in its female employees except marriage. The Civil Service, while producing experts in parlour-tricks such as Austin Dobson, A. B. Walkley and Edmund Gosse, seems incompatible with genius. This caution also influences her style.

Another vice incident to woman at present is spiritual pride. She has found the first steps of man's journey upwards quite easy. He had pretended they were difficult, so he gets what he deserves if woman assumes that all the other steps are just as easy, and that the government of empires is as easy as getting a university degree. This attitude is a little irritating. Everything becomes *so* simple. The mother soul of which Mrs Pethick Lawrence talks is going to solve problems that have vexed civilisation since the beginnings by sheer motherliness and soulfulness. The possession of the vote is going to release women wage-slaves from the power of the capitalist. Women estimating their future activities tend to become presumptuous persons such as Nietzsche described as 'those who "briefly deal with" all the real problems of life, death, and eternity'.

An example of this is *The Consumer in Revolt*. There is much ability in Mrs Billington Greig, but there is little that speaks of it in her book. The first chapter, which says in twenty-three pages what would better have been said in six, is devoted to an exposition of the fact that man sometimes produces goods and sometimes consumes them. Therefore the social system will be hopelessly one-sided until there is an organisation to uphold the claims of the consumers. These are 'a pure product, clean and honest, being what it professes to be; a product at a fair price; a sufficient variety of products to allow of reasonable choice; and a sufficiency of all kinds of products'. They must insist, too, that the products are made under fair conditions of labour. And they are to revolutionise the struggle against capital by using the 'double-edged strike, a strike from two sides, in which, while the workers strike, the consumers employ a potential or positive boycott'. The obvious objection to this, that this would lead to the trustification of industry, is whirled away with a rattling facility. 'But this policy, too, can be met. The consumers and workers together can start their own manufactories, and such ventures would be economically sound and safe.' The mind reels at the idea of consumers withdrawing their capital from profitable capitalist concerns to start a factory on a non-profit-making basis with the certain difficulty ahead that a capitalist combine would attempt to corner the raw material. Moreover, no scheme which leaves the question of land untouched is sound. There would be certain difficulties before a committee of railway men and railway passengers could start an opposition line to the Midland, or of colliers and coal consumers could open out new coal mines. Problems are never so simple as all that. The idea of The Consumers' League is material for a not too long magazine article.

Mrs Billington Greig holds it as a grievance against the producer that he so often produces shoddy and adulterated goods. She loses the beautiful spiritual significance of adulteration, which is a form of philanthropy probably originally designed by the Charity Organisation Society. The consumer who produces nothing, but lives on rent and interest, need fear no adulterated goods. Adulteration is devised by the benign capitalist to console the workman for his shiftlessness and stupidity in not being able to make a living wage. Although he cannot indulge his appetites, he shall at least have the illusion of so doing. For instance, the capitalist recognises the desire for salmon as a constant quality in the composition of Englishmen. A small proportion of the nation eats fresh salmon, a large proportion eats tinned salmon. Why should the remainder, worthless as it may be, not have at least an illusion of salmon? Hence the capitalist ingeniously provides the obscene kind of salmon paste sold in the Euston Road and Villiers Street. This method of pauperising the poor can only be stopped by giving the people higher wages. The Consumers' League could do little to that end.

Another example of the 'so simple' attitude of women is the philosophy of Olive Schreiner, whose *Dreams, and Dream Life and Real Life* has just been re-issued in a cheaper edition. Olive Schreiner is less a woman than a geographical fact. Just as one thinks of Egypt as a foreground for the Pyramids, so South Africa seems the setting of that warm, attractive, aggressive personality. Her work is far inferior to her. *Woman and Labour* was slow and vague, though its heart was in the right place. *The Story of an African Farm* was a good novel spoilt by an illicit attempt to improve the reader's morals. In *Dreams* she wrote of an abstract spiritual woman, just as Adam Smith wrote about an abstract economic man. To avoid the incomplete conclusions which are consequent on writing about abstractions she attempted to write in a poetic style, although at all times she has lacked the 'fundamental brainwork' needed for poetry. Her real line was probably realism, for that, in its surrender of the selective power, needs little brainwork; Zola wrote charming novels on no basis whatsoever. Moreover, her style is too humourless for poetry. When Woman and Wine come leaping towards the Hunter they announce themselves as 'the twins, Sensuality', as if sensuality would ever be anything so morally unassailable as twins, which are most commonly found among the more respectable poor in rural districts. The occasional note of private and confidential enlightenment over commonplace facts is subtly absurd. 'Then the sun passed down behind the hills: but I knew that the next day he would rise again.'

Her philosophy tends towards the most undiscriminating asceticism. 'By having the hell of a time we shall have the heaven of an eternity' is not a syllogism. The extremely depressing career of Woman, who left the garden of Pleasure because Duty with his white, clear features came and looked down at her, and who decided to seek the land of Freedom down the banks of Labour through the waters of Suffering, seems to be planned by use and wont rather than by the findings of an individual and inquiring morality. Just as the kind-hearted outside broker, on his way home from the bucket shop, tries to save his soul by giving his spare pennies to any drunken beggar he passes, so women try to earn salvation quickly and simply by giving their souls up to pain. It may only be a further development of the sin of woman, the surrender of personality.

Miss Louise Heilgers' novel, *The Naked Soul*, is another example of the 'so simple' attitude. I call it a novel because, although its style recalls the appendices to Mr Havelock Ellis's great work, it is not true. At least, I hope not. Miss Heilgers belongs to that school of fiction led by Victoria Cross, Elinor Glyn and Dolf Wyllarde, who imagine that by cataloguing stimuli one can produce a feeling of stimulation: as though one could convey the joys and miseries of drunkenness by enumerating the public-houses in the Harrow Road. Miss Heilgers reminds one of a south coast watering-place called Deal. There are more public-houses per head of the population in Deal than in any other town in Great Britain. But the atmosphere is neither exhilarating nor deplorably alcoholic: the sight of a public-house becomes monotonous, that is all. Similarly, though there are more appalling incidents per page in *The Naked Soul* than in any other book I have ever read, it is very dull. Or perhaps I should say that it is too technical for the lay reader.

The Freewoman, 12 October 1912

Two Books by David Graham Phillips

The Conflict and *The Price She Paid* by David Graham Phillips

Miss M. P. Willcocks has told the gospel of David Graham Phillips in an earlier number of *The Freewoman*, and has told how he contemplated the muddled world in an ecstasy of loathing, and found it a toy in the weak, fat hands of the parasite woman.

It is to buy gauds for these parasites, gauds wrung from the sweat of millions, that men strive and agonise and let their better selves go to the wall. But the gauds do not satisfy; the women must have ever more and more . . . The stored-up wealth of the race is spent, not in building the future, with endowments of science, art and letters, but in feeding the appetites of these rapacious cormorants, the parasite women.

His soul had taken vows of chastity and poverty. Except the Magnificat, there is no literary expression of class-hatred so sincere and dignified as the works of David Graham Phillips. He could write seriously and simply that 'the much talked-of difference between those born to wealth and power and those who rise to it from obscurity resolves itself into little more than the difference between those born mad and those who go insane'. This modern St Francis, who longed to found a world of saints of austere and busy lives, was defeated by the world against which he warred in an essential matter. In spite of a genius for vehemence, a subtle sense of character and an intuitive power of observation, his style was vulgar. That partly came from the fact that there has never been in America any popular uprising in favour of style as there has been in England. While we were learning from the *Yellow Book* school to be dainty with our words, the Americans had given themselves to the pursuit of strange religions, and the modern mind appears to find religion and style incompatible. Hence Mr Phillips could, without fear of rousing popular opinion, write such fumbling and common sentences as this description of a drawing-room: 'There were no messy draperies, no fussy statuettes, vases, gilt-boxes and the like.' And, worst of all, Phillips had to live in the very thick of the ugly world he hated. For years he was a journalist. One thinks of him sitting in a newspaper office, hotly thinking out his gospel, while rattling tape-machines and ringing telephones, and the clamour of many Americans at work drove peace and dignity from his being. The world revenged itself on the modern St Francis by taking from him the purity of his self-expression.

Although Phillips was only forty when he died, he left many novels behind him. *The Conflict* and *The Price She Paid* are the two most recently published of these. Both preach that the rich shall be sent empty away when the spiritual food of the world is set in the banquet-hall. In *The Conflict*, which is the story of the corruption of municipal politics in an American manufacturing town, Phillips describes the course of a love affair between Jane Hastings, the daughter of the multi-millionaire who owns Remsen City and the sweated millions who make its wealth, and Victor Dorn, the socialist carpenter, who is trying to stir up the sweated millions to revolt. Here Phillips touches something that ought to be beautiful. The men of the commercial and financial world are the merest accident of a complicated social system; their work has nothing to do with the satisfaction of the natural hungers of mankind. But the navvy, the sailor or the miner are essential to humanity. The navvy has pierced the hillside with a tunnel, the sailor has faced furious seas, the miner has gone into dark places inhabited by perils. All of them have taken some risk and won some victory over the fear of death. It is natural that a woman should desire the father of her children to be among the victorious. Probably middle-class women will unexpectedly hasten the social revolution by becoming weary of bearing the children of men who are about as essential to the State as typewriters and fountain-pens, and much less important than a dynamo.

So the love of Jane Hastings ought to have been a fine return to elemental things. But it is Phillips' gospel that nothing can make the rich man's daughter worthy of the poor man's son. She has been fed from her childhood on the flesh and blood of the poor, and it has worked like poison in her veins. When she tries for Dorn's sake to help the people, she can only do it by philanthropic doles that kill the spirit he is trying to waken in the slaves. Her love for Dorn is a conscious and artificial thing, provoked in a desire to kill monotony. Just as other idle people go in for art, so she deliberately seeks for love, who ought to come suddenly to intercede with time for the claims of eternity. And her victory over Dorn means the entrance of caprice into a well-ordered life. She distracts him from his work, and even plans that if they marry he must leave the people and become one of her class. The consummation of the love affair must be a disaster, yet both Jane and Dorn should have been splendid lovers. It is an abortive masterpiece of fine emotions, like Wordsworth's later or Masefield's more recent poetry.

He gives Dorn the victory. He turns away from Jane to his work. And suddenly love comes to him, and he perceives that Selma Gordon, the Russian Jewess with whom he has been editing his socialist weekly, is the most desirable woman on earth. With characteristic severity Mr Phillips denies Jane love. The nearest she gets to it is by entering into a sexual relationship of a severely disciplinary nature with a doctor with coercive ideas on diet and early rising.

This complacency over the frustration of the strong passion between Jane and Dorn is characteristic of Phillips. At first sight it looks as though he despised love. But he did not. He merely disbelieved that it was possible for such disfigured beings as the men and women of the modern world to create anything so wonderful as love. Two things Phillips worshipped, and those were love and women. It was his tragedy that in this world he could find only lust and prostitutes. That was what gave his work its ecstasy of indignation.

Mildred Gower is another parasite woman to whom Phillips denies the possibility of love. *The Price She Paid* is the most fierce feminist tract that ever was written. That it should have appeared as a serial in the pages of a frivolous American magazine, sandwiched in between photographs of Maud Allan in moonlight and Mr Chesterton in fancy dress as Dr Johnson, and other such mountebanks, shows that the Americans are better epicures of life than we are. The English magazine, with its eternal love story which always ends in at least the registry office, represents the hopeless struggle of an over-sexed nation to get as much excitement out of sex as is compatible with monogamy. The American magazine, with its bright-eyed interest in science and everything else, has recognised that thought itself is great fun. In their search for intellectual excitement the public lightheartedly entertained the most revolutionary attack on the standards of honour held by women that was ever made. And a civilisation must stand or fall by its standards of honour. It was when the sense of honour of Englishmen became so artificial and unspontaneous that the duel had to be abandoned, that men enclosed the land of the poor, and prepared to sweat children in factories.

The Price She Paid shows the evolution of a parasite woman towards independence. Before she graduates in freedom she has to struggle against the mastery of four men. The sudden death of Mildred Gower's father left her penniless. Her only refuge is marriage with General Siddall, a drunken and dishonest little millionaire, whose views on women have a rather physiological bias.

> I'm going to make careful inquiries about her character and her health. If those things are all right I'm ready to go ahead . . . I can't stand a sickly, ailing woman . . . I wouldn't marry one, and if one I married turned out to be that kind, I'd make short work of her. When you get right down to facts, what is a woman? Why, a body. If she ain't pretty and well, she ain't nothing.

This marriage is mere prostitution. But Mildred does not feel like a prostitute because she has been married in church. But she soon finds that she has to pay a price for her respectability. The prostitute gets paid in cash down. Mildred never gets paid at all. She is allowed to wear the clothes the General buys for her, but she never has a farthing to spend. Her jewels are taken from her every night by her husband and locked in his safe, lest she should steal them. Her husband is determined to keep her penniless, lest she should evade his power in any way.

This condition of things seems to Phillips typical of what marriage may become. If women sell themselves to the highest bidders, they must expect to have rough husbands. In the vicious competition the women themselves have provoked by their greed only the brutes can conquer. Besides, Mildred deserves nothing better. She is doing no work. She deserves no payment at all, still less honourable treatment.

But latent in her is a spark of genius for freedom. She sells the gold bag which her husband has been forced to allow her to keep in her hand – that obviously being the only true home of a handbag – and with the money travels back to America. She intends to work for a living. It is an incredible decision for a woman of her class, and when she announces it 'her mother looked at her with eyes full of the suspicion one lady cannot but have as to the prospects of another lady in such circumstances'. And her mother was quite right. Quite unconsciously she abandons it. An old admirer, Stanley Baird, provides her with money to support her while she studies for grand opera.

Baird is another type that oppresses women. At first sight he seems Mildred's friend, for he encourages her to go on and make a career. But his own reason for desiring her to make a career is that she may become a more valuable and admired possession. At the same time he prevents her making herself fit for a career by making constant demands on her charm and companionship, by leading her into a busy social life. Late hours, rich food and stuffy rooms snap the strong stem of her health. Worst of all, he reconciles her to this life by never exacting any value for his money. Because she is not living by the sale of her body she feels satisfied that she is leading an honourable life.

That genius for freedom reasserts itself, and she leaves Baird and tries to go on the musical comedy stage. At once her beauty and her voice get her a leading part. But at the same time they attract the desires of Ransdell, the producer, and he asks her to become his mistress. When she refuses he cleverly uses the unreliability of her voice, due to her own laziness and self-indulgence, to prove to the manager that she is incompetent. So she is beaten again, but this time only by her own defection. 'If your voice had been all right,' says the wise theatrical manager,

if you could have stood to any degree the test he put you to, the test of standing alone, you'd have defeated him . . . He wouldn't have dared go on. He's too shrewd to think a real talent can be defeated . . . You know the conditions of success now. You must prepare to meet them. If you put yourself at the mercy of the Ransdells – or any of the petty intriguers that beset every avenue of success – you must take the consequences; you must conciliate them as best you can. If you don't wish to be at their mercy, you must do your part.

So she goes away and devotes herself to making her voice, which is already perfect in tone and method, reliable. Then the fourth man assails her independence, and he is the most dangerous, because his claim is legitimate by every court of reason and sentiment. They love each other. But Mildred knows that if she gives herself up to this man, who is a distinguished lawyer, before she has made any career for herself she will lose her personality. So she goes back to her singing lessons. When at last she becomes a prima donna she has lost all joy in her art in the drudgery of developing a voice in spite of natural disadvantages. But she has the joy of liberty. She need pay no price to anybody for the bread she eats, in coin of either body or soul.

The life of Mildred Gower, who had to spend the beauty and passion of her youth in seeking what she ought to have had as a birthright – the right to work – is a parable of the life of David Graham

Phillips. He was the divine sort of ascetic; he neglected the beauty of the present, not because he feared it, but because he had seen the vision of a greater beauty to be made by fiery spirits such as himself. He neglected the beauty of the present because he had an imagination. It is only uncreative artists with second-rate imaginations, such as Oscar Wilde, who can abandon themselves wholly to the present. It is only the highest kind of genius that can make the best of both worlds. Phillips could not aspire to that. He was a great moral genius and a pioneer of new and terrible standards of honour that will change the world. He will not even attain immortality. The fate of Ebenezer Eliot, who lost his audience with the repeal of the Corn Laws, or the missionary who was slain by the cannibals to add a more memorable feature to the feast with which they were celebrating their conversion to Christianity, is the ultimate lot of all propagandists. But Phillips's idealism protects him from success and oblivion for many years to come. He is a fire at which many generations shall warm their hands.

The Freewoman, 10 October 1912

The Fool and the Wise Man

The Woman Thou Gavest Me by Hall Caine, *The Passionate Friends* by H. G. Wells

A Manchester bookseller, provoked to articulateness by the Press on the subject of banned books, said surprisingly: 'People in Manchester are very particular about what they read. Hall Caine, H. G. Wells and Corelli are not a bit more read than Arnold Bennett, Galsworthy and Hichens.' Only by marrying that bookseller and by living with him for years could one come to the roots of this marvellous classification. He may have divined the common fate which undoubtedly lies before Mr Caine and Mr Wells. Their books get longer and longer. Some day the parlourmaid, pushing back the study door against the rising tide of manuscript, will discover the distinguished author suffocated by the proof sheets of his new novel. And there is a tie between their latest productions. Both take the position of woman with an extreme seriousness which we must find very flattering.

To us intellectuals *The Woman Thou Gavest Me* has a personal appeal which *The Passionate Friends* has not, for the heroine, Mary O'Neill, is undoubtedly drawn from Mrs Beatrice Hastings of *The*

New Age. Her incapacity for forming friendships with her own sex and her extraordinarily rich emotional life constantly remind us of *Pages From an Unpublished Novel.* She was naturally pure, blind-pure, and this quality was fostered by early upbringing in a convent, the atmosphere of which was perhaps all that could be expected of an institution whose Mother Superior had first been found on the doorstep at six o'clock in the morning dressed as Bacchante with a cluster of grapes in her hair and an extremely unconvincing story on her lips. That had, of course, an effect on the discipline. For instance, Mary's favourite novice eloped with the father confessor and maintained him in London in a way that would now be interfered with by the Criminal Law Amendment Act (1912). From this stimulating atmosphere Mary was torn by her father and forced into a loveless marriage with Lord Raa. On their wedding-night she rebuffed his advances in a scene that would look well on the cinematograph, and henceforth they lived a celibate life. Unfortunately poor Lord Raa fell in with one of Mary's schoolfellows from that phallic convent and naturally ceased to be a celibate. About the same time Mary fell in love with an Antarctic explorer. It was the kind of chaste love which one stucco angel perched above a sausage-maker in Kensal Green Cemetery might feel for the angel perched above the draper across the path; but the convent breeding would out. 'I did not knock at Martin's door. I took hold of the handle as one who had a right. It turned of itself and the door opened. My mind was in a whirl, black rings were circling round my eyes, but I heard my trembling, quivering, throbbing voice, as if it had been the voice of somebody else, saying: "Martin, I am coming in."'

The Antarctic explorer, ignorant of Mr Caine's artistic economy of material, left the next day: but of course there was a baby. For the rest of the story Mr Caine suffers from a perpetual cold in the emotions: there is an extraordinary indecency about catarrh. As soon as Mary finds out that she is going to have a child she runs away from the Isle of Man to London, wishing that she had never left the sympathetic atmosphere of the convent. She had no money but was at first succoured by the one respectable schoolfellow of whom we hear, who had taken up rescue work; probably to keep in touch with things. However, this aid fails her and she has fallen into dreadful poverty when she receives the last blow: it is rumoured that the explorer has been lost in the Southern snows. Thereafter her story, apart from its general bearing on the segregation of the feeble-minded, has the same moral as Tennyson's 'Maud': always keep a halfpenny for the *Star.* The young man in 'Maud' languished on the Breton strand because he had not the sense to read the papers to see if he had really winged his man. Mary never had the curiosity to buy a paper to see whether the rumour about her lover was ever verified. So, lonely and penniless, she is about to sell herself on the streets to get money for her starving child when the explorer embraces her in Piccadilly Circus. That catarrh of the emotions impels Mr Caine to shatter the obvious happy ending and to kill her off by a catastrophe unparalleled in English literature: she dies of cold caused by drying her baby's more intimate garments – I have not the happy domestic touch that enables Mr Caine to be more explicit – on her own body when she was too poor to afford a fire. By the time one reaches this tragedy one is soggy with viscous emotion, like the toast under a poached egg.

The immense significance of this work lies in its binding. It is rich and restrained. It is the red of the suburban dining-room and has a loathsome granulated surface that sets the fingertips in a frenzy. To pamper the eye still further it is adorned with deep black lines, heavy gold lettering and two unconvincing designs of the dandelion rampant and couchant. One envisages the hundreds of thousands of quite repulsive people who will buy this book: people who live in unspacious houses and perform tedious duties and slake their voluptuousness on caraway seeds and the sermons of Mr R. J. Campbell and such mean pleasures. So now they are going to listen to Mr Caine on the wrongs of woman as they have listened to Mr Lloyd George on the wrongs of the poor. It will probably have the same effect on them. Just as this squalid mass that makes the damned compact Liberal majority has given doles like Old Age Pensions and the Insurance Act to the working class and kept them all the more the expropriated classes, so it will give women a few little liberties and grind them down into the profounder slavery. The vote and economic independence must be used to subserve the institutions that break the teeth of the hungry who bite into the earth to find their souls' appropriate food; the old Christian ideals of self-sacrifice will shackle them like irons. Though the monkey may have its chain taken off it will have to go on grinding the barrel-organ.

In its way *The Passionate Friends* is just as fantastic as *The Woman Thou Gavest Me*. It is infinitely nobler than Mr Wells's last book, *Marriage*. It has no such mean heroine as Marjorie, that born pawnbroker cheated of her destiny, who was continually termed by her creator 'gallant' but who would have faced life gallantly only under the cheerful gleam of three golden balls, who indeed showed no signs of ordinary pluck until her husband had been partially introduced into a hyena. May it be that we shall never see her like again. And the first thirteen pages of *The Passionate Friends* stand among the most beautiful achievements of Mr Wells's art of elucidating emotion, whereby some passion that dipped in the waves of one's soul like a storm-tired bird suddenly soars upwards to the sunlight, splendidly, enlighteningly recognisable. The first chapter, with its brooding over a dear wilful child in gusts of naughtiness and sickness, with its yearning past the impassable barrier of parentage towards free communion with the soul of this child, is among the very greatest artistic representations of parenthood. It is certainly the only literary expression of the pride of fatherhood which is wholly free from the suspicion of being mere male clucking over a female achievement. But for the rest the book rubs on one's nerves just like the binding of *The Woman Thou Gavest Me*. The skin of one's brain is dappled with goose-flesh at the irritating surface of the style. That pointillist way of suggesting a vivid event obscured through the mists of time by reference to the spotted canvas of the memory is used again and again: 'I do not know if indeed we raised our voices, but my memory has an effect of raised voices . . .' And every now and then Mr Wells, with a benevolent air of giving us a treat, ladles bread-and-milk into our angry adult mouths.

I hurried through London into Surrey, and in my father's study, warned by a telegram, I found a bright-eyed, resolute young woman awaiting me, with the quality about her of one who embarks upon a long-premeditated adventure. And I found too a family, her sisters and her brothers, all gladly ready for me; my father too was a happy man, and on the eighth of November in 1906 Rachel and I were married in the little church at Shere. We stayed for a week or so in Hampshire near Ringwood – the season was late that year and the trees still very beautiful . . .

and the cows all looked as if they had been painted by Sidney Cooper. This film of pretences that falls so surprisingly on the quality of Mr Wells's prose, like gilding on bright steel, which was not at all in *Tono-Bungay* and but little in *The New Machiavelli*, is a deliberate vice. It is the pusillanimous effort of a fierce brain to seek conformity with the common tameness, the lapse of a disorderly prophet who does not see that to be orderly is to betray his peculiar gospel. And besides these flaws the quality of the book's substance is curiously troubling. One feels as though one were going through a new country in the train and not liking it nearly so much as one had expected.

The Passionate Friends is the story of Lady Mary Christian and Stephen Stratten, two lovers of the same age and upbringing, who had 'the love of coevals, who had been playmates and intimate companions, and of whom the woman was certainly as capable and wilful as the man . . .' They knew 'real love, you know; the real thing . . . I don't mean the mere imaginative love, blindfold love, but love that sees . . .' In this passion one believes, but the story drops away from the burning core like the draggled tail of Halley's Comet. Lady Mary, with that curious unaristocratic preoccupation with the material perquisites of aristocracy which Mr Wells finds a symptom in modern womanhood, would not marry her lover because he was poor. She did not believe that she could live beautifully without the spacious backgrounds of luxury, long drawing-rooms that make beauty captive by some trick of colouring, wide gardens disciplined by centuries of culture into something more than grace. So she married Justin the millionaire and Stratten went away to the South African War. When he came back they tried to be friends and became lovers; when Justin discovered them she again refused to trust herself to shine apart from her setting. She sent her lover away and continued to live with Justin and bear him children, while Stratten married a phantom doormat called Rachel who lives to Mr Wells's eternal shame in one sentence: 'It sounds impudent, I know, for a girl to say so but we've so many interests in common.' After eight years Mary and Stratten met again by accident in a hotel in Switzerland. Though they merely talked for a morning calmly, like brother and sister, an enemy reported the meeting to Justin. To avert a threatened divorce case and save Stratten from disgrace Mary took a fatal dose of chloral. It is in keeping with the loose texture of the book that she is undeterred in this last step by any thought of the shadowy infants she is alleged to have produced. But the book, coming to a crisis by an accident, is bound to pass in smoke. For an accident being without a motive is an event without a soul and therefore useless in art. *The Passionate Friends* dies of that fatal meeting in Switzerland as *The Ordeal of Richard Feverel* dies of that wanton bullet.

But through this curious chink of brain that has somehow come away there pass the finest thoughts, the bravest speculations that bridge possibilities as steel bridges span dark rivers, the most delicate dreams. The passages on the history of labour that sprawls unwritten over the wide page of India are unsurpassable. The industrial suggestions make one wonder whether the life of the woman of today would not be a thing of merely richly coloured promise if the energies of the Victorians had not been spent in pushing women into the constructive business of commerce rather than winning them the dusty hall of the super-schoolmistress. The letters from Mary on the position of women are a rather florid elaboration of a point that Mr Wells has raised more than once before. She argues that the work of social reconstruction which Stratten and his kind advocate will come to naught so long as women who are specialised for sex have nothing to do but prowl one of the kitchens and nurseries where others are doing their appointed work, and rob men of their patient accumulations . . . The remedy that Mr Wells points towards is granting freedom to women that they may turn to honourable service and creative work. But this, though it would make sexual aggression a more honourable combat between equals, might almost intensify the problem. For it is true that men often turn willy-nilly to the business of love-making as a steamer, however urgent for far seas, must call at the coaling station; for some great thing they have to do they need the inspiration of an achieved passion. A man may find that for lack of a certain woman he can no more fulfil an enterprise than a scholar could write his book without a British Museum reading ticket. If women take up these heavy tasks they may find themselves terribly compelled to descend pitilessly yet with infinite remorse upon the reluctant lives of their lovers. Surely the only way to medicine the ravages of this fever of life is to treat sex lightly, to recognise that in this as in philosophy the one is not more excellent than the many, to think no more hardly of two lovers who part soon than we do of spring for leaving the earth at the coming of June.

Mr Wells suggests no remedy but exhortation for the curse of jealousy, though he writes:

> The deepest question before humanity is just how far this jealous greed may be subdued to a more generous passion. The fierce jealousy of men for women and women for men is the very heart of all our social jealousies, the underlying tension of this crowded modern life that has grown out of the ampler simpler life of men. That is why we compete against one another so bitterly, refuse association and generous co-operations, keep the struggle for existence hard and bitter, hamper and subordinate the women as they in their turn would if they could hamper and subordinate the men – because each must thoroughly have his own.

But the question arises as one finishes *The Passionate Friends* whether Mr Wells's attitude to life does not create an atmosphere that is favourable to that poisoned growth. This perpetual deprecation of rash defiances, this tolerance of flinching and weakness, this constant subordination of the quick personal wisdom to the slow collective wisdom, makes for selflessness. And jealousy is the complaint of the incomplete self. The woman who is acting the principal part in her own ambitious play is unlikely to weep because she is not playing the principal part in some man's no more ambitious play.

The New Freewoman, 1 October 1913

'*Happy is the country where they know at whom to throw their bombs,*' *Rebecca West exclaimed in June 1913 on a trip to Spain (while King Alfonso was being specially guarded). England had become intolerable to her. Previous holidays had taken her to the English countryside where she 'could contemplate the innocent activities of the natives as a virgin martyr new to Heaven might survey the gambols of the Cherubim. But it has suddenly come about that England is no place for a respectable virgin martyr. It blunts the fine edge of the sword of the soul to live in a peace maintained by the torture of women.' Government and police repression of the women's movement had become intolerable. Rebecca West's remarks remind us that many women intellectuals and artists took the mistreatment of their sex very seriously indeed.*

There are several other articles from The Freewoman *and* The New Freewoman *which are excluded for reasons of space. In a piece on Chesterton, Rebecca West says that his 'worst blasphemy lies in trying to preach the Gospel when heaven has sent him down a comic song'. She praised the first performance of* The Cherry Orchard, *and in a review of M. P. Willcocks's novel* Wings of Desire, *says: 'In the panoply of our newly-found emancipation we women are as serious as a little girl in a new pelisse: we dare not unbend in so much as a smile.' Reviewing W. H. Davies's* The True Traveller, *she takes a pot shot at the Press:*

No man could ever be so impossibly moral as the average journalist is, when writing. Although he lives in the heart of the modern Babylon, he knows no evil. When he writes of the drink question it is plain that he himself is Grand Master of the Rechabites. When he supports the blocking of the White Slave Traffic Bill it is not of ill-will; but the subject brings a blush to his cheek, and he thinks us unkind to discuss it. Not only the vices of men, but even the common passions of humanity are unknown to him. Pain he does not dread, for he scorns the suffragette who cries out against forcible feeding; nor fear either, for he despises the railway-shunter for making a noise about the risk of losing a leg. Even hunger he has never felt, for he reproves the unemployed for wishing too eagerly to fill their empty stomachs. Above all, he has Christian charity. From a careful study of the leaders, reviews and dramatic criticisms of the *Daily Telegraph* I know there is no politician who is not honest, no author who cannot write, no actor who cannot act. Truly, there are still saints among us. The Vicar of Christ upon earth is not the Pope, but the editor of *The Times*. Just as in the United States, after the Civil War there was little current coin, but too many unrealisable 'greenbacks', so we today have too little of the coin of good deeds to pass from hand to hand, but are flooded with paper virtue.

And her comment on Oliver Onions's In Accordance with the Evidence *includes further rebukes to those who claim to be or to love 'the weaker sex'.*

. . . If the art of life is largely the art of selection, it is no use painting a woman as pure and good and also showing her grossly selecting death instead of life in the important matter of marriage. It is strange how this lack of selective power, which is censured as 'bad taste' in art or dress, is excused when it touches marriage. The Norwegian antifeminist, August Strindberg, admits quite shamelessly that not once but three times did he choose a woman of evil disposition for his wife. And I learn from the pages of the weekly journal of a certain suffrage society that women ought to be enfranchised because some of them are fools enough to take husbands who afterwards chastise them with pokers, and mad enough to stay with them after they do it. As a matter of fact, the wife of a vicious husband ought to be cut by society as a person addicted to low company, unless she deserts him.

Part II

Battle-Axe and Scalping Knife

Essays (complete) from *The Clarion*,
September 1912 – December 1913

Editor's Introduction

Many socialists remember Rebecca West only for her sharp anti-communist polemics in the 1950s. It is for this reason particularly that I wanted to reprint these early political essays.

Rebecca West became a political writer on *The Clarion* in 1912, and continued writing for the paper until December 1913. Robert Blatchford, the editor of this socialist newspaper, had asked her to join the staff after reading her attack on Sir Almroth Wright, the notorious anti-feminist, in *The Freewoman*. 'What vigour, what aplomb! . . . I wouldn't have missed it for a pension. It's like a ride on an aeroplane; so exhilarating, so breezy; it is also irresistibly funny.' A keen fighter himself, he greatly admired her 'handling of the battle-axe and scalping knife'. 'She is a heavenly fighter and I wish she were leader of the opposition in the House of Commons or that she was there as a Socialist M P.' His daughter Winifred who also worked at *The Clarion*'s office at Oakley House, Bloomsbury Street, used the same figure of speech. 'She is one of the sturdiest and most gallant wielders of the battle-axe it has ever been my luck to see.'

The part played by *The Clarion* in Labour history is important enough to describe more fully. The first issue appeared on 12 December 1891. Forty thousand people bought it and it had soon established itself as the most popular radical journal of the day. (Blatchford himself was editor of the paper until 1910; he retired, discouraged, from the Socialist movement in 1914, but the paper continued to be published until 1935.)

Though a socialist paper, *The Clarion* gave space in its columns to many other topics than socialist questions; it was highly original, colloquial, and constantly interesting. As Margaret Cole wrote: 'There never was a paper like it; it was not in the least the preconceived idea of a Socialist journal. It was not solemn; it was not highbrow; it did not deal in theoretical discussion, or inculcate dreary-isms. It was full of stories, jokes and verses – sometimes pretty bad verses and pretty bad jokes – as well as articles. It was written in

language that anyone could understand, "with no middle-class unc-
tion", to quote an unemployed carpenter friend of Thompson's; it
believed that anyone, whatever his condition or education, who
could read plain English could be made into a socialist, and that
socialism was not a difficult dogma, but a way of living and thinking
which could make all men behave like brothers in the ordinary
pursuits of life. In the confidence that its readers would back it up, it
carried William Morris's gospel of fellowship throughout the industrial areas in homely terms which Morris would never have been able
to use; it made Socialism seem as simple and universal as a pint of
bitter. It is pleasant to notice that Morris, two years before his death,
expressed his appreciation of "Mr Blatchford's *Clarion*".'

Something too should be said about Robert Blatchford, *The
Clarion's* editor, for it is not difficult to see what might have appealed
to the young Rebecca West about his political philosophy and his
personality. Born in 1851, the second son of a strolling comedian and
an actress, he was largely self-educated, and always greatly admired
Samuel Smiles's famous book *Self Help*, despised by many of his
socialist friends. After a brief apprenticeship and six years in the army,
his writing career began in 1882 with a piece in a local paper. He
wrote a weekly column in the Leeds *Toby*, a satirical journal. Later he
moved to London with his family, then back to Manchester to work
full-time on the *Sunday Chronicle*. It was the move back North
which probably led to his conversion to socialism, as his particular
kind of socialism was very much a reaction against the cut-throat
competitiveness of industrial society. He was one of the founders of
the Manchester Fabian Society in 1890 and as he became more and
more deeply involved in the labour movement his articles in the
Sunday Chronicle became more and more socialist in their views.
When his editor protested at this in October 1891 he left the paper,
and with four other members of staff, decided to start a socialist
weekly – *The Clarion*.

Having established the paper, he then turned his energies to forming a Socialist Party which would be social democratic rather than
merely 'labourite' (as he now, with disillusion, saw the Independent
Labour Party). By 1893 the Clarionettes, a district group within the
socialist and labour movement, was formed, with himself as leader,
and composed of *Clarion* readers. These Clarion organisations included groups with wide interests, political, social, recreational and
educational. Blatchford himself believed he had a mission to educate
people into socialism. He was a rationalist, much influenced by
theories of evolution, and attacked organised religion in his paper. He

wrote one of the most successful pieces of propaganda in the history of the British labour movement, *Merrie England*, written first as a 'series of letters on the labour problems addressed to John Smith of Oldham, a hard-headed workman, fond of facts' which was serialised in *The Clarion* (these serials more than doubled the circulation). In 1894 it sold 20,000 copies as a shilling book, and then, published at one penny, sold over a million copies. The *Manchester Guardian* wrote that 'for every British convert to socialism made by Karl Marx's book *Kapital* there were a hundred made by *Merrie England*.'

There were numerous other Clarion organisations through which people could learn about socialism – Cinderella Clubs for slum children, Clarion Scouts, Clarion Vocal Union and Glee Clubs (with a Clarion song book), Clarion Handicraft Guilds, Holiday Camps, Clarion Vans which toured the country on propaganda campaigns, Clarion Cycling Clubs, Field Clubs, The Clarion Fellowship For Clarion Sympathisers. In 1909 a woman's paper (edited by Winifred Blatchford), *Women Folk*, was produced. In the first decade of the twentieth century the Clarion movement reached a remarkable peak.

As Judith Laird and John Saville have said (*Dictionary of Labour Biography*, Volume 4), 'Blatchford was a passionate critic of the social evils of capitalism and of the ways in which human nature was warped and twisted by competitive individualism. Above all he believed that "the best way to realise Socialism – is to make Socialists", and that the most effective way of making Socialists was by the use of reason to dispel ignorance.'

Blatchford's zestful approach to life and socialism must have appealed to Rebecca West as much as her wit and vigour appealed to him. Her articles for *The Clarion* are a revelation. They are concerned among other things with women's work in and outside the home. They were thorns in the left side of the Labour Party, a brave attempt to keep it honest in relation to women's issues. The articles which follow are a remarkable expression of what might be called syndicalist feminism, socialist in spirit. They are notable not only for the power of analysis of specific events, but for their shapely transcendence of polemical forms. They survive because of their wit and sheer intellectual exuberance. Their potential bite never hinders the flight of her mind. She called Swift an angel of polemics whose tongue often got the better of his wings. She is indeed archangelic in wielding the terrible swift sword. But angels are reputed to be androgynous and the redeeming and endearing feature of Rebecca West's prose is its source in a celebratory female sexuality. While so many British reforming temperaments have seemed rooted in celibacy and self-denial, it is refreshing to read a freedom fighter who not only recognises but revels in female sexuality. And when she tells us that good food, good books and pretty clothes are as necessary to working women's liberation as equal pay and intrepid trade unions, the modern feminist senses a kindred spirit.

Rebecca West encouraged the pleasure principle in her writings on feminism and socialism, as Robert Blatchford and the Clarion movement had done even earlier for a generation of socialist men and their families. This was a dangerous doctrine she espoused, in an age when working women had less access to information about birth control – that it was not necessary to deny the body to free the spirit. So, while these essays are specific to events in the struggle for suffrage, they are not dated by the still-surviving Victorian valuing of female self-sacrifice or the non-conformist imagination.

But Rebecca West's outspokenness did not come from arrogance. She spoke her mind as instinctively as the lion roars. There is no preacher's tone, no prejudice, no looking down from on high with 'pro-proletarian spectacles'. In *The Clarion* she had a larger audience than in *The Freewoman*, more space in which to develop her ideas. She was increasingly caught up in the passions of the feminist cause – passions particularly violent at this time because the Women's Suffrage Amendment of the Franchise Bill was in the process of being defeated.

With Rebecca West's column on the front page next to Robert Blatchford's, feminism and socialism with unbridled wit and intelligence, *The Clarion*'s columns surely brought more than one penny's worth of pleasure to many homes on Friday nights. Take, for example, a characteristic broadside against Lloyd George. In September 1912 Lloyd George presented a Village Institute to Llanystumdwy, his boyhood home in Wales. When suffragettes interrupted his speech to ask for votes for women, the crowd beat them, stripped them to the waist and threw their bleeding bodies into the village pump while Lloyd George went on with his speech about British 'fair play and personal chivalry'. Blatchford demanded in *The Clarion* that 'missionaries should be sent to Llanystumdwy at once' to relieve the savages of 'misogynistic superstition'. Rebecca West called Lloyd George 'The Minister of War for Llanystumdwy' and warned men that the Liberal Party, careless of the liberty of women, will be just as careless of the liberty of men, as witnessed by the fraud of the Insurance Act, 'a very ugly and deliberate device to break trade unionism'. She called for equal pay and equal opportunity as well as votes 'before the populace of Llanystumdwy have time to give any more demonstrations of the beastliness of men'. Lloyd George ought to 'disenfranchise Llanystumdwy for the next two elections. That would give them something to talk about in the long winter evenings at the village university.'

One has to check the date again, for her essay on 'Blacklegging and Timidity' is so alive to present problems – the weakness of teachers' unions, State jobs for women doctors at low pay, the exploitation of women workers to avoid paying a decent wage to men, the refusal of capitalists to equalise wages by pretending 'that women have no dependants'. ('A woman, according to the capitalist is an air bubble blown between earth and sky, with no human ties of any sort.') Accepting 'the swindle of underpayment' we not only injure ourselves but also the community. 'The capitalists suck strength out of an exploited class which enables them to exploit other classes.' 'The real objection to the control of the women's movement by the middle class is the extreme danger of a disassociation between the emancipation of women and the emancipation of workers. Otherwise the emancipation of women may only mean their exploitation.' She blamed the WSPU for using paid organisers who left their jobs and homes; she believed that the only way to organise was *in* and *by* the workplace, converting each industry, each factory to the feminist cause. Window smashing was less effective than the revolt of 'wage slaves in the bird cages of servitude'. When reading *The Clarion* it is well to remember that the pages of many papers during the years of the suffrage movement were full of the cries of women confused by labour's demand for yet more sacrifices on their part. While it is true that certain groups, such as the Co-operative Women's Guild, some union organisers, some intellectuals, were steadfast within the labour movement, women were too often told that socialism must come first, that they could not work for both at the same time.

Like Robert Blatchford, Rebecca West saw the Labour Party's treachery in 1912 when it 'sold itself to the Liberal Party body and soul' by repudiating its pledge to oppose the Liberal Government for refusing to grant votes for women. 'At its best the Liberal Party is a jellyfish . . . At present it is lying on top of the Labour Party. Through the transparent jelly one sees dimly the programme of socialist ideals which those who have gone before wrote in their heart's blood. To be wiped out by the Liberal Party is a more inglorious end than to be run over by a hearse.'

Rebecca West never failed to see the connection between militancy and the larger feminist movement. And she recognised the formidable amount of social reform legislation which was generated by the suffragette movement – twenty-eight laws passed in a decade.

She and Blatchford inspired each other to ever greater and greater feats of political journalism. On 28 February 1913 Blatchford produced a modern sequel to Swift's 'Modest Proposal' called 'A Short Way With The Suffragettes'. 'Cut off the women's heads, my countrymen; cut off their heads while there is yet time. Don't flog them, nor brand them or they will be wanting to do the same to us. Cut off their heads and get rid of their rebellious brains and silence their exasperatingly logical tongues. Cut off their heads and show them that if we cannot reason we at least are men. Cut off all their naughty heads: it will buck up the Dean of St. Paul's no end.'

While the new Swift so disposed in one column, the new Wollstonecraft proposed in the next that the burning of the tea house in Kew Gardens was an example of 'the mildness and militancy'. Since the Franchise Bill had been 'strangled by the fat hands of fools and knaves' a violent vengeance was to be expected.

She was ruthless on settlement houses and district visiting. 'Charity is an ugly trap. It is a virtue grown by the rich on the graves of the poor.' She dealt savagely with the idea that women and the poor have a 'lower standard of comfort'. She never ceased to plant her darts in the flanks of the young Labour Party, and dealt sharply with the socialists who were still 'ape men' on the subject of women. She continued to press for education for working women and supported Mrs Bridges Adams's Working Women's Movement, which had established a labour college for women called Bebel House. She attacked eugenics, and was deeply suspicious of the male mission to make woman womanly. 'It recalls a painful incident that occurred to my sister and me some years ago in a public park at Harrogate. We were selling *Votes For Women* and we offered one to a dear old lady in rustling black silk and widow's bonnet. With superb vigour she raised her umbrella and brought it down on my sister's head, remarking: "Thank God, I am a womanly woman!" and since then I have noticed that womanliness is a virtue claimed only with aggressive intent.'

The violence of official and public reaction to the suffragettes is difficult to comprehend now. Rebecca West was struck in the throat by a hysterical policeman with a quivering Adam's apple, pelted with herrings when she spoke to the striking dock workers, for not being a mother. The sight of several policemen hurling Margaret MacMillan, who worked for children's education, nursery schools and infant welfare, down the steps of the House of Commons affected her deeply. Once your own body has been assaulted by the law, it is very difficult to hold it in respect. Forcible feeding was the ultimate legal assault, comparable only to legalised rape.

It has not always been easy for historians to admit that such suffering, humiliation and death were necessary so recently to win such a simple right as votes. Rebecca West reported that she and many other friends of Emily Davison were glad that she had died under the feet of a horse rather than at the hands of prison doctors who forcibly fed her after she had thrown herself five flights down the prison well and was too injured to protest. Rebecca West wrote: 'Today Jack the Ripper works freehanded from the honourable places of Government: he sits on the Front Bench at St Stephen's with those vast public sepulchres of conscience in White Hall, and works not in secret but through Home Office orders and scarlet robed judges. Scotland Yard is at his service; the medical profession up to the President of the Royal College of Surgeons, places its skill at his disposal, that his mutilations may be more ingenious. And for his victims he no longer seeks the shameful women of mean streets. To him, before the dull eyes of the unprotesting world, fall the finest women of the land, the women of the most militant honour and the wisest courage.' To the women she wrote 'We must drop this masochist attitude of long-suffering which is the mistake of the revolutionary movements, and show ourselves an angry England.'

Rebecca West's first experience with spies, a species of humanity she was later to study in great detail, was in the suffrage movement, spending a 'quiet day with the constitutionals'. At a conference on the 'Cat and Mouse Act' she found that the police spy disguised as a journalist, whose reports had brought long prison sentences to many women in the 1913 trial, was insolently taking notes at the meeting. What kind of Government was it, she asked, which forced a young artist like herself to attend meetings instead of writing fiction? There was no place for the woman artist to feel joy; instead she was outraged at finding herself furious 'at the system of malicious espionage he represented', with 'murder in her heart'. (There is a police file on Rebecca West in the Home Office papers.)

Virginia Woolf argued that we would never produce a 'Judith Shakespeare' as long as women were allowed so little freedom and experience of the world. At twenty, Rebecca West had had enough experience for any ordinary lifetime. Repeatedly in her early writings she observed the 'havoc men and women make of life if they refuse to love life for its own sake, but covet the trappings thereof'. Two months after her assault by a policeman, she found some relief from the harrowing experience of 1913. She went to a music hall to see

Gaby Deslys dance, and she was delighted. The sight of this 'magnificent straight-backed chorus girl' held up 'hope for womanhood'. When she crossed the Palace stage she turned the audience's thoughts to May mornings, and ices and money enough to go where you like. Now if most of us crossed the Palace stage, we would turn the audience's thoughts to November evenings and cold cocoa and thirty shillings a week in the Post Office.' She objected to the Bishop of Kensington's denunciation of Gaby Deslys's scanty garments and told him he would be better occupied providing clothing for Mary Brown and her four children. It didn't matter whether Gaby Deslys danced in a 'crinoline or a cobweb, compared to the real problem of underfed and under-clothed working people in London. Poverty is the most obscene immorality.'

An Orgy of Disorder and Cruelty
The Beginnings of Sex-Antagonism

With the modesty for which he is notorious, Mr Lloyd George celebrated his birthday last Saturday by presenting, far from anony-
mously, to Llanystumdwy, the home of his boyhood, what the *Daily
News* called 'a village university'. It was a village institute. He found
himself unable to perform the act of generosity without the support
of his wife and family and five MPs. 'In the absence of Mr Winston
Churchill, the ceremony of opening the outer entrance was performed by Mr Masterman MP, who was presented with a golden key
for that purpose, and upon reaching the institute, the door of that
building was opened by Mrs Lloyd George, to whom another key had
been presented.' The whole George family was present in ecstasies
over the noble deed. Miss Megan Lloyd George, that unremarkable
child whose bare legs twinkle across the stage of English politics, was
photographed all day, playing with daddy or pushing a go-cart in the
garden. The festivity was as characteristic of Mr Lloyd George's
generosity as of his modesty. The institute was built with £1,000
which was awarded to Mr Lloyd George in a libel action. We may
receive the statement without rapture if we reflect that he charges his
unhappy country £5,000 a year for his services in hatching addled
Insurance Acts. It was a debauch of vulgarity. And there was something sinister about it. No one would mind if the George family went
to Blackpool for the day and ended up by changing hats and singing
comic songs on the promenade. But this brandishing of the simple
pieties and Christian virtues under the camera's eye is false and
dangerous. So no one need have been surprised when the celebration
suddenly turned into an orgy of disorder and cruelty, a letting loose of
Hell.

Some suffragettes turned up at the opening ceremony. They reminded Mr Lloyd George that the question of the enfranchisement of
women had not been settled. They were tactful. They did not point
out the plain truth – that it is galling for women to be cheated out of
their citizenship by such an inefficient person as Mr Lloyd George.

They made remarks such as 'Votes for Women', and expressed disagreement with various challenging statements that he made. Nothing they said could have aroused the fury with which they were received. A gentleman named Mr P. W. Wilson, who occupies a confidential position in the Liberal world, claims to have made a protest.

'Remember,' he exclaimed, when he saw a fellow-Liberal scratching a suffragette, 'she is a woman!'

He was thereupon hustled, and quite rightly, too, for making such a silly remark. The questions were not in the least provocative of scratching; and had the questioner been a man, there was not the slightest reason why he should be scratched any more than a woman.

To prove that everything is for the best in the best of all possible worlds, Mr Wilson tells us that afterwards one of the men who had hustled him came up to him and, touching his hat, begged his pardon. How like the vanity and littleness of liberalism to record solemnly a triviality like that when describing a scene as brutal and perilous as a battlefield!

The population of Llanystumdwy showed clearly that, though it had been given a village institute, what it really wanted was a village shambles.

Think of a mob of screaming, shrieking men, convulsed with liberalism, throwing themselves on singlehanded women, beating them with sticks and stones, tearing out their hair in handfuls, and stripping them down to the waist! Think of them dragging the bleeding bodies of their captives towards the village pump, pitching them over hedges, and trying unsuccessfully to dip them in the river!

Then listen to the speech with which Mr Lloyd George was leading their hearts heavenwards:

There is no country where political warfare is fought under stricter and more honourable rules of fair play and personal chivalry than in Great Britain. That is a worthy pride and boast for this land, and they fight all the more effectively because they fight honourably.

The right honourable gentleman broke the chain of his argument for another distinguished son of Llanystumdwy. Seeing a suffragette pinioned by this fellow, who was pummelling her face with his fist, 'I am sorry in my heart,' he complained, picturesquely. 'I would do my best to protect their lives, but I cannot be responsible any longer.' It was only by a miracle that his fellow countrymen did not take the hint.

It is impossible to take this scene as a mere bit of rowdyism. It happened under the auspices of the Chancellor of the Exchequer, and it was performed by the supporters of the present Government without fear of arrest. It is an event of profound significance.

One quite obvious lesson that women may learn from it is to be seen in the attitude of the Press. Things like this have often happened before. It has long been the custom of stewards at Cabinet Ministers' meetings to commit vindictive and often indecent assaults on suffragette interrupters. There have been attacks on the lives of many suffragettes – sometimes unsuccessful, as when a young Liberal of Dundee demonstrated his enthusiasm for retrenchment and reform by winding Miss Adela Pankhurst's scarf round and round her throat until she nearly choked; sometimes successful, as when, a stone's throw from the Mother of Parliaments, Cecilia Haig was kicked so that, after a lingering illness, she died. Of these things the Press has been silent. Now for the first time it has begun to recognise and speak about them. But not from any sympathy with the women's cause.

They have their own axes to grind. The Tory papers want to discredit Lloyd George, and to this end they use the pain women have suffered for their principles as coolly and calculatingly as they use his blunders over the Insurance Act. The Liberal Press use it to show what women must expect if they go in for militancy of the Dublin variety. Partisan Liberals neither think nor remember: they simply see that scratching and stripping women is a possible way of revenging an insult to their great god, and give the suffragettes fair warning.

This callousness should teach suffragettes two lessons. Firstly, that they cannot win their cause by mere virtuosic exhibitions of courage. Courage requires an audience of heroes. If Gladys Evans dies in Mountjoy Prison as a result of being forcibly fed, the public would stand it. There is no limit to what the public – the great mass of tired, weak souls, broken and killed by the capitalist struggle – will stand. It might make a certain amount of stir if that bloodthirsty stutterer, Mr J. L. Garvin, could so far subdue his natural loathing for suffragettes as to use them as a weapon against the Liberals. And the perception of this callousness should make us the more determined, if the more calm, to take a share in government. Since men take the assault of women so calmly we may judge that their self-sought task of the legislative protection of women will be done without zeal.

The second lesson is one for men. It never seems to strike men that a party which renounced the principle of liberty, when dealing with women, might renounce them when dealing with men. When Lewis Harcourt told the working women of Rossendale Valley that he would not give them votes because he did not believe they were as fit for self-government as his wife, it never struck the voters of Rossendale Valley that their member had confessed his disbelief in democracy.

It never struck them when the Government insulted women, gave them false promises, and shut them up in prison on faked charges and forcibly fed them, that this was not a firm with which an honest man would deal.

Then one morning the working men of England are dumb with amazement when they find that the Insurance Act is a fraud and the instrument of fraudulent societies, and a very ugly and deliberate device to break trade-unionism. Even since then they have voted for the Liberal at Crewe and Hanley and Cardiff and Midlothian. Perhaps now it will seem to them that a party led by a gentleman who turns his eyes up and thinks beautiful thoughts while his supporters light-heartedly hurl women over hedges can't be much good.

But this incident is of more than political interest. It is typical in the bitter thoughts which it must arouse in every woman of the disturbance in the relationship between men and women which this repression of the suffragette movement has brought about. It is a fact, minimised by the good nature of everyone concerned, that the present structure of society automatically compels women to be oppressed by men. The social liberty of a respectable woman is circumscribed by the vices of men. A woman who wishes to go about London alone by night or to look into shop windows in Bond Street in the afternoon encounters unpleasantness due to the accidents of the man-made social system. There is even an idea that women should regulate their dress according to men's lack of self-control rather than their own comfort. The Vicar of Lee, for instance, is always hoisting distress signals in the parish magazine (I presume, at the spiritual state of his male parishioners) begging women not to wear tight skirts because of their effect on men. He abstains from considering the fact that it is more comfortable for a woman to walk with two and a half yards of stuff hanging from her hips than with five.

And at the back of these little, worrying interferences there is the great economic grievance of women: that they are not given equal pay for equal work, that they are not allowed equal opportunities of education and profession.

But these were difficulties which women understood quite well arose out of the accident incident to a changing civilisation; some of them she felt she had brought on herself by the parasitic part she played in past ages. So she was perfectly willing to do her part in clearing up the muddle. That this was going to be tedious, onerous work she quite well understood. That is why being thrown over a hedge when she had offered to do her part seemed so unkind. It makes women doubt the Russian saying that the heart of man seems more like a menagerie. And that is the beginning of sex-antagonism.

And the worst of sex-antagonism is that there is such a lot of admissible evidence. If, for instance, some sentimental person like the Bishop of London, who likes talking about that sort of thing, had met those battered suffragettes on Saturday and said: 'My dear ladies, you are neglecting the true destiny of womanhood; you ought to be the mothers of men.' The suffragettes would be quite reasonable if they answered: 'Men? Ha! Those were men that tore the clothes off our backs and the hair off our heads. There seems quite enough of them to go on with without bringing any more into the world.'

And that's a very sensible point of view. Like all terrible and wicked things, sex-antagonism has a sound logical basis. So let's solve this business of votes before the populace of Llanystumdwy have time to give any more demonstrations of the beastliness of men.

And in the meantime Mr Lloyd George must be made to put his pious reflections into practice. A nice way of doing it would be to disenfranchise Llanystumdwy for the next two elections. That would give them something to talk about in the long winter evenings at the 'Village University'.

The Clarion, 27 September 1912

Women and Wages

Blacklegging and Timidity

In the *Daily Citizen* of 9 October there was a sentimental quotation, seemingly of feminist import, from *The Shipping World*. A new Act in the States has decreed that every vessel navigating on the American coast or the great lakes must carry a wireless operator; and it furthermore provides that women are eligible to qualify as operators.

And why not? [asks *The Shipping World*]. The invention opens out a new career for women, in which their special abilities can be used to the best advantage. If acuteness of hearing, rapidity of decision and suppleness of wrist and fingers count for anything, then, surely, the Marconi house on the bridge deck seems to be the natural goal for a self-reliant woman with cool nerves and efficient brain.

It is an alluring picture, and one flattering to women. In the mind's eye one sees the Marconi operator sitting gracefully at her work, with a rose in her hair, surrounded by votive offerings from passengers, operating much, much better than any mere man ever did. And, apart from *The Shipping World*'s idealisation of the prospects, it does seem an interesting new occupation for women. Women have had to settle down to occupations which were too tame for men and in which there are few opportunities for the adventurous-minded. The young woman who wants to see over the edge of the world would probably love the life of a wireless operator.

Yet, 'I fear the Greeks even when they bring gifts,' said the one wise Trojan, when he saw his fellow-Trojans dragging the wooden horse into Troy. I fear the Marconi Company even when they bring gifts.

Ah! Here we have it. Here is the powder in the jam, the snake in the grass, the wolf in feminist's clothing. I thought there must be some reason for this sudden lyric outburst of feminist enthusiasm. 'Probably she will be less expensive to the shipowner than the male operator, and quite as reliable.' One might have remembered that the capitalist respects woman in only one capacity; not as the worker or the wife or the mother, but as the blackleg. That takes the pride out of the working woman. If she becomes a Marconi operator on these terms, no matter how efficient and plucky she may be, she is living on the wages of dishonour. She has bought her job with the flesh and blood of her fellow man.

Though it is galling for the woman worker to know that she is not loved for herself alone, she may get a good deal of satisfaction out of the encouraging words that are let fall by the capitalist on the make. For instance, there was that remarkable wave of feminism that passed over local authorities four years ago, when they became obliged to appoint school medical officers. All over the country councillors enthusiastically declared to one another that it was imperative that children should be attended to by women; that men were far too coarse and tactless to deal with them; that every woman (even though she be a doctor) is a mother at heart . . . and that while men doctors were asking £250 a year they could probably get women for £150. The wiles of the municipal seducers were in vain. Women doctors, being in the main middle-class women, had savings and homes to fall back on; so they stood loyally by their male colleagues and refused to blackleg. Not one woman doctor in Great Britain applied for a £150 post. And there was an abrupt subsidence in the wave of feminism among local authorities.

What reason is there that women should play the part of blacklegs?

The underpayment of women is one of those 'ninepence for four-pence' tricks that capitalists have ever loved to play on the people whenever they had the chance. Capitalists have said to women: 'We deduct fourpence from your wages so that we can pay men larger wages, and then they can support you as their wives. So in the end you will make at least ninepence out of it.' It is only an excuse for sweating more money out of the people. It pretends that women have no dependants. A woman, according to the capitalist, is an air-bubble blown between earth and sky, with no human ties of any sort. True it is that man recognises that first imperative necessity which is plain to the lowest savage, the duty to provide for the next generation. But there is another duty which is patent only to the more civilised (if one was a really bitter feminist, one might say that that was why it fell to the women), and that is the duty to provide for the old. Miss Grace Neal, of the Domestic Workers' Union, states that it is the rule and not the exception for the members of her Union to send money home to support their parents. And sometimes widowhood lays the burden of both generations on a woman.

Women ought to understand that in submitting themselves to this swindle of underpayment, they are not only insulting themselves, but doing a deadly injury to the community. The capitalist sucks strength out of an exploited class which enables him to exploit other classes. An example of the infectiousness of poverty and the persistence of disease is the terrible economic condition of Edinburgh, which is directly due to the Battle of Flodden Field in 1513. Most of the able-bodied men were killed off and their widows had to set about earning a living for their fatherless children. They got 'woman's wages'. That meant that wages all round were depressed, and capitalism in Edinburgh got a good hold over labour by planting its feet on a solid substratum of the blackest and most helpless poverty. Labour has never shaken itself free.

How can women bear to be willing instruments of this crime against themselves and the community? The industrial women seem to consent to the indignity without resentment. Every woman who has risen from the floral stage of political activity (that is, the Primrose League), or the vegetable stage (that is, the Women's Liberal Association), must admire the suffragettes. Yet we may wish that they had spared a little of their dear irreverence and blessed pluck to stir up the industrial women to revolt. We have clever Miss Pankhurst trying to get the vote and earnest Miss Macarthur trying to organise trade unions; but seemingly we have no women who have read the signs of the times, who have discovered that political power and trade unionism are pin-pricks in the hide of the capitalist monster. Where are our women syndicalists?

Ladies of Great Britain, we are clever, we are efficient, we are trustworthy, we are twice the women that our grandmothers were, but we have not enough devil in us. We are afraid of going back to first causes. We want to earn good wages. But we try to do it by being amenable and competent wage-slaves, and thus pleasing the capitalist. We never try to do it by fighting the capitalist and turning him out of the workshop. The other day Mr Ramsay MacDonald complained that women do not make good enough socialists for him. The whole trouble is that women make socialists which are just good enough for Mr Ramsay MacDonald. They accept as doles from the capitalist class what they should take as rights. Wherever one gets a gathering of women socialists, one gets a programme of such charity gifts from the State as free meals and school clinics for children: excellent things, but dangerous unless taken discontentedly as niggardly instalments of a long-due debt. They should watch such things critically lest their children grow up in servitude. A slave is more of a slave when he is well fed than when he is hungry.

It is strange that women who are independent and fearless in private life should not introduce their independence and fearlessness into their public life. This occurs to me especially in connection with elementary-schoolteachers. The cheerfulness with which they have shouldered the responsibilities thrown on them by the free meals and medical examination of schoolchildren explains why the children love their school and their teachers. Yet they submit to being paid salaries of from one-half to two-thirds the amount paid to men for similar work. They submit in spite of the fact that they could end the injustice in a week by a strike. What could the Government do if women teachers struck? There are no hungry teachers walking the streets, so degraded by poverty that – God forgive them and punish the capitalists – they will help to drag their fellows down to poverty, too, by blacklegging. The women teachers of England have their remedy in their own hands.

Yet not only do they not use it, but they consent to remain members of a quaint body called the National Union of Teachers, which, although it exacts an equal subscription from men and women alike, maintains this principle of unequal payment. The scale which it suggests for certificated class-teachers is quite a humorous little effort. Apparently the male class-teacher is intended to get married at once, as his minimum salary is higher than the female's. True the difference is but £10, but the maintenance of a family can be the only excuse for any difference at all. His maximum salary is £200 against the female's £160. Puzzle: If the N U T thinks a class-teacher can keep a wife on the £10 surplus, how many children does it expect him to rear on the £40 surplus? Surely the birth-rate can't be going down!

I am no teacher, but I don't think much of that Union. I like to get value for my money, and a union that takes my money and does not give me equal benefits with my fellow-unionist is no use to me. Decidedly the women members of the N U T ought to withdraw their support from their ungracious colleagues and form a union of their own.

But what is the explanation of the meekness which makes such impositions on women possible? It is perhaps nothing disgraceful to ourselves, nothing that need make us doubt our worthiness as citizens of the ideal State. Nietzsche says that a man who is aiming at Supermanhood passes through three phases: the camel, the lion and the child. At first the soul becomes mastered by the idea of duty and self-sacrifice. It desires to be a preserver of life. Thus far have women gone. They have no time to travel further, having left the home so recently. 'But when the camel is loaded, it goeth to the desert, and there it is transformed into a lion.' The soul finds that the life for which it has sacrificed itself is in its present state hardly worthy of preserving. It turns to rend and destroy life, that out of its wreck it may make a new and more beautiful life. To this stage have men come.

Let women make haste to become lions, and fearlessly attack the social system. So that together men and women may be transformed for the last time into the child, who, untroubled with the consciousness of material things, is concerned only with love and happiness.

The Clarion, 18 October 1912

The Labour Party's Treachery

What Is Lloyd George?

The past week has seen a national disaster, more sordid and squalid than any tragedy of war or shipwreck. The dull days of the South African War, black as they were with death and defeat, were brightened by the thought that the dead had given their lives for their country. But the present calamity is not a tragic consequence, but a violent destruction of our ideals. The repudiation by the Labour Party of its pledge to oppose the Government if it refuses to grant votes for women shows that the people have entrusted their deliverance to men destitute of honour.

To treat this as a national disaster is not to exaggerate the importance of Woman Suffrage. The point lies not in the merits of Woman Suffrage at all, but in the fact that the Labour Party has refused to carry out a principle for which socialism has always stood; that it has made a promise and broken it; that it did this out of cowardice; and that it has sold itself to the Liberal Party body and soul.

We all of us know that it has always been an understood thing that the Labour Party admitted women to its ranks on equal terms and preached their equality wherever it could. It lost nothing by this, and gained a good deal. The women were used as much as possible as speakers and workers, and this gave the socialist movement a double supply of brains. If Eleanor Marx, Beatrice Webb, Mrs Despard and Mary Macarthur had not been allowed to use their gifts in the socialist organisations, it would have been a lot the worse for socialism. The support of Woman Suffrage was therefore not only a matter of principle, but also of gratitude. So when it was found that in the present Parliament the Labour Party held the fate of the Government in its hands it seemed inevitable that votes for women would be one of the first concessions wrung from the Government.

There was a double reason for rejoicing over this when the Government brought in its Franchise Bill. That the Labour Party could get votes for women was certain; and that it would have to show a little spirit and independence in doing so, and dissever itself from any alliance with the Liberal Party, was another joyous certainty. For some time past no sane person would have attempted to cook a soft-boiled egg on the revolutionary fire of the Parliamentary Labour Party. But the coming of George Lansbury, whose daring rectitude expressed itself in splendid, shameless words and deeds, seemed to herald a better time. Mr Ramsay MacDonald's pledge at the Albert Hall that his party would turn out the Government if they did not give woman suffrage showed a definiteness that was as welcome as it was surprising. Mr Philip Snowden, by his activity in this question, showed signs of fulfilling the promise of sincerity and passion that he had given when he first entered the House, 'the sea-green incorruptible, speaking on the Address', as Wells described him, 'a slender, twisted figure, supporting itself on a stick and speaking with a fire that was altogether revolutionary'. We had lost sight of that man. We were glad to see him again. There was just a chance that now there was this fine, daring thing to do, the Labour Party might become once more the fiery-hearted band of spiritual adventurers that one had thought it was, when one first joined the movement.

They were cleared of this suspicion on Monday. Mr Ramsay MacDonald had allowed himself this lapse into a definite promise only because he had never meant to keep it. Mr Philip Snowden had allowed himself the preparations for battle only because he had meant to postpone the battle *sine die*. At a special conference between the Labour MPs and the National Executive of the Labour Party, the Labour MPs resolved to break the pledge Mr MacDonald had given on their behalf. They unanimously – for George Lansbury was not present – decided neither to turn out the Government for its refusal to adopt woman suffrage nor even to vote against the third reading of the Franchise Bill. The National Executive, which represents the movement throughout the country, wanted them to keep the pledge. There was no pressure on them to commit this dishonour. They contrived it out of their own hearts. Crooked are the ways of the professional politician, who leaves his worker's heart behind him when he leaves his work and becomes a busy parasite like the rest of his fellow members.

One might have expected some opposition in the way of honesty from some of the lesser MPs, who have not been corrupted by success. But, perhaps having heard the rumour (of course, quite untrue) that Mr MacDonald will soon be offered the position of groom-in-waiting to the young Prince of Wales, they thirst to follow in his footsteps. Besides, they have the same idea of politics as the docker who has interrupted a socialist speech about the tyranny of the Port of London Authority with the remark, ' 'Ere, this ain't politics. Give us your views on Welsh Disestablishment, and then we'll listen.' Mr George Roberts (of Ipswich) solemnly declared that not even for woman suffrage would he imperil the causes of Welsh Disestablishment and Home Rule. It needs a divine discontent to revolt against the conditions one is accustomed to, but a penny-dreadful imagination can always luxuriate in thoughts of the simple and pious Welshman and the oppressed Irishman. I would almost believe it if I was told that Mr MacDonald had committed these follies through too much anxiety over the poor souls in the Balkans. Much of the rottenness of the Labour Party is due to excessive indulgence in the milder and less expensive Christian virtues uncontrolled by common sense.

There is no such excuse for the letter from Mr MacDonald which appeared in the *Daily Citizen* – fit setting for such a jewel – on Saturday. In order to justify turning his coat he attacks the Women's Social and Political Union. Naturally, as the attempt of middle-class

women to organise a revolt that could only be adequately felt by
working-class women, the WSPU is bursting with vitality and
faults. But Mr MacDonald does not take advantage of his opportunities. He peevishly relies on mis-statements. In a sentence of ninety-
four words there are only thirty-seven that matter, and they convey
an impression which is not true. 'Should the women by any mis-
chance fail to be included in the Reform Bill, the suffering will not be
upon the rich women who would be enfranchised because they pay
taxes, but upon the poor working woman.' This insinuates that the
WSPU is asking the Labour Party to fight for a property franchise.
This is not so. Ever since the Government's adoption of manhood
suffrage the WSPU has dropped the Conciliation Bill and demanded
adult suffrage.

He goes on to say that

if the working women of the country only knew what has been going on for
the last two or three years, it is not a sex, but a class war that would be
declared against the wealthier sections of women for whose stupidity and
vanity they have now to suffer. It is not men who have stood in the way of
their enfranchisement, but a small section of the women themselves.

There are other whimpering allusions to 'the havoc these militants
have done, both to public opinion and to individual tempers', and 'the
criminal proceedings which now stand as the only serious barrier
between women and the franchise'.

Now, it is true that the feminist movement will not reach victory
until it is more of a working-class movement. But the militant
movement – unwise, incoherent and limited as it has often been – has
made victory possible by showing us what men and women really
are. The plucky, hopeless raids, the hunger-strike and forcible feeding
gave us a sudden vision of the funds of courage, faith and honour that
lie in the hearts of women, to be spent some day for the world's good.
And from the ringing cheers raised by the honourable gentlemen in
the House when it was decided not to prosecute the policemen who
had been guilty of indecent assault on the suffragettes during Black
Friday, we learnt for all time how fitted Parliament is to govern
women. But all this hardly needs arguing, and one dislikes haggling
over so gallant a movement with a knight who has always gone forth
to battle with a hot-water-bottle tied to each stirrup.

But one's heart is melted by some closing sentences of Mr Mac-
Donald's letter: 'I wanted to elaborate this, and explain in detail why I
have come to such a conclusion. Unfortunately, I can't do it this
week for reasons which I have explained. But during the next few

days I shall find some pious and ennobling explanation of why I ate my words, or my name is not Pecksniff.' Well, I admit that Mr Ramsay MacDonald did not write that last sentence, but anyone with clairvoyant gifts can hear him thinking it. I am deeply touched at the thought of Mr MacDonald spending the next few days in absolute seclusion, studying the works of the Jesuit fathers for hints on how to behave in a hole.

The newspaper which gives publicity to this experiment, in making the best of a bad job, provides a leading article to match. It is naturally annoyed that the WSPU is going to oppose the Labour candidate at three-cornered elections. So it produces a feeble and attenuated red herring. 'Those who turn against their best personal friends – the friends who have helped them with money and service – may also be expected to turn against the movement which first gave them a platform and which from first to last has been loyal to the cause.'

Of course, this argument is quite unsound. The suffrage movement cannot be expected to grow old open-mouthed in gratitude because Mr Keir Hardie patted it on the head when it was young. There is no doubt that this present punishment for present scoundrelism is richly merited. Yet there is also no doubt that the moral effect of it will be lessened by the public's knowledge of the undemocratic government of the WSPU. No one expects a huge organisation to be run on debating-society lines, and the impossibility of such action was proved by the failure of the Women's Freedom League. But an important change of policy ought – less as a matter of ethics than of common sense – to be laid down before the members by a referendum. When four leaders of the WSPU differed, and Mr and Mrs Pethick Lawrence could not endorse Mrs and Miss Pankhurst's policy of attacking property, this neglect of the feelings of the led became painful. It is not only a question of the presence or absence of the Lawrences, but of the ultimate effectiveness of the policy. Unless the Union as a whole is convinced that this 'irritation strike' (to use a syndicalist phrase) is right, it will only succeed in irritating the members.

But however despotic and foolish the government of the WSPU may be, is this any excuse for the Labour Party's repudiation of its principles? And does it excuse the Labour Party becoming footman to the Liberal Government? Just as some men go to the public-house and come home to beat their wives, so the Labour Party goes to talk to Mr Asquith and comes home to beat its principles. They trot from lobby to lobby, voting against the reduction of the tea duties and a

Single Chamber in Ireland to please their master. They acquiesce in crimes such as the National Insurance Act, that quaint tax on employing power, and the raising of the Plimsoll mark. And what a master! At its best the Liberal Party is a jellyfish. Sometimes the milk of human kindness which flows through it, instead of blood, gets heated, and then it flops about and tries to do good. This warm milk enthusiasm soon evaporates, and it lies inert. At present it is lying on top of the Labour Party. Through the transparent jelly one sees dimly the programme of socialist ideals which those who have gone before wrote in their heart's blood. To be wiped out by the Liberal Party is a more inglorious end than to be run over by a hearse.

But something has happened which should have startled the Labour into action, however deep its apathy. We all know what happened at Llanystumdwy. That women were scratched and bitten and had their hair torn out is admitted by everyone, even the most rabid anti-suffragists, who was present. There were worse outrages. 'I have been doing this kind of protest ever since the WSPU began, six years ago, but of all such meetings that I have attended this one excelled in brutality and indecency. I am not a young woman, I have a grown-up family, but it makes my face burn with shame to think of the way these fiends touched me.' There was painful corroboration of these complaints in certain Press photographs which had to be suppressed.

In the House of Commons last week Mr Lloyd George said that 'the whole of that story' of the assaults at Llanystumdwy 'is not merely grossly exaggerated, but nine-tenths of it is unutterable falsehood'.

What is Lloyd George?

This is no ally for the apostles of freedom. Mazzini, who released Italy from Austria, would never in his most desperate hour of need admit among his helpers men of tarnished honour. He saw evil as a growing, creeping thing, that would spread from one man's soul to another's and finally to the ideal itself. 'By their fruits shall ye know them,' said another, who was a practical politician if he was nothing else. He was so practical a politician that he died on the cross. Mr Ramsay MacDonald would, we know, always avoid such regrettable excesses.

I think we should have worn mourning last week. It is true that we have been saved the necessity of worrying about the reversal of the Osborne Judgement. The trade unions had better keep their halfpence out of mischief. But we are bankrupt of political ideals, for we paid them to bankers who have absconded. We dreamed of a country 'where the State is the Church and the Church the people; three in one and one in three', a commonwealth 'in which work is play and play is life; three in one and one in three', a godhead 'in which all life is human and all humanity divine; three in one and one in three'. And now we see the stuff of which we were building that State: whimpering betrayers of trust, the companions of liars, the treasonable sellers of their own flesh and blood, three in one and one in three, we must begin to build anew.

The Clarion, 25 October 1912

The Future of the Middle Classes
Women Who Are Parasites

Life ought not to be divided into watertight compartments. Apparently feminism seems a simple matter to many suffragettes, like floating a patent medicine. One advertises the principle of the equality of the sexes with immense vigour and publicity until the public begins to swallow it. As to the effect it has on the public the suffragette cares as little as the patent-medicine vendor. Indeed it is often explained at suffrage meetings that the women's vote will have no appreciable effect on the social structure, and will simply act as a *police des moeurs* to suppress the White Slave Traffic. It is strange that the middle-class woman, who forms the backbone of the suffrage societies, should believe that one can superimpose the emancipation of women on the social system as one sticks a halfpenny stamp on a postcard. For in the social developments consequent upon the emancipation of woman she will probably play a great and decisive part.

For the middle-class woman comes of a class that is in a state of chaos. The present position of the middle classes may be symbolised by a certain distracting disturbance of the residents of Hampstead. On a hillside starting at Church Row and extending down to the Finchley Road there is an area of immensely valuable house property. Those who dwell in Fitzjohn's Avenue and the surrounding parts have arrived at the summit of the middle classes. After that they can only soar upwards to Park Lane. They have everything that money can reasonably be expected to buy, and certainly more than is good for them.

Yet at the bottom of the hillside there is a railway goods yard. That means a persistent and uproarious disturbance of the middle classes every night in the year. Engine whistles shriek, trains puff and rattle, men shout, and there is that particularly maddening reverberation of buffers all night long. Up in Fitzjohn's Avenue members of the middle classes may be dying, and members of the middle classes may be being born – these last in the minority, for the birth-rate is very low in such parts – but this infuriating disturbance goes on. There is also the uncomfortable circumstance that every now and then a shunter gets crushed or a boy gets mauled to death by a runaway capstan, but these things rarely come within the cognisance of Fitzjohn's Avenue. Even without that the night is made hideous.

Now the people in Fitzjohn's Avenue are the railway shareholders and directors. It was entirely on their shoulders to organise the railway system so that the goods yards and sidings were at some distance from human habitation. It was their business to discover that all those vans that are shifted about are not really necessary: most of them work about six months out of a life of seventeen years, and spend the rest of the time wilting in sidings and being repaired. But they did not take the trouble. So now the world of work, which they refused to organise economically and justly, has its revenge on them by destroying their night's rest.

There you get the position of the middle classes today. It used to be imagined in Victorian days that to be a member of the middle classes was to be in a position of perfect security. One rose from the working classes by the practice of what one Samuel Smiles called 'self-help'; that consisted of practising the baser Christian virtues in order to steal the job of the man above you. Thus one attained to the middle classes, and after an unexciting life, died, leaving a large middle-class family, perfectly confident that they, too, would have large middle-class families. There would, please God, always be a sufficient residuum of the self-helpless, idle, thriftless and drunken to do the work.

But now there is no such feeling of security. The special circumstances which helped the middle classes to this prosperity do not now operate. The wealth that flowed into England at the beginning of the last century was largely due to the fact that after the industrial revolution the manufacturer found himself in power over a vast reservoir of amenable labour. Trade unions were still illegal combinations, so the adult worker was cheap indeed, and cheaper still the labour of little children. Out of this slavery England sweated enough wealth to enable herself to resist Napoleon without unduly feeling the financial strain. Thus she was able to pursue her commercial way unruffled at the time her European rivals were hopelessly overcome by the Napoleonic Wars. Again, we see that the poor, in asking for a greater share of the national wealth, are neither thieves nor beggars, but simply workers presenting an account for services rendered.

But England has outlived these advantages. The European countries have recovered and, with wits sharpened by adversity, are formidable rivals. The middle-class man is hard hit by this readjustment of things. Moreover, his two errors of judgement are coming home to roost. First of these is the idea about the thriftlessness and worthlessness of the working classes. The working classes have rebelled against him; and they are so clever and so fit that they have got a good deal out of him already and they are going to get a lot more. Free education, free libraries, the Workmen's Compensation Act – all such things as those come out of the middle-class man's right-hand pocket. His other error of judgement, snobbishness, which makes him love all lords as one should only love the Lord, makes him feel deeply surprised when the rich and great do not assist him in his hour of need, but pick his left-hand pocket with their demands for rent for their overpriced and capriciously disposed-of land. Between them he is plucked very clean. That is, of course, only from his own point of view. But it is perfectly true that there is a very black future for the middle-class man. There is not the slightest prospect of his being able to live up to his present standard of comfort for more than one generation.

That means all hands to the pumps. The middle-class woman will have to come out and work for her living. Not as the exception, as it was ten to twenty years ago; not in the minority, as it is now; but as the general rule. The middle-class woman will have to stop being a parasite.

There is no question that she will be able to compete equally with men. But what will happen next? What will be the effect on the labour market?

Many advocates of the economic independence of women appear to think that by qualifying for a trade or profession one automatically guarantees oneself a living in that trade or profession, and that this principle operates just the same no matter how many other people qualify. That is the type of mind that believes that technical training is the solution to unemployment, and that peace on earth and goodwill to all men will be secured by the multiplication of trade schools to infinity. Trouble is never settled so easily as that. Thirty years ago in the West Riding of Yorkshire a textile designer could make five pounds a week. Now, years of technical classes have turned out scores of trained textile designers who can hardly command twenty-five shillings a week. And similarly the entrance of all these trained and efficient women into the market will, although the feminist pride engendered by the suffrage agitation will probably prevent them from being blacklegs, lower the rewards of labour. This will be particularly so in the case of the occupations taken up by middle-class women, which will be mostly of a distributive or not directly productive nature, such as stockbroking or the practice of law and medicine. Thus life will become more than ever intolerable for the middle classes.

So the entrance of the middle-class woman in the labour market will precipitate a social revolution.

There are two possible social revolutions which would relieve the strain. There is the progressive revolution: a social readjustment which would enforce a more equal distribution of wealth, a repudiation of the claims of rent and interest, and a capture of the national resources for the workers. This revolution will be necessary if women are to stay in the labour market. But if women are withdrawn from the labour market and maintained as parasites the other revolution will be necessary. That is the reactionary revolution, which could take the form of a return to the happy conditions of the early eighteenth century, when the middle classes built their prosperity on the solid foundations of the slavery of the working classes.

That such a revolution is in the sphere of practical politics is shown by the vicious anti-democratic temper of the middle classes today. The loathing of trade-unionism, free education and restrictions on child labour, that is a popular feature of the Conservative Press; the acquiescence of the public in Lord Devonport's attack on the dockers and the callous attitude of the crowds to the women who collected for the dockers' wives and children; for the shameful apathy with which England allowed Frederick Crowsley to be sent to prison for inadvertently preaching the Sermon on the Mount – those are signs of the times. And the instrument of this passion against the people is already forged. The Conservative Party of last century was an essentially aristocratic party formed in the mistaken idea that liberalism threatened the privileges of the landowner. But the lawless and bellicose Conservative Party of today is essentially middle-class. Mr F. E. Smith is the most middle-class man who ever lived. Yet such a frenzied figure has never before intruded on the stage of English politics. For such impudent activity over great issues, for such flippant values of life and death and liberty, we must look to the French Revolution. From this reactionary revolution, however coercive and violent it might be, there would be no prudish shrinking on the part of the Conservative Party, any more than there would be any effective opposition to it from the Liberal or Labour Parties.

And this reactionary revolution is an absolute necessity if middle-class women are to be maintained as parasites. The parasite woman costs money. The nation is not wealthy enough to support a non-productive class. We only produce £25-worth of goods per head of the population. We practise the most determined concentration of wealth, one-tenth of the population own nine-tenths of the accumulated wealth, and one-fifth of the adults take to themselves two-thirds of the annual product and leave only a third to be shared by the four-fifths who are manual workers. Our poverty may be measured by reflecting how small a proportion of the nation is kept in comfort and how still smaller a proportion is kept in luxury by the poverty of these four-fifths who are never lifted clear of the subsistence level. So we may assume that if middle-class women are to remain parasites these four-fifths must remain at the subsistence level. It is not only a question of whether slaves will submit to supporting women, but whether women will submit to being supported by slaves.

Issues as grave as this are raised by feminism. That is why women should not concentrate their intelligences too fixedly on the vote without preparing for the tremendous issues that follow. And that is why socialists should regard the woman's movement as something more important than the fad of a few propertied ladies and women as humble beings to be satisfied by pious opinions concerning the advisability of free milk for babies. When woman came out of the home she came bringing not peace but a sword. Great things depend on how she uses that sword.

· *The Clarion*, 1 November 1912

The Danger of Having Only One Eye
Suffragists and the Irish Party

The attitude of the Labour Party towards the suffrage amendment to the Home Rule Bill was most significant. Their nervous enthusiasm, which began with Mr Snowden's excellently lucid speech and declined into Mr MacDonald's brief murmurs of approval, was a sign that the Party has found its repudiation of the pledge to turn out the Government over woman suffrage very expensive. Mr MacDonald's imitation of the Almighty has deceived no one. All over the country socialists have been telling him very loud and clear that he has done wrong. It is bad to be pricked by one's conscience, and far worse when public opinion is on the side of the conscience. The Labour Party, perhaps for the first time, really wishes that it could carry a suffragette amendment to the Franchise Reform Bill. And the result of the Home Rule Bill amendment was most disheartening.

The granting of votes to Irish women, by substituting the local government register for the parliamentary register for elections to the Irish House of Commons, is obviously right and just. Of the hundred thousand women this would enfranchise, seventy thousand would be working farmers. So the democratic objection (usually raised by democrats of the type of Comrade Fred Maddison) that only idle women of the leisured classes would be enfranchised, does not stand. The Irishwoman deserves her vote, for she is not a luxury, but a working partner in the firm. The idea of sloth as an agreeable feminine characteristic – an idea that has arisen since the industrial revolution took the married woman's work out of the home and left her comparatively idle – has never been popular in Ireland. It never could be in an agricultural community, where so much work, such as dairying, has to be done by women. In the sense that Irish women are more intimately concerned with the business of life, they deserve a vote almost more than English women.

The only scruple that could deter a sane person from voting for this amendment was a doubt as to whether the Irish Parliament should not be allowed to settle this matter for itself. But the Imperial Parliament ought to see that the Irish franchise is reasonable, particularly in view of Mr Redmond's notorious lack of ideas, which renders him credulous. If he read *The Eyewitness* with too close attention and proposed to introduce a fancy franchise excluding all Jews, temperance lecturers and persons named Samuel, it would clearly be the duty of the Imperial Parliament to intervene. As it happens, he seems to have read *The Times*, for he shares its conviction that women are either vice-presidents of the Anti-Suffrage League or brazen hussies. He has already exhibited his fantastic prejudices on this point by bullying his party into voting against or not voting for the Conciliation Bill last March. That killed the Bill.

So as a reward the Liberal Party, while removing the Post Office Savings Bank from his control, have left him power to suppress foot-and-mouth disease, swine fever and women. And his party will let him suppress the women. Except the eight members of Mr Healy's 'All-for-Ireland' group, there is not one Irish member who stands up to Mr Redmond.

It is a strange party. One could judge of its futility by its leader, just as one could pronounce on modern liberalism by looking at a photograph of its leader and marking the foolish, legal face, the lips pursed and jaw protruded with the sham dignity and strength of a third-rate actor. Mr Redmond is the blood brother of Mr Asquith. He means nothing. He is a battering-ram of a man; grown by Ireland to get Home Rule as belligerent animals grow horns. He is as specialised, as implacable, as incapable of differentiation as a steam-engine. The party he leads would naturally be a limited thing that has never developed beyond the crudest individualism and *laissez-faire* doctrines. It has hardly ever used its place in Parliament except to protest ignorantly against wars, on quite the wrong grounds.

Yet there is a glamour about the Irish Party. We see them against the background of an Ireland laid waste by Cromwell's sword and later laws that made the selling of a Catholic by his brother fair commerce, rewarded by the State. We think of their country as a ragged old woman, beautiful with sorrow, who needs only the gift of liberty to become beautiful with youth. Now that these deliverers have cast off English rule Ireland will begin to blossom like the rose.

But the trouble is that Ireland has been blossoming like the rose for some time past, and the Irish Party does not like it at all. Up till 1880 the whole force of the aspirations of Ireland was directed to nationalist propaganda. Members of Parliament returned from defying the English to fire with their rhetorical genius the brooding, miserable people. This segregation of a revolutionary class was bad for the Irish. Idle themselves, they had a feeling that Ireland was yet doing great things. They lived by proxy.

Then came Sir Horace Plunkett, an unromantic figure – a Protestant and landowner, own brother to a peer, and a man of dull speech – on the unromantic errand of organising co-operative agricultural societies of farmers. Suddenly the practical genius of the Irish was inflamed. The Irish Agricultural Organisation Society was founded. Since then it has organised creameries so that the Irish farmer gets as well paid for his butter as the Dane; it has sent instructors to every district to teach the farmers scientific methods of tillage; actually it prevailed on the Government to form a Department of Agriculture, and saw to it that the State hovers in the background as a friendly backer when co-operative societies borrow from the Joint Stock Bank to build their creameries. The IAOS has found a triumphant agricultural syndication in Ireland which ought in time to make it as prosperous as this growing land of industrialism.

But all these things came about without the help of the Irish Party. The Irish Party has only one eye, and that it keeps fixed on the question of the Irish Parliament. It had been born like all human creatures, with two eyes, but it had shut the other just as one does when looking down a microscope. So at first it did not see the IAOS and when it did, it dismissed it as an inessential. When the IAOS prospered and began to absorb the energies of the people, the Irish Party's indifference turned to hate. It clamoured that the Department of Agriculture should withhold grants from the IAOS on the ground that it was a political society of anti-nationalist aims. And eventually it did. The IAOS now receives no subsidies from the State.

Now the Irish Party has come into its own. They start their task of establishing the Irish Parliament with the faint resentment of the finest citizens and, what is even worse, the support of the gombeen men, the moneylending publicans who battened on the farmer while he was still enjoying the beauties of individualism. If the co-operative workers also make the mistake of seeing with one eye and withdraw in mistaken fastidiousness from political action, we may yet see politics regarded in Dublin as they are in America – as a lucrative profession unsuited to gentlemen.

That's a sad end for a noble cause, to which fine men and women gave their lives. It should be a lesson to suffragettes who look at the world in a one-eyed way. The movement grows more and more specialised. In its early days it dealt boldly with the wrongs done women by the industrial system and spoke out plainly on subjects such as the dismissal of married women teachers. Now it is concerned chiefly with the dreary tactical struggle for the vote. Not from any ill-will, but simply because it was felt to be irrelevant. A suffrage speaker was forbidden last spring to announce from a suffrage platform that a fund had been started for the relief of the dockers' wives and children. Criticism of the suffrage movement is not, as some people believe, the real sin against the Holy Ghost which only the masculine prejudice of the disciples prevented them from denouncing more explicitly. It is because there is just as much courage and genius in the suffrage movement as there ever was that one wishes that it would keep in closer touch with the only movement that could make feminism possible. Otherwise it may go on in a horrible success, growing more battering-ram leaders like Mr Redmond, and at last find itself sitting in power in a world where no one can be truly free, which it has not altered in its progress. Then in desperation it might turn to silly, violent legislation like the flogging clauses of the White Slave Traffic Bill, which propose to make the world a better place for women by making good men degrade themselves by torturing bad men. In fact, the women might fail as badly as the men.

The Clarion, 15 November 1912

The White Slave Traffic Bill
The Archbishop's Blood-Lust

The trouble, as usual, begins at the top. Born of parents who have never been weakened by poverty, the upper-class woman passes through a healthy babyhood and girlhood spent in the open air to a life of leisure. All the resources of civilisation are commandeered to make her a peculiarly fine, vivid human being with keen sensations and strong faculties. Yet from the perfected miracle civilisation asks nothing.

It guarantees her an excellent living without the slightest exertion on her part, and lets her loose in her unemployed strength and beauty. Motherhood exhausts not a tenth of her time or energy. She cannot become an artist, for art is not produced by idle people. If she has the scholar's mind, she may keep an intelligence, as other people keep dogs, feeding it on lectures and such very digestible forms of culture. In these circumstances Satan finds work for idle hands to do.

There remains to her the resource of sex. She gives herself up to the development of her sexual attractiveness, she makes the toiling earth subserve it. For the adornment of her body to that end have sprung up those surprising institutions, the great drapery stores, with their amazingly unstandardised goods, and all sorts of curious, rather amusing occupations are carried on – beauty-doctoring, hunting for the pelts of rare animals in distant snows, fantastic hair-dressing, and diving for pearls in foreign seas.

Naturally, such a highly organised department of life is efficient. Sex, which ought to be an incident of life, is the obsession of the well-fed world. With all the wonderful things to do in life, men are constantly distracted by the desire of beautiful, luxurious women. But the women, using their double power of sex and superior economic position, make their own terms. Men cannot have them unless they undertake to support them – an undertaking which becomes more and more exacting every year as this expensive worship of sex raises the women's standard of living and incomes remain stationary. So most men have to wait until their prosperous maturity before they marry. The passion which these parasite women inspire, being based on no pretence of comradeship or equality, is not such as commands faithful waiting, so men visit the vagrant passion of their youth on the daughters of the poor.

The rich are the real procurers of the White Slave Traffic. The poor are in their net. They are betrayed by the passionate atmosphere which the rich women create into the hands of the rich men, who will not pay them well for any service except this. There is a very real direct compulsion in these things. The domestic servant who, after being victimised in her situation, has to go to the infirmary ward, is often condemned to prostitution as inexorably as though a bench of magistrates had pronounced her punishment. And still stronger is the indirect compulsion that sternly reminds women that if they will indulge in honest work they will be very badly paid for it. Prostitution is a peril that hangs over the economically insecure girl, just as consumption threatens delicate women. And, worst of all, just as the spawn of a pond-bottom produces strange and ugly things, so muddy poverty produces natural prostitutes, women born with an appetite for shame.

Ultimately this evil recoils on the rich:

> As rich men die in many a town
> Of sickness from the poor men blows.

There are no limits to the ugly physical consequences of sin, nor any rest for those who have defiled the loveliest thing on earth. There is a vague sense of shame and unhappiness about everything connected with sex which makes people too miserable to think clearly on the subject. Instead of thinking, they occasionally rise to their feet and begin blazing away at prostitution with any old musket that happens to be handy.

The Criminal Law Amendment Bill is the latest old musket. It is a Bill to suppress the White Slave Traffic. Is there a White Slave Traffic? I think so, and you think so, and so does the House of Commons. But where it is carried on, and to what extent, none of us really knows. Those of us who have an ideal of a parliament as a research laboratory in which social questions will be weighed and analysed and finally understood will feel indignant that the House of Commons started to legislate on this subject without having the slightest expert evidence as to what it was legislating about. True it is that once there sat in the Mother of Parliaments a gentleman who had founded his fortune by judicious investments, personally selected from helpless alien immigrants, in the White Slave Traffic. But it is now some years since he passed away on the brink of the peerage. In default of this expert knowledge, the House legislated on hearsay knowledge of the investigations of Scotland Yard, which is notoriously uninterested in the subject, and facts supplied by bodies of sectarian, Puritan and even remarkably vulgar (as in the case of that society which objected to the statues on the British Medical Association offices in the Strand) bias, with admittedly no systematic means of getting information. We can hardly imagine the Wages Board Act being drafted and passed by a parliament that had not the vaguest idea of how many employers or employees there were, where or under what conditions they worked, and what pay they got. The Government might at least have appointed a Royal Commission to find out what the White Slave Traffic is.

The first and best clause of the Bill permits any constable above the rank of sergeant to arrest a person suspected of procuration without a warrant. There is, of course, the danger which was urged in the House, that innocent men will often be arrested. It did not seem to strike the members that the present laws empowering constables to arrest suspected prostitutes without a warrant are sometimes used to persecute innocent women, particularly of the working classes. Let men also endeavour to live above suspicion. True it is that a simple-hearted policeman, brought up by a pious widowed mother in the rural simplicity of Chipping Sodbury, might make some awkward mistakes in his zeal to protect innocent girlhood from voluptuous and mercenary manhood, rounding in, perhaps, on his first day's duty a South African millionaire of sixty-three with his titled bride of nineteen. For, after all, some prostitution is protected by the law. We could do away with all need for the intervention of the law by giving every girl a full measure of knowledge and economic freedom. But that is rank feminism and socialism. Since we prefer to have a State that, by keeping its girls ignorant and poor, renders them liable to be carried off to South Africa by procurers, we must give policemen power to arrest the procurer on the quay, however many inconveniences arise.

More controversial were the clauses which compel the landlord to evict the tenant who has been convicted of using his house for the purpose of habitual prostitution. It was urged that this will have the effect of raising rents for prostitutes, who are already shamefully victimised in this way. Since it is an economic axiom that the consumer always pays the tax, we shall probably hear more than ever of the rise in the cost of living under Free Trade. The other illuminating objection to this clause is the naïve complaint that a landlord could not be expected to know what happened on his property. Could anything be a more cynical confession of the profound immorality of private property? And can one imagine a respectable person, with a house in Queen's Gate and a life membership of the National Liberal Club, getting married, begetting a family, and going to meet his God without every having the curiosity to find out whether he drew his income from brothels? This is moral imbecility.

So, too, is the enthusiasm over the clause that inflicts flogging as punishment upon procurers who have been twice convicted. One might perhaps call it something worse, but it is backed by an archbishop. The Archbishop of York, at a meeting at the London Opera House, made a speech such as Mr Garvin would make if he were suddenly saved.

> They wanted increased power and increased punishment. (Cheers.) It was said that they must never use the lash lest they degraded the criminal or the man who flogged. Degrade whom? Degrade the villain who had sunk to cowardly devilry to obtain the carefully contrived ruin of innocent girls? He defied them to degrade a man of that class. (Cheers.) And as for the man whose unwelcome duty it was to inflict the punishment, he would fulfil it if thereby he thought it would render less likely the ruin of one innocent girl. (Cheers.)

This seems rather ignorant nonsense. It was put still more crudely by another bloodthirsty Christian who solemnly urged in support of the clause the fact that Christ whipped the money-changers out of the temple. But Christ never stood beside the triangles holding a blood-stained lash; he only indulged in a free fight of propagandist intention, such as all social reformers from suffragettes backwards have enjoyed. Our instincts tell us that normal, healthy people do not flog other people any more than they skin live cats in the back gardens. And many psychologists hold that flogging is the amusement of men of evil character, holding out Nicholas Udall, the famous 'flogging headmaster' of Eton, and a man of many vices, as the historic type. As a patriot, I object to men of this type being made government servants.

I doubt, too, the moral effect on the man who is flogged. If one arrests a man for a violent offence and then commits officially sanctioned violence on him, one probably leaves him with the impression that the world is a violent place, and that his abductions are not really wrong but only unpopular.

He will probably go out with a wilder conception of the forcible demonstrations possible on this disorderly earth, and ideas of revolvers and Sidney Street sieges in the last resort.

Besides, the irrelevance of it! When I read in my paper that Mrs Emilius has been convicted of selling her daughters, aged fifteen and seventeen, into prostitution, I loathe her far more than any murderer. She is, in sober fact, worse than a murderer, for she has broken the spirits of her daughters and probably pronounced a deferred death-sentence over their bodies. But I do not want her to crush her finger in a door-hinge or fall downstairs. I take no interest in her physical feelings. I don't believe she has any. I can't imagine what she looks like: I find it hard to believe she is made in human form. I don't want her to be punished; I simply want her to be suppressed.

And so she is – for twelve months. At the end of that time she will be free to practise her maternal virtues again.

And if in her place had stood some Napoleon of the profession, like the man who died recently in this country after having organised an army of touteneurs here and in the United States to rake the poorer manufacturing towns for girls to draft to the wealthier cities, he could not have been sentenced to more than two years. That is the maximum penalty for procuration. Amusing rogues get seven years for swindling people who have not the wit to look after their own money. But that is an offence against property: this is merely an offence against the person.

Of course, this is wrong. But so is flogging; and just as ineffectual. If I should ever meet a tiger walking down Piccadilly with a half-chewed baby in its mouth, and I managed to muzzle it, I should take it to the Zoo and leave it there for good. In my wildest moments it would not occur to me that my duty to the innocent babyhood would lead me to flog that tiger, keep it locked up for two years, and then let it loose in Piccadilly again. Neither the flogging nor the short imprisonment would cure it of its tigerish taste for babies.

I think we ought to treat procurers as tigers. The mistake archbishops make is in thinking that a procurer is a man who might have been an archbishop if he had not taken to procuring instead, and that he only needs a flogging to help him proceed on archiepiscopal lines. But the procurer is an immutable specialised type, whose energy has been concentrated by degeneracy into an insensibility to the fine things of the flesh and the cold execution of premeditated villainies. We have a right to protect ourselves from his talents. His existence is a riddle, and he might as well solve it from behind prison bars. The long sentence must be tried. In cases of Napoleonic crime that has corrupted continents, life sentences must be used.

But that would need a great campaign behind it – convincing the Houses of Parliament that an offence against the human body and soul should be punished with the same deliberation, dignity and severity as an offence against property. If the Archbishop was expressing anything more than the merest outburst of the blood-lust he has been obliged to suppress since taking orders, here lies his chance.

The Clarion, 22 November 1912

The Divorce Commission

A Report that Will Not Become Law

Suffragettes are often denied the justice that one expects from civilisation, such as a fair trial in an open court and police protection from assault. They receive surprises; such as the acquittal of the Pwllheli gentleman on a charge of assaulting a suffragette at Llanystumdwy in face of the sworn evidence of a police constable and several unbiased witnesses. But while they are irritated and obstructed in all these minor ways the woman's movement wins triumphs in strange battlefields far enough from the political citadel it is attacking.

The latest triumph is the recommendation in the Reports of the Royal Commission on the Divorce Law that a woman shall be able to divorce her husband for adultery. This adoption of a feminist reform is the more amazing when one considers the composition of the Commission. It consisted mainly of people impervious to ideas. The Majority Report was signed by such Conservative temperaments as Lord Guthrie, whose treatment of the wife in a certain divorce case once roused the bitterest criticism that any divorce-court judge has provoked in modern times, and Mrs H. J. Tennant, a Liberal woman, tarred with the Downing-Street brush. The Minority Report was signed by the Archbishop of York, Sir William Anson, an antifeminist too uninteresting to be really dangerous, and Sir Lewis Dibbin, unremarkable save for being a pious lawyer. Yet there was such a pressure of public opinion that this unpromising assembly had to concede this demand of the suffragists. The suffrage movement has organised the pride of woman into a conscious militant body of which every statesman is as nervously conscious as he is of the German navy. The distant voice of Christabel Pankhurst has coerced the Commission into supporting the feminist revolution.

For this penalising of the adultery of men is not merely the opportunity of release for many unhappy women, but it is a revolutionary proclamation that women have souls and that men are not as beasts of the field. The argument that women did not mind their husbands committing adultery rested on the assumption that women are such materialists that, so long as their bodies are not assaulted and they get food and clothing, they will put up with any spiritual indignity. And the argument that a man must not be punished for his adultery rested on the assumption that a man is always a little unsteady on his moral legs, and that when he descends to the gutter he is only fulfilling the law of his being. Men ought to feel the deepest gratitude for the adoption of this feminist reform.

When we consider the other new extensions of the grounds of divorce, which consist of desertion for upwards of three years, incurable insanity after five years' confinement, habitual drunkenness and imprisonment under a commuted life-sentence, we must not be diverted into the advocacy of ideal conduct. Doubtless the perfect husband would wait a lifetime for his wife to return to him, and the perfect wife would never weary of helping her husband fight the passion for drink. But it is not the State's part to decide whether a marriage is so unhappy that it has become dangerous to society and ought to be dissolved. For we must have happiness at all costs. Submission to unhappiness is the unpardonable sin against the spirit just as submission to poverty is the unpardonable sin against the body.

There is a parallel between the poor and the unhappy in their ultimate mischievousness to the State at large. When one section of the community sinks into poverty it infects the whole community with its misery. It depresses the general level of wages, it overcrowds into tenements and creates disgraceful housing conditions, and helps the capitalist class to sweat more wealth and get its heel on to the worker's neck. In the end they disturb the peace of even the most comfortable by pestering them as ugly and ill-mannered tramps and beggars. And so the unhappy take their revenge on society; for they, too, create an atmosphere of depression, and they, too, become tramps and beggars. Just as the pavement artist cadges pennies by the display of a withered arm so a man whose wife is in an asylum soon begins to cadge affection. So obviously pitiful is his case that he can easily induce some other woman to take his wife's place. And if there is the least streak of the brute beast in him he will be tempted to use the economic and social insecurity of her position to bully her and threaten her with desertion. Whereas if the Report becomes law, ladies, if courted passionately under disadvantageous circumstances, will be able to say: 'How long did you say your wife had been in an asylum? Four years? Very well, we can wait another twelve months.' Thus unhappy people will be freed from the temptation of becoming mischievous.

Moreover unhappy marriages ought to be suppressed out of deference to the child.

I have read in an anti-suffrage publication that wife-beating is not a serious offence because many women like to be beaten and thus feel that they have really married a man. But such scenes of masculine dominance, delightful as they may be to the participants, are bad for the children. Childhood needs rest and placidity more than it wants the benefit of being brought up in a Christian marriage. It is more important that a child's nervous system should not be jaded than that its father should remain with a drunken mother in order to please the Archbishop of York. It is obvious that in the trinity of the man, the woman and the child, the child is the most important person, and that if the companionship of the man and the woman hurts the child it must be forbidden. Divorce may easily be not an indulgence, but a duty.

Not even the signatories of the Minority Report, who object to all extensions of divorce, have a word to say against the recommendations of the Majority Report that divorce should be made accessible to the poor. The Commissioners recommend that cases in which the joint income of the petitioner and respondent is under £300 a year shall be tried in local High Courts by a local commissioner, with simplified procedure and a special table of costs. Up till now a working-class man and woman simply could not get a divorce, however hard their case, on account of the prohibitive cost of bringing a case in the High Court sitting in London. The obvious unfairness of this is increased by the greater harm that an unhappy marriage can inflict on working people. A well-to-do man with a drunken wife has the pity of his friends, and is probably able to send her away to some home; the artisan whose drunken wife comes to his place of employment loses his job. And a deserted wife of the working class with half a dozen children has no marriage settlements to fall back upon. The addition of desertion to the list of grounds of divorce is also of special benefit to the working classes. A working man whose wife elopes to America cannot possibly afford to trace her and obtain witnesses to prove her adultery, nor is it a task that the most Marxian socialist could possibly expect the State to undertake. Now the simple proof of her absence for three years solves the difficulty.

So the issue of the Majority Report seems an occasion for rejoicing. But we must temper our elation with the thought that it will very likely never become law.

Of course, no one would grumble at delay. The Divorce Law framed by the Divorce Commission of 1850 was not put upon the Statute Book for seven years. But in the present state of party politics it is likely that the present Commission will not even have that luck. For the Liberals will not touch it. In time of peril they always shed their liberalism and start wooing the Nonconformist conscience by such dainty devices as flogging procurers. The Conservative Party, when it returns to power, will stand for a more forcible reaction to barbarity and piety than anything we have seen in our life-time. The Labour Party will do nothing, as usual. Those Labour members who are not too much under the refining influence of liberalism to discuss such a delicate matter, are too busy with soul-stirring reforms like Welsh Disestablishment.

Yet this is a question that socialists must press home. The foulest insinuations were made by witnesses before the Commission against the working classes. The extreme beastliness of the immoral poor was, so far as one could gather, only matched by the beastliness of the pious poor. For the President of the Mothers' Union stated that the working women she knew objected to the cheapening of divorce on the ground that adulterous couples would then be able to marry and 'they feel that it will be an injustice to themselves that a neighbour who has sinned should be allowed to marry again and be made respectable by law'.

It is for socialists to disprove this cant by agitating on the side of sane reform. The fate of the Commission lies in their hands. For the candid admission of the Commissioners that the reforms affect chiefly the working classes is sufficient to make Parliament shelve them for ever.

The Clarion, 29 November 1912

The Personal Service Association
Work for Idle Hands to Do

Charity is an ugly trick. It is a virtue grown by the rich on the graves of the poor. Unless it is accompanied by sincere revolt against the present social system, it is cheap moral swagger. In former times it was used as fire insurance by the rich, but now that the fear of Hell has gone along with the rest of revealed religion, it is used either to gild mean lives with nobility or as a political instrument. A man who has spent his life in selling adulterated food to the poor gives a hundred thousand to a hospital and buys a title, which brings him a puzzled respect from a people perplexed by the tradition of an honourable peerage, artificially perpetuated by the *Daily Mail*. Peers ride forth to war against Land Inquiries, flapping the blankets which, should heavier taxes be imposed, will not be given to the tenantry next Christmas. And nothing could be meaner than the way the charitable have of capturing the moral value of the situation by quoting, 'It is more blessed to give than to receive.'

Women know the true damnation of charity because the habit of civilisation has always been to throw them cheap alms rather than give them good wages. On the way to business men give women their seats in the tube, and underpay them as soon as they get there. In politics women are denied the right of self-government, and are given doles like the White Slave Traffic Bill, fatuous measures that do no good, but confer an irritating sense of obligation. Moreover, apart from this charity between the sexes, there are certain forms of philanthropy that press very heavily on the working man's wife. While her husband is out of work she has to bear the brunt of district visiting and, if she lives in London, the Personal Service Association.

This Association has its home in one of the gloomiest streets in Bloomsbury, where there stands a red building that looks like the public baths. And a public bath it is in a spiritual sense, for here the rich resort to purify themselves in the waters of charity. It is the Passmore Edwards Institute. Under its roof is a settlement, which is a place where the well-to-do come and hatch out the elements of virtue which lie (so distressingly dormant) among the poor. It is an excellent refuge for young people who cannot get on with their families. But as some people are too delicate to risk total immersion, the Institute also provides a shower-bath. Instead of living among the poor, one may do things in moderation and occasionally call on them.

'The Personal Service Association,' as one of its leaflets explains, 'aims at affording men and women of all classes some opportunity for social service by asking them to visit regularly, as friends and helpers, one or more families under the carefully organised system of the Association.' The insufferable air of forbearance about that statement brands the Association. They must know perfectly well that if they tried to visit the families as anything else but friends, the families could request the police to eject them. Yet, reading on, one gets an impression that the Association is doing the poor a favour by not taking their temperature and giving them cod-liver oil during the visit. In this spirit they send their members to visit families which have come under various charitable societies, such as the Central (Unemployed) Body, the Charity Organisation Society and the After-Care Association for the Recovered Insane. 'The ideal visitor will enter into every detail of that family with sympathy and interest; he will follow up the lives of the boys and girls, enter into their hopes and fears, their work, their amusements.' He is to do everything except give them money, thus proving himself the more like the Providence which, we are told, is always watching over us.

From the correspondence from visitors which is printed in the annual report, I judge that he is actuated by the same spirit that drives me to the Zoo. In every line I can detect the zoo spirit, the benevolence that offers buns through the bars on an umbrella-point. 'For dumps, depression, dreariness and "the heart-ache and the thousand natural shocks that flesh is heir to", I know of no better antidote than Personal Service visiting,' cries E, jubilantly. 'I have found the families I look after self-respecting, hard-working and kindly,' declares D, patronisingly, and does not inquire how it comes about that self-respecting and hard-working families need 'looking after'. And C says:

As a member of this Association, who has been absent from London for long intervals in the course of the past year, I am glad to have this opportunity of saying that I believe much good can be accomplished, even although the worker is unable to pay regular weekly or even fortnightly visits, provided he or she has obtained the confidence of the family visited.

I rejoice to think that C, having been left alone with the family plate of Mr James Huggins (Bricklayers' Union), has now gone to the Riviera with an easy mind.

Most philanthropic literature, like *The Times* leaders, seems to be written by someone eating very resilient toffee in a state of moral indignation. So I am not surprised when the Association's leaflet disclaims all such sporting intention, and declares in muffled sentences that it 'would urge primarily that the Personal Service movement exists to encourage the ideal of citizenship, and also the ideal of the corporate responsibilities of all classes to one another'.

The examination of a list of prominent members of the Association who are going to practise this noble aim is most disquieting.

By good luck I have not yet come under the care of the Charity Organisation Society or the London Mendicity Society, and they sound ungentle institutions. I would rather be attended to by the After-Care Association for the Recovered Insane, for it sounds tenderer. Well, if I had slowly fought my way back to sanity after a long period of mania, would it be fair to send Mr J. L. Garvin to visit me? Ten minutes of his passionate conversation on the subject of Belfast and the Balkans would shatter the work of months. Can an Association that exposes the poor to such perils claim to be philanthropic? In such a state it would shake my nerves to be visited by Lord Northcliffe, that eager recipient of the gossip of murderers' widows. And a visit from Mrs Herbert Samuel would cause prostration. One would think helplessly of all the delicate subjects one must avoid – silver, India, money-lending, wireless telegraphy and all the other corporate responsibilities of all the Samuels one to another . . .

I can imagine that some working women would object to being visited by the anti-suffragist Mrs Humphry Ward, whose one real flash of imagination – an assertion that an artisan, his wife and three children can be amply fed on eighteen shillings a week – is not so well known as it ought to be.

And then that business about the election petition would make Lady Wimborne's reception uncertain, notwithstanding that she was acquitted of all blame. The respectable poor have such a prejudice against appearances in the Law Courts.

This mingling of the rich and the poor will not do. There are too many irritations between them as there must always be between honest men and thieves. Least of all, can there be any easy relationship of patronage and respect between the rich and the poor woman. For both are failures. The rich woman is the most expensive luxury the world has indulged in. She is the most idle human being that has ever secured the privilege of existence, and, with her furs and jewels and silks from strange places, commands more service than any emperor of the past. And her achievements are nothing. Art and science are beyond her grasp, and her growing sterility stultifies the last reason for her dependence. Perhaps she feels the tragedy of her incompleteness, but luxury has bred a hard pride into her.

And hard work has made the poor woman ugly and clumsy. The working woman, whom childbearing and continual drudgery have made a bruised and withered thing at forty-five, feels herself an offence against beauty and life. She is too weak, too tired to shift the blame to those who ought to bear it, and feels humiliated.

The poor and rich can only meet when the poor have been exalted and the rich humbled by some moral passion. There lies the true significance of the feminist movement.

The Clarion, 13 December 1912

A New Woman's Movement
The Need for Riotous Living

Perhaps if I had been a railway shareholder I should have been more interested in the case of Driver Knox. For those who know about these things tell me that a man who can get drunk on two small rums must have an economical nature, and would probably make the company's coal go twice as far as anybody else would. But the real interest of the case lay in the determination of his employers to buy their employee, body and soul, off duty as well as on duty. If Driver Knox had caught measles, the company would have remained calm; but they became anxious when he imperilled his immortal soul.

This anxiety can very often be detected in the relationship between masters and men, and is a curious form of penitence. The rich perceive that they are giving the poor a very bad time in this world. But that is quite irremediable, and probably, since the heavens permit it, ought to be. So they coerce the poor into virtue, and thus make them sure of a good time in the next world.

One sees this attempt to provoke piety in the poor in orphanages and other charitable institutions where the inmates are quite defenceless. A year or two ago I went to see a village home for little girls that lay somewhere in the flat dullness past Barking. It was a very ugly place. Little mud-coloured brick villas, flanked by spiky evergreens that looked dusty with boredom, looked over flat lawns and fields at other little mud-coloured villas. The children seemed well nourished and not unhappy, though it was strange that all – except those who had been disfigured by disease – were designed for domestic service. No woman could believe that all those little girls had the right temperament for that occupation. And this tendency to regard little girls as made by the gross from the same pattern prepared one for the hard deficiencies of the institution. There was not a fleshly vanity in the place. There were no pictures on the walls; no lost ladies of old years to kindle the imagination with their beauty, no vision of other countries and the past. There were no good books even for the older girls, only sentimental tracts that were really inflated prospectuses of the simplicity of the Christian life. And the austerity of the furniture passes description; in its gauntness it reminded one of the ribs of a London 'bus horse.

It is no use saying that the funds of the institution will not run to luxuries. If the benevolent take on the responsibilities of these children's lives they must be prepared to give them 'bread and roses', not merely 'crust and cabbages'. And yet I have a suspicion that roses are not considered good for the indigent. For it is strange to note with what hostility the rich look on the timid attempts of the poor to grow some roses. The mildest amusements of the rich become the vices of the poor. The canon's lady who holds the district where I live in the hollow of her hand forbids waltzing in the local girls' club, on the ground that the initiation of the sinful pleasure would ultimately lead them to low dancing-halls. She shows no penitence at having let the world get into such a rotten state that there are no healthy amusements left to the poor. But there are acidities quite unconnected with any fear of immorality. It is amazing how angrily the well-to-do speak of the poor girl's love of finery. Yet there is really something very hopeful about the pert face of a Cockney beauty, smiling at life from under a wide and worthless hat tipped with nodding, spurious plumes. She is a better rebel than the girl who accepts her poverty as a matter of fate and wears its more durable badge of drab garments and sailor hats, for she perceives that life ought to be hung with flags, and that the ugliness of the world is a stupid convention. A similar idealism moves the waitress who, twittering like a little London sparrow, quite ridiculous, quite charming, carries on a flirtation under the sour gaze of her customers. Her sub-consciousness has reasoned that the Creator cannot have destined her to spend ten hours a day bringing unpleasant food to people she doesn't know or care twopence about for five shillings a week, while he may have destined her to love and be loved. I admire these attempts to get on with the business of life in spite of the absurdities of civilisation.

The relations between the rich and the poor are often paralleled by the relations between men and women, and it is so in this case. For the working woman is invited by men to lead, as the price of their respect, a grey life of unexuberant decorum and contempt of all the good frivolities of the earth. That is the real meaning of the mysterious sentence, heard sometimes from the unregenerate: 'Women don't need such big wages as men, because they have a lower standard of comfort.' It obviously does not mean what it says, for it is obvious that everybody wants as much comfort as they can get. If I refuse to give up my seat in the tube to a woman with a baby on the ground that, because she went to an elementary school when she was young and I went to a secondary school, she has a lower standard of comfort, I am not only a cad, but also an unimaginative liar. My motive would be pure selfishness. And pure selfishness is the motive of men's desire to repress women. Anti-feminists, from Chesterton down to Dr Lionel Tayler, want women to specialise in virtue. While men are rolling round the world having murderous and otherwise sinful adventures of an enjoyable nature, in commerce, exploration or art, women are to stay at home earning the promotion of the human race to a better world. This is illustrated by the middle-class father who never goes to church himself, but always sends his wife and daughters. But the highest form of virtue men can imagine is asceticism. But it happens that ascetics are 'gey ill to live wi''. So they absolve their wives from the sacred duty of renunciation of all fleshly vanities and, supported by some lingering memory of the old Catholic idea that a woman ought either to be.a wife or a nun, put it all on the spinster.

The schoolmistress is an example of this enforced asceticism. She does work of the highest importance, requiring not only a brain, but a heart. For the work she has done in the elementary schools in connection with the Free Meals and Medical Inspection of schoolchildren she can claim to be among the most efficient and humane public officials we have. We ought almost to allow her special privileges. But instead we bully her into an elaborate pretence that she is not a human being at all, but some undecorative kind of vegetable. We impose on her a tradition that she ought to dress dowdily. We turn her out of her school if she takes any prominent part in political affairs, although we are worse than foolish if we want our children to be brought up by a mind so vacuous that it has no political opinions. If we are well-to-do, we object to her continuing to teach after she has proved herself human by marrying. And we underpay her miserably, so that she wastes half her efficiency in trying to make ends meet, as one tires oneself out trying to hold on a large hat in a gale. When she is in training at college she is underfed. But then, of course, wherever women are gathered together for the purpose of work their spirits are tamed by partial starvation. The students at Newnham and Girton are weakened (some of them for life) by underdone joints and rice puddings. In YWCAs the boiled egg is of more importance than it ought to be, and there seems far too much bread-and-butter in the world. Nurses in hospital usually enjoy a diet much too unpalatable and restricted for any better-class child of ten. The air of extreme solemnity possessed by many professional and business women is largely due to over-familiarity with milk puddings.

Another aspect of the artificial asceticism of woman is the sacrifice of personal liberty she has to make before she can get a respectable roof over her head. If she is sufficiently prosperous to avoid the slums she must go to a YWCA and whatever her private convictions may be, step into an evangelical *mise-en-scène*. She may be fortunate enough to find a comfortable branch, but she may chance on one where the founders – although the YWCA is not run at a loss, and the inmates owe nothing to charity – gratify their appetite for vicarious piety. They rip phrases from the Gospels and hang them on the walls in the starkness of black print, unmitigated by the presence of other pictures. They insist on public prayer at certain hours. Public prayer at half-past eight in the morning, with the cold light falling through a basement window on to the dirty cups and saucers on the breakfast table, promotes atheism more effectively than all the publications of the rationalist Press. And those of us with passions for going to suffrage meetings and music-halls – both excellent enthusiasms – must restrain ourselves, for we must not stay out later than half-past ten. But there we are in the same position as the inmates of 'philanthropic' institutions such as Hopkinson House (which pays a sleek five per cent), who, although they may be women of forty holding responsible educational positions, must not dare to stay out a moment longer.

Decidedly what we need is a militant movement for more riotous living. Schoolmistresses must go to their work wearing suffrage badges and waving the red flag. The ladies of Hopkinson House must stay out till two in the morning, and then come back and sing outside till the doors are opened. And we must make a fuss about our food. 'The milk pudding must go' shall be our party cry. I can see in the future militant food raids of the most desperate character. I see the inmates of the YWCA inflamed with text-burning on Hampstead Heath, pelting the central offices with bread-and-butter and threatening a general massacre of hens if the boiled egg persists in prominence. Armies of nurses would visit the homes of the hospital governors and forcibly feed them with that horrid breakfast dish, porridge and treacle. And in Simpson's some day the blenching stockbroker shall look down the muzzle of the rifle and hand over his nice red-and-black beefsteak to his pale typist ... Wages would go up then.

But that is a dream. But not an unromantic one. The modern psychological theory of insanity states that impulses can never be killed, but only scotched; and if one denies an impulse its natural outlet, it will find an unnatural outlet. It may be that the repression of the animal in woman, with its desires for food and freedom and comfort, accounts for her greater liability to nervous irritability and hysteria. If so, then what has always been a racial danger is becoming more and more dangerous every day, as women take more and more part in the world's business. Many of the evils of our social system spring from perversities that arose when all education and much of the land was in the hands of monks and nuns who were professedly leading unnatural lives of repression. And in the same way the lady – who is simply the well-repressed woman – may be a source of danger to the State. So that though the doormat type of anti-suffragist is

disgusted by the women who struggle for material comfort for themselves, we are doing sound service to the State by our selfishness.

The Clarion, 20 December 1912

Christmas Shopping
The Psychology of Regent Street

The West End shopping area is a hateful place. The arrogant stone
pillars of the great shops pretend that their trade is carried on magnificently, while it is really based on a foundation of squeezed-out
small tradesmen, unprosperous factory hands, sweated home-
workers and anaemic shop-assistants. And Granville-Barker described the goods in the windows in *The Madras House*:

A hat as little like a hat as anything on a creature's head may be. Lace.
Flowers of a colour it never pleased God to grow them. And a jewelled feather
– a feather with stones in it. The rest ought to be called a conspiracy in three
colours on the part of a dozen sewing-women to persuade you that the
creature they have clothed can neither walk, digest her food, nor hear her
children. Now, can that be beautiful?

And those women who spend their mornings hovering round drapery shops are hardly dignified; they remind one, in their obvious
ignorance of what they want and their occasional bursts of predatory
enthusiasm, of a hen picking at random round a rubbish heap. And
shop-assistants, those uncannily elegant and passionless beings, are
slaves in that their occupation demands incessant and promiscuous
politeness. The temporary irritation ought to be the right of all.

That is why shopping is more cheerful at Christmas than at any
other time. People do know what they want and shop-assistants
occasionally lose their tempers. The people who are jostling each
other in Regent Street by artificial light have an exciting meretricious
charm. The changing pattern of lights reflected on the wet roadway,
the taxis that sweep by brightly and silently like dragonflies, the hard
brilliance of the shop windows and the towers rising blackly out of
the warm haze into the chill blue night, are a little too theatrical but
quite amusing. As this is the haunt of wealthy folk there is no jarring
ethical appeal such as greets one in the Commercial Road, where a
mission invites you to 'sign the pledge and enjoy Christmas without
hurting yourself'. The only jarring note was struck by a poster of the

Pall Mall Gazette which announced at every street corner (on a day which we all know to be 18 December), 'Christmas is Coming'.

But there is the Christmas mood, a kind of purring of the soul, which makes one tolerate these platitudes.

Yet there are baffling things in Regent Street which make one stop and think at any season. There is, for instance, an amazing exploitation of feminine underclothing; chiefly corsets. Now, corsets are not beautiful things in themselves, and I understand from the harsh words of scientists that they are no better than they should be in their ultimate results. And their cumulative effect as one walks down Regent Street is appalling. Once, when I began an article in another paper with the remark that there are two kinds of imperialists, imperialists and bloody imperialists, a vicar's wife wrote to tell the editor that my use of foul language indicated a coarse nature. Yet, condemned as I am of vicars' wives, I blush to see a windowful of waxen princesses, clad only in corsets and muslin flounces, grouped smilingly round another similarly clad princess, who is standing on one toe and extending her other foot high in the air behind her. I find this spectacle, as the other quaint tableaux which arise out of the habit common to the wealthy of delighting to see their garments exhibited in the street before they buy them, strangely humiliating.

I find it rather sneakish too. Recently Mlle Gaby Deslys made a sensation by appearing in a sketch at the Palace in not quite the customary amount of clothing. But there was one excellent point about her performance. She took the full responsibility of this exhibition. She associated herself with the petticoats and faced the attitude of mind which this display provoked. I do not see why the respectable ladies who shop in Regent Street should be allowed to exhibit their clothes in this furtive, anonymous and impersonal manner. If they wish to do provocative things they ought to do them boldly as professionals and not skulking as amateurs. For amateurs, be they gentlemen jockeys or amateur actors, are those who want the thrill of a profession without risking the social stigma that may attach to it. And the rich woman, with her increasing immunity from all work in the home and her increasing devotion to self-adornment, is becoming an amateur of provocation. She uses her position of economic security to avoid the results of her skill. So a cruel and insatiable demand for sex springs up, which is eternally satisfied by the women of the poor.

From the six underclad princesses I turned to a shop where I suddenly found myself among people who I concluded to be of a serious turn of mind. For they were buying books. It seemed a characteristic of the English attitude that this noble enterprise was being carried on in the basement.

I hovered about them apprehensively for a long time, for their proceedings seemed ill-regulated. Keats and Shelley were being bought, but so were anthologies, and anthologies are mischievous things. Some years ago there was a rage for chemically predigested food, which was only suppressed when doctors pointed out that since human beings had been given teeth and digestive organs they had to be used or they degenerated very rapidly. Anthologies are predigested food for the brain. When we have to read Stevenson and Herrick in snippets it is all up with England. I came to the conclusion that all was up with England, for they were buying anthologies by the bagful.

Then the clear voice of a saleswoman brought me understanding. She said, 'So you will have the Milton, madame. Or perhaps you would like something in the Persian yapp line?' Then I saw what these wretched people were up to. Persian yapp (which has nothing to do with Peruvian bark) is a kind of leather used for binding minor poems. These people were buying books for the binding. The lady preferred the Persian yapp line, bearing Ella Wheeler Wilcox under her arm and not John Milton, who was clad in a foppish lavender shade of soft leather. One realised with a start that nothing was safe from this passion for ornament, and at the same time how mean a passion it was and how solely concerned with material things. These Christmas shoppers would take a book of poems, a miracle of passion and wonder and proud blasphemies of things as they are, and make it an excuse for a note of pretty colour in a drawing-room. They have no concern with the beauty of the spirit, but turn from it with vulgar suspicion, as a thing they cannot touch and valuate.

When I left that shop I walked to the end of Regent Street, and there I bought a copy of the *Suffragette* from a cold and tired and gallant seller. It struck me, on the way home as I read the announcement of the deputation of working women who are going to St Stephen's when Parliament reassembles after the New Year, that this was the true festive spirit. The excellent thing about the suffrage movement is its insatiable appetite for life.

Of course, this deputation is going to be ineffective. No deputation that did not succeed in getting hold of Mr Asquith's head and banging it against a stone wall twice a second for two hours could make any real impression on him. For he is that type of Englishman who, one feels, must in early youth have heard his Aunt Matilda say that the dear child bore a striking resemblance to Napoleon and has lived up to it ever since by cultivating a general insensitiveness towards life.

This gallant little deputation will go out and become simply another opportunity for a pouter-pigeon's exhibition of 'dignity' and 'firmness'. The worst thing about the woman's movement is the extent to which it has had to advertise this most insignificant of all political personalities.

The deputation itself will have a very bad time. The women will be knocked about the streets in a violent and indecent manner, they will be tried and sentenced in an insulting manner with all kinds of brutal jokes, they will be tortured in prison. We know quite well that there is no end to the courage of suffragettes. But there is also no end to the beastliness and baseness with which they will be fought. And the nation will stand it.

The nation will stand anything. We socialists ought to know that. The nation that mocked the dangers of the miners and the railway-men and the poverty of dockers, that permits Sir Edward Grey and Mr Lloyd George (the Minister of War for Llanystumdwy) to remain in the Government, is not likely to care for the subtler grievance of the women. It seems a pity that the suffragettes should spend themselves on war with such dishonoured enemies before such an apathetic audience.

And we must not forget that whatever disaster occurs, the Labour Party is entirely to blame. A month or two ago they had the power to coerce the Government into settling this business with peace and honour. They betrayed their convictions. So did St Peter when the cock crowed, but this is a comfortable case with no repentance. For at the present there is every likelihood that even if the Reform Bill does not include women they will not dare to vote against the third reading, so thoroughly besotted with liberalism are they. Any further manifestation of militancy lies at their doors. It is strange enough that they should be the begetters of a thing which, rash and unwise as it may be, is yet of a strong courage and sincere purpose.

The Clarion, 27 December 1912

The Prig in Power

Whom God Hath Joined McKenna Puts Asunder

Last week a Tory paper sent a message asking me to write an article on an exploit of the Home Secretary. The exploit sounded so incredible that I came to the conclusion that the message must have gone wrong in the telephone, and I took the extreme step of buying the *Daily Mail*. There I saw it in print. The Home Secretary has established himself as a matrimonial censor with compulsory powers. I distrust McKenna's intelligence, for few men have expressed themselves on the subject of woman suffrage with such feeble venom, but I cannot believe that this title of Home Secretary gives him power to settle the domestic affairs of all Englishmen. Yet he had taken upon himself the responsibility of forbidding John Williams, the man who is now lying under sentence of death for the murder of Police-Inspector Walls at Eastbourne, to marry Florence Seymour and legitimatise his unborn child.

Now, this is villainy.

To begin with, it is an impudent misuse of the powers which his high office in the State gave him over John Williams. The details of the Eastbourne murder have left me, difficult as they were to grasp through the incomplete reports of a protracted trial, but the sentence and its meaning are clear. It was pronounced that John Williams had killed Police-Inspector Walls; and that thereby he had shown himself governed by such dangerous impulses that he must not be allowed to walk abroad to hurt his fellow men. We think weakly and hysterically, so we have not learned the lesson of the zoo. It does not occur to us to realise that the tigers and wolves made in our shape are only following the law of their own nature in doing tigerish and wolfish things, and that it is childish to punish them. The clean cage with room for pacing and no restriction on any appetite save the appetite for human flesh is the perfect penal system. But we prefer violently to kill our tigers and wolves in a disgusting manner. So far we are all revengeful fools together and equally guilty with McKenna.

But McKenna has gone one step further. Society has handed John Williams over to him to see that he is safely hanged – no more no less. McKenna has tortured him. For in the open world behind him he had left a girl of twenty-one who was going to have a child. They appear from their references to each other in court to be sincerely devoted to each other. After he was sentenced to death and knew that he had to leave her for ever, he wrote to the Home Secretary: 'I want to marry my girl, Florence Seymour, before her child is born.'

The Nonconformist conscience was ruffled. Probably it seized a pen and wrote, frantically: 'You didn't ought to have a girl. If you had gone to church regular like me, you wouldn't. Anyway, she must be a brazen hussy. And marriage is out of the question. Nice people like me and my wife get married. Where would the respectability of it be if low creatures like you and Florence Seymour were allowed to do it too?' But a sense of dignity of his position restrained him. So almost by return of post Williams got the curt reply: 'I am in receipt of your letter and am unable to accede to the request therein contained.'

It is amazing. First of all, it is an unjustifiable restriction of liberty. To a man in the position of John Williams it is ungracious of us to refuse any reasonable request. We are putting out the light of his eyes, surely he may look his last on whatever he will. So long as we secure our victim for the gallows, what does it matter what he does in the few weeks' grace we grant him?

But it is worse than a mere restriction of liberty. It is a question of torture. Like everybody else I am a coward. I have never been in prison (which I know is a shameful admission for any woman in such a time of war as this), but I am quite sure that a few days of prison life, even under short sentence, would leave me a thing of raw nerves. If in addition to the solitude and the routine I was under the shadow of an impending violent death I should be mad with fear. Old superstition and violent repentances would possess me, events would assume the immensest values, my mind would brood on the past, finding opportunities for remorse. Any imaginative person can reproduce the state of hyperaesthesia in which John Williams must be living today.

In this state McKenna's decision may affect him in various ways. It is a psychological possibility that he may feel acutely his sin against Christian marriage. The respect for it is woven into the very texture of us all. Those advanced minds who believe marriage to be a trivial superstition never act on their convictions, and the people who practise promiscuity make up for it by theoretically upholding indissoluble marriage. It may well be that, just as the weak hands of dying men pluck up rejected creeds, so Williams is tormented by a sense of sin. In which case McKenna has no right to forbid him to make peace with his God.

But that is only a possibility. What is an absolute certainty is that he loathes to leave Florence Seymour to endure unmarried motherhood. In this he obeys the ordinary tradition of Christian society. A man who leaves a woman when she is going to have his illegitimate child is considered a cad. Williams is willy-nilly made a cad as well as a murderer. He must think, as he sits in the condemned cell, that through his deed the girl he loves is henceforth a pariah. For an unmarried mother is the most outcast thing on earth.

We, as socialists, primarily concerned that life should be beautiful, know that this is nonsense. It matters far more that a woman should have a beautiful and healthy child than that she should have a legitimate child. But the fact remains that most people do not think like that. They will treat Florence Seymour as an unclean person who has been meddling with important things in an unpleasant manner.

There may be some high ideal at the back of their minds – some feeling that the girl has done a sacred thing too carelessly – but the fact remains that the mob is instantly subdued by a marriage certificate, however post-dated, which looks more as if it were an expression of the vulgar desire to tie up the world with red tape. A supremely proud soul in Florence Seymour's position might have disdained conformity to the laws of the world that killed her lover. But Florence Seymour is just an ordinary human being with the softnesses and superstitions common to us all. 'Why cannot we marry?' she said, after her child was born a few days ago. 'My baby would have had a father.' She wants to live the ordinary life of pleasant, warm contacts with friendly people of her own kind. She wants to bring up her child in an atmosphere of dignity and respect. Instead, all her life she will be insulted. Men will treat her as though her barriers were down to all comers. Women will not take the trouble to discriminate her from the prostitute. Henceforth she is a broken thing.

That is what John Williams must brood over till he dies.

It is not even a legitimate form of torture. For quite as much as it punishes John Williams does it punish Florence Seymour; and she, though judged by society to be a disorderly and uncontrolled person, has not brought herself within the clutches of the law. And most of all does it punish the most guiltless being concerned, their child. Some ex-official of the Home Office, interviewed by a Sunday paper, said in defence of McKenna that if Florence Seymour had married Williams her child would have been branded as the child of a murderer, whereas now it will only be described as 'illegitimate' – 'not an uncommon description'. Neither is 'cripple' an uncommon description, but that does not make a cripple any the happier. An illegitimate child has a bad time before it. It is exposed to material loss – Florence Seymour's daughter will not be able to inherit the sum of money which has been left to John Williams, or in the event of his decease, to his heirs – and to a life-long irritation. Vulgar people will be rude to her, respectable people will avoid her, everybody will whisper about this scandal of her birth. She will suffer a subtly corroding sense of personal cheapness. McKenna has spoilt her life. Yet she has done no harm.

This new principle, which holds that so long as we make a criminal smart it doesn't matter if we punish an innocent person at the same time, is most damnable.

When stupidity became inflamed with blood-lust over the Criminal Law Amendment Bill it was openly adopted by the House of Commons, which decided that so long as flogging hurt the procurer it did not matter if it also perverts the flogger. The mass of Englishmen are not so brutal. If it were proposed to preclude all executions with a fantasia of emotional torture so that the murderer might be prepared for death by seeing his child strangled under his eyes, we should rebel. We cannot be so obtuse as not to realise that a deed is cruel unless it leaves corpses about and some blood. If we have any imagination whatsoever, we must see that in compassing the misery of three human beings McKenna is a very dangerous criminal. If there is any hanging to be done . . . But we must not be infected with the hysteria of revenge. That can do no good to Florence Seymour. Nothing can now, for her child is born.

It only remains for us to recognise that, just as we would not allow a butler who had stolen all the forks to remain in charge of the spoons, so we must not allow McKenna to remain Home Secretary. There has been a suggestion that he felt that these people had had plenty of time to get married before, and that they had forfeited their opportunity. It is not the place of the Home Secretary to inculcate neatness and punctuality, and it reveals amazing stupidity if McKenna thought it was. But there is something worse than stupidity in this affair. It is priggish, tyrannous and merciless. The spectacle of the Nonconformist conscience awkwardly imitating Nero on the airy assumption that, as the victims are disorderly persons down on their luck, no one will mind, is the quintessence of cadhood. The present Government is a grievous affront to our national honour. This mishandling of the weak and helpless is the last straw.

At last we have a definite and certain answer to that ancient riddle which has provoked so much discussion: 'Who was the worst Home Secretary?'

The Clarion, 10 January 1913

First Result of the Franchise Bill

The Moral Degradation of the Ministry

Asquith has been able to break his pledge that the House of Commons should vote freely without Cabinet pressure on the woman suffrage amendments to the Franchise Bill, thanks to the marine-like credulity of the private member. Through various prudently talkative underlings he has spread it abroad that should any suffrage amendment pass he will resign his office. And actually people believe it. It is said that many pledged suffragists of average sincerity have been hoaxed by this preposterous threat, and have been terrorised into agreeing to vote down woman suffrage, even at the cost of their own souls. The Irish members, those reactionary heirs to a revolutionary idea, are only too glad to believe it. For the most part their credulity is a matter of malice. But the credulity of many Liberal and Labour members is obviously a matter of cowardice. But if they had not been stupid as well as timorous, they would have defied it.

For there are two important reasons why this threat should fail to terrify a mouse. They both depend on the same notorious fact – the extraordinarily uninspiring nature of Asquith's character. There is no Prince Charlie about Asquith. However righteous his cause and however desperate his peril, no Flora Macdonald would risk her life to smuggle him from the country. Strong men would never drink with tears in their eyes to Asquith over the water, nor would beautiful songs to Asquith in exile be composed by a sorrowing peasantry. His lack of romantic atmosphere is so obvious that he cannot keep it from himself. He knows quite well that were he to leave the Liberal Party he would take with him no enthusiastic band of eager-eyed young followers who would go with him to the jaws of death. Rather would he share the fate of Lord Rosebery who, as superannuated prima donnas archly sing 'Comin' Thro' the Rye', exercises his haggard gift of oratory in facetious speeches at village flower shows. He prefers the heavy burden of office. The front bench is always the front bench, even if it be in opposition.

Moreover, let us suppose that, in some excess of sulkiness and hatred of the light, Asquith did resign from the Government. There would be an impressive public meeting, where he would pose as the great man shedding the purple and lifting the imperial crown from his brows rather than betray his principles: there would be a ponderously tragic residence at his country seat, where, with luck, tourists who made a sufficient noise on approach would see the leader of men in exile, brooding over past greatness, with bent head and folded arms. And the Liberal Party would go on exactly as it did before. For Asquith, like McKenna or Runciman, is not part of the living tissue of liberalism, but rather its dry bones. He has never been a popular idol, and neither his worst enemy nor his most fulsome friends have ever accused him of providing the ideas of the Liberal Party. Such personalities never count. His coming or going would merely precipitate an election that is very near at hand. True it is that this would imperil both Welsh Disestablishment and Home Rule, but these questions are insignificant beside woman suffrage. Let the Welsh Nonconformists demonstrate their piety by bowing humbly to Heaven's will. And the Irish members deserve to be punished for voting down Snowden's amendment to their own Bill. Under cover of their devotion to Home Rule, they lie supine in the crassest, most reactionary individualism, and no one will ever know why the Labour Party feels called upon to risk its own soul for the sake of such as these.

Credulous is the kindest word one can apply to a man who is a pledged suffragist and betrays woman suffrage because of a hypothetical event that will not happen and would not matter if it did.

Another appeal to the sheep-like traits of man was made by Winston Churchill and Lewis Harcourt, who have been buttonholing the more impressionable suffragists in the lobby and telling them that should any suffrage amendment pass, they too would resign from the Cabinet. This is a much more dangerous threat than the other, for they are really valuable for the purpose of party window-dressing. Churchill goes down to the provincial hustings and plays like a fountain, drenching his audiences with political passion. Harcourt fulfils his destiny by being a perfect gentleman, and thus reassuring the Whig aristocrats who fear that liberalism is being defiled by intimacy with that dangerous member of the working classes, Mr Ramsay MacDonald.

The joke of this threat is that they will resign in any case. If the suffragist members have blood in their veins and stand by their pledges, they will certainly use that as an excuse for withdrawing from the Cabinet. But if the House succumbs, as usual, to bullying, they will simply find some other excuse. For they have never felt at home in the Liberal Party. Churchill was converted because he was young and full of visions, and liberalism on the threshold of power seemed a god of high purposes worthy of service. Harcourt finds himself a Liberal because his ancestors of the eighteenth century were Whigs and his family has always been too stiff with pride to change its position. They are both of them gentlemen of a past epoch. They hark back to England of that joyous time between the sixties and eighties, when the aristocracy, as well as bubbling like champagne with scandal, had the most glorious opportunities for important and irresponsible activities. In the diplomatic service men showed a vast amount of easy cleverness in dealing politely with large issues. It was a great game and they played it confidently with no angry, honest demos to wave moral standards in their faces. The machinery of democracy was an amusing toy, too, and the voters just sufficiently educated to form a gullible, intelligent and enthusiastic audience. On these two platforms aristocrats strutted as gods, apparelled like gay dogs. For those were the last days of dandyism.

Decidedly Winston Churchill and Lewis Harcourt are political gay dogs. And F. E. Smith yearns towards doggishness (as would all Smiths that would fain not have been born Smiths). They have imagined a party of leisured people with a tradition of pride and administrative efficiency, who shall make all England as quiet and orderly as the great houses and rolling parks of their own homes. Within the next year or so there will come to birth the Young Tory Party. At best it will be a formless thing with a vaguely benevolent land policy and a sincere but featureless imperialism. But first Tariff Reform must be shorn of its food taxes, which operation is being carried on daily by Lord Northcliffe in the *Mail*, what time Garvin shouts in distress to the unanswering stars.

A suffragist member who sacrifices his cause to these brothers in vanity will feel a knave in the present and no end of a fool when the Young Tories burst upon the future.

It has been widely stated during the week that if the suffrage amendment is not slain before birth by the individual scoundrelism of members of the Cabinet, it will be slain after birth by their collective scoundrelism. To prevent the House of Commons taking advantage of Asquith's pledge the representative system goes overboard. If the House passes Grey's amendment, which moves that 'male' shall be deleted before 'person' in the first clause of the Franchise Bill – which must be agreed to before the House can deal with the question of qualifying women at all – the Bill is going to be dropped. Harold Baker's Plural Voting Bill will be substituted and the suffragist interpolation will be impossible. That is, the expressed will of the representatives of Great Britain will be set aside by half a dozen of the least important Cabinet Ministers. The Reform Bill need never have been passed. This melancholy gang of misogynists has brought us back to 1832, and if they get back to power they will probably rescind the Magna Carta. The country ought not to submit to this sort of thing, if only out of respect for our ancestors. They went to all the trouble and expense of breaking the Duke of Wellington's windows, killing Charles I and frightening King John in order to create a certain illusion of democracy in the State, which we meekly hand over to Asquith when he asks for it.

These parliamentary manoeuvres remind one once more of the intimate connection between anti-suffragism and certain qualities that make one's existence on earth a thing not perhaps to be actively discouraged, but at least to be deplored. All drunk men are anti-suffragists, as every by-election worker knows. So are Lib-Labs. So are the two worst women novelists that ever disgraced their sex by a split infinitive. So is the lady who writes in the *Anti-Suffragist Review* that the vote may raise the wages of working women and that 'for this reason, as well as for many others, the enfranchisement of women is to be deprecated as a danger to the national prosperity'. So are the Samuels. So are the *Pink 'Un* and *Town Topics*.

This is the cause to which the Labour Party has directly subscribed by announcing so long ago that the Liberals need not fear any effective opposition from them if they betrayed woman suffrage.

The Clarion, 17 January 1913

Socialists and Feminism

The Fate of the Limited Amendment

A spiteful, unmarried female churchwoman brought up on the knees of curates. That is how I strike a gentleman living at Petersfield. The high quality of imagination which has enabled him to detect the curates' knees in my article alone differentiates him from many other correspondents who have been angered by my protest against Mr McKenna's prohibition of Florence Seymour's marriage. They are all men. No woman has spent her time in writing the sentence which, in one form or another, I have read constantly during this week: 'In the eyes of all right-thinking persons there is no stain whatsoever upon Florence Seymour and her illegitimate child.'

Now, I am not the sporting editor of *The Clarion*, nor have I really a black heart, or I would, as a new winter game, advise every correspondent who asserts that an unmarried mother suffers no social discredit to announce casually before a few friends that he and his wife are not legally married. My arguments would then be enforced by his wife. If he required any further conviction, let him consider that a servant who has an illegitimate child loses her situation, that the Board of Education suspends the certificate of a schoolmistress, that no hospital nurse or typist would expect for a second to keep her position. And as for the illegitimate child, I have already pointed out that a sum of money has been bequeathed to John Williams, or, in the event of his decease, to his legitimate heirs. Thus the child has been deprived of a start in life. And the social stigma is an indefensible but quite real consequence of the degradation of the unmarried mother. The child sees its mother shunned by the godly, associates itself with her disgrace and grows up to think of itself as a pariah. The recklessness and solitude of such a position is shown by the fact that a large proportion of the unmarried mothers in workhouse wards are themselves illegitimate. For these reasons, I repeat that McKenna has wantonly used his power to inflict serious economic and social damage upon a woman and child absolutely outside his jurisdiction.

A curious thing is that many of my correspondents appear to regard marriage as a dangerous institution to be actively discouraged at any cost. They are still obsessed by that old-fashioned division of life – so popular in the nineties – as a perpetual general post of childless men and women, changing partners whenever emotion dropped the handkerchief. Times have changed. With a romantic conception of life we have perceived that it is only the abnormal types – the super-normal, such as the artist, too closely bent upon art to choose wisely the one lasting love and impelled by a passion for research into emotion, and the sub-normal shabby Bohemians and the feeble-minded – that stagger from marriage to marriage. The normal citizen, if every church, chapel and registry office were burnt to the ground, would continue to enter into permanent monogamous unions. And if our divorce laws were improved, we could at least say that if marriage does nobody much good it does nobody any harm.

But even if marriage were a dangerous institution, the readers of *The Clarion* have no right to sacrifice Florence Seymour as an unwilling martyr to their principles.

For she expressed her desire to marry John Williams. I do not care what her motive was – whether it was a fine determination to proclaim to the last her loyalty to her lover, or whether it was anxiety to put herself right with the grocer's wife. The point is that she wanted to do it. It may be the desire of a fool or a knave or a weakling, but we have no right to stand between a human being and its desires unless they take the form of an attack on others. To the contemplative mind that is the magic of socialism: when men and women, free from the pressure of poverty, really express themselves in their actions, there will be possible a new art, a new philosophy. This determination to save the soul of Florence Seymour against her will reminds us how unregenerate we socialists really are. From afar off we have seen the pleasant fields of socialism, and we have hastened to peg out our claims without troubling to wash our hands and change our clothes. Two notable vices have we retained. First this desire to save souls against their will, which makes our representatives in the House so ready to fall in with the heavy-handed compulsory benevolences of the Liberals, such as the Insurance Act or the Mentally Deficients Bill. And second comes in a lingering anti-feminism, banished from the brains of the movement, but occasionally visible when the ape-man in us stirs himself. A portent of the weakness and carelessness with which the Labour Party has subsequently treated the question of woman suffrage was the attitude of the Miners' Conference a year or two ago on the employment of pit-brow lasses. Argument to the effect that miners preferred to keep their wives and daughters sitting in a parlour eating bread and honey hardly rang true. More convincing was the candid admission that the lasses' jobs were wanted for old and infirm miners. That a conference of the most organised and advanced section of industrial workers should solemnly agree to insure themselves at the expense of a much poorer body of workers was significant. It showed that the feminist movement had to some extent had a more *succès d'estime*. The Labour movement had given a gala reception to the suffragettes on their frontage; but in the hinterland are dark masses of sex-antagonism. So socialists may vote quite fearlessly for the limited amendments.

It is possible that this sex-antagonism may even project into the frontage if the womanhood suffrage amendment to the Franchise Bill is rejected by the House of Commons, as seems very probable. Those who are pledged to democracy by reason of their connection with the socialist movement, but who have not received the inner light, will breathe a sigh of relief and turn to face the other amendments, most important of which is the Dickinson amendment to enfranchise all women over the age of twenty-five who are inhabitant occupiers or the wives of inhabitant occupiers. This the unsaved Labour member may be tempted to vote against because it is 'undemocratic'. But quite apart from the fact that it will enfranchise the wives of working men, it is his plain duty to vote for it.

Any measure – even the conciliation amendment, which will enfranchise hardly two million women to ten million men – that puts women among the electorate must be supported for two reasons. Firstly, because the consideration of women in the mass as potential voters, even if the number of actual voters be very small, amounts to an admission on the part of the British Constitution that women are not imbeciles. And secondly, because the majority of members of Parliament will (once the thing is done) dislike having to seek the suffrage of women electors, and will feel sourly towards all women. There will be a sudden decline in the wave of post-prandial maudlin kindliness towards women which has recently been the curse of the legislature and government departments. No longer will telephone-girls be warned against accepting pots of hydrangeas from plausible strangers in the tube. Legislation concerning women will be done directly at the stern behest of the women electors, and there will be no more voluptuous indulgences of the protective instinct.

It may be argued that such a restricted franchise would bar the way to womanhood suffrage. But this temporary check will be of short duration, and might be of positive value in stimulating working women to get their vote for themselves instead of merely abusing the WSPU for trying to get it in a middle-class way. The WSPU is an eminently abusable body. I think that it wasted a wonderful oppor-tunity when it encouraged its working-class members with a genius for revolt to leave their mills and go to south coast watering-places to convert retired Anglo-Indian colonels. If the mill-girls had stuck to their mills, the teachers to their schools, the shop-assistants to their shops, and had preached revolt in their own circle, England might have been covered by now by a network of disaffected industries, clamouring for political and economic emancipation. As it is England is merely starred with groups of sympathisers too heterogeneous for effective action and too largely composed of middle-class women to organise industrial revolt. Not that the middle-class movement is to be despised: this impulse of its women towards political service of the State may prove the redemption of the materialistic section of society. But the fact remains that the working woman has not been organised into a feminist army. But whose fault is that?

Were the Pankhursts and the Kenneys the only able women in Lancashire that when they went to London the movement had to follow them? It is a mystery why the Lancashire women, impressed as they undoubtedly were by those first acts of militancy, did not start a movement of their own in accordance with their democratic ideals. That they had the brains to do it we know from the history of the trade unions. That they had the courage we know from those working women who, as members of the WSPU suffered imprisonment and hunger-strike. Only the will was lacking. But it is there. Since the mere campaign of the middle-class woman has aroused such protests, it is safe to foresee that their enfranchisement would stimulate the working woman to action. There need be no fear that they would permit a limited franchise, with its implied insult to the working classes, to remain for long on the statute book. Indeed, they must if they would dissociate themselves from the ugly campaign of anti-suffragism. A typical example of anti-suffragist tactics was observable in Mr Garvin's proceedings at the beginning of the week. In the *Observer* he had a leader arguing that since women do not risk their lives for the State they do not deserve votes. It is obviously a more necessary and dangerous business to write an article on the Balkans (signed at both ends) than to have a child. Apparently he himself came to the conclusion that this argument seemed a little thin, so he made up for it by an article in Monday's *Pall Mall Gazette* which was headed, 'Lives of Ministers Threatened: New Menace of the Suffragettes.' In reality, one gathered from the article that a reporter had gone down and chatted to the policeman in charge of the umbrellas at Scotland Yard, who had remarked that these 'ere Suffragettes were a 'isterical lot, and there warn't no knowin' what they'd do next. There was also some gossip about Mr Birrell being seen home by two policemen. This may be true (perhaps a precaution against the White Slave Traffic). But in sober truth there was not a shadow of evidence for the monstrous charge of murder so lightly made.

The Clarion, 24 January 1913

Quiet Women of the Country
The Impartial Speaker

The scuffling of lawyers with precedents and the cowardly submission of the average man when hit over the head by a legal technicality makes Parliament contemptible. There has been no more exasperating demonstration of the villainous tendencies of the political machine than the Speaker's malicious perversion of Parliamentary procedure which killed the Franchise Bill. It is laid down by Erskine May that if irrelevant amendments are interpolated in a Bill it must be withdrawn and reframed. This is a very necessary protection against the snap-division and such party manoeuvres. By no effort of the imagination could it have been meant to apply to such a unique situation as that created by the Franchise Bill. The existence of the suffrage amendments had been published and discussed for months; their effect was obvious. The Cabinet, candidly advertising its intention of shirking its responsibilities, was inadvertently giving the House an opportunity to really make the laws, as our misguided ancestors believed that Members of Parliament would. It was not an attempt at fraud, but an attempt at democracy, and it was as preposterous to defeat it by this well-meant ruling of Sir Erskine May as if two policemen were to arrest each other for loitering.

It is a matter of malice. *The Times* suggested this misuse of a precedent nearly a year ago, but suddenly became silent on the subject. It was a line of attack that required secrecy for success. Apparently the question was learned by that well-known anti-suffragist, Sir Frederick Banbury, who afterwards suggested the point to Mr Bonar Law; and the required answer was learned by the Speaker, also a well-known anti-suffragist. In all probability it was a plan approved by Unionist anti-suffragists alone, for Liberals – with the exception of Mr Harcourt and Mr Churchill, whose party loyalty is at a low ebb – would hardly desire to put their party in such a position. Thus, so far as the malice of the ruling class is concerned, only a small and inconsiderable group are concerned. But insulting to the whole of Parliament is the way in which the Speaker has sat quietly with this ruling in his mind while the House discussed the fate of the suffrage amendments again and again. This artificial business of government cannot be done with dignity. I can imagine, in a more passionate world, the Speaker as a controlling monitor of an eager assembly of enthusiastic legislators, helping them to attack wisely the mountain of work before them. I can imagine him in the kind of conference of businessmen which we have the right to expect today, as an intelligent officer. I dislike to think of him as a parrot pretending to doze on his perch, with his feathers ruffled round him and his eyes veiled with a film, who suddenly starts up and dislocates the conversation by a seaman's oath.

But the mischief is done. It is not even resented. The Government has breathed a sigh of relief, and has informed an indifferent House of Commons that they will give facilities to the Conciliation Bill next session. They found the experiment of giving facilities to the Conciliation Bill enjoyable and easy. That hefty Machiavelli, Mr Asquith, talked seriously to Mr Redmond about the embarrassment of the Government, so that the Irish members flocked like sheep into the lobby against the women. And subtler Mr Lloyd George used this Franchise Bill, whose corpse now lies at the feet of Sir Frederick Banbury, to induce the weaker Liberal suffragist members to vote down the limited franchise. We have had enough of that sort of facilities. We would almost go to prison to avoid them. So long as Cabinet Ministers are knaves and private members fools, a private Bill is doomed. If the Liberals are in power, we have Mr Asquith, Mr Harcourt and Mr Churchill to take the ambitious private member on to a high mountain and tempt him with the kingdoms of the earth.

And when the Tories are in power we will have Mr Smith and Mr Chamberlain offering friendship and preferment on the same terms. That this is so speaks of the corruption of the Cabinet system, but the Cabinet system is with us and we must use it. When we go into shops we are sometimes served by people who ought never to have been born. But we do not drastically remedy this error. We buy what we want and go away. And similarly, though we may hope to abolish the party system after we have got the vote, we have to get the vote with its help.

The suffragettes are asking Mr Lloyd George and Sir Edward Grey to subordinate all other considerations to woman suffrage, and to resign from the Cabinet if a government measure is not forthcoming. That they will not do. These are not the days of miracles. We are beaten beyond all hope.

It is strange that we should be beaten by such poor stuff. Mr Arnold Ward's mother and Mr McCallum Scott's mind – nimble as a pantechnicon – are strange things to subdue a Parliament. And Mr Harcourt advertised the perfectly beastly nature of anti-suffragism in his speech in the abortive debate on the Grey amendment. It was a little less objectionable than his remarks to the deputation at Rawtenstall when, with an unpleasant moist little smile, he alluded to the 'physiological disabilities' of women which forbid their enfranchisement. To sanctify his remarks he produced a quotation from Herbert Spencer – who was ever undone by his love of classification – to the effect that all women are morally and intellectually deficient. In case Herbert Spencer·would not convince the honourable members that they had one and all been born of the feeble-minded, Sir Edward Clarke, that well-known authority on morals and the intellect, kindly lent his name to a statement which suggested that his choice of friends must have been singularly unfortunate. To give the last touch of distastefulness to this exhibition, there was an attempt at 'quiet dignity' in an allusion to 'the attempt to burn my home – or rather the children's wing'. Long may the little Harcourts remain unburned; but there is really no more reason that they should not be burned to death than that Cecilia Haig and Mary Clarke should have been kicked to death outside St Stephen's three years ago. The Government chose its own weapons of murder and sudden death and it is too late to whine. For theirs is the bloodier sword. There was danger as well as folly in this speech which, in its 'manliness', might have been made by a tipsy squire of the eighteenth century at a hunt supper. No better and fuller exposition of his cause could have been made even by Mr Churchill, that pathetic figure whose lack of political success is an eternal warning to opportunists that there are some souls for which the devil does not care to pay a price.

This ragged army, which marches from victory to victory over us, has no support among the brains of the land. They rely, as they tell you in a peculiarly irritating phrase, on 'the quiet women of the country'. By this they do not mean the kind of quiet women who went with Mrs Drummond to see Mr Lloyd George and Sir Edward Grey to explain how, as tailoresses and nurses and laundresses, they enjoyed belonging to a privileged sex. I grasped what they meant three years ago, when I stood outside Palace Yard and saw the police assaulting a woman who would not give them a tricolour flag she was holding. They bent her backwards and shook her by the shoulders, sawing away with their nails at her hands so that she might drop the flagstaff. On each side of me stood a group of women applauding this demonstration of the chivalry of man and the weakness of women. Inside Palace Yard stood a knot of the womenfolk of the members; their smooth faces bore the expression of those who knew themselves capable of everything and thought nothing worth the doing except the adornment of their own supremely valuable type. Round this insolent conviction had grown a certain vileness, as appeared in their delighted contemplation of the assault. Decidedly they were hurtful parasites. And to my left stood three Jewish prostitutes, their languid and depraved faces shining, leprous with pearl powder, in the shadow of their rabbitskin hats. Decidedly they, too, were hurtful parasites. They laughed a little more honestly than the women inside the railings, but at the same things. All of them liked watching the brutal virile movements of the great policemen, and they abhorred the woman's lack of submission and loved to see her beaten down.

These are the quiet women of the country. Quiet they can be, for their duty lies plain before them and they are not averse to it. And certainly they have made the country what it is.

Not surprisingly, the victory of the quiet women of the country has been celebrated by the crash of breaking glass. Always the victories of this kind of woman have cost the country dear. We must see that the right people pay the price. Not the suffragettes, to whatever violence they may have been tempted by this insult to every divine thing that moves women to energy, but the Government who have insulted Florence Nightingale for the sake of Nell Gwynne.

The Clarion, 31 January 1913

A Training in Truculence

The Working Women's College

It is a very serious thing that working women do not take a more active part in Labour and trade-unionist organisations. In trades confined to women one understands that the workers have the militancy sweated out of them by evil conditions, but even in the prosperous mixed unions women appear to feel that so long as they support them by funds and obedience they may leave the government of the unions to men. But men should never govern women, for it makes the men purr with self-admiration and the women whine with self-contempt. One would not wish women to become the kind of bureaucrats that the men's unions have in certain cases brought upon themselves, for it is one of the chief dangers to feminism that women may learn to play the fool as successfully as men. But one would wish them to lead by the ardour of their propaganda and the pride of their policy. One would wish them to form the most aggressive quarter of the Trade Union Congress, instead of merely the distinguished handful that now represent their sex.

I saw in my own education some of the things which eat the power out of women. My fellow-pupils and I were not deterred from preparing to earn our livings, because it was evident that for the most part our parents would refuse to support us in idleness; but it was tactfully suggested to us that, rather than attempt to storm the world by genius and personality, we had better court it by conformity to convention and 'lady-likeness'. It was as though one should train an odalisque as a typist, but instruct her to keep her yashmak on in the city just in case a post should fall vacant in some harem. 'To take a strong line on anything' was to be regarded as carrying dynamite in one's head to the public danger. As a child of fourteen I was nagged and worried for wearing a Votes-for-Women badge; and then attention was distracted from me by a luckless little girl who had been converted at an evangelical meeting and whose salvation was considered in the worst possible taste. Moral passions were discouraged, and there was engendered in the girls a habit of compromise and avoiding decisions. Power does not lie that way.

Moreover, on every essential point where lying was possible, my teachers lied to me. On the subject of history their mendacity reached its height, and they preached pessimism with a very strange vigour. I cannot conceive of any honest adult looking on England today without feeling the same horror and indignation that would possess the spectator who saw two railway trains crash into one another because a too economical board of directors had removed a signal-box. But England black with industrialism, foul with poverty, irridescent with the scum of luxury, was held up to my infant eyes as the noblest work of God and the aristocracy. I was exhorted to glory in industrialism and pity such savage parts as Ceylon and Burma, where you may travel for years and never come on anything like Wigan and Burnley. A stainless history of England was produced by the process of elimination. I was never taught that in the fifteenth century there was a green and happy England in which the common labouring man was neither starved nor landless. I was never taught how this class was betrayed into poverty: how, after the quick decline caused by the royal debasement of the currency, the landlord and the farmer slowly bled the labouring classes till they fell weakly into the hands of the capitalists at the beginning of the nineteenth century. As do all the young and helpless, I fell a victim to the passion felt by so many unenterprising persons of quiet life, such as are often found in the teaching profession, for anecdotes concerning Napoleon. Yet I was never taught that England conquered the Corsican by the power of her purse, which was swollen by profits squeezed out of the tortured labour of slave women and children. I was never taught that England had been governed for centuries by cheats and bullies who impoverished the country man by land-grabbing and deported all the fine blood that dared to rebel, leaving our England to be peopled by the slavish and dull-witted. Now, knowing these things, I am a patriot. I see England as a fair maiden who has been delivered over to the dragons and mauled and maimed, but yet has so strong a spirit that she is immortal and to be rescued whenever we have the courage. But then I saw her as Jane Cakebread among the nations, born a sinner and not to be reclaimed even by the inspired ministrations of Mr Joseph Chamberlain.

I escaped from this pessimistic conception through a lucky chance that snatched the blessings of education from me at the age of fifteen, and an aversion to honest work. These left me free to study life from the angle of the suffrage movement, which removed any inclination I might have had towards meekness and unqualified admiration of the Government. But had I been a little less fortunate I might have been intellectually seduced into being a lady-like pessimist. A girl who goes to an elementary school is taught the same lies that I was in the same atmosphere of sex-subordination. And she has no leisure in which to stretch herself and find out what she really is. Not for her are the outdoor exercise and the long walks that give one fearlessness. Not for her is the unchecked desultory reading which is the proper food for every hungry mind. Even if she does not belong to the class where even the babies have to earn their keep and does not spend her evenings sewing hooks and eyes on cards, she will be busied by housework. If she belongs to that rapacious organism which preys upon itself, the large family, her chances of developing are small. Mr John Burns has patted the large family on the ground that he himself was the glorious culmination of a family of eighteen; but school doctors know that large families are commonly inadequately fed and clothed and receive only the slightest attention from their mother – a person whose feelings Mr John Burns left out of account. So the elder girls have the cares of the family on their little shoulders and come to nothing except tired nursemaids. And this is wrong, for youth must be selfish so that in maturity it shall have more to give away.

This appropriation of the girl's leisure leads to a superstition that she needs no joy. When parents have the opportunity of sending away one of their children on a holiday-fund excursion, they always send a boy, for a daughter is more useful at home. Parsons and such persons of authority are always ready to organise games and interesting classes for boys and men; women, they feel, should be busy elsewhere; or they stretch a point and permit a thrilling lecture on mothercraft – possibly a discourse with lantern slides on the more hygienic kinds of feeding-bottle. I have no doubt that the fall in the birth-rate is partly due to the unbridled way in which parents and the educational authorities thrust babies on the little girl.

When the girl comes to wage-earning adolescence she may either pass into the extraordinary isolation of domestic service and have very little chance of playing any part in organisation, or she may go into a factory. The opportunity for revolt is there, but one cannot blame her if she does not take it. She is usually paid poor wages and lives more thinly than a man, and the imprisonment of her youth has kept her from sport and discussion and all profitable idleness where men cultivate the insubordination and aggressiveness that save their souls. Public opinion frowns on her if she thinks that debate on the conditions under which she works is more important than darning her stockings. So, like all people who do not think, she cannot fight. Thus she corrupts the labour world by practising the milder Christian virtues.

But the women workers can now turn to Mrs Bridges Adams and say, 'Come down and redeem us from virtue.' For after a year's eager organising she has formed a Working Women's Movement that, to quote from her leaflet, means 'to meet by means of well-equipped colleges controlled by working-class organisations, the growing demand of working women for the education necessary to fit them to take their place beside their men comrades in the industrial, political and educational work of the Labour movement'. Already Mrs Bridges Adams is installed as Resident Principal of the first of these colleges, which she has christened Bebel House. This is no attempt to provide an academic education. It is a technical school under the control of the trade unions and socialist organisations for the training of 'an organised body of disciplined, militant working women, combining confidence in themselves with an intelligent knowledge of their position as workers, who will, by constructive educational work, increase working-class discontent and help to organise that discontent under the banner of organised labour'. These 'un-sexed viragoes', as *The Times* will ultimately call them, are to study economics and industrial history, logic, rhetoric and the theory of evolution.

'It would be foolish to pretend that such a fragmentary and partisan course is our ideal.' But we are living in a transitory time and fight behind barricades. There is not only the need for knowledge that will enable propagandists to explain that socialism is not a bomb thrown at the natural institution of society, but a well-considered medicine for a diseased community. And our leaders must be armed against the improper uses to which the poor put their education. A working girl who stands up against her master suffers not only the initial disadvantages of youth, poverty and liability to dismissal, but also his caddish misuse of his knowledge. He can stun her with his vocabulary alone. With a shower of addled economic terms flying about her ears she retreats to her comrades, almost persuaded that the shareholders, though they must have their twenty per cent, will not be in the least perturbed if the factories are shut down for good in consequence of the girl's strange demand for fifteen shillings a week. She knows that it must be a lie; but it is demoralising and saps the courage to be defeated in argument. And still more knowledge is needed by those who argue with the nimble Conciliation Board. It is needed even by the trade unionists who have victory in their hands, lest they become selfish class-individualists and forget that their industry stands or falls with the other industries, not only of this country but of the whole world. The workers trained at Bebel House will always remember not only social democracy, but also the International.

The Clarion, 14 February 1913

The Mildness of Militancy

A Storm in a Tea-House

When the Speaker gave his malicious ruling on the Franchise Bill and the corrupt House of Commons accepted it, it was plain that whatever Mrs Pankhurst desired in the way of vengeance would come to pass. Woman suffrage had been strangled by the fat hands of fools and knaves, and it is not the temper of Mrs Pankhurst or her followers to be gentle with fools and knaves. If it had been her will that Mr Asquith should ascend to Heaven by the aid of dynamite, many women would have been delighted to arrange the dynamite. I should have been very sorry if they had done so. I dislike the duty imposed on me by the suffrage movement of constantly writing about this least remarkable Yorkshireman who ever lived. But I should dislike still more writing about his corpse. For then I should have to show a decent respect to the dead.

But just as there is no limit to Mrs Pankhurst's power to command violence, so there is no limit to her clemency. We ought to be grateful to the WSPU for setting an example of good temper and forbearance at a difficult time. It speaks worlds for the benevolence and sanity of the suffrage movement that, stung as it is by treachery, it should punish the country for its disgraceful toleration of Parliament's villainy by such mild disciplinary measures as have been used during the past week. Some of them were of debatable wisdom, it is true. One wonders why active young women should destroy beautiful flowers when the Albert Memorial still stands in Kensington Gardens and there is gunpowder in the land. And the cutting of telegraph wires gives an opportunity for the nepotism characteristic of the Government. Very probably we shall find on the opening of Parliament that all the unemployed members of the Samuels' and Isaacs' families (to say nothing of Mr Lloyd George's private secretaries) have been appointed at salaries of from £800 to £2,000 a year to sit beside telegraph poles, and see that nothing happens. But the other forms of militancy could excite no sane person's serious disapproval. Certainly the destruction of golf greens seems an inadequate revenge on the sluggish nation, but it is one way of approaching people who have entrenched themselves behind petty preoccupations. I love going to music-halls; but if the angels of God coming down to put the hosts of Belial to the sword should by accident knock out the skylight of the Palace, I should not lose my temper. I should feel grateful to them for drawing my attention to the event (particularly if it was a really good fight). And similarly the destruction of golf greens is a crude way of calling golfers to higher things.

It is true that the women have burned a tea-house in Kew Gardens, but it was only a little one. And I can understand why they attacked this place of innocuous pleasure, for I spent a little time of sleepy pleasure there one sunny day last summer. At the next table sat a dear old parson with silver hair and gold-rimmed spectacles, and a pale young curate. During the three-quarters of an hour I was there they talked with a delicate gravity and an air of profound culture about a correspondence in the *Spectator* about the decay of the subjunctive mood in modern English. The burning of the tea-house was an honest attempt to overcome the difficulty felt by all reformers of getting in touch with people who are snowed under by decaying subjunctives. No doubt the parson and the curate are now, in some refined Anglican manner, busy wishing the suffragettes at the devil. But when women have been insulted and exasperated as the suffragettes have been, they are glad to have enemies they can strike on the mouth rather than passive spectators who lift no hand to help.

I have no idea why the public should suddenly show a maudlin affection, such as they usually reserve for the royal family, for the late tea-house, but I can quite understand why all those who love the good, the true and the beautiful must unite in deploring the bomb outrage upon the house at Walton Heath that Sir George Riddell was about to hand over to Mr Lloyd George. So beautiful a friendship as links Mr Lloyd George to Mr Riddell (as he was until two or three years ago) ought not to be shadowed with violence. Mr Riddell owns a newspaper called the *News of the World*: a journalistic 'fertiliser' (that is how the politer gardening papers put it) that nourishes the imaginations of a million and a quarter Englishmen every Sunday morning. It is some years since he made the acquaintance of Mr Lloyd George. Subsequently it was noticeable that the *News of the World* dropped its gospel of romping imperialism and supported the People's Budget. This act of friendship did not go unrewarded. The Birthday Honours List declared that England delights to honour the man who gives his grateful country the *News of the World*. It is unfortunate that this act of violence should have unveiled the tender relationship between these soldiers who have fought shoulder to shoulder for the purification of England. Liberals must understand the situation and realise that, invaluable as is the moral support of the *Daily News*, His Majesty's Government must also be buttressed up by the *News of the World*.

How deeply the Lloyd George family has taken this affair to heart may be judged by the fact that as yet no photograph has been issued showing Miss Megan Lloyd George wheeling her go-cart round the ruins.

Now, that is all the militancy that has been used up till now. Personally, I think it is a pity that it has been used. It is great fun to send the respectable into hysterics, but it distresses me to think of young women tramping round the suburbs firing pillar-boxes after a hard day's work, or missing their night's sleep and catching cold running about golf links in this dreadful weather. And I really do regret those orchids. Moreover, I doubt whether the public can in the long run be terrorised, being three parts brute and unlikely to flinch at sending out Maxim guns against the women. But I defy any unbiased person to reflect on this history of the past few weeks – on Mr Asquith's obstinacy, Mr Harcourt's and Mr Churchill's squalid dishonesty, Mr Lloyd George's half-sincere, hysterical duplicity and the Speaker's deep malice – and not regard these outbursts as legitimate tantrums.

If Mrs Pankhurst and the WSPU had had the mildness of the dove and the wisdom of the serpent, this militancy would certainly not have happened. But as they are fallible flesh and blood, something was bound to happen. And it says much for their self-control that there has been nothing worse than these quite discreet and controlled attacks on unimportant property.

Yet there is death in the air. As I write there comes the news that one of the women who burned the tea-house will probably pay for her offence with her life. She has been forcibly fed, and the food has been poured into her lungs, and this has caused septic pneumonia. It may be that before these lines are printed Mr McKenna will have tasted first blood.

Perhaps I overrated the importance of those orchids. Perhaps, so long as the country tolerates a state of things which drives women of fire and honour to seek such torturing ways of death, it is right to destroy all the lies of beauty that pretend that the world is a fine and lovely place. Perhaps it is right to punish the gross for their destruction of the spiritual beauty of revolt by destroying the tangible beauty which is all they can understand. But I think that if this girl dies and if they kill Mrs Pankhurst, the retribution will not stop at the destruction of orchids. For it is a very clear case of murder. A report signed by Sir Victor Horsley and Dr Agnes Saville, published in the *British Medical Journal* and widely circulated, pointed out the extreme danger of this injury to the lungs following on forcible feeding. So when

Mr McKenna ordered the prison doctor to inflict forcible feeding on the girl he knew what he was doing. And the prison doctor who was criminal enough to obey knew what he was doing. And when the law countenances murder and sudden death, the people will take murder and sudden death as the law of their lives. Those of us who know the spirit of the militant movement from within know that if Mr McKenna takes to murder, his victims will very quickly and very efficiently be avenged. And it is hard for the most moderate of us to say why they should not. The country will be plunged into a time of sudden assaults and terrible martyrdoms. And the issue will be quite clear, even for the most law-abiding of us. For on the one side there is the guilt of a few score damaged golf greens and a burnt tea-house; and on the other is the guilt of murder. The choice between law and justice is an easy one for courageous minds.

The situation promises tragedy in the near future, not only for the women, but for the whole country. We are paying the price for our toleration of a Government that upholds the cause of anti-suffragists and the will of the parasite women.

> The harlot's cry from street to street
> Shall weave old England's winding sheet.

Better is the silence of the broken suffragette in the prison cell.
The Clarion, 28 February 1913

The Nature of Woman

Every Home a Little Earlswood

The Nature of Woman by Dr Lionel Tayler

I love the intellectual modesty of the Fabian. Dr Lionel Tayler demonstrates it beautifully by his first attempt at literature, *The Nature of Woman*. He announces on the fly-leaf that he is going to do it again in the 'Type Problem Series': *Woman – Her Life and Development* (in one volume). Having thus settled you and me and the Virgin Mary, he is going to tell the whole truth about *The Science of Life* (in separate parts). When bound, this latter work will certainly be the book sealed with seven seals which is mentioned in the Revelation of St John. 'And no man in heaven nor in earth, neither under the earth, was able to open the book, neither to look thereon.' For his literary manner is terrible. He tells us that he is a biologist (though the

biological section of *The Nature of Woman* contains nothing that
was not known to all those of us who went to school after the passing
of Mr Forster's Education Act of 1870), but that is no excuse for his
style. He begins a sentence with a panegyric of conjugal love, and
after twenty-four panting lines is in at the death with a discussion of
classical education. He does not so much split his infinitives as
disembowel them. He encourages a most devastating eruption of
footnotes, side-headings and appendices. And there is a roguish
charm about his comments. There is no other writer in the world
who would quote the assertion that 'male and female He created
them', and add, quite without irony, 'But will England accept it? I ask
myself this question, but I cannot say.'

But Dr Tayler's thoughts are very white and pure, recalling in their
disorder a draper's shop on the last day of a great white sale. He has a
mission. Woman has gone wrong. Dr Tayler will save her. He admon-
ishes her with the same inspired suggestiveness with which
Macmahon encouraged the Negro trooper who had suffered endless
insults and mockery from his white comrades rather than not fight
for France: '*C'est vous qui êtes le nègre, n'est ce pas? Eh bien . . .
continuez de l'être, continuez de l'être.*' He merely cries through two
hundred pages, 'Be womanly! Be womanly!'

For a certain reason I heard the word 'womanly' with alarm. It
recalls a painful incident that occurred to my sister and me some
years ago in a public park at Harrogate. We were selling *Votes for
Women*, and we offered one to a dear old lady in rustling black silk
and widow's bonnet. With superb vigour she raised her umbrella and
brought it down on my sister's head, remarking: 'Thank God I am a
womanly woman!' And since then I have noticed that womanliness
is a virtue claimed only with aggressive intent. When women want to
suggest that providence has been unkind to other women, even to the
matter of their sex, they point to their own womanliness. But used
otherwise than spitefully, the word merely means a capacity to deal
effectively with the events that come a woman's way, just as manliness is a capacity to deal effectively with the events that come a
man's way. There is no evidence for the assumption that womanliness is a psychological condition antipathetic to manliness. From the
biological researches of the Mendelians we know that woman is half
formed of maleness. For the cell is formed by the union of the sperm
and the ovum, and while the ovum may be male or female the sperm
is invariably male. Therefore while a man consists of maleness plus
maleness, a woman consists of maleness plus femaleness. And there
is no femaleness that has any effect upon the organism beyond

deciding the disposition of the reproductive tissue and the resulting modification of physical structure. There seems no difference of mentality. There is no study mastered by men that women cannot master, and no virtue honourable to men that dishonours women. Some claim that things disgraceful to men, as cowardice and quiescence, are permitted to women; but these are prostitutes. Women only differ from men in that they have not been geniuses; but that is because they have lived virtuous and normal lives. And genius is the abnormal justifying itself. Men who are conscious of deep imperfections, of madness and sinfulness and spiritual failure, know that they are condemned by the laws of life, and to escape that condemnation they make themselves one with life by some magnificent act of creation. Women have had no such heavy debts to pay, for the domestic life admits only lesser sins, and they could put themselves right with life by childbearing. They have not proved themselves incapable of genius, but they have been excused it.

But Dr Tayler considers womanliness to be a state of holy and sickly imbecility. Woman is sacred only if she fulfils two conditions. She must be physically so feeble that she cannot play games or take any exercise, and creep along from petty sickness to petty sickness to the malady of motherhood, over the painfulness of which he gloats sentimentally. She must also have lost her reason. He insists on the moral necessity of her imbecility because he declares that if she uses her reason she will quarrel with her husband. And anyway: 'Woman is a bad reasoner at best, but she is a good intuitionist if her powers of mind are given free and healthful scope.' This meaningless chatter about intuition is due to the duplicity of women. When one tells a fool something and the fool wants to know how one knows it, and one cannot be bothered explaining one's mental processes, one alludes mysteriously to 'feminine intuition'. It is a social ruse, like telling the parlourmaid to say 'not at home'. Most of us believe in intuition, 'instinct that has become disinterested, self-conscious, capable of reflecting upon its object and of enlarging it indefinitely'. But even Bergson admits that the truths discovered by intuition must be apprehended by the intellect. And so a woman without an intellect would be no more in touch with intuition than one of the lions in Trafalgar Square.

But Dr Tayler is determined to have his woman imbecile. Rather than she should read even *The Science of Life* (in separate parts) he wants her to look like Raphael's Madonna. (Raphael, by the way, painted his Madonnas from unmarried ladies; but it is true that the phrase by which Dr Tayler describes the unmarried lady of today, 'the unchosen of her type and kind', hardly applies to them. It is no good talking scandal about Queen Elizabeth, but they really were not quite nice.) And he lays down a scheme of national education which is to provide England with a harvest of prolific female imbecility.

Latin, Greek, German and mathematics are not to be taught; only domestic economy and the three Rs. From nine to seventeen girls are to be 'under the control of woman teachers specially trained to sympathise with and draw out in healthy directions womanly ideals, and themselves of some feminine charm and insight'. The strongest woman may blench at the thought of her daughters being given over for eight years to the care of self-consciously charming young women (certified as such by an enthusiastic sub-committee of voluntary workers on the LCC) with nothing more to do than dangle visionary babies before them and discourage their intellects. From seventeen to twenty-two the now adolescent imbeciles are to study

the many-sided demands and wonders of home life; child psychology; human physiology; dietetics and cooking; hygiene and housekeeping; choosing a house; the ordering of a home; how a library may be acquired; pictures and their value; wallpapers, furniture, windows, and how these may be hygieni- cally and aesthetically treated; the stages of life; nursing and management of disease.

To these may be added the making of toffee; an acquaintance with God; choosing a toothbrush; and the comprehension of the Absolute. Only by such painstaking researches can we furnish girls with the proper equipment of a wife and a mother; which any sane woman knows consists half of knowledge that any quick-witted girl can pick up in six months, and half of qualities that spring from a fine and exuberant character. And if we claim to be able to educate these others into existence we will end by having classes for affection and honesty in our elementary schools.

Now, at first sight this seems merely comic quackery. But it really is rather disgusting. Dr Tayler's scheme – and it is blood-brother to a number of such experiments incubated by eugenicists such as Dr Saleeby – is simply an attempt to stimulate the sexual and maternal instinct in children. It is a crime against the clean sexlessness of childhood. Little girls have no maternal instinct. They like playing with dolls, for it is a handy way of gratifying the dramatic instinct, though toy soldiers have a stronger appeal to all children but those too dull for the effort of organisation. And they like to play with babies now and again, just as they like playing with puppies and kittens because the vitality of young things is very pleasant. But the maternal instinct is latent till maturity, as all strong passions must be. One wonders at the clayish emotional substance of people who imagine that the desire for children is an appetite for nursemaiding that can be coaxed in children like an appetite for milk puddings. This attempt to produce precocity is, of course, quite against the interests of the race, for if all girls of sixteen wanted to have children they would, and the stock would degenerate. The immediate result would be a generation of the very nastiest and most self-conscious little girls the world has ever seen, such as are foreshadowed in a sentence of Dr Saleeby's description of a similar nightmare system of education. 'If only one girl who reads that lecture' – Ruskin's 'Queen's Gardens' – 'can be persuaded in the beautiful phrase to be found there that she was born to be love visible, how excellent is the work we shall have accomplished!' A bishop who did not love prohibition once declared for England free rather than England sober, and one wonders whether England sterile is not better than England simpering and priggish.

But when Dr Tayler has created this army of feeble-minded but determined mothers, he does not know what to do with them. He strongly disapproves of the State endowment of motherhood, being unable to believe that a woman would ever stay with her husband unless he had the power of the purse. His ideal is the 'complete economic dependence of the married woman on her husband, and of giving her full practical rights down to the extent of shutting up an idle husband in a labour colony and obtaining work for him under compulsion for her support'.

Dr Tayler may be the future parent of The Science of Life (in separate parts), but he has not reflected that it is unwise to make a child's nature depend on the variable economic position of its father. He has not reflected that a woman may sometimes need a child who is in no sense necessary to the man she selects as its father. He has not reflected that society does not gain at all if the research scholar, bound by genius to an unprofitable vocation, is driven into a labour colony by his resolutely philoprogenitive wife (already the mother of thirteen). He has not reflected on the obvious injustice of paying what he deliciously calls a 'marriageable living wage' to the father of seven, the father of one, the sterile husband and the bachelor; nor does he remember in advocating this inelastic wage that the strain of supporting a large family is variable, rising slowly and steadily to a climax and then diminishing. But Dr Tayler is a bad reasoner at best.

There are many other aspects of Dr Tayler's book with which I would like to deal; particularly the historical section, in which he has consulted his own intuition rather than any more serious authority. But this book is bad for me. My sex vanity awakes and roars triumphantly in its cage. As a self-denying ordinance, I suspend operations until the publication of the great work that really ought to succeed on its delicious title alone: *The Science of Life* (in separate parts).

The Clarion, 7 March 1913

The Isles of the Wicked

The Sin of Imprisonment

The suffragettes appear to have scored a complete victory. Nobody really wants to kill them except Sir Frederick Banbury; and somehow that does not matter. The general tendency of the House of Commons during the debate on forcible feeding was to snatch at any remedy that will keep the suffragettes alive. That good old man, Mr Joseph King, wants to rub the suffragettes with dugong oil. This extraordinary desire is probably due to the persuasive eloquence of some American commercial traveller who has renewed hope of thrusting dugong oil on to the English market, which has always rejected it hitherto. But at least that scheme has the virtue of being good for trade, which is more than can be said for Mr McKenna's cat-and-mouse system of licensing. This will work out so that a suffragette will be able to commit her horrid outrage, be sentenced to six months' imprisonment, and be released after five days' hunger-strike. She will then spend the next six weeks getting up her strength so that she can commit another outrage, be sentenced to six months' imprisonment in addition to the unexpired term. And again she will hunger-strike and be released. And so on until the English lady develops some camel-like adaptation of digestion to this rhythmic alteration of feeding and fasting. This scheme obviously leaves the position exactly where it was. But the nation will pretend to be impressed by the merest temporising, rather than murder the suffragettes. For letting the suffragettes die in the hunger-strike would be a very flagrant form of murder. The infliction of capital punishment has the superficial justification of 'an eye for an eye'; but there is no justification for dealing death as a penalty for window-smashing.

Now, it is worth while considering why a nation not prone to mercy should shrink from this crime. Both reason and instinct are for making murder a recognised resource of humanity. A walk down the Strand shows us that the phrase 'all human life is sacred' is about as significant as the statement that 'God is Love'. Poverty on the one hand and gross privilege on the other have made many believe that mistakes, perversions and sins can only be remedied by a nicely directed Maxim gun. And, as well as being useful, murder may be amusing. In the Renaissance, that holiday of crime, mercenary assassins took a real pride and pleasure in their profession, and there were many enthusiastic amateurs, such as Benvenuto Cellini, who never forgot to thank God when his knife slipped neatly into an enemy's back. There, indeed, lies the real reason why murder must not be popularised. It is an activity too natural to the human animal. I live in a garden suburb where the conviction of one's neighbours' sin is very strong and the hedges are very low. I can quite easily conceive that, given a lawless twist in the atmosphere, I should be unable to have tea in the garden with my family because the Buddhist on my right was peppering the Freethinker on my left with grape-shot. That would be inconvenient. Moreover, I am a tender-hearted person, and even when the battle was done and we had the garden to ourselves, the cries of the wounded and the wails of the repentant Buddhist would distract me from my tea. For a tormented creature binds all other creatures to it in its torment. Though we detach ourselves from our victims in the moment of our strongest hatred, we remorsefully identify ourselves with them in their agonies: and our sympathy for other people's victims is always unbounded.

Such are the disadvantages of murder under private enterprise. The disadvantages of murder under State control are quite as obvious. A murder trial can easily corrupt England. The Crippen trial, for instance, swept over the country like a pestilence. The lickerish air of expectancy with which it watched the miserable little man tracked down at sea by wireless telegraphy; the snuffling of the pariah dogs of the Yellow Press round the relationship between Crippen and Miss Le Neve; the hot breathing of the crowds round the slow, careful trial; and the bubbling of gross things in the mind that come from the contemplation of violent squalor, until the music-halls echoed with rollicking jests concerning the hangman's scaffold. These things are defilements of the fabric of our national life. Cruelty may cleanse the State of twisted lives; but it is like radium, a healer that eats away the hands of those who use it. And this condemns not only the murder of the suffragettes and the more formal execution of murderers, but also imprisonment.

'Imprisonment' is a mere euphemism. It is as much a lie as the expression 'rescue home' which commonly denotes a place where young girls are forcibly detained to do laundry for excessive hours and no pay. We recognise now from the sinister demonstration of the habitual criminal that imprisonment does not mean reformation, so we pretend that it means segregation. We want a zoo for wild humans; an airy place of clean cages with strong bars. Thither we could go on Bank Holidays and converse, in complete safety to our pocket-books, with such delectable rascals as Von Veltheim and D. S. Windle. But unfortunately this kind of comfortable segregation is impossible for human beings, for it costs too much.

So if Polly Flinders steals her mistress's silver spoons we sentence her not only to six months' imprisonment, but to lots of other things which are not on the statute book as legal forms of punishment. To begin with, we shut her up in the power of staff wardresses who, we know, from the fact that human clay is not fit to have unlimited power over helpless people, will probably ill-treat her. Today in the asylums no medical superintendent dare vouch for the safety of his patients when his back is turned, and they are left to the mercy of the attendants; and the temptation to cruelty is much greater when the victims are not only helpless but in disgrace. Having provided Polly with the perpetual excitement of an umpireless fight with dehumanised officials, we shut her up for twenty-two hours out of the twenty-four in a little stone cell without the means of keeping herself properly clean, in cold and heavy clothes adhering to the pattern introduced into our prisons in the reign of William and Mary. When her nerve gives way and she seeks relief in healthy insubordination, we put her in an underground punishment cell to be reformed by pitchy darkness, wet floors and foul air. And we inflict on her a method of life that brings on her – in nine cases out of ten – indigestion and insomnia. We turn her out at the end of her sentence broken as though we had had her on the rack.

And prison must always be a vile and beastly place. It is the last home of revenge: the last place where cruelty is legalised and encouraged to be efficient.

Yet it is absurd that crime, the instrument of imperfect minds, should compel us into the degrading commission of cruelty. From that the better economic conditions of a socialist State will partly relieve us by putting an end to the pitiful crimes of hunger and the irrational acts of those whose brains have been corroded by poverty. And the courageous wreckage of institutions would free us from crimes of fear. 'As for murder and such like offences,' says Mr E.S.P. Haynes in *The Great State*, they are nowadays far more often the results of the economic pressure under which we live than of any innate evil in men. It is merely silly to kill a wife or concubine when there are means to divorce the one or to make decent provision for the other. The want of these things manufactures fifty per cent of our murderers. It is equally absurd to kill an illegitimate child if its birth does not pillory the mother so that her earning power is reduced exactly in proportion to her necessity for more. There again is a class of offence for which the Great State will leave no inducement. . . In the end I conceive that the Great State will have little more to consider in the way of crime than those inevitable clashes of jealousy, the Crime of Passion. Sordid crime will disappear; only romantic crimes are peculiar to men or women of no wide intellectual interests or recreations who, by reason of their limitations, cannot shake off the obsession of a particular person or a fixed idea.

But for the irreducible residuum of naughtiness there is a remedy that was brought up – of course, in the wrong connection – by Lord Robert Cecil in the debate on forcible feeding, in which he intervened in that well-intentioned deafish manner with which his family always faces the rising tide of democracy. He suggested that the suffragettes should be deported. He has forgotten our last experiment in the deportation of rebels, when we transported to Australia the leaders of the Labourers' Revolt against rural conditions. They left the countryside to be peopled by the dull and the slavish, and in their disgrace founded a glorious colony. But deportation is the only way to prevent ourselves being provoked to cruelty by such mischievous gadflies of society as the incurable cheat, the procurer, the habitual drunkard. 'Perhaps islands will be chosen,' says Mr H. G. Wells in *The New Utopia*, in the chapter devoted to such a scheme,

islands lying apart from the highways of the sea, and to those the State will send its exiles, most of them thanking Heaven, no doubt, to be quit of a world of prigs. . . . About such islands patrol boats will go, there will be no freedom of boat-building, and it may be necessary to have armed guards at the creeks and quays. Beyond that the State will give these segregated failures just as full a liberty as they can have. If it interferes any further it will be simply to police the islands against the organisation of serious cruelty, to maintain the freedom of any of the detained who wish to transfer themselves to other islands, and so to keep a check on tyranny. The insane, of course, will demand care and control, but there is no reason why the islands of the hopeless drunkard, for example, should not each have a virtual autonomy, have at the most a resident and a guard. I believe that a community of drunkards might be capable of organising even its own bad habit to the pitch of tolerable existence. I do not see why such an island should not build an order for itself and manufacture and trade. 'Your ways are not our ways,' the World State will say; 'but here is freedom and a company of kindred souls. Elect your jolly rulers, brew if you will, and distil; here are vine cuttings and barley field; do as it pleases you to do. We will take care of the knives, but for the rest – deal yourselves with God!'

The Clarion, 28 March 1913

'Autumn'
The Fate of the Drudge

The majority of women one knows are struggling towards something outside the sphere of their immediate human relationships. Of the girls who were at school with me nearly all, married and single, have joined in that splendid – even when it is blind and incoherent and has its blood in its eyes – assault on the social system which calls itself the suffragist movement. Some have gone to the university to pursue wisdom for its own sake; others have studied medicine or have joined the glorious and sweated profession of nursing; and many have become teachers. But there is a minority which has had nothing to say to the world: that has relapsed into the isolated homes of their husbands or parents. Outside their most intimate relationships they have taken nothing from life and given it nothing. It is true that they were of old the dullest-witted pupils. Yet a very large anti-feminist section of modern opinion says that they were quite right; that it is necessary for women to hold themselves from life and lead purely animal lives.

Now, I should not mind being some sort of animal. I should love to be a cat, and lie in a basket by the fire all day and go out on the tiles all night. And the life of a tiger seems attractive; even in captivity. It must be great fun to escape from a menagerie and liven up a rural district. But the animal life that the Eugenics Society orders women to lead is not nearly so amusing as that. If a woman's husband is rich she must lead the cloying life of a prize pedigree pig. And if she is poor she must live the life of a pit pony in a district uninspected by the RSPCA. For she is to be debarred from all activity save the organisation of her home life. This means that if she has any money she will hire specialised workers to do her domestic work and be idle herself. And if she is poor she will live in a rabbit-hutch handsomely provided with an unworkable kitchen-range, for which she will not be able to buy enough fuel, and try to make her family happy and comfortable by adulterated food and shoddy clothing. To this existence, which is all that industrialism has left of the domestic life, anti-feminists desire to consecrate woman. She must not be educated lest she should learn that there is a world beyond four walls. She must be debarred from the labour market and treated with contempt if she remains unmarried. And once she is a wife and a mother she must lay her soul in the scullery. It sounds a little dull: and the growing revolt of women against marriage under such conditions shows that it is. Yet it may be that sometimes, distressed by the sight of the woman worker under capitalism – the laundress rotted by her poverty, the waitress with shadows under her eyes – we may think that the half-witted and prolific may after all be the most fortunate type of woman.

But she is not. That is proved very convincingly in 'Autumn', a short story that is contained in the collection called *Married*, by August Strindberg. Strindberg could not write. These stories are chiefly remarkable for a queer haste and ineffectiveness and insincerity, as though they were written on telegraph forms with the end of a burnt match by a lost soul. Their real interest lies in the fact that Strindberg was the greatest European anti-feminist of the century, and being (by a curious coincidence) certifiably insane he has expressed his gospel with a candour that makes the enemy blaspheme and the police intervene. He was a specialist in a kind of grey indecency that incites one to virtue. After his recital of his depressed adulteries (mostly entered upon in a vain attempt to show his wife that he really was a man) one's lawful husband becomes magnificent in his uniqueness. He makes one proud of being a woman. The only mortifying thing about his career is that he got three women to marry him, and not one of them had the wits to put him in a lunatic asylum.

He hated women. Yet he needed them, for he wanted to have children. He was very fond of children, and if he had been taken in time and taught not to use improper language he would have made an excellent nurse. His own virtues were those commonly considered feminine. He seems to have won his wives by being at times of crisis an efficient substitute for a general servant. 'I was your nurse then,' the oppressed husband cries to his wife in one of his plays, 'I saw that you brushed your hair, that your boots were mended; I took care that a dinner was being cooked in the kitchen.' He omits to state whether he cleaned her teeth, but he convinces you that if he was sober and an early riser he was well worth £20 a year and beer money. However, his wives, being ladies of forcible – and in one case evil – character, found themselves unable to respect him; and they henpecked him. Therefore all women of spirit were from Hell. And unmarried women are cursed in terms which I find it hard to explain, but which we can all enjoy: 'Old maids, rejected by men as no good. Why are so many women unmarried? They all boast of proposals and yet they pose as martyrs! Higher interests! Latin! To dress in low-neck dresses for charitable purposes and leave the children at home neglected!' This last sentence baffles me. Apparently the austere methods of the Charity Organisation Society are replaced by something more thrilling in Sweden; but the children are untraceable. Anyway, it is all very dreadful and the only kind of woman to be permitted is Lily, the wife of the secretary to the Board of Prisons.

Lily fell in love with an ordinary man of no special brains or character. She married him and was his loyal wife, and did all the work of his home. She bore him many children and reared them. While he went to his dronish office-work her tasks multiplied every year and the work became more ravenous of her time, her youth, her beauty and her health. 'Her shoulders were a little rounded; much bending over the cradle, ironing-board and kitchen range had robbed her back of straightness. Her plaits were thinner than they had ever been, and a faint suggestion of silver lay on her hair.' One does not doubt that a woman ought to bend over the cradle; she would insist on doing so under any social arrangements. But one wonders whether it is not blasphemous for a woman to lay her strength on the ironing-board and burn her brightness to ashes on the kitchen range. She might have cried, like the woman in 'Getting Married':

When you loved me I gave you the whole sun and stars to play with, I gave you eternity in a single moment, strength of the mountains in one clasp of your arms, and the volume of all the seas in one impulse of your soul. A moment only: but was it not enough? Were you not paid then for the rest of your struggle on earth? Must I mend your clothes and sweep your floors as well? Was it not enough?

But she would have met her match in Strindberg, whose prudent comments on marriage run:

She darned his socks without the slightest feeling of degradation and asked for no thanks. She never even considered him indebted to her for it, for did he not give her and the children new stockings whenever they wanted them and a good many other things into the bargain? But for him, she would have to go out and earn her own living, and the children would have to be left alone all day.

But for him there would be no children to leave alone, but for her he would have to pay someone to look after the children. One almost wishes that neither of them had existed at all, so depressing is the thought of a lady who is so moved to gratitude at the thought of receiving new stockings from her lawful husband.

But it might be that as Lily had allowed herself to be absorbed into her husband's personality her husband would love her as himself. But she had become to him something like the nursery wallpaper. 'He had neglected her during the last twelve months – not so much from indifference as from respect – he always saw in her the mother of his children.' But when he went away on a tour of the provincial prisons he could forget domesticity, which 'lay behind him like a stuffy bedroom', and think of the wife he had once loved:

In the evening solitude, emptiness, coldness. He felt a pressing need to talk to her. He fetched some notepaper and sat down to write. But at the very outset he was confronted by a difficulty. How was he to address her? Whenever he had sent her a few lines to say that he would not be home to dinner, he had always called her 'Dear Mother'. But now he was not going to write to the mother, but to his fiancée, to his beloved one. At last he made up his mind and commenced his letter with 'My Darling Lily', as he had done in the old days. At first he wrote slowly and with difficulty, for so many beautiful words and phrases seemed to have disappeared from the clumsy, dry language of everyday life; but as he warmed to his work, they awakened in his memory like forgotten melodies, valse tunes, fragments of poems, elder-blossoms and swallows, sunsets on a mirror-like sea. All his memories of the springtime of life came dancing along in clouds of gossamer and enveloped her. He drew a cross at the bottom of the page, as lovers do, and by the side of it he wrote the words: 'Kiss here' . . .

But somehow he felt that he had shown his naked soul to a stranger.

Now an exchange of love-letters began. So beautifully wrote the woman that was left in the drudge that he fell in love with her once more. And by the time he was able to return to his home he would not bear to face the thing that he had made:

He shrank at the thought of finding her with a kitchen towel in her hand, or the children clinging to her skirts . . . Should he ask her to join him at Waxholm, in the Stockholm Archipelago, at the hotel where they had spent so many happy hours during the period of their engagement? Splendid idea!

So they met on the happy island of their honeymoon. As soon as she arrived he noted sourly a great change: 'Ten years stretched between her and the picture of her which he had had in his mind.'

But they made the best of it by an uneasy sentimental journey to the house where their first child was born, and returned to a tête-à-tête dinner. He began magnificently. 'He took the bread-basket and offered her the bread. She smiled. It was a long time since he had been so attentive.' The quiet glow that suffused her heart on account of the stockings blazed into a flame over the bread-basket. And after dinner he asked her to sing to him. 'And alas! Her voice was thin and shrill and emotion made her sing out of tune. At times it sounded like a cry from the bottom of a soul which feels that noon is past and evening approaching.' The poor drudge was not yet forty. 'The fingers that had done hard work strayed on the wrong keys.' So he went to bed and left poor Lily to talk to the landlady of spring onions and woollen underwear.

After another day of bickerings and shamed silences they went home by the night-steamer, dropping into the even tenor of married life. 'They went downstairs into the saloon as soon as they got on board. For appearances sake, however, he asked whether she would like to watch the sunset; but she declined.' Apparently Strindberg could not conceive of a man and woman looking at sunset together unless they were the worse for passion. 'At supper he helped himself and she asked the waitress the price of black bread.'

So the too-devoted wife becomes a widow. The drudge has nothing more to give; and what she gave before was not of so precious a quality that it could change her husband from the mean clay he was and make him kind. She is as unlovely in her destitution as any old beggar sitting by the roadside. But Strindberg says that that is all right. It would be rough luck if we had but one life to live; but one lives 'twice if one has children, three times if one lives to see one's grandchildren'.

But the sin against the Holy Ghost, the honour of Sir Rufus Isaacs, the poverty of Mr Lloyd George and the abominable brats this unamiable pair would have brought into the world – these are things no man can think on and live.

The Clarion, 4 April 1913

The Sex War

Disjointed Thoughts on Men

We have asked men for votes, they have given us advice. At present they are also giving us abuse. I am tired of this running comment on the war-like conduct of my sex, delivered with such insolent assurance and such self-satisfaction. So I am going to do it too.

Men are poor stuff.

Messalina was no better than she ought to have been. Mrs Brownrigg flogged her 'prentices to death. Mrs Humphry Ward is a shocking bore, and Eve brought sin and death into the world. But my sex has produced nothing like Mr J. L. Garvin, the Editor of the *Pall Mall Gazette*. I want Mr Garvin to be disfranchised. I want him to be imprisoned for life. I want to get up monster petitions against him, hold protest meetings and pass strong resolutions with no dissentients. I want him to be deported to St Helena or marooned on a desert island in company with a hyena of good digestion. For I have just been reading his leaders in Monday's *Pall Mall*.

The first is entitled 'The Year of Mourning', and celebrates with solemn, ghoulish enjoyment the anniversary of the Titanic disaster. It is redolent of such simple piety as fills one when writing a letter describing one's Sunday evenings in London to a bachelor uncle who is a Plymouth Brother and has £10,000 in Consols. Its use of small capitals tugs at the heartstrings.

'A year ago,' says Mr Garvin, 'the mightiest construction in which man ever rode over the seas struck an iceberg, and in four short hours carried two-thirds of her human cargo into Eternity in the Titanic. The daring race of JAPHET challenged the gods. With face upturned to God, the voyagers in the Titanic went to their death.' Nothing is said about the proportion of the children of third-class passengers who were obliged to turn up their faces to God:

They died a death which has made them immortal in human story . . . What, then, is to be said? The lesson has been taken to heart by the shipping companies. . . But we look, and we trust we do not look in vain, for higher and deeper results. First we look to see the arrogant pride of man in the work of his own hands abated . . . The belief in the material is a very disquieting symptom of the day. It is one manifestation of the valour of ignorance. When one of the greatest triumphs of man's skill and ingenuity is suddenly and utterly overthrown, there is a lesson for him to learn which is patent to any who believe that the spiritual side of man's nature is meant to dominate the whole.

Mr Garvin does not point out the shocking manner in which the American millionaires who sent out the liner with neither seamen nor boats had overlaid their spiritual side. He passes on tactfully to the dead:

Amid all the signs of degeneracy [that is you, because you read *The Clarion*, and me because I write for it] the Anglo-Saxon race can rise to a height not inferior to its proudest traditions. All that has gone to make the blood great was displayed – fortitude, constancy, self-sacrifice, self-control. In their last agony they reached the height of the great ideal with which St Paul cherishes the doctrine of the Resurrection.

One can see Mr Garvin brooding over the soft, maudlin sentences and sucking their sentiment like toffee. 'Had I not heard the clarion-call of politics,' he must have murmured, 'what a mystic I might have been. A poet, perhaps; Francis Thompson at his best. Or a priest.' Then his face changed. He remembered that fate had called him to be the leader of the Tory Press and ever to attack women and the weak for his country's sake. 'Curse it, the world wants blood!' he cried, and started his second leader. The release of Mrs Pankhurst from Holloway Gaol after nine days' starvation inspired him:

If the police force of the country is not adequate to the safeguarding of property it might well be spared the duty of protecting the advocates of crime from the crowds which are justly incensed at their audacity. The attitude of those who attempt to prevent suffragette meetings under present conditions is thoroughly warranted, however distasteful may be its aspects of violence.

In other words, man may take an arrogant pride in the work of his hands if this includes a clod flung in the face of a suffragette in Hyde Park. 'The protection of the law is practically suspended, except for criminals. If that goes on much longer, the country will find its own weapons. They will not be dainty, but it will be impossible to censure them.' In fact Mr Garvin wants the public to lynch the women. He wants the spiritual side of man's nature to direct a hail of stones and refuse on the women in Hyde Park. He wants the suffragettes to be torn limb from limb in order that they may show fortitude, constancy, self-sacrifice, self-control. He wants them to suffer such injuries that they will be able to see for themselves if there is anything in what St Paul thought about Resurrection. And if there is any response to this wicked incitement it will not be Mr Garvin who will pay the price: it will be some wretched little Cockney office-boy, blinded with hysteria, whose poor blood fevers easily at such weak violence as this. As usual he will fight from the editor's chair. I give him one more chance and challenge him to go to the next Pavilion meeting and attempt to lynch Mrs Drummond. But I do not think he will rise to the occasion.

Men are very poor stuff.

The debate on the Cat-and-Mouse Bill made one stroke one's skirt with pride. In a House pledged to woman suffrage, eight members voted for Mr Keir Hardie's amendment, which called upon the House to decline to proceed with any coercive measure against suffragist prisoners until the Prime Minister redeemed his pledge to make the Government responsible for the further progress of a woman suffrage measure that had passed its second reading. Two were Tories and six were Labour members. In the debate the members peevishly rebuked the suffragettes as a seasick man might rebuke the Atlantic in a gale. That extraordinary person who ought to be secured for the nation and kept on view in the British Museum, Sir Arthur Markham, made a remark which sounds as if it had been taken from an eighteenth-century jest-book. 'If I had my way,' said he, 'I would hang anybody who was convicted of throwing a bomb or of being in possession of a bomb, whoever it was, whether their life was in danger or not.' Thus the folly of the Commons. There was also the crime. Sir J. D. Rees, who swoops down greedily on every evil piece of legislation as the vulture swoops down on the festering corpse, accused the Hume Williams' amendment of encouraging 'the Home Secretary to let loose every ordinary prisoner in gaol, for there are very few prisoners whose health is not seriously or permanently affected'. That is a more terrible indictment of our prison system than ever Charles Reade or Oscar Wilde could pen – the lips that said it were so unpassionate, so unrepentant.

Oh, men are very poor stuff indeed.

And I begin to doubt whether they are ever reasonably efficient in the sphere in which they have specialised. They do not claim to be good. Collectively they do not claim to be beautiful, though private enterprise in this direction is brisk. But they certainly claim to be clever. And looking round at that confusion of undertakings which we call the City one begins to doubt. One doubts it still more if one ponders on the law which men have had to themselves since the beginning.

The law is badly done. It is preposterously expensive. One may be sued for libel and find oneself, if the plaintiff happens to be penniless, bankrupt in order to pay the cost of one's defence. Divorce is a luxury. One could have four operations for appendicitis as cheaply as one can get rid of one cruel and adulterous husband. Yet one buys skill on the one hand and merely a hearing on the other. It is intolerably tedious. It may, as it did in a famous case of infanticide, keep a prisoner waiting for months between her arrest and her trial. It is brutally cruel, even for the untried. It secludes prisoners on remand, makes them do menial work and subjects them to an unnatural order of life, that in conjunction with the strain of awaiting trial, often unfits them to defend themselves.

And it is discourteous. The proceedings of the fine flower of the law, the Bench, make one wonder whether man is not the imagination of some immortal but aberrant mind. One must avoid the temptation to treat as typical the buffooneries of Mr Justice Darling, whose only successful joke was getting appointed to the Bench. It is only fair to say that the event was not wholly unconnected with his services to the Conservative government at a by-election, and was greeted by protests from the Bar of that day. But generally speaking the tone of the Bench is low. The Divorce Court is a terrible place where two bleeding people come to tell the story of how they got their wounds; and when they have told it, Sir Bargrave Deane asks them to repeat it much louder. Deafness is his attempt at judicial dignity. A commercial summons might seem an innocent thing; yet it rouses the worst passions of Mr Justice Scrutton. And Mr Justice Lush abandoned himself to tantrums at the trial of Mrs Pankhurst. When she desired to tell that tale most relevant to her defence that the law is so unsafe in the hands of men that no decent woman can submit to it, of how a certain judge of Assizes was found dead in a disorderly house, he flew into a temper and sentenced her to three years' penal servitude in the face of a strong recommendation to mercy.

Oh, men are miserably poor stuff!

The Clarion, 18 April 1913

The Life of Emily Davison

I never dreamed how terrible the life of Emily Davison must have been. Yet she was to me quite a familiar personality ever since I first met her just after her first imprisonment four years ago. She was a wonderful talker. Her talk was an expression of that generosity which was her master-passion, which she has followed till today she is beggared even of her body; it was as though, delighted by the world, which her fine wits and her moral passion had revealed to her, she could not rest till you had seen it too. So I knew her, though I never spoke to her again. I saw her once more; last summer I saw her standing in some London street collecting for the wives and children of the dockers, her cheerfulness and her pyrotechnic intelligence blazing the brighter through a body worn thin by pain and the exactions of good deeds.

But for her last triumph, when in one moment she, by leaving us, became the governor of our thoughts, she led a very ordinary life for a woman of her type and times. She was imprisoned eight times; she hunger-struck seven times; she was forcibly fed forty-nine times. That is the kind of life to which we dedicate our best and kindest and wittiest women; we take it for granted that they shall spend their kindness and their wits in ugly scuffles in dark cells. And now in the constant contemplation of their pain we have become insensible. When enlightened by her violent death, we try to reckon up the price that Emily Davison paid for wearing a fine character in a mean world, we realise that her whole life since she joined the Women's Social and Political Union in 1906 was a tragedy which we ought not to have permitted. For if, when we walked behind her bier on Saturday, we thought of ourselves as doing a dead comrade honour, we were wrong. We were making a march of penitence behind a victim we allowed the Government to do to death.

Emily Davison was a woman of learning: she had taken honours in both the English schools of Oxford and classics and mathematics in London University. When she became a militant suffragist she turned her back on opportunities of distinction as a journalist and teacher. More than that, she entered into a time of financial insecurity; no comfortable background offered her ease between her battles. And eight times she went to prison. So many women have been brave enough to pass through prison unconsumed that, doubting if our race could furnish so much courage at one time, we have come to wonder whether prison is such a place of horror after all. But it was a hell through which she passed eight times. Once, indeed, the law of the land pursued those who maltreated her in gaol. A more than common ruffianly gang of visiting magistrates, who turned a hose of icy water on to her as she barricaded herself in her cell against forcible feeding, had to answer for their offence in the law courts. But we have her own description of an ordeal when her tormentors kept well within the law:

On Wednesday 19 June, from 10 a.m. onwards, we were kept in solitary confinement.

On Saturday we decided that most of us would barricade our cells after they had been cleaned out. At ten o'clock on the Saturday a regular siege took place in Holloway. On all sides one heard crowbars, blocks and wedges being used; men battering on doors with all their might. The barricading was always followed by cries of the victims, groans and other horrible sounds. These sounds came nearer and nearer in my direction. My turn came. I fought like a demon at my door, which was forced open with crowbars till at last enough room was made for one of the besiegers to get in. He pulled open the door, and in came wardresses and a doctor. I protested loudly that I would not be fed by a junior doctor, and tried to dart out into the passage; then I was seized by about five wardresses, bound into the chair still protesting; and they accomplished their purpose. They threw me on my bed, and at once locked the door and went off to the next victim.

If we subjected the most infamous woman, expert in murder, to such mental and physical torture, we should make ourselves criminals. And this woman was guiltless of any crime. Such torture, so unprovoked, would have turned most of us to the devising of more bitter violence against the Government; but there was a generous twist even to her rebellion. She longed not for a satisfying revenge, but for the quickest end to the tormenting of her friends. And then it was she conceived the idea of the need for a human sacrifice to buy the salvation of women:

I lay like a log for some time. When I did recover a little, I got up and smashed out the remaining panes of my window, then lay down again until I was able to get out into the corridor. In my mind was the thought that some desperate protest must be made to put a stop to the hideous torture which was now being our lot. Therefore, as soon as I got out I climbed on to the railing, and threw myself out on to the wire-netting, a distance of between 20 and 30 feet. The idea in my mind was 'one big tragedy may save many others'; but the netting prevented any severe injury. The wardress in charge ran forward in horror. She tried to get me off the netting, and whistled for help. Three others came and tried their best to induce me to go into my cell. I refused.

After a time their suspicions were allayed, and the matron came through into the ward to visit some of the prisoners; while she was there the wardresses relaxed their watch, and I began to look again. I realised that my best means of carrying out my purpose was the iron staircase. When a good moment came, quite deliberately I walked upstairs and threw myself from the top, as I meant, on to the iron staircase. If I had been successful I should undoubtedly have been killed, as it was a clear drop of 30 to 40 feet. But I caught once more on the edge of the netting. A wardress ran to me, expostulating, and called on two of my comrades to try and stop me. As she spoke I realised that there was only one chance left, and that was to hurl myself with the greatest force I could summon from the netting on to the staircase, a drop of about ten feet. I heard someone saying 'No surrender!' and threw myself forward on my head with all my might. I knew nothing more except a fearful thud on my head. When I recovered consciousness, it was to a sense of acute agony. Voices were buzzing around me; in the distance someone said, 'Fetch the doctor.' Someone tried to move me, and I called out, 'Oh, don't!' Then the doctor came and asked for me to be moved to a cell close by. They lifted me as gently as possible. He asked me to go to hospital, but I begged him to leave me there – which he did. I also managed to say, 'For heaven's sake, don't feed me, because I shall fight.'

That was a year ago. For twelve months she was brooding over this plan to close a bloody war by giving her body to death. We belittle her if we think that her great decision can have made that decision to die an easy one; her last months before death must have been a time of great agony. To a woman of such quick senses life must have been very dear, and the abandonment of it a horror which we, who are still alive and mean to remain so, who have not even had the pluck to unseat the Government and shake it into sense, cannot conceive. And this decision was made by a soul harried by a body whose state was such as would have killed the courage in most of us. For the harsh treatment to which she subjected herself was nothing to the treatment she received from the prison officials, and between the two her body was shattered:

To my amazement the doctors came to forcibly feed me that afternoon. The operation, throughout which I struggled, caused me such agony that I begged the three comrades who were released that afternoon to let friends know outside what was being done.

From that time on they fed me twice a day, in spite of the torture it caused me, until Thursday when, to our intense relief, they fed me only once. We all said that any food that could have been poured into us in a second operation could not possibly have done us the good that the relief from a second torture did.

Meantime nothing was being done to make my condition better. My head was dressed on Sunday. Nothing further was done to it. By the examination I knew that besides the two injuries to my head the seventh cervical vertebra was injured, and another at the base of my spine. They seemed very much worried about my right shoulder-blade. The sacrum bone was also injured, not to mention the many bruises all over my arms and back. All the vertebrae at the back of the head are very painful, and it is torture to turn.

From these injuries she never quite recovered. Till the day she died her spine still hurt her. Twelve months of misery of body and soul we inflicted on her by tolerance of this vile Government.

Many of the women in that funeral march were weeping; the sight of the broad arrows on her purple pall kept me from tears. Surely it was the most merciful thing that ever befell Emily Davison that her death, unlike her life, was unshadowed by prison walls. To the end the sunlight was on her face. Mr McKenna had no part in her sickroom; he paid no delicate deathbed attentions with the stomach-pump and nostril-tube. I was glad that for her executioner she had an unmalicious brute. But except for these kind circumstances of her death it was all grief.

When I came out of the memorial service where, in our desire to testify that the way of high passion which she had trodden was the only way, we had said and sung rather inadequate things over her coffin, I heard that Mrs Pankhurst had been re-arrested. And for a moment I was choked with rage at the ill-manners of it. Imagine a government arresting an opponent simply and solely to prevent her doing honour to the body of another opponent! But then I realised what it meant. Mrs Pankhurst was very ill, so ill that her nurse had tried to dissuade her from rising for the funeral, lest she should die on the way. And now she was taken back to Holloway and the hunger-strike. I felt a feeling that is worse than grief. It was the feeling that one has when one is very ill and has not slept all night. There comes an hour in the early morning when one realises that one will not sleep again for a long, long time; perhaps never. So now it was not only that England had passed through a hot restless night of delirious deeds. But England has murdered sleep. Before us stretch the long, intolerable weeks during which they are going to murder Mrs Pankhurst. During that time we shall know no innocent rest, and surely some plague should fall upon us afterwards.

They have released her since. It must be for the last time. We dare not bear the double guilt of the death of Emily Davison and of Mrs Pankhurst. We must avoid it at the risk of turning the British Constitution upside down, at the risk of driving from the Cabinet 'the best-dressed man in Parliament', at the risk of breaking Mr Asquith's evil, obstinate heart. We must drop this masochist attitude of long-suffering, which is the mistake of the revolutionary movements, and show ourselves an angry England. We must have a demonstration in Trafalgar Square that will tell an astonished government that positively in the beginning of the twentieth century, in the centre of civilisation, after seven years of Liberal government, there are still people who object to the murder of women. And when the Government absurdly asks: 'But what are we to do?' we must tell them that we prefer law-breakers to be at liberty; that if the women must burn grandstands they must; but that at any cost these wonderful law-breakers must go free, for they are the stuff of which England is built. And if the Government dislikes the resulting state of chaos it can give Votes for Women.

What a foe we have to fight! Can we hand Mrs Pankhurst over to that foe? This mishandling of women has its roots in horror. Doctors know that there is an obscene kind of madness that makes men torture women. Twenty-five years ago London was sick with fear because one such maniac crept through the dark alleys of Whitechapel mutilating and murdering unfortunate women. In those days people cursed him. They tried to hunt him out of his black hiding-place and make him pay for his crime. But today Jack the Ripper works free-handed from the honourable places of government: he sits on the Front Bench at St Stephen's or in those vast public sepulchres of conscience in Whitehall, and works not in secret but through Home Office orders and scarlet-robed judges. Scotland Yard is at his service; the medical profession, up to the President of the Royal College of Surgeons, places its skill at his disposal, that his mutilations may be the more ingenious. And for his victims he no longer seeks the shameful women of mean streets. To him, before the dull eyes of the unprotesting world, fall the finest women of the land, the women of the most militant honour and the wisest courage. How times can change in a quarter of a century!

And the backing behind this Government! The *Manchester Guardian* whimpered evil of the dead last week; so party passion can turn fools to knaves. The unspeakable *Pall Mall Gazette*, whose pages in their technical excellence and spiritual nauseousness remind one of an efficiently managed sewage farm, had a vulgar leader with a comic title on the death of Emily Davison. The dreary mob of Pecksniffs and heavy-jowled stockbrokers that stand behind these papers! And poverty has made many allies for the perverted Government. Near King's Cross there was a horrible crowd that jeered at the hearse. Old men, that looked like wicked little boys, little boys that looked like wicked old men, lively young prostitutes with bare arms scrawled with tattooing, old women putrescent with sin. They cried out lovingly upon the name of one Jones, the King's jockey, for these were betting people. Again I was glad that Emily Davison was killed by a horse and not by the kind of person she was fighting with.

Now that she is laid to earth, will we break up the procession and melt into the wicked crowd? Or will we continue to follow in the hard path of tolerance and defence of a cause that is fighting under extraordinarily difficult and perplexing conditions, till her spirit, eased by our achievements, may rest in peace, all being won?

The Clarion, 20 June 1913

The Sheltered Sex

'Lotos-Eating' on Seven-and-Six a Week

'We know that we are the sheltered sex and lie enfolded by man's protection and respect; therefore the demand for the suffrage so rashly made by some of our sex is an impertinence and an ingratitude.'

At a recent conference on the National Insurance Act Mr Handel Booth M P and Mr Kingsley Wood of the L C C complained that God had forgotten us, for the actuarial calculations of the National Insurance Act had not been fulfilled. It appears that 'the claims of women for sickness benefit under the Act are of a most extraordinary character. In one society, in which there are men and women, there are two women to every man on the funds and the women remain on twice as long as the men.' So 'appalling' are these claims that some of the big approved societies are threatened with bankruptcy.

In parliamentary debates on woman suffrage the physical weakness of women is so vividly presented to us that for days one hardly dares to dine more heavily than on a split mangold-wurzel at Eustace Miles. But on this occasion it was assumed with a strange readiness that we failed not in the flesh but in the spirit. The official opinion was tartly put by Mrs Handel Booth: 'Of course, it is much more comfortable to have seven-and-sixpence at home than seven or eight shillings at work.' The question of comfort hardly arises when one is dealing with sums of seven or eight shillings, but the lady's meaning is plain. The woman workers of the country are dissimulating the glow of health which is the reward of honest toil and have taken to 'lotos-eating' on seven-and-sixpence a week. They are malingering.

They are doing it in hot-eyed battalions, in luxury-lusting armies. In one district where there are 17,000 women on the books of the National Federation of Women Workers 130, drunk with sloth, are living like the lilies of the field on sick-pay, which now amounts to 4d per head per week instead of the actuarial guess of 2½d.

The name of this Scarlet Babylon is Cradley Heath.

Only once have I seen a group of Cradley Heath chain-makers. The course of treatment that they suggested to me was six weeks in a nursing home, a long holiday on the Mediterranean and a large income for the rest of their lives. I do not say that this was what they wanted; for, poor dears, they had never heard of happiness, so could never articulately desire it. Nor was it exactly what they needed: for only some miracle from above could repair the injuries they had incurred in their slavery. It was merely the least that any person of common honesty could do to pay off the heavy debt that the world owes to those desecrated makers of its wealth. So if it were true that the women of Cradley Heath were malingering I should congratulate them on at last having got back a fraction of the arrears due to them. It is therefore with positive regret that I state that a special representative of the National Federation has been down to Cradley Heath and has found that, although under the beneficent reign of the present Government it is now possible for the women to earn fifteen shillings a week if they work ten and a half hours for seven days a week, they are still subject to weaknesses of the flesh. Even they become unfit to carry on the graceful feminine occupation of chain-making and are genuinely ill.

Cradley Heath is only one place where women are horribly and abnormally ill. For, of course, woman is not a natural invalid born to shed a sickly sweetness from a Bath-chair. Yet in Cradley Heath 8 per cent of the women are receiving sick pay; in Acton the laundresses are almost as expensively unhealthy; and among the weavers of Lancashire and Yorkshire there are 15 per cent of the women receiving sick pay as against 9 per cent of the men. In fact, wherever there are married women workers the proportion of sickness is terrifying.

Now it is the habit of men to say that the woman with the child in her arms is the ideal which they all serve and respect, but I have noticed that this respect for motherhood is usually produced as an offensive weapon against women who are not mothers when they demand the ordinary privileges of humanity. As an extreme instance of this, I remember that at Leith docks, on the one occasion when I so far broke a natural habit of silence as to address a public meeting, a gentleman at the back of the crowd repeatedly threw a herring at me for the reason, so he said, that I was not a mother. And if an unmarried lady wishes to be admitted to the Bar or to make a wage of more than two pounds a week she is always irrelevantly reminded of the beauty of motherhood. But beyond these assaults on spinsters there is little tangible honour paid to the mother. There is something careless and sinister about the human mind that makes war on its own kind. It did so without shame at the beginning of the nineteenth century when English manufacturers founded their wealth on the bloodstained labour of little children. It does so now in its industrial exploitation of the mothers of the race.

About three-fourths of the women in this country are married or widowed; so every girl ought to be treated as a potential mother. I do not mean by this that the happily sexless little children in our elementary schools should be bothered by attempts at the premature stimulation of their maternal instincts, either sentimentally or by lectures concerning the feeding of babies. If after these millions of years women will not love children unless they are caught in infancy and inoculated by celibate schoolmistresses and middle-aged doctors with magic lanterns, let the race die. But rather let us recognise that all good things spring from three square meals a day. Elizabethan England was a nest of singing birds because a not yet enslaved populace had beer and meat pasties for breakfast, and Beethoven transcribed the music of the spheres because he ordered dinner for six when he dined alone. If we want to make every woman a Madonna we must see that every woman has quite a lot to eat.

But the working woman never has even enough to eat. From a starved childhood she emerges to a starved adolescence. Taking an ascetic standard, I understand that if one is determined to keep alive one can do it on ten shillings a week: and if the effort is not to be unendurably uncomfortable one must have fifteen shillings a week. If I have ever to face the prospect of living on either of these sums I shall turn to whatever branch of crime lies nearest. But the majority of my sisters are my moral superiors. Of the little princesses of the textile trades, the girls in the cotton mill, 85 per cent make under fifteen shillings a week; and more than half of them do not make ten shillings a week. In the other textiles 98 per cent do not make fifteen shillings, and three-fourths of them do not make ten shillings. And in the clothing trades 97 per cent of the girls do not make fifteen shillings and 88 per cent do not make ten shillings. In laundries and dyeing- and cleaning-works 98.8 per cent of the girls do not earn fifteen shillings and 92 per cent do not make ten shillings a week. Therefore the mass of women of the working classes pass through adolescence that is on the whole uncomfortable and in the majority of cases a prolonged starvation. This means that at the critical years of her life when she ought to be storing up energy for herself and for her children she is spending it recklessly for the benefit of the capitalist. Not only the joy of her youth goes to the making of shoddy and elastic web (think of it! such silly little accidents of civilisation) but the health and future of her children. And she is beggared in other ways than this. It is notorious in a certain town built of biscuits that love comes to the factory-girls there by ugly ways, with mean happenings; it is not that the heart of man is really wicked, but that on the given data the men cannot respect the girls. The capitalists can buy their whole time for seven shillings a week, they are sluttish with poverty and dazed with overwork and underfeeding: quite obviously an inferior species.

The capitalist pretence that the average working girl works merely for pocket-money and is supported by her father is a subtle joke. Where in our England are the prosperous fathers who can support their daughters in whole or part till the age of eighteen?

So, diverted from normal development at the very beginning, the woman enters as an adult a labour market where comfort is still not bestowed for the asking. It appears that more than half of the women employed in factories and workshops are under the comfort line and one-fifth of them under the starvation line. A fourth of the cotton workers and three-fourths of all other textile workers do not make fifteen shillings a week. And 60 per cent of the women in the clothing trades and 71 per cent of the women in laundries and dyeing- and cleaning-works do not make fifteen shillings a week. It is evident that the majority of working women are unable to make a wage sufficient for their own support. This is bad enough if we take them to be an army of spinsters. But we know for certain that more than one-fifth of the total number of women employed in factories and workshops are married women and widows, and there are probably many more women who are not so described only because rumours have reached them of legislation affecting the employment of wives. We have no means of knowing how many of these support dependants, but having regard to the strong social tradition in England during the last century which discourages married women from working except under the stress of necessity, we may assume that the majority are supporting others besides themselves.

The smallest sum on which a family of average size can subsist is one pound a week. In the cotton trades only 40 per cent, in the other textile trades only 5 per cent are making a pound a week. Lumping the figures together it appears that only three-twentieths of these workers are making what one-fifth of them must make or starve.

The fractions don't fit. I am inclined to think that it is the missing twentieth that is malingering.

The margin of starvation is really greater than these figures suggest, for the selected trades are comparatively favourable as regards wages. And the employer usually takes advantage of the strategically weak position of the mother who will take any work rather than see her children suffer; so it is probable that it is the unmarried woman, who being without ties can bargain fearlessly, who gets the bigger wages and not the married woman worker. We must add to the poverty of the married woman worker the fact that she is tormented by society through her motherhood. It is bad enough that her children should grow up in poverty, for she suffers not by her own hunger alone but by theirs also; but it is worse that they should do it remote from her eye and from her care as she works all day in the factory for a pittance that does not allow her to delegate them to the skilled charge of other women. When she comes back tired in the evening to her double task of housework the bond between her and her children may be snipped by the sharp scissors of irritability. For no civilisation has ever so burdened woman so heavily before as the capitalist does today by making her a factory-hand by day, domestic drudge by night. The human frame is not built for such a strain.

Such are our lotos-eaters. But, now that Mr Handel Booth (who is Mr Handel Booth?) has publicly denounced them they shall not have many more of those seven-and-sixpenny debauches. For though his origin is wrapped in obscurity there is one thing certain about him: he is a bottle-washer to the present Government and a blood-brother of Mr Lloyd George. And when he complained that the women's claims were 'appalling' and that 'something would have to be done' he was breaking the news that a revision of the Insurance Act is contemplated by which the women's sick benefits shall be reduced or their contributions raised. 'We women know that we are the sheltered sex and lie enfolded by man's protection and respect: therefore the demand for suffrage so rashly made by some of our sex is an impertinence and an ingratitude.'

The Clarion, 4 July 1913

The Sterner Sex

Whitehall and Pimlico

The other day a cousin of mine was married. Though what God or myself had to do with it I do not know, but I was obliged to go to church. I object to going to church except to hear the Athanasian Creed, which stretches the power of belief and leaves one with the same pleasant, warm, tired feeling as an attack of yawning. All the same, I found myself one day last week in the porch of a sombre building adorned with stained-glass windows which proved that the Apostles liked aniline dyes and everything handsome about them: I faced an usher whose eyes dropped doubtfully on the books I held in my arms. I had caught them up carelessly as I left home to read in the train, and it was an unfortunate coincidence that they happened to be the latest batch of literature issued by the Divorce Law Reform Union. With an air of resource he conducted me to a pew in the transept where any disturbance I might make would be quite ineffective ... The organ began to play a Nocturne that Chopin wrote for George Sand when he loved her; their shades were drawn down by the music from the skies and looked in at the church windows. 'I wish they wouldn't bring us to such ugly places!' they grumbled. Perhaps, forgetting their last discords, they looked at each other and smiled a little. 'Things were prettier with us in Venice, weren't they?'

That horrid interior, distempered a deep drab picked out with a lemon-coloured dado, turned the sweetness of the music sour; and I opened 'Marriage and Divorce', a pamphlet compiled by the secretary of the Divorce Law Reform Union, which is largely concerned with the findings of the Royal Commission on Matrimonial Causes. That is the body which sat for three years and issued a Majority Report containing recommendations of the utmost importance to the working classes. Because it deals with sex and shocks the Archbishop of Canterbury neither the Liberals nor the Conservatives will ever have the pluck to carry it into law. Thus do men perform the task of government. My eye fell on an extraordinary conversation between Lady Frances Balfour and the Bishop of Birmingham:

'We have had evidence put before us,' said Lady Frances, 'that there are men who live on the prostitution of their wives. Is such a wife, being a Christian, to stick to her husband and to do as he commands her?'

'Yes,' replied the Bishop, probably plucking at the edge of his apron, 'I am afraid so.'

I felt sorry that I had come to church. It was true that Norwood is not in the diocese of Birmingham, but I did not wish to encourage the Church of England at all after this. The lack of pity for hurt flesh, the tolerance of squalid sin!

But a shadow fell across my book and I looked up into the candid gaze of two blue eyes. The bridegroom stood beside me, extending a slender hand and smiling shyly and frankly, but quite without coquetry. The sun lay on his fair head like a benediction, and no fretful or angry passion had ever lined that boyish brow: only the gentlest words had shaped that mouth. Personal grace of a high order was accentuated by dainty dressing; his frock-coat fitted him like the pelt of a young antelope, and his trousers had a silvery gleam like willows seen at twilight. He was like a pure white rose.

How can I tell you how this flower-like radiance of untainted youth

affected me, who had just come from Fleet Street? Suffice it to say
that hastily I closed my book and put it from me, lest his eyes should
fall on the – to his young mind – strange and disturbing title. I had an
impulse to raise his gloved hands to my lips: only by some such
old-fashioned courtesy could I express the million mingled feelings of
love and pity, foreboding and strong hope, that rose in my heart as I
saw this young creature, so grave, yet so unsuspecting of life's darker
side, standing on the threshold of his new life. I did not do it. People in
Norwood are so ununderstanding. He murmured a few graceful
words, his delicate skin suffused with a flush, and flitted on.

An hour or so afterwards I threaded my way to my aunt through a
number of people who were eating oyster patties and meringues for
the same excellent reason that they had previously gone to church:
because my cousin was being married. My aunt shook my hand
warmly, looked out of the window into the garden, and said with deep
feeling: 'I shall never see geraniums and calceolarias again without
remembering how I lost my little Rachel.' Our conversation was at
first disconnected, for it seemed that I had been dropping pamphlets
on cheap divorce all round the wedding breakfast, and people were
constantly retrieving them and bringing them to me. Then, casting a
glance to where a trembling but composed figure stood beside my
cousin's athletic form, I asked:

'What does this young man that Rachel's married do?'
'Nothing. He's in the War Office,' replied my aunt, and her attention
wandered again. 'I always think there's something depressing about a
bridesmaid if she's over twenty. Poor things, they can't help feeling it . . . Yes,
Cyril is in the War Office. Your uncle is very pleased about that. He said to me
last night, quite impressively, that a government worker is in as secure a
position as any member of the royal family.'

I was glad that my cousin had chosen her husband from that
sheltered parterre, the Civil Service. When I go down Whitehall and
meet all the cool and uncreased young men emerging from the cloister of their offices, I feel as one does when visiting an Irish convent
boarding-school where girls of good family learn to paint on satin and
play the harp; one feels one's voice a little loud, one's boots a little
large. There is something appealing about the turning of the middle-class man to the refuge of unresponsible administrative work: the
working man knows peril in his various occupations, and all women
may die through motherhood; but he alone walks always in the
sunlight, almost as happy as the capitalist. And so England would
have her manhood. Do not the Insurance Commissioners congratu-

late themselves on the fact that they are spending thousands not on sick or maternity benefits, but on the employment of unskilled clerk labour? I see a day when the manhood of England will spring like a lily from an office-stool. All the same, I felt that there was a certain exuberance about the statement that a government worker is in as secure a position as any member of the royal family.

For Whitehall leads to Pimlico. And in Pimlico there are a number of government workers who seem in an extraordinarily insecure position. It is true that they are not decorative persons like Cyril, whose personal appearance is, as I have explained, such that no one could raise a hand against him save in the way of kindness: still, their humanity entitles them to a certain measure of justice. On 1 July a notice was put up in the yard which announced that the rate of pay for making soldiers' drab jackets was altered from 2s 11½d to 2s 6d: which meant a reduction of from 1s 6d to 2s on weekly earnings which now average 17s 4d. It was a reduction that one cannot ascribe either to the law of supply or demand or too much gold. It was simply an air of pure devilish thrift on the part of the War Office: the Army Clothing Employees' Union has just forced them to raise the rate of pay for making scarlet uniforms by 3½d, and it is now trying to make the other workers pay for this generous rise. So six hundred women marched up Whitehall to the War Office. Cyril, I believe, watched them from behind a blind. Cyril's superiors received them with politeness and promised that, pending the arrangement for a round-table conference, the reductions should not be carried into effect. Meantime, the authorities are hunting for some justification of the prejudice that equates in the official mind like a blind-eyed toad: that some women of exceptional skill make 25s a week at this work, and it is not the will of God that a woman should earn more than a pound a week. And the need for keeping down expenses is so great . . .

Good God enlighten us! Which of these two belongs to the sterner sex – the man who sits in Whitehall all his life on a comfortable salary, or the woman who has to keep her teeth bared lest she has her meatless bone of 17s 4d a week snatched away from her and who has to produce the next generation on her off-days? I remembered a member of the Army Clothing Employees' Union that I met a week or two ago: her brown hands were strong, every sentence she spoke bit into the truth, she had the faculty of deep and rowdy laughter. I looked at Cyril. He had sat down now and, with a solemnity that lay prettily on his Dresden-like charm, was toying with a vanilla ice. I had a vision of the world fifty years hence, when we have simply had to take over the dangerous adventures of the earth. I saw some bronzed and travel-scarred pioneer returning from the Wild West with hard-earned treasure, buying a fresh and unspoiled bridegroom who had hardly ever stirred from the office of, let us say, the Director of Public Prosecutions. I saw a world of women struggling as the American capitalist men of today struggle, to maintain a parasitic sex that is at once its tyrant and its delight . . . We must keep men up to the mark.

The Clarion, 18 July 1913

Dog-Wagging

The Revival of the Constituent

I found six Scottish bailies in my front garden this afternoon. It was, I regret to say, a mistake: they had come to see not me but the notorious evil-doer to plate-glass windows who lives next door. All the same I grasped them warmly by the hand and shamelessly kept them as long as possible. For these were members of the deputation of forty Scottish bailies and councillors who had come to see Mr Asquith and tell him that the Government's attitude to woman suffrage is not only an insult to God, but may cost them a Liberal seat or two at the next election, and as I was bred in Scotland I felt very proud of them, and the spirit which had made them take the extreme step of coming to England. Scotland has come out of the militant suffrage agitation very well indeed. There is something magnificently dramatic about the way the Scottish woman, dressing in darker colours and giving up more of her youth to study, has quietly gone about her warfare. All through my childhood two silver-haired sisters flitted daintily through the grey squares of the new town of Edinburgh, contriving tea-parties and other forms of good works for the insatiable poor of St Giles's Cathedral. A month or two ago they were sentenced to stiff forms of imprisonment for the raffish-sounding crime of setting fire to a racecourse grandstand. And now they have flitted just as daintily away from the new town to – the police would like to know where, for they were released only under the Cat-and-Mouse Act. And the Scottish public has not been so brutally insensitive to events as the English. I don't know whether you English realise that never yet have the Scottish prison authorities resorted to forcible feeding. The common people who weave the fabric of life on which art and learning are mere embroideries are determined to weave it more delicately. That

is why they have sent their representatives to protest against its
defilement by blood.

But the bailies had a political significance that was almost as
important as their moral aspect; for they came to remind Mr Asquith
that the dog must wag the tail and not the tail the dog; that if the tail
insists on movement unsanctioned by the dog, it is a case of St Vitus's
Dance. That has always been Scotland's point of view. To such nice
recognitions of cause and effect she owes her pre-eminence in science
and the law. But England has never been quite clear on the point; her
strength has always been emotional rather than intellectual. What is
her great and perilous game of imperialism but becoming the administrative tail of some such treasure-land as India or Africa, and then
proceeding to wag the dog? In this matter her belief has at least
apparently served her well, .but, indeed, it has not in the manner of
her own government. Freed by the male franchise from the unchecked domination of the land-owning class, we have allowed the
administrative class, the mere tail we invented to flick the flies of
disorder from the common hide, to become the governing class.
There can be no more damning indictment of the nation than the fact
that it allows Mr Asquith to decide the question of woman suffrage. Is
not the idea of letting Mr Asquith decide anything on earth not
enough to blot out the sun in heaven? He would make an excellent
butler. I can imagine that owlish solemnity quite good and happy
polishing the plate or settling a question of etiquette in the servants'
hall. Such flunkey minds, afflicted at birth with an irremedial lack of
dignity, must inevitably be attracted by the elaborate insincere ceremony of party politics. It is wrong of the true masters of the State to
leave their house unsupervised for so long, for these flunkeys burn in
an attic oil that was meant to light a hundred rooms and waste on one
banquet food that should have fed a village. And there is no bravery in
their debaucheries, no purpose in their violation of precious things.
Mr Asquith, undistinguished even in his crimes, expedites by his
clumsy thwackings at women from behind the bars of authority no
such clever plans, often for the common good, as did the Borgias by
their poisonings.

To this, the chief of all flunkeys, the Scottish bailies appeared
suddenly, even horribly; for they recalled the existence of the rightful
master of Parliament – the constituent. He was as startled as a curate
would be if he met the Holy Ghost in Hyde Park. He never doubted
his existence and, of course, it's all very well in its way, but hang it
all! there are decencies to be observed! It used to be the pleasant habit
of constituents to be shadows that rose from the registry on polling

day, and were reabsorbed therein after they recorded their votes. Occasionally a constituent might, if he attained to a more tangible substance by the possession of money and helpful motor-cars come to town and be introduced to the Strangers' Gallery, and to that one good thing connected with the Liberal Party, strawberries and cream on the terrace of the National Liberal Club. But always he knew his place. And he was not concerned with any such immediate question as the Cat-and-Mouse Act; it was one of the good points that he was never interested in what was happening today next door, but always in what happened round the corner three weeks ago. I live in Middlesex; my neighbours are never tired of spending the evening in elementary schools protesting against the Welsh Disestablishment Bill. In Wales, I believe, the live question is Home Rule, in spite of the fact that Ireland, far the most practical of nations, has forgotten about Home Rule, and is much more interested in the syndicalist development of agriculture. If the constituent has a tender heart and civilised instinct, he should read the articles on Bulgarian atrocities in the *Daily Telegraph* and fix his attention on some peasant crucified on some far-off hillside. He must spend his tears on him; he must not let his eyes wander to the nearer torture of Mrs Pankhurst, whom Mr McKenna means to starve to touching distance of death in Holloway, and then to dismiss, so that she may die at home and not in prison. So he may enjoy guilt and escape blame. The constituent must not object to things like this. That is not playing the game. It is making politics personal.

So the flunkeys of the Government turn frightened faces towards this new kind of constituent. They do well to be alarmed, for the man who escapes the extraordinary human belief that because a thing is done in the next street by people we know it must be quite a normal thing, and not a hellish rite performed by the Devil, is the man who makes effective resolutions. 'What shall we do? He's going to make trouble . . . Hadn't we, this once, better give in?' 'No! Think, if he finds out that the legislative machine really moves he'll want it to go on moving. He'll want it to do things.' So, with sullen faces, they cluster round the mysterious machine, which is so well oiled when the rich touch it and so rusty when the poor tear at it, and will not do the constituents' bidding.

That would have been the danger. The Scottish bailies might have become foolish with victory, and might have cried out to the people when they got back to Scotland:

See! We have stopped the torture of women. Let us now stop the torture of men. The Leith dockers are born into a cat-and-mouse life. For two days their employers let them work and earn pence, but on the third day they must gnaw the crusts of the bread of yesterday and slip back into the prison of hunger and weakness. They, too, must be saved – the Government must release them!

And from the heights of Edinburgh they would look down in amazement on the harbour of Leith. There, lying like black lizards on the Firth of Forth, are many warships full of guns and men to hold the dockers in check; the very strangest cure for hunger. If Mr Asquith had received them with decency and been convinced, they might have hoped that the Government might intervene here in kindness and tried to conciliate the dockers. But as it is, the way that suffragette prisoners are treated is a guide to all other fighters. It teaches us that the Government is not ashamed to rob and assault the poor and unprotected; that the land is given over to a pirate class, and that we must, for the love of our country, pray for labour unrest as the parsons pray for peace.

The Clarion, 25 July 1913

A Quiet Day with the Constitutionals

Last Thursday I went to a conference organised by a committee, including Miss Margaret MacMillan, Sir Edward Busk and Mrs Cavendish Bentinck, to consider the Cat-and-Mouse-Act, and the quickest way towards its repeal. I expected to be bored, as I would be at a conference convened to discuss the undesirability of typhoid fever and the quickest way towards its abolition: the vileness of the germ is not more inarguable, and the sewer is not more hospitable to such loathsomeness than is the Home Office. But I was not bored. Indeed the nearest thing to the proceedings of the day that I can think of was the bull-fight I saw in Seville two months ago.

When I went into the Conference three very noble people were discussing the medical aspect of the Cat-and-Mouse Act. There was Sir Victor Horsley, who spoke with an air of delicate disgust, and Professor Waller, tolerant of the Home Secretary as he would be to a feeble-minded thief. And there was Dr Alice Corthorn, an Empire-builder more pleasing in the eyes of any merciful God than Cecil Rhodes; for it was she who worked so magnificently among the plague-stricken natives of India. They told us that starvation was not, as Mr McKenna imagines, merely the extremity of hunger, to be comfortably cured by a square meal. It is a deadly assault on the body. From laboratory experiments it is known that from the very first day it does more than drain away the nourishment stored up by the tissues of the body: it deteriorates the very structure of the tissues and gives the living body over to rapid degeneration. But Mr McKenna does not know that. With the contempt for expert knowledge which might be excused in a grocer newly elected to an education committee, he consulted no doctors when he drafted the Act. No doctor has anything to do with its administration; he leaves detectives, the kind of man one calls about a lost dog, to decide when the prisoners are sufficiently recovered to be dragged back to prison and starvation. All this the scientists said very solemnly, with the reverence for the human body that one finds in great doctors, and wistfully: they felt that the little people who sit in offices were condemning themselves to unutterable shame and guilt by their refusal to listen to wisdom.

Then we turned to a discussion of what we were to do to rouse the country to demand the repeal of the Act. But first Alderman Sanders stood up in the hall and drew the chairman's attention to the fact that a police spy was sitting among the delegates and taking notes. He spoke with a personal note of indignation which we could understand: for recently, without one shred of legal justification, the police took into custody his wife, Mrs Beatrice Sanders, and induced that malevolent judge, Mr Justice Phillimore, to inflict on her a sentence of fifteen months' imprisonment. The only offence alleged against her was that she kept the accounts of a society not declared illegal; and the person now performing the identical duty still goes free. Things like this are terrifying. In such days we dislike any police-spy, and this one was recognised as the reporter whose perversions of Mrs Pankhurst's speeches were partly responsible for the sentence of three years which was her death-warrant. To breathe the same air as one of these ferrets was a new experience to me and I rose from the Press table to see him better. He was a sleek-haired young man, almost grossly respectable in appearance; yet he was a very sinister figure. I remember once seeing a gang of convicts waiting in the rain on the platform at Clapham Junction. Their poor stupid faces were evil with passion and in their ridiculous dress their stunted bodies showed contorted with passion; they were disgraced by their chains. But this man was disgraced by his liberty. He was so sure of protection by the law that he sat at ease with his notebook open on his lap, smiling insolently up at the men and women who crowded round him, infuriated by the system of malicious espionage he represented. He had the right to swear us into gaol, he had the right to come among us and lie us into crime; the law loved his ill-doings. But the meeting was quicker to attack than the law to protect; a woman moved that he should be carried out, and the delegates surged towards him. With the air of being a perfect gentleman even though we forgot ourselves the police-spy vanished through the swing doors.

But think of my feelings. For I found myself half up the gangway with murder in my heart. Now, what sort of a condition of things has the Government brought about when a person like myself, too lazy to be fond of fighting and possessed by a passion for the peace and order in which alone wisdom and art can be made, feels moved to assault a perfect stranger simply because he is the accredited representative of law and order?

Then the Conference settled down to deliberate what they could do to suspend the operation of this Act and ultimately repeal it. 'We will hold conferences in all the big towns,' said many of the delegates, 'the men voters will fight the Bill when they understand.' Men voters fight any Act!

Can you conceive of any enormity that the Pecksniffs who read the *Daily News* would not pray God to bless and which the Kipps who read the *Daily Mail* would not stomach after a week? There is a blight fallen upon England. So it is easily understood that the Conference, though not with any militant intention, decided to send a deputation then and there to discuss with Mr McKenna this matter of life and death; for so it was at the moment, Mrs Pankhurst having been in Holloway for four days.

I did not want to follow that deputation. I was extremely hungry and I wanted to write a short story. The satisfaction of those needs lay on the Northern Heights, but as a conscientious journalist I went to St Stephen's and waited on the pavement outside the Strangers' Gallery, thinking of tea and my heroine with melancholy intensity.

But suddenly I saw a sight which gave me quite a new emotion. I do not know whether you have ever seen an elderly and heavily built lady thrown down a flight of stairs by half-a-dozen policemen. It gives one a peculiar buzzing sensation in the head. And when you look again and see that two more elderly ladies behind her are being thrown from side to side as dockers pass sacks of grain into a hold, the sensation increases. It may be that then it should happen to you as it happened to me, that a policeman in a state of hysteria with quivering eyelids and twitching Adam's apple should strike you in the throat. But that is not essential to the thrill. Sufficient is the climax, which is reached when the first elderly lady is pitched forward on to the dusty pavement and is seen to be Miss Margaret MacMillan.

Miss MacMillan is one of the few constructive statesmen of this country. She organised the idea of the school clinic. I need not tell you who read *The Clarion* of the work she did in Bradford and the work she is doing in Deptford. Thanks to her there is now no child of school age in Deptford who needs any medical attention and does not get it: even the child, rejected of the hospitals, who is 'just ailing' and has no organic disease, gets his chance in the open-air school. The working men and women of the neighbourhood mention her with the deepest gratitude: many of them owe the life of their children to her. Can you say as much of any man in the House of Commons? You know you could not. There they serve neither the eternal nor the temporal ends of their country. Her influence on legislation affecting school-children is too great to be estimated. Without her we would not have had the medical inspection or the feeding of schoolchildren. If she had walked into the House of Commons and said, 'Gentlemen, I need this as a playground for the children of Westminster,' they should have listened to her with perfect courtesy. But she made no such interruption of proceedings. She simply went into the lobby and waited to see what would happen to the deputation of her friends. The police, who are reduced to nervous wrecks by the constant nagging of the Cabinet Ministers and their underlings, lost their heads at the sight of Mrs Pethick Lawrence, and decided to clear the lobby. They did it as I have told. That it was not more good-tempered jostling is proved by the fact that Miss McMillan was unable to attend the evening meeting of the Conference owing to her injuries. The police probably let themselves go, feeling sure that, unlike Miss Queenie Gerald, she had no really enthusiastic friends in high places.

I have put it without passion. I have not told you of what the women outside thought and felt when they looked on this new device of the dignity of the Mother of Parliaments. It ought to be enough for you that Margaret McMillan was kicked and shaken and flung down a flight of steps by a band of policemen. This is a thing that cannot be undone. Ours is the guilt. We have let this ferment of coercion and hysteria go on too long.

The Clarion, 1 August 1913

Mother or Capitalist?

What the World Asks of Women

One would be appalled if one heard two old gentlemen of the professional classes who had just picked up a lost baby in the Edgware Road, wrangling as to whether they ought to inject typhoid germs into it, on the off-chance that it was one of the unfit. And if one is sensitive one may be appalled by that section of the new Local Government Report on Infant Mortality, in which we read of a controversy between Dr Newsholme and Professor Karl Pearson, in which the latter objects to attempts to reduce infant mortality on the grounds that they 'merely prevent the weeding out of the unfit and ensure the survival of an excessive proportion of weaklings'. It is surprising that Dr Newsholme, instead of telling the police to keep an eye on Professor Pearson, actually argued with him seriously, pointing out that the causes of infantile mortality are largely evils of environment, which act as powerfully on the supposedly fit survivors as on the unfit baby martyrs. This controversy, so entirely sincere and self-satisfied, and so profoundly contemptuous of ordinary human values, gives one an idea of the streaks of prejudice and mis-understanding that shoot through even such a noble and industrious piece of work as this. And one of these streaks is the constant abuse of the working-class mother.

Like the landlady's cat in the music-hall song, it was always she who did it. Just as its lean body slinks round the chair legs under perpetual suspicion of having stolen the salmon and broken the china, so she steals through the Report under a reproach of, one way and another, killing her baby.

'The widespread ignorance of mothers ... child neglect ... the industrial employment of married women is an important factor ... wives and mothers with no domestic training...' One has an impres-sion that woman has just insisted on taking the job of childbearing away from the Local Government Board, which would have been delighted to do it for half the money, and is making a mess of it. One blushes for one's sex's unwomanly aspirations. But let us take this matter of 'widespread ignorance among women' as to satisfactory methods of rearing children under the adverse conditions of town life, which is alleged to be 'an important factor in producing excessive infant mortality in the more densely populated areas'. This is an unkind way of putting it, with a capitalist bias. We have exchanged instinct for intelligence: the more civilised a woman is the further she leaves behind her the instinctive knowledge of the animal concerning its young. 'Widespread ignorance' is therefore a natural consequence of evolution. In the case of the poor woman it is removed by printed leaflets issued by municipalities, all of which contradict each other. Should any London mother of an impressionable nature receive all the leaflets on baby-feeding issued by the Metropolitan Boroughs, her baby would run a risk of being fed forty times a day, or if she decided not to obey contradictory instructions, never at all. And Medical Officers of Health find themselves unable to agree as to the preparation of artificial foods, and even as to the time when a baby should be weaned, a problem that has been before the universe some time. How much simpler it would be if the mother, instead of tackling the baby single-handed with a leaflet or two, could effectively dispel her ignorance by enlisting the co-operation of a doctor, a trained nurse and two nursemaids!

Everyone is ignorant about babies; the well-to-do girl is not taught at her mother's knee to mix the baby's bottle, but is as uninterested in and ill-informed about babies until motherhood comes upon her as any other girl. But she can buy the knowledge of those who have given their lives to the study of babies when she needs it. It is a pity that these virtues which are most admired in our sex are so largely matters of money. One doesn't become a prostitute if one has a little money; and for a few hundreds a year almost anyone can be a serene and efficient Madonna.

I am afraid that Dr Newsholme does not regard health visitors as an inadequate and slightly offensive substitute offered to the poor woman for the skilled service the rich can command: I am afraid he thinks of them as missionaries. For his belief in the death-dealing influence of women can best be demonstrated by the conclusion he draws from the comparison between Nelson and Burnley. Both are prosperous cotton-weaving towns, but Burnley has an infantile mortality of 210 per 1,000 and Nelson has an infantile mortality of only 77 per 1,000. Burnley has a population of 106,000 crowded together in a density of 23 to the acre, as against Nelson's 40,000, with a density of 11 to the acre. Burnley is an old town with an old-fashioned form of refuse destruction, lying low round a central basin. Nelson is a modern town with a new form of refuse destruction, standing high on a windswept position that catches a good rainfall, in the midst of grazing-country. From these facts Dr Newsholme turns away with the remark, which probably makes him popular among the working women of Burnley, that it is probable that in Burnley the extensive employment of unmarried women in factories leads to their becoming wives and mothers without any domestic training and with indifferent habits of cleanliness. These supposed influences do not, however, appear to produce the same effect in Nelson . . .

where the same proportion of women work under the same conditions! And this strange fixity of idea is noticeable when Dr Newsholme declares the industrial employment of married women is one of the most important factors in causing infant mortality, although he has to admit that the infant death-rate is as high in the textile districts in places like Durham and Glamorgan, where the employment of married women is non-existent!

Why do they all do it – bishops, and John Burns, and all the serious-minded? It can't be all mere sex-antagonism, mere trumpeting, to put the woman in her place. It is done too fervently, too nervously for that. Is it not that to blame the mother makes them feel that they are doing something, and that it salves their conscience for turning their backs on the really great factor in the question? They feel that they couldn't deal with poverty wallowing in the sty of industrialism, who is the real murderer of the child. It is so much easier to accuse working women of feeding their babies on pickles and tea than to accuse society of poisoning these babies long before their little bodies come into being: of sucking the blood of the fathers that begot them, and making the mothers that bore them tired and fretful with thin living. Sixty per cent of the deaths of babies under three months are caused by what public health slang calls 'the group of five': premature birth and congenital defects, injury at birth, want of breast milk, atrophy, debility and marasmus. These are troubles that come to the unwelcomed fruit of a stock too blown upon by poverty for reproduction. To blame the mothers for these deaths would be to insult hurt things.

And the children who are born untainted by their parentage – for the life germ is strangely incorruptible and most babies are born healthy – are exposed to risks of a kind for which we women are not responsible. The Report says:

Of domestic insanitation, overcrowding and lack of cleanliness are probably the most important. For the infant this usually means exposure to a stuffy, dusty atmosphere, very variable in temperature; it implies, for the bottle-fed infant, insufficient or unsatisfactory arrangements for storing food and the consumption of food which may be partially decomposed and probably is uncleanly. The fact that in tenement dwellings refuse is often stored within the living-room, and in other forms of houses commonly close to the kitchen, adds to the possibilities of mischief. The yard may be paved or imperfectly paved, dirt then being trodden into the house. The sanitary convenience may be in an unsatisfactory condition and give off noxious effluvia. From these sources organic filth is trodden into the house. Similar domestic contaminations may result from the streets being unpaved and unscavenged, or only imperfectly kept. Household refuse may have to be taken through the house, or even through the living-room. Infective material may also be blown into the house or may be brought in on shoes, or carried by flies bred in fixed ashpits or any other accumulations of refuse.

I do not see that the least ignorant or the least industrially employed woman can do anything here.

I think you ask too much of mothers if you ask them to protect their children from such dangers. Even were it possible, why should mothers spend their whole existences on struggling for their children against dangers imposed, not by them nor by God, but by the profiteering capitalist, who decrees unwholesome poverty? Isn't there something impertinent in the demand that women should have to labour to rear children 'under the adverse conditions of town life'? Presumably the children, when rescued, will grow up wage-slaves among these 'adverse conditions', rear other little wage-slaves and die. One must be sure that life is worth while before one burns to pass it on. So before we kill the mothers in women by this unpleasing present and that hopeless future, let us send out the capitalist to fight the Angel of Death whom he called down to this massacre of the innocents.

The Clarion, 19 September 1913

On Mentioning the Unmentionable
An Exhortation to Miss Pankhurst

On September the twelfth I spent one penny on the *Suffragette*, and I got too much for my money. For it was a paper rendered wholly undesirable and to people with a sense of humour and a sense of beauty wholly unreadable by a certain preoccupation. The first paragraph which inspired me with terror was headed 'The Penalty of Ruining Girls', and it began cheerfully:

> In California, where women have the vote, a very serious view is taken of offences against young girls. That this is so is proved by the sentences imposed on two wealthy married men – Maury Diggs and Drew Camminetti.

Drew Camminetti has been convicted of taking a schoolgirl, Lola Morris, from San Francisco to Reno, Nevada, for immoral purposes and has been sentenced to five years' imprisonment and ordered to pay a fine of £1,000. Maury Diggs was convicted for the abduction of Martha Warrington, a school companion of Lola Morris, and has been sentenced to twenty years' imprisonment and ordered to pay a fine of £4,000;

and it went on to approve these sentences.

Now, that paragraph is a portent. It has three defects which, as a suffragette, I do not like to see in the official organ of the militant movement. It is inaccurate; it is hasty; it is prejudiced. It is inaccurate in that the sentence was not passed on Diggs and Camminetti till 17 September, and then Diggs was sentenced to two years' imprisonment and a fine of £400 and Camminetti to eighteen months' imprisonment and a fine of £300. It is hasty because it takes no cognisance of the particulars of the case. I agree with the *Suffragette*, that Diggs and Camminetti would not have been sentenced like that in this country; but I do not therefore weep for the sins of my country. I consider that the White Slave Law under which they were prosecuted is a piece of puritanic legislation which pretends to protect women and really thrusts them deeper down into subjection by refusing to recognise their moral responsibility. It provides that if a man takes a girl under twenty-one from one State to another he can be prosecuted. It is not taken into consideration whether she is willing to go or whether he means to marry her on arrival. The dangers of such a law are obvious. We know quite well that the average girl of nineteen or twenty is, unless she is feeble-minded, perfectly able to look after herself. To make her irresponsible concerning the disposal of her body fosters an undignified and sneakish sense of irresponsibility in her own mind, encourages her parents to keep her ignorant, and puts an unfair amount of responsibility on men. That such a crude piece of lights-out-at-eight-o'clock legislation should be held up to us as a result of what we may hope for when we get the vote is quite intolerable. Moreover, I dislike the attitude which is displayed in sentences such as this: 'Men of the country will be startled at such sentences, because the laws which they have made and administered so tenderly as regards themselves, enable them to ruin a young girl almost with impunity.' The wretches ... These generalisations flagrantly aren't true. No candidate ever mentioned 'improved facilities for ruining young girls' in his election address, and surely the practice is regarded with some distaste by the majority of men. And I do not see any great reformer writing such a sentence. One must love humanity before one can save it. Hate fortified by inaccurate information will take you nowhere; except to such triumphs as the flogging clause of the Criminal Law Amendment Act.

I passed on to a very sensible paragraph on the Dublin strike which pointed out that

for the killing of men in Dublin and the bludgeoning of women and children the Government are, of course, primarily to blame. But a very large share of the Dublin tragedy rests upon the official Labour Party, which long ago allowed the Government to initiate the policy of violent repression at the expense of women.

That is the kind of point that ought to be driven home, and I read on with interest till I came to: 'An Announcement. Our readers will be interested to know that the articles on venereal disease and social purity by Miss Christabel Pankhurst which have appeared in the *Suffragette* will, with some other articles by her on the same subject, be published in book form by Messrs David Nutt.' These articles contained but bluff and hearty assertions of the undoubted facts that most men are immoral at one time or another, and that it is horrible to be a prostitute and – a rather irrelevant *QED* – therefore women ought to have votes. However, it does no harm to rub these facts in. Underneath was more good news. 'We have to announce, in addition to the articles on venereal disease and its prevention now appearing, a new series of articles on Women in Fiction . . .' Art and hygiene hand in hand.

I then turned the page and came to the gist of the matter. 'The Dangers of Marriage (1)' by Christabel Pankhurst. Thencefrom I dropped into a flood of pathology and came up soaked with information concerning venereal disease. I have since regained calm by reading the *Morning Post* in a devotional manner. Now, taking into consideration that Miss Pankhurst is just about as much married as I am and just as much a doctor, I exhort her as one completely ignorant young woman to another. I say that her remarks on the subject are utterly valueless and are likely to discredit the cause in which we believe.

The case, of course, is presented as badly as possible. It is a case so strong that it stands by itself. That the race should be poisoned and deformed by sexual disease as one may see in any workhouse ward or doctor's consulting-room is a thing horrible enough to galvanise the ordinary reader without copious quotations from American doctors who touch the subject with that juicy sentimentality characteristic of a certain breed of transatlantic scientist. Miss Pankhurst goes in too much for exact but unenlightening detail. If the angel who has evidently visited Miss Pankhurst had bade her denounce instead the sin of gluttony she would surely not have begun by describing, moment by moment, a bilious attack. And the rashness of her assertions! She assures us that: 'Nerve trouble is also on the increase, we are told, the rush of modern life, telephones and motor-cars being, as people fancy, the reason of it. The real cause is syphilis.' Perhaps Miss Pankhurst is now puzzled at a certain coldness noticeable in those of her friends who have had nervous breakdowns.

But the real crime in Miss Pankhurst's article is her attitude towards those who suffer from sexual disease. She begins splendidly with the sweeping statement: 'Men before marriage and often while they are married contract sexual disease from prostitutes and give this disease to their wives.' With a sharp pang one will see Miss Pankhurst on the Day of Judgement, sweeping all our fathers and husbands and sons down amongst the goats. She elaborates her point of view with vehemence:

Never again must young women enter into marriage blindfolded. From now onwards they must be warned of the fact that marriage is intensely dangerous, until such time as men's moral standards are completely unchanged and they have become as chaste and clean-living as women.

These consequences are not only suffered by the persons who wantonly contract syphilis in the course of immoral living. They are suffered by innocent wives . . . and numbers of women who have inherited from their forebears the terrible legacy of suffering . . . and there are men who also suffer, though they have learned so little by it that they seek in immoral intercourse new infection, which they in turn transmit to generations yet to come.

Enough has surely been said to prove the dangers of marriage under existing conditions; to show the injury done to women by the low standards and immoral conduct of men.

Dear lady, behind whom I have been proud to walk in suffrage processions, this is rather a partial view. If we take it that your statements are literally true, have you no pity for the immoral men? We must be sorry for the man who loses the bright glory of love on the streets. He lives in a city and leads a tame life till he becomes tame and loses the wild thing's scorn for a pleasure that is stale, unecstatic, grimy. All the time he is invited to brood on sex by us, by women. For there is the army of rich parasite women who have nothing to do and no outlet for the force in them except to play with sex and make life its gaudy circus. And there is the other army of women who will beseech him to buy their sex because it is the only thing they have that will fetch money. The fallen man may be something that quite certainly no woman wants as a lover and he becomes very soon something too cheap and dirty to have much to do with, but he is as much a victim of social conditions as the fallen woman. Moreover, had Miss Pankhurst studied the subject for more than three weeks she would have known that disease strikes down for the most part the young; that most of its victims are mere youths, sometimes perilously ignorant, who are bewitched by tawdry lures before their maturity has shown them the difference between the white, flashing thing of passion and the shabby substitute sold by gaslight.

But this scolding attitude of Miss Pankhurst is not only ununderstanding, it is also a positive incentive to keep these diseases the secret, spreading things they are. Doctors who were studying this matter long before Miss Pankhurst or I were born have complained bitterly that their efforts will come to nothing so long as sufferers are intimidated by a hostile social atmosphere into being afraid to acknowledge the nature of their illness and thus to seek advice as the best way of treatment. As the great Duclaux said: 'The struggle against syphilis is only possible if we agree to regard its victims as unfortunate and not as guilty . . .' Only so will sufferers be encouraged to come forward and acknowledge themselves centres of infection. Let Miss Pankhurst ask herself: Would any of those hundreds of thousands of people who have innocently contracted such diseases – who have inherited it, who caught it while attending to the sick, who have been infected by the use of a cup or towel that had previously been used by an infected person – be likely to be frank about their malady in a social atmosphere influenced by 'The Dangers of Marriage'?

The strange uses to which we put our new-found liberty! There was a long and desperate struggle before it became possible for women to write candidly on subjects such as these. That this power should be used to express views that would be old-fashioned and uncharitable in the pastor of a Little Bethel is a matter for scalding tears.

The Clarion, 26 September 1913

Lynch Law

The Tragedy of Ignorance

Tonight as I came home in the tram a bricklayer was cast out into the windy starlight because he wanted to fight another bricklayer who had spoken slightingly of a certain forward of Aston Villa. His enthusiasm was hot-eyed and ridiculous. Quite evidently it confused the discussion of the game. Even so the indignation of Miss Pankhurst's partisans when her opinions are questioned confuses the discussion of feminist problems. I find this kind of personal passion in the suffrage movement almost disgustingly childish even when it leads to discourtesies as amusing as Miss Amy Haughton's. Miss Haughton will perhaps forgive me if, as I have been writing about woman suffrage on and off for seven years, I cannot suddenly convince myself that I am too young to deal with the topic. These personalities make decent discussion, the fearless slinging-out of the truth about to find out which end comes uppermost, quite impossible. We have none of us staked out a claim on any particular part of the world of ideas. It is our business to follow the vein of truth wherever it leads us and whatever the theories of our nearest and dearest may be.

In a recent issue of the *Suffragette* Miss Pankhurst published a characteristically good-tempered and courteous article entitled 'Attacks Answered'. Yet still I doubt the usefulness of her articles. It is long since one objected to the public discussion of venereal diseases, but I believe that Miss Pankhurst discusses them in a way that will defeat her own ends. I was severely shaken by her article on the chastity of men. I should have suffered a certain agony if I had seen an article dealing with the health of women in similar detail printed in a man's paper and freely read by men. Surely this affront to the modesty of men is the very thing that Miss Pankhurst should avoid, for modesty, so psychologists tell us, is a thing that loves clean living. Much more powerful than moral enthusiasm is the disinclination of the immaculate flesh to risk the soilure of the streets. The body loves beautiful things – sunlight and the sea and swift running – and this thing against which we are fighting is not a beautiful thing. We are playing the game against ourselves if we shock the body out of its fastidiousness by coarse description.

And still I deplore the rancour against men. It would be as well if Miss Pankhurst would put a note at the head of her article: 'For man read immoral man.' Otherwise there is a terrifying savagery about generalisation such as this: 'Although by medical means and healthy living men can gain control over themselves they renounce that control and stimulate their desires by foul thinking, by obscene words, sights and acts, by alcohol and . . .' The sentence rises well to its climax. But even had she added such a note I would quarrel with her for severity. It is for this reason that my charitable *Suffragette* correspondents accuse me (with a certain gusto) of approving of the immoral proceedings of such men and their ghastly consequences.

Yet if I say that consumptive patients ought not to be kicked down-stairs, but should be treated in sanatoria, the ordinary mind will understand that I am not encouraging mankind to contract consump-tion and then marry and beget consumptive families. The ordinary mind might even go a step further and agree that if kicking down-stairs became the recognised treatment for consumption consump-tive patients would become shy about acknowledging their disease and would creep among us furtively, themselves in agony, actively disseminating infection. This abuse of the diseased seems to me quite obviously bad business.

But the Puritan may answer me: 'This is mere opportunism; I must be just. The immoral man deserves to be hated, therefore I must hate him!' Myself I cannot reach this pinnacle. I have a frightened con-tempt for the immoral man, as I might have for a poor maniac who rushes about squandering time and money on dropping pennies into automatic machines. The deadly certainty of the proffer of the coin, the deadly certainty of its acceptance! When I feel more charitable I think of the words of Havelock Ellis, the great psychologist who has thought more deeply on these things than any other man of science:

The man who is run over in crossing the street, the family poisoned by unwholesome food, the mother who catches the disease of the child she is nursing, all these suffer as the involuntary result of the voluntary act of gratifying some fundamental human instinct – the instinct of activity, the instinct of nutrition, the instinct of affection. The instinct of sex is as fundamental as any of these, and the involuntary evils which may follow the voluntary act of gratifying it stand on exactly the same level. This is the essential fact, a human being in following the human instincts implanted within him has stumbled and fallen . . .

But if the Puritan convinced me that the human being by stum-bling has lost its divinity and become meet for hatred, I should still ask her not to hate. I have by me the most terrifying photograph I have ever seen in my life. A hundred men are standing round something in the principal square of a certain American town and looking at the camera with the pride of a legitimate and satisfied hatred. Every one of those hundred faces is the face of a devil. One would not think that human eyes could look so hot and narrow, that human mouths could raven so. Yet the hatred that turned them from men to devils was indeed legitimate. They had come out to lynch a Negro for rape. He lies, a torn thing with curious cuts, at the feet of a man who looks most like a devil. Rape is the most appalling crime there is; yet it would have been far better had they hated it a little less and left the

Negro in the county gaol. For by their violence, in the strangest way, they duplicated his crime. But now there were a hundred guilty men instead of one.

Even so I can imagine that the suffrage movement might become corrupted by just such hatred. By too eager pursuit of lust it might duplicate and multiply the savage irrationality and indiscriminate destructiveness that is the simple essence of lust. We see abroad in the regulations of the *maison de tolerance* how a contempt for an immoral person, given its head and encouraged, may become a hellish cruelty threatening even the innocent. At first men expressed their contempt for the girl who committed the sin of social self-sale by taking away her right to the law's protection. That feeling grew and grew. Now it is an obscene brutality that, if a penitent girl runs away in loathing from the wretched house, uses the police to drag her back to prostitution and her angry keepers. That is what hatred, growing from the very soundest moral basis, can do for a nation! Let us learn from the vices of our masters.

But if Miss Pankhurst is willing to lynch the immoral man what method will she use? 'When women acquire the necessary influence, political and social,' she says, 'they will have it in their power to convince men that to live cleanly or to be cast out from the society of decent women are the alternatives open to them.' So, portentously, says Mrs Ethel Snowden in *The Feminist Movement*. This is all very well. Most decent women are careful of the company they keep. But how are they going to find out whether a man is living cleanly or not? It is a vice that is most easily hidden and there is no phrase like 'British Constitution' and 'Truly rural' that breaks upon the voluptuary's lips. A society that consciously tries to discover the undiscoverable will find itself the prey of the tattler, the lickorish-lipped retailer of gossip, the secret enemy. And sooner or later the baffled Puritans would foregather and whisper: 'We can't get at it! We can't get at it!' And they would begin to fence in the flower-beds with prohibitions and put up notices to keep joy off the grass: to eradicate vice they would root up liberty. Why should we resort to these frenzied expedients of hate? If we socialists found ourselves confronted with a community where the men had drunk themselves into brutishness and habitually beat their wives and starved their children until they passed away in the repulsive agonies of delirium tremens, we would not mount tubs and remark: 'You brutes, you drink!' We would begin by saying: 'You must be very uncomfortable, being so awfully drunk and all that. We have built an inebriates' home round the corner that you might find useful.' And then we would deliberate and say: 'These

men are working too long hours. They didn't make enough money to
give them decent satisfying food. Their housing conditions are bad.
They want less work, more money, better homes; and lots of amusing
things – parks, picture-galleries, sports, theatres . . .'
Where does the analogy break down? Almost at once. If the brutishness of the men were connected with sex we would immediately go
into hysterics and weep and greatly add to the disorder of the scene.
But if we kept our heads we would reason through to conclusions just
as economic though more complicated. Plainly moved by economic
forces are two important classes of seller and buyer. The women who
come, with their pride of sex torn and draggled from the start, from
mean and poverty-staled homes; and the men of a class rotten with
too much leisure, undisciplined by effort, without moral standards
because – and let us suffragettes be warned! – it has preferred large
expressions of moral aspirations and aversions rather than clean-cut
ideas. The problem of these two classes is clearly economic: so, too, is
the problem of the other people who play this gloomy game. They are
not compelled to it by either poverty or luxury. Yet they are compelled to it. For we have no Dionysiac festival, and when the human
heart turns aside from the unsatisfying routine of modern industry it
turns aside to no such clean orgy of riot and free-spent strength. Such
adventurers must satisfy themselves with the poor glamour of the
streets. If the woman goes out she must stay there always; and
though the man comes back he is not less beggared.

We cannot bring this tragedy to a happy ending by hating a bad man
here and a bad man there. We must design life anew as though we love
all men.

We have the wits to do it too. At this moment I feel joyously
confident of the female wits, for I have been reading Sir Almroth
Wright's *Unexpurgated Case against Woman Suffrage*. It is the
worst book ever written and distressing. I have horrible nightmares of
Sir Almroth Wright's limp sentences wandering through the arid
desert of his mind looking for dropped punctuation marks. They have
a brooding look in their eyes like childless women, for every sentence
ought to have a little meaning clasped in its arms, but these have
none. This book is the tragedy of my life. Months ago when it was
announced by the publishers I promised myself the joy of tearing it
limb from limb. And now it has no limbs – only two rudimentary
organs embedded in a mass of protoplasmic jelly. Sir Almroth Wright
imagines that woman does not deserve a vote because she is the
'insolvent citizen'. She does not earn her keep. Apparently motherhood is an extravagant hobby of hers which she carries on simply to

give trouble. It would be brutal to remind him that she was joint-producer in the home of all England's wealth till that doubtful blessing, the industrial system, came along; and that since then the greatest fortunes have been piled out of the work of sweated women. The other rudimentary organ is a belief in the imbecility and immorality of women. 'There are no good women, only women who have lived under the influence of good men.' This is the oldest pot-house epigram in the world. There are lapses into comedy:

That not very unusual type of spinster who is in a condition of retarded development (you will find this kind of woman even on county councils) is completely unconscious of the sexual elements in herself and in human nature generally. Nay, though one went from the dead, he could not bring it home to her that unsatisfied sexuality is an intellectual disability.

I glory in the idea of Sir Almroth Wright's uneasy ghost explaining matters to the startled and dismayed members of the Women's Local Government Board Society.

Miss Pankhurst at her worst is worth ten Sir Almroth Wrights.

The Clarion, 17 October 1913

The Bishop's Principles
Our Case against the Church

I want more than anything in the world to read the hearts of men and then decipher history. Yet I cannot read the hearts of bishops. Constantly as I read the papers I come across their sayings, and always they are baffling and incomprehensible to me. For this reason I can rarely obey my lady-like instinct to read *The Times* and the *Morning Post* or any of those nicely printed journals where bishops most do congregate. And so when they invade *The Clarion* I must ask them to speak the word that will make all plain. I do not understand Bishop Welldon's statement on feminism. I can understand his claim that 'women in Christendom today enjoy a position of greater freedom, respect and dignity than was theirs before Christ was born or than is theirs now in the countries which do not bear His name'. It would seem to me not surprising that the world had advanced in two thousand years; and I note in non-Christian countries an absence not only of feminism, but also of syndicalism, aviation and the Russian Ballet. But all the same I can understand the propagandist spirit that makes Christ the determining factor of the progress of feminism. What I cannot understand are 'the two essential Christian principles' from which Bishop Welldon imagines feminism to spring.

Firstly, there is 'the obligation of personal purity upon all men and upon all women'.

Now, if I were not a human woman I should tell Bishop Welldon to consult Miss Christabel Pankhurst on this point. If the Church has ever laid any obligation of personal purity upon all men it has certainly never enforced it. It could not, for in this business of purity it has had no philosophic basis. In a hysterical revolt against the excesses of decadent paganism it set a high and mischievous value on celibacy which did its best to destroy the fabric of European humanity by tearing out the strongest thread: for the finest and most spiritually minded men and women went at the bidding of the Church into monasteries and convents and did not reproduce their kind. The Church taught men to regard woman as the thing of the flesh luring them from the sexless pursuits of the spirit. It counted every wife and mother as having won a victory in this disgraceful game. I think we see traces of this not only in the general attitude of contempt for women and the unpaid business of motherhood, but in many of the irritating barbed-wire prohibitions against which all active women must trip now and again. It is at the back of the minds of the authorities who object to married teachers: they feel that a wife and mother is an unclean being who ought not to be allowed to go freely to and from her work, but ought to be decently secluded in her home. It gives rise to the superstitious regard for virginity, as was recently displayed by the Bishop of Willesden, who issued a circular to the householders of his diocese asking them to take note of the fact that many rescue workers stated that a large proportion of their cases were domestic servants who went out to daily places. Therefore he requested them to make all their servants live in, and not to give them many evenings out. Enclosed in the suburban kitchen they could not sin; they could only want to do so.

I admit that this is a way of securing their virtue. It is capable of application to many sections of society. If the mine-owners will provide shake-downs and free meals in the pit we shall soon put an end to the drinking which is so regrettable a feature of many mining districts. *The Clarion* staff will be allowed out once a week to see the Albert Memorial and the Natural History Museum, but will otherwise live a blameless life under lock and key at Worship Street. Such virtue that is mere nullity and fencing-off from opportunity satisfies the Church. The really dreadful aspect of the statement brought forward by the Bishop of Willesden is that it points to the fact that there are thousands of women who do not get the chance to become wives and mothers. Their employment in the home does not bring them in contact with men. Probably they are girls from the provinces who have had to leave their home and their social world to come to a city where they have no friends. Or they may come from a class so distracted by poverty that all things happen dishonourably. But that does not worry the Bishop. So long as they answer in all particulars to the Church's description of unmarried women, what does it matter if they are bored and lonely and resentful at spending their lives in tending other people's homes and children?

That has always been the Church's attitude to women. It has always been purely sexual. So long as it maintained among women a certain physical decorum and corresponding ecclesiastical labels it was careless of the happiness of their souls. Now it often abandons even the insistence on the physical decorum and concerns itself solely with the labels. We have not forgotten the bishop who told the Divorce Commission that if a husband drove his wife on to the streets it was still her duty to cleave to him and be a faithful and obedient wife.

The second essential Christian principle is 'the reverence of man as the stronger for woman as the weaker'. Personally I have never found myself moved to drop on my knees before the infirmity of an ancient cab-horse, nor does my spirit bow before the pitiable intelligence and character of Mr McKenna. Weakness is the sign of an organism ill-designed for its work. A Church which boasts that its members are inflamed with a passion for the unfit is an unreasonable and dangerous thing. But the cool assumption that woman is weaker than man is impertinent. A bridge that stands the strain of whatever traffic may pass over it is strong: woman, who is physically the bridge over which passes the traffic of life, stands the strain. The muscular development that makes men good navvies would hinder her in her special work; she lacks it by her fitness to her function. Of course, if Bishop Welldon is referring to anything but the physical weakness of women he is not to be argued with. One shuns the company of the man who is convinced that his mother was a fool.

Not from such barren soil as these essential principles springs the strong tree of feminism. Nor can I see how they are 'the only firm, true, pure and sacred basis of human society'. They do not touch economics, which constantly preoccupied the mind of Christ. It is because the Church builds on emasculated pious opinions such as those rather than the naked and direct anarchist teaching of Christ

that the attempts of the more respectable suffragists to capture the
Church Congress seem to be so futile an expenditure of force. The
spirit is not there. All through the day after the Senghenydd disaster
the joy bells of Canterbury Cathedral pealed merrily: to rejoice over
the wedding of two people – I cannot find out who they are – called
Prince Arthur of Connaught and the Duchess of Fife. That is characteristic of the Church. It is a symbolist thing. It incites mankind to
concentrate its pity on the figure of one man out of many who were
crucified; and when it communicates with mankind it deals only
with its leaders, with royalty and government. And if we trouble to
carry our battle into this camp of sleeping soldiers, sleep will fall on
us also. We may get our vote through the influence of our respectable
friends, but we shall move snoring to the ballot.

The Clarion, 24 October 1913

Our Second Treachery
The Desertion of Jim Larkin

One day this summer I sat in the company of a few respectable
persons of socialist sympathies – one a prospective Labour candidate
and a well-known trade-union leader – who explained to me how
wise the Labour Party had been in not taking the obvious course of
running this Government round the room by the hair of its head and
forcing certain concessions out of it. To insist on even the moderate
reform of woman suffrage would have been unwise, I was told. For it
would have been monstrous to imperil the stability of the Government until the wrongs of Ireland had been redressed by Home Rule. I
who am Irish laughed. Only in England does one find passion expended by the clear-headed on the nationalist movement, that emotional camp-fire round which dance the gombeen men, the money-
lending publicans who battened off the distresses of the farmer and
the peasant, and would be glad enough to have a parliament of their
own where they could entrench themselves behind the double barrier
of economic and political power. It has demoralised the proletariat:
because the ostensible war for Irish liberty was being carried on in
another country by a specialised class the common people could drift
on in their muddle of poverty, drunk with the self-satisfied inertia of
those conscious of serving a lost cause. And we know what the
specialised class has become: the most loutish collection of conserva-

tive prejudices that even St Stephen's ever housed, with no economic theories newer or more generous than *laissez-faire*, and no enthusiasms save anti-socialism and anti-feminism. Could any nation survive the disgrace of suffering the great-jawed and low-browed John Redmond to be its leader?

My country, I thought, had grown out of that enthusiasm. That strange awakening of the long-dead drama in the Dublin Abbey Theatre was a portent that Ireland had ceased to be a down-at-heels dreamer, and was going to be a strong and romantic maker of life. Under Sir Horace Plunkett and George W. Russell Irish agriculture – such a hopeless, hungry thing when left to develop on the individualist lines of the Nationalist Party – had become a prosperous co-operative industry. The Irish Agricultural Organisation Society – which, in spite of the Nationalist Party's bitter opposition, is helped by the State – is one of the few definitely civilising and constructive forces in modern Europe. And I had heard, too, that the Irish industrial world was subject to a similar inspiration; for in the last three years the progress of the Irish Transport Workers' Union under Mr Larkin had pointed to the fact that the imagination of the industrial workers was turning to just war, and that they had one splendid warrior. I could see Ireland changing from a marsh that bred in its hungry dwellers a low fever of sentimental loyalties and inactive enthusiasm to a land of sane people, turbulent with reasonable passions.

But I was wrong. We are the same Ireland still. At first our folly was not our fault. The nation was too long on the rack of English oppression, and became delirious with pain. Now we have had time to become normal again. But, like a child that has been petted and humoured when its illness made it peevish and strange, we keep up the peevishness and strangeness long after our illness has left us. The fact of the Dublin strike shows that Ireland was getting well at last. The fact that the priests of Dublin have been able to incite the people to a hysterical attack on the Englishwomen who were taking the strikers' children to English homes not famined by industrial war shows that Ireland is still pretending that it has no self-control, but is a whimpering, broken, raging thing. As the cases of Mrs Montefiore and Mrs Rand are still *sub judice* I refrain, with extreme difficulty, from saying exactly what I think about the charge of abduction and what I believe to be the truth about the evidence. I may at least say that if all Ireland can do with Grace Neal, that most valiant and disinterested of trade-unionists, when she comes over on an errand of goodwill is to hoot and hustle her, it deserves to be governed by the

English Parliament. I can think of nothing worse to say. And when I hear that the priests inflamed the passions of the mob against Mrs Rand, herself a Catholic lady, by declaring that she was an agent of the White Slave Traffic, I can only marvel that the same phrase catches the ears of English and Irish geese. If one wants an English goose to put flogging on the statute-book or an Irish goose to turn and rend its best friends, one need only mention the White Slave Traffic. Can Ireland not understand that the three hundred families to which the children would have come would have felt themselves bound not to take advantage in any way of the children's unprotected condition? Until it realises that the world is full of friendly and honourable people, that the earth is buttered thick with kindliness, it will continue to be the same narrow, Nationalist – what a poor, limited, little ambition nationalism is, when one thinks of the word! – cockpit of prejudices that it is!

I blush with shame not only at the hurt and insult which have been bestowed on the Englishwomen, but at the picture of foaming epilepsy that is drawn in the following paragraph from the *Daily Telegraph*:

The attempt to take fifty children to England last night by the Laird Line boat from North Wall was frustrated. A body of about twenty-five Catholic clergy were present to witness the boat's departure, and they surrounded one woman who was going aboard with a child in her arms. As the woman tried to force her way through the crowd a cry of 'Rescue the child!' was raised and a wild scene followed, both the child – about four years of age – and the woman being roughly handled. Ultimately, with the aid of the priests, the child was removed to a place of safety by a workman, and subsequently it was explained that the child, whose mother is dead, was being taken to England by its father.

I am sorry that Ireland must show its devotion to the Virgin Mary and her infant son by this kind of child-mauling. I am more sorry still for the part played by the priests. 'With the aid of the priests' the child was removed from a peril which the priests had brought upon her. For this is a priest-made agitation, calculated with a nice eye for dramatic effect. I am not a bigoted anti-Catholic. I believe that Catholicism has sweetened Irish life and given it a certain decorousness and purity. But the Church itself makes it no secret that it is completely careless of the economic fate of its children. It has consistently ignored the economic teachings of Christ, and simply teaches its members to remain in the state to which it pleases God to call them; and this attack on the trade-unionists is part of this policy. The Archbishop kept his letter warning the parents not to send their children to atheist and Protestant homes until it fell like a bombshell among mothers who, naturally highly strung after weeks of poverty and fear through which Dublin has been passing, were further unnerved by the wrench of parting with their children. Yet this scheme had been declared openly enough; prudence and common decency should have compelled the clergy to formulate their charges against the women of the *Daily Herald* League so that parents could have been warned in good time, and the women themselves could have had the opportunity to disprove them. But it was not the intention of the clergy to investigate the truth. They wanted to have a dramatic incident that would demoralise the ranks of the strikers and leave Larkin with a disaffected army to resent the sentence which a sheep-like jury has brought upon him from an embittered judge. They know their flock. They are right.

Years ago there was a man called Charles Stewart Parnell, who could have delivered Ireland from this insane preoccupation with the dry husks of political power and given her her own parliament to play with. There came to him a time of peril: it was the extraordinary will of God that Murphy, who is now the oppressor of Dublin, was able to seize on his weakness; for Murphy has been a rich man from his youth up, and that was all that counted with the pawnbroking gang that then, as now, made up the controlling force of the Nationalist Party. He deposed Parnell from the leadership of his party, and so killed him.

Even so will the Irish workmen who believe this lie of the abduction of children for White Slave or Protestant purposes depose Larkin. They will inflict a deep injury on themselves and on their class: for they will become accustomed to the sight of their beloved children in hunger and distress, and therefore be more deeply rooted in the vice of endurance of poverty. Very probably they will trot back to work at the tail of the priest's black gown and sell their souls at Murphy's terms, and thus chain their subject class more heavily. They will refuse to let Larkin save the factories of Ireland as the indifferent agriculturist once refused to let Sir Horace Plunkett save the fields of Ireland. They will prove themselves astonishingly of the same betraying blood as Murphy. Like him, they will condemn their country to more years of feverish slavery to frustrated effort.

There is no help for it. No blame certainly for the Englishwomen who organised this plan of transportation which has caused so much trouble; they could hardly be expected to know that so much folly lived today. There can be only strong sympathy for Larkin in his hour of desertion, and for us of Irish blood a deep wonder and a deep

remorse that our loyalty has turned so easily once more to black
treachery.

The Clarion, 31 October 1913

Mr Chesterton in Hysterics

A Study in Prejudice

In these days I am constantly meeting a certain type of self-satisfied
young person who imagines that he is saved as a social and spiritual
man because he drinks beer in a priggish manner and experiences
feelings of sentimental distension on such occasions as sunset, and
that he has solved the problem of poverty because he dislikes Mr and
Mrs Sidney Webb. Such persons state that it is Mr G. K. Chesterton
who has made them what they are. I believe them. I have the greatest
admiration for 'Tremendous Trifles' and the other fairy-tales –
Heavens! How I can see Mr Chesterton's beaming face crying
happily, 'But that's just it! Life is a fairy-tale!' Heavens! – but I believe
his view of life to be based on a misconception. To put it in a
theological way, he denies that God made the brain as well as the
heart. He despises wisdom. He does not know that he who lets the
strong beast of his hatred rage through an uncharted world may find
that it has defied the dwelling of the Holy Ghost. As I dislike intensely the condescension with which he slaps the working man on the
back I rarely read his political articles. But last week I was sent The
New Witness of 30 October which contained an article called 'I Told
You So'. There is no sentiment in that article which would not be a
credit to an inhabitant of heaven: in fact it makes one desire to send
Mr Chesterton thither at once. The conclusions of that article are
corruptingly foolish and wicked.

The subject is that recent incident in Dublin, when the strikers'
children who were being sent over to English or Belfast homes were
assaulted by priests and 'Hibernians', and prevented from leaving the
city. This incident seems quite full of beauty to Mr Chesterton. Like
all sentimentalists he is cruel: the thin wail of the hungry teaches
him no truth. There is obvious picturesqueness about a priest walking in his black cassock through a little world of ritual. There is a
certain juicy sentimentality to be extracted from the spectacle if the
priest happens to be leading a little child by the hand. So that is the
picture he has made for himself of the situation in Dublin. So he turns

angrily on Mrs Montefiore, the chief organiser of the scheme for finding homes for the children of Dublin until the famine in Dublin is less bitter a thing, and tells her that she and her friends are the servants of evil because she is a woman; she is a Jewess; and she is a philanthropist of the Webb school.

I am not prepared to deny the first allegation. I object passionately to the use to which it is put. Mr Chesterton, whose grip on public affairs is the most tenuous thing about him, has no right to treat the woman who in Australia was the boldest opponent of conscription, and in Africa did her part in organising the Rand miners for their present battle, as a cheeky intervener in the rising of the people. Yet he airily sweeps her into the ranks of an alleged feminist movement which is 'like an idolatrous procession cutting across and stopping the march of modern men in revolt'.

I myself have never been able to find out precisely what feminism is: I only know that people call me a feminist whenever I express sentiments that differentiate me from a doormat or a prostitute. But it is obviously as imbecile to say that the feminist movement shows a 'priggish imperviousness to the instincts of the sexes and the institution of the family' as it would be to say that it shows 'a priggish imperviousness' to the greenness of grass and the shrinkage of the ancestral caecum to the appendix. It is as likely that the human race should agitate for pink grass and the restoration of the caecum as that it should become impervious to the instincts of the sexes and the institution of the family. And not the very blindest fool could see any indication of any such imperviousness in the *Daily Herald* League scheme. I find it almost incredible that, while Dublin is crying out to us of the black things of reality, Mr Chesterton can be sentimentally enjoying the thought of the wickedness of parting a mother and her child. He cannot know the horror of a city sacked by a strike. He surely must know that a woman hates to see her children starving, even in the institution of the family. He surely must know that industrial war such as this puts many women in the horrible dilemma of choosing between stinting the born or the unborn. He surely must know that many women who are nursing their babies are torn between their impulse to deny themselves food for the sake of the older children, and the impulse to go on nursing their babies. He surely must know that just now, when every available garment is pawned and the winter is coming on, many women feel a knife in their heart every time they look at their children. There is one point when it is permissible to break up the institution of the family; that is the point when it is changing from an institution to a mausoleum. In

Dublin it had begun to change. And that is why the mothers were ready and anxious to hand over their children to the care of the Englishwomen. They had the instinct for life, which is the strongest of all the instincts of the sexes.

As for the point that Mrs Montefiore is a Jewess, I simply do not know what to say. My first name will undoubtedly bring this portion of my article under Mr Chesterton's suspicion, but I swear that I am not a Jewess and that I am not a Samuel. But I loathe this anti-Semitism as I loathe the devil. I think the ferment of Celt and Saxon that makes up our British blood is so wonderful a thing that we need fear no other race alive. I have an insular pride in the fact that those who are responsible for the revival of this insane cowardice, Mr Belloc and Mr Chesterton, are both of French blood. By their howlings against aliens they prove themselves more alien from our clean hearth than any poor Polish Jew who comes to make our wealth in Scottish mines, and infinitely alien from the British heroes who, with the nervousness of uncourageous men, they love to celebrate.

And incidentally Mrs Montefiore is not a Jewess.

Mr Chesterton will say that that is no matter!

The mere name Montefiore, strangely enough, would not suggest to an Irish labourer a Celtic legend about a mountain of flowers. It would rather suggest another mountain remarkable for the quality of its sharpness; one that is even sharp enough to call itself Montague. I believe Mrs Montefiore's generosity to be entirely genuine; and quite unconnected with the mere 'philanthropy' of international financiers. But I am not talking about what I think; but about what the Dublin populace might rationally have been expected to think. And I say the mere surname of one of the great Jewish financial houses has probably done more harm than we can easily cure.

To the end of my days I shall have in my heart this exquisite picture of an Irish dock labourer restrained from handing over his starving child to a comfortable home because the organiser who took down his name bore the name of a banking firm . . .

Think of it. And such a banking firm: one of the least public and the most upright in its dealings. One might as well imagine a London dock labourer blenching because a Mr Van Raalte came to speak with Ben Tillett on Tower Hill. This is not my nasty superciliousness: it is a correct estimate of exactly what the name Montefiore conveyed to the members of the Irish Transport Workers' Union. When Miss Larkin was asked by a speaker at the Albert Hall (who had probably got the idea from this mischievous source) whether Mrs Montefiore's name had roused much prejudice in Dublin, it was the first time she had heard it was Jewish. We Irish have one kind of sanity. Never once was this race prejudice exploited in Dublin: a 'White Slaver' the priests called Mrs Montefiore, but not a Jewess.

Now we come to the third point. According to Mr Chesterton, the people who tore the children from the women to whom their parents had gratefully entrusted them were not driven by priests:

> They were driven by a human and hearty hatred of the spirit and power of Sidney Webb: a hatred of high-minded, high-handed, conscientious, officious, efficient, insolent philanthropy . . .
> Poor people are people with not enough money. They are not people with not enough organisation, or education, or parental responsibility, or parental leisure. What we ought to have sent, what we ought to be sending, to the poor Dublin parents is money . . .
> If I give a man coffee, I tell him to drink the coffee; if I give him threepence, I give him tea or coffee or any other beverage that can be so procured. Now the stamp and brand of Webb sociology through all its windings is that it will not give the poor money – that is, freedom to the extent of threepence. That abominable brand burned on the forehead of the socialist philanthropists in Dublin. They would feed the children; they would not pay the parents to feed the children.

This sounds well. It is simple. It is direct. It is from the heart. It is mischievous nonsense.

Mrs Montefiore is – I know she will understand me – a socialist that the Webbs would not touch with a barge-pole. She did not descend upon Dublin in her luxurious steam yacht with bags of Jewish gold, which she would not hand over to the strikers because she was afraid they would spend it on drink, but which she would disburse in railway fares to remove them to Fabian-staffed barracks. She was sent over to Dublin by the workers of England. Three hundred trade-unionists and socialists of England, many of them Catholics, had written to her saying that they would take one Dublin child or more into their homes until the strike was over. I have seen those letters. They were from working people: they breathed not Webbery but brotherhood. (Why does Mr Chesterton pretend to believe in a benevolent God and yet think he peoples the earth with nothing but Webbs and Samuels?) The majority of them plainly stated that they were not in a position to send money: 'A slice off the loaf won't make no difference.' 'We can put up another cot in our kiddies' bedroom.' 'The children must be of school age, as I go out charring in the morning and can't look to them.' That was the spirit. That there were three hundred manifestations of that spirit is one of the most glorious things that has happened during this glorious time of unrest. If one has a cantankerous nature and a short memory about half-fares, one may claim that the children might have been maintained at home on the money spent on their fares. It may be my feminist 'imperviousness to the instincts of sex and the institution of the family', but I am perfectly certain that sum of 7s 6d (which was all that was spent on the children who went to Liverpool) would not maintain a child for long with prices as they are today in Dublin. Nor do I think the strike will be over in a period that could be covered by a pound, which was the most that was expended. I do not blame Mr Chesterton for not knowing these details. I suggest that before abusing Mrs Montefiore and the feminist movement he might have found them out. He makes another point, which shows us the frame of mind which permits him this kind of impertinence:

I should have thought that anyone who had so much as seen an Irish priest (even in the distance) would know what he would say in answer to Mrs Montefiore, or another, if they promised not to violate the Catholicism of a little boy or girl. He would say: 'But Mrs Montefiore would not know she was violating Catholicism.

Catholicism is not a topic. It is not something one can mention on Tuesday but not on Friday. It is a way of looking at everything there is in the world.'

The priests said nothing half so pretty. They were too busy getting hold of Grace Neal by the shoulders and shaking her, too busy picking the identification off the children's jerseys in order to make confusion, too busy inciting their Hibernians to strip naked a luckless father who was trying to send his child out of Murphy's ravaged city to a Catholic home in Belfast. But if they had, what an exposure of Catholicism! So it is not a natural flowering of the instructed spirit. It is an artificial thing that must be clamped on by bars of compulsion which have to be constantly screwed tight by priests. Well, Mr Chesterton may have his own way about that. We only ask him to remember that Rebelhood is a different thing. It is a natural flowering of the spirit as it moves among events. It is not an artificial thing that is clamped on and will stay clamped on even when one is writhing in the paroxysm of anti-Semitic or anti-feminist hysterics. I beg him, in the face of this amazing display of distaste for research in fact, to remember that true Rebelhood is the precious product of discipline and sanity: that a rebel who is inaccurate and mad is a traitor.

The Clarion, 14 November 1913

Another Book Which Ought Not to Have Been Written

Insults and Privileges

The Fraud of Feminism by Belfort Bax

There is a journalistic curse of Eve. The woman who writes is always given anti-feminist books to review. Thus to earn my keep I have read the fluffy yet resistant matter of Dr Saleeby, and consequently felt as though I had swallowed a feather-bed. I have watched Dr Lionel Tayler's interminable sentences crawl along like a centipede gone lame in every other foot. I have been enveloped in the fog-like featureless gloom of Sir Almroth Wright. And now I have to diagnose the obstinate case of Mr Belfort Bax, whose fever against women has burst out for the hundredth time in *The Fraud of Feminism*, which Mr Grant Richards is offering to England for half-a-crown. It is written in 'the hope that honest, straightforward men who have been bitten by feminist wiles' – probably a misprint for wives – 'will take a pause and reconsider their position', and it is one of the most distressing books I have yet endured. It is like answering a call on the telephone and hearing no words but distant shrieks and groans and thuds. Woman is doing something dreadful: what it is one can't, from Mr Bax's disordered sentences rent by intractable commas, quite make out. Like Bishop Welldon, Mr Bax considers woman a physical failure. It has never broken upon their minds that in valuing a machine one should consider its efficiency rather than its mass or weight. Probably if one went often enough to the British Museum one would find Mr Bax and the Bishop kneeling side by side in silent adoration before the thigh-bone of a mammoth. Inflamed with pride by the knowledge that their sex holds the record for Indian-club swinging, they term women the weaker vessel. I do not know how they account for their presence among us except by the successful physical efforts of an endless chain of weaker vessels all well up to their job.

I forgive the Bishop for this contempt for women because he has pledged himself to stand by St Paul, but I do not forgive Mr Bax. With him it is no such mistaken loyalty, but simply carelessness in choosing his women friends. He states without shame that one out of four of his women friends are subject to periodic attacks of mental instability, and gives us an unpleasant impression of the sane ones by affirming it 'a fact, undeniable to all those not rendered impervious to facts by preconceived dogma, that, as I have elsewhere put it, while man has a sex, woman is a sex', and quotes approvingly an elaboration of this theory by a gifted young man named Weininger who, like the other great anti-feminists, Nietzsche and Strindberg, went mad. If, like Mr Bax, we take his experience as the basis of a generalisation concerning all women, it is clear what must happen to any organisation that is in the hands of women. In a hospital, for instance, twenty-five per cent of the nurses are liable at any moment to rush from ward to ward in the throes of 'outbreaks of fury wanting all the characteristics of womanhood' and 'driven by a morbid and uncontrollable impulse to such acts' as 'tearing up clothes, breaking windows, etc.'. (I quote from Mr Bax's illustration of the neurotic excesses of women.) The other seventy-five per cent, though spared by the hysteric scourge, are yet women: therefore they go about their duties in a distracted manner, and foregather in little groups to murmur hungrily of love. Similar deplorable scenes would be witnessed in the telephone exchange, in every big shop, in every school, in every home. If we were sickly weaklings, the whole race would die of our sickliness.

But I speak to the dead. I peep and botanise on Mr Bax's grave. His arguments ought to be left in peace.

Still, *The Fraud of Feminism* ought to be read because it inadvertently contains some quite useful information which is a powerful argument in favour of the revolt of women against any kind of social or political control imposed by man. It is impossible to quote it, because Mr Bax's habit of writing at the top of his voice positively prevents one from believing what he says. But he is undoubtedly correct in his argument that in theory and practice the law often favours the woman. For instance, the right to maintenance belongs solely to the wife, and no woman, however wealthy, need pay a farthing towards the support of her husband, even though he be crippled and disabled for work, unless he becomes chargeable to the parish and renders her liable to a pauper's rate. It is also true that a wife can leave her husband without proper cause and yet claim maintenance from him. A husband cannot sue a wife for money lent to her. If a wife commits tort against third parties, such as libels and slanders, the law holds the husband responsible. When a wife proceeds to file a petition for divorce her husband has to advance her costs, which he cannot recover from her on the failure of the suit even should she possess great wealth. A married woman is exempt from the ordinary liabilities incurred by a male trader as regards proceedings under the Debtors Acts and the Bankruptcy Laws. And even when the statute-book is innocent of any such sex-bias the woman is often favoured in the administration of the law. It is unquestionably true that if a man brought a breach-of-promise case he would have to face the derision of a court that would sympathetically greet a woman plaintiff in a precisely similar case, and that would even forbear to prosecute her should she commit perjury. And there is no more amazing excrescence on the nature of man than the tolerance displayed by judges and juries towards the vile crime of vitriol-throwing. Mr Bax quotes a case in which a Belfast jury awarded a nurse a hundred pounds damage for breach of promise, although it was admitted by her Counsel that she had thrown vitriol over the defendant; and the case of the woman who threw vitriol over a sergeant at Aldershot, and was sentenced to a mere six months' imprisonment without hard labour – less than many a suffragette has got – is typical of this shocking abortion of human charity. In these cases, as in the case where a woman was acquitted for an admitted attempt to shoot the local postman in the head, there is often the sentimental excuse that a ruined girl must take the only chance she has of revenging herself on her heartless betrayer. Although it is plain that if a girl turns to so vile an assault on his flesh as vitriol-throwing she was a thing apt for vileness from the first. But the criminal woman is treated tenderly even when she has not the flicker of a halo, but is simply a thief and cheat:

At Ledbury Petty Sessions a woman in the employment of a draper who had purloined goods to the amount of £150 was acquitted on the ground of 'Kleptomania', and this notwithstanding the fact that she had been in the employment of the prosecutors for over five years, had never complained of illness, and had never been absent from business; also that her landlady gave evidence showing that she was sound in mind and body. At the very same sessions two men were sentenced respectively to eight and twelve months' imprisonment for stealing goods to the value of £5.

In February 1902, a woman clerk aged twenty-six pleaded guilty to a charge of embezzlement, at Birmingham. She had

entered the prosecutor's employ in 1900, and in June last her salary was raised to 27s 6d a week. The defalcations, which began a month before the increase, amounted to £134. She had falsified the books, and when suspicion fell upon her destroyed two books in order, as she thought, to escape detection. Her Counsel pleaded for leniency on the ground of previous good character and because she was engaged! The Recorder merely bound her over, stating that her parents and young man were respectable, and so was the house in which she lodged!

It makes one wonder. Can it be that we are spoiled darlings of our lords and masters, who have no right to ask for decent pay for our work because we are so handsomely tipped for our sex? Why was it that I never noticed this atmosphere of tenderness and inexhaustible charity? Could it be because I have not yet stood in the dock? That is it. I have never gone away to yacht in the Mediterranean on money borrowed from a blind and paralysed husband whom I have left in Marylebone Union with a stream of solicitors' clerks depositing on his hard pillow writs for libels and slanders that I have committed, to say nothing of my legal claim for maintenance. Nor, after dragging my husband to bankruptcy by my reckless enterprises, have I forced him to pay out his last penny so that I can advertise my business in the divorce court. I have never perjured myself in a breach of promise action. I have never thrown vitriol over even a private, and my relations with the local postman are formal but friendly. (How one's negative virtues mount up!) I could never purloin goods to the amount of £150 before I was caught, and no employer would keep me long enough as a clerk to give me time to get more than the petty cash. Indeed my inherent disabilities shut me out from any participation in this feast of chivalry and good will.

To this banquet one must be conveyed by Black Maria. Not until one is crudely vicious does one's sex really inspire tenderness and confidence. For in every case the seeming privilege springs from false male value, which desires to make women cheap and base. Lawyers think that a wife has a right to maintenance because her husband has depreciated her sex value, and, of course, a woman has no means of livelihood except her sex. The same abominable theory is at the back of the detestable breach-of-promise law. The law cannot bear to think of a woman possessing property of her own: if the husband has not got hold of it he deserves to go on the parish. A husband who lets his wife get out of hand and go about libelling and slandering and filing divorce petitions and failing in business is a poor thing who ought to pay for his weakness: if he had hit her on the head in the right place it never would have happened. A vitriol-thrower is obviously a womanly woman: that is, being uncontrolled, unfastidious, and energetic, she is the kind of woman who easily becomes men's property on easy terms. Her charred victim must have been tactless and no man of the world, without knowledge of how to hand this kind of person over to the police. As for the thieving shop-assistant and the embezzling clerk, the justices of the peace and the jury evidently judged them on Mr Bax's assumption that while man has a sex woman is a sex. £150 and £134 are bagatelles: is it not positively our duty to smile through

our curls and twitter that six and five make nine? How more important is the question, Do we lodge in a respectable house? If we do, we
are plainly without sin.

Every one of these privileges is an inducement to women to
become weaker, slacker, more irresponsible.

The Clarion, 21 November 1913

Much Worse than Gaby Deslys

A Plea for Decency

I want to say a few things concerning the behaviour of Mlle Gaby
Deslys, but I find myself at a disadvantage. Everybody else who has
intervened in the discussion has first put themselves on a sound
moral basis by pointing out that, of course, they have not seen Mlle
Deslys. The Bishop of Kensington hasn't, Mr Shaw hasn't, Miss
Christabel Pankhurst hasn't and I gather that Miss Thompson hasn't,
nor Mr Blatchford either. I have, which shows conclusively the kind
of person that I am.

But, really, it was very nice. I grant that the play in which she
appeared was so incredibly witless that it can have been written only
by a National Conference of Village Idiots. But in its real purpose of
exhibiting a great many beautiful ladies it was very successful. The
ladies were beautiful. The ignorant greatly overestimate the beautify-
ing effects of theatrical make-up. If a girl looks pretty on the stage she
is almost certainly pretty off the stage; so we were looking at some
really wonderful and praiseworthy achievements of humanity. And I
fail to see why, when industrialism has made most of us so extremely
plain, we should not have the opportunity of looking at the women
who have managed to be beautiful. Of course, I might go to the
National Gallery and look at St Helena, or to the British Museum and
look at Clytie, but I take a great delight in the movement of living
things, and I will have my magnificent straight-backed chorus girl.
There was one indeed who seemed to me to hold up hope for womanhood. A fairly intimate knowledge of theatrical history enabled me to
calculate that she must be forty-five: yet her hair rose from her
smooth brow in the strong waves that show vitality, the line of her
chin and jaw delicate and uncoarsened by age, her body was straight
as a pine tree, and she moved proudly. Maturity had merely ripened
her: it should. The tired drudges who are grey-haired and bent-backed

at forty-five have been mutilated by society. The woman was the pattern of what nature meant a middle-aged woman to be; and though I know quite well that the musical-comedy and music-hall stages are in certain respects remarkably like the Pit, I am grateful to them because their women set up a high ideal of physical excellence.

But Mlle Gaby was much more than that. I do not mean that I would trust her with the management of the women's movement during Mrs Pankhurst's absence. I can't imagine anything with which one would trust her. The fact is that she is not quite human. When she frolics on to the stage and purrs impudently to the audience, it is as though one's Persian kitten should suddenly stand upright on the hearthrug and, flourishing its dainty paws, should sing 'We Won't Go Home till Morning'. One could no more be scandalised by her brevity of dress than one could be distressed at the Zoo by the gazelle's refusal to wear anything but its horns. Her occasional vulgarity is no more disquieting than would be a saucy gleam in the eye of the giraffe. She is a happy child who dances because she is tingling with life. When she crossed the Palace stage she turned the audience's thoughts to May mornings and ices, and money enough to go where you like. Now if most of us crossed the Palace stage, we would turn the audience's thoughts to November evenings, and cold cocoa and thirty shillings a week in the Post Office with the prospect of three-pence a month extra under the Holt Report. We feel the difference with shame and hate the dingy world of work that has made us what we are. We ardently desire brightness and health, and rebel against the dispensation of gloom and sickliness which is the work of poverty. This is the state of mind that will save the world. Therefore Mlle Gaby's performance is neither immoral nor non-moral, but definitely moral.

I do not believe that any performance which depends on the physical exercises, such as dancing, of a beautiful and healthy person can have any immoral effect on a normally clean-minded audience. The Bishop of Kensington referred in the course of his letter on Mlle Deslys to a 'positive morality', which her performance was violating. There can be no such thing as positive morality any more than there could be one course of treatment for all the patients in a hospital. The social system has put us into so many holes that it has no right to ask us to obey the same rules. It's as right for a starving man to steal as it would be wrong for Lord Abinger to try to recover his taxes in this way; it is as right for a suffragette desiring to stop the forcible feeding of Rachel Peace to punish the quiescent property-owner as it would be wrong for me to break Mrs Humphry Ward's windows; it is as right for a Dublin docker to let his children go hungry as it would be wrong for any other man to shirk his duty. Morality must not be a solid unyielding thing like the old-fashioned seawalls that so often fell in ruins, but must be ready to give to pressure where it is stronger, yet yield no inch further than it must, like the seemingly carelessly scattered lumps of granite that keep back the sea so much more strongly. All we know of morality is that it must be the kind of conduct that is instinctive to a healthy body : for if it conflicted a virtuous people would be doomed to extinction, which is absurd. That was the mistake of the medieval Christians who, fearing the flesh, drove the best men and women into the monastic life and left Europe to the seed of the unspiritual. A healthy body means a strong, sensitive nervous system that will perceive and understand the emotions of others, thereby ensuring an unpriggish altruism which is the secret of virtue. Therefore I believe that the sight of beautiful persons is a moral tonic.

And as for the other people, who make ugliness out of beauty because their minds are unclean, it is our duty to let them get all the uncleanness they can out of the spectacle. 'If a man or woman is a pig with an unpleasant taste for doubtful and dirty things, ought his or her taste to be encouraged?' That is what Hilda Thompson asked in last week's *Clarion*. I think it ought. Sin makes for death, otherwise it would not be sin. If a person has a rottenness in his heart which shows as an instinct for some sin, let him sin and sin until he dies of his sin. All through the upward struggle of life clumsy and inefficient species were evolved whose continued existence brought life no nearer to complete consciousness, and which were enemies to other and fitter species. These mistakes were corrected by death; they perished of their own clumsiness and inefficiency. Is that not one of the reasons why we want liberty, that the men who are clumsy and inefficient in their souls shall no longer be protected by their economic position but may perish of their sins – and that those who have the instinct of life in them need not be turned by poverty to foolish vices? Let every man follow his destiny. 'If so,' Miss Thompson goes on, 'what is the objection to the White Slave Traffic, for instance?' The real objection to the White Slave Traffic is that both men and women buy and sell against their wills. Men buy because they are bored either by luxury or by poverty. Women sell because they are hungry, or if they make enough for bread, because they crave for gaiety, or because they are feeble-minded and allowed by a careless State to fall prey to any man. If the only traffickers were men and women in whose hearts imagination and the love of beauty had no place, who were so blind to love

that they could buy and sell it without shame, let them have their
sterile joy. So they will live without power over men and presently
die, leaving none of their stock to corrupt the world. If a man execute
himself no one can blame the executioner: he must have been moved
by an imperative need.

This is not moral anarchy. I believe in prohibitions. I think that
healthy-minded people should be protected from certain indecencies.
The Bishop of Kensington was offended by Mlle Gaby's lack of garments. The following letter, which I print over an assumed name, is
an example of the lack of garments:

West Ham

Dear Madam,

I hope you will excuse me taking this liberty. We have been readers of *The
Clarion* for nineteen years, and I want to ask some of your kind readers if they
could assist me with some cast-off clothing for myself and four children. I
want to go out to work to help my family, as things cannot go on as they are. If
I had something decent to wear I might get some daily work. I have three
boys, ages from 13, 11 and 6 years, and a little girl 2 years, and they are so
badly off for clothes that I am ashamed to look at them, and it breaks my heart
to send them to school. My husband's work is so bad that he can't get more
than 24s, some weeks it is less. This week we had 21s, and as he works away
from home I am bound to give him 1s a day; he has to pay 4d railway fare out
of that, and our rent is 6s 6d. So you see the remainder is not enough to buy
food for us all, so if any of your readers can help me with some old garments
for my children and myself I will go out to work. I can put my baby girl in the
day nursery for 3d a day. I must go and do something to help, for we cannot
live on 10s or 11s a week, which is what it amounts to. Yours, etc.,

'Mary Brown'

Now, is that not indecent? The Bishop is shocked at the idea of one
healthy and well-nourished young woman voluntarily assuming
becoming and comfortable scanty garments. I am shocked at the idea
of five ill-fed and ill-housed people compelled by society to wear
unbecoming and scanty garments. Quantitatively and qualitatively I
win! Is it not disgraceful that a woman who has brought four children
into the world and left them there under these disadvantageous
conditions should have to wear cast-off clothing? Is it not disgraceful
that once she has got a decent covering to herself she should have to
go out and leave her family? I know that it is more pleasant to talk
about jolly and pretty and notorious people, but let us think hard of
'Mary Brown'. Is it not more blunting to the sword of the spirit that
we should live in a world where 'Mary Brown' and her children and
their like are starved into weakly shadows of men and women? I give

you my word, Lord Bishop, that had you not reminded me so vividly I should never have remembered whether Mlle Gaby had danced in a crinoline or a cobweb. But every time I go out I see poor and sickly people; and every time I grow more callous to poverty and sickliness, those aggressions in life. There lies your work. Rescue me from that indecency. If you or any other of the members of the Episcopal Bench who have recently come under the eye of Mr Blatchford and myself care to send garments for 'Mary Brown' to *The Clarion* office we shall be pleased; and lay readers of our sheets are also asked to 'take up this moral question and see this through'.

The Clarion, 28 November 1913

Some Race Prejudice
Packs and the Caste System

During the past few days citizenship has dropped from my shoulders like a mantle. For fate has thrown me of late into the company of a little yellow man who looked as though he had been quaintly carved and neatly lacquered, rather than come as naked living flesh from the Creator: he is a Japanese student of English literature and a learned man. His studies in the subject are indecently profound: his investigations into the works of dead authors, such as Shenstone and Henry Mackenzie, are unholy bodysnatchings from the quiet and honourable graves of literature. There is no English author whom he has not swallowed whole. Indeed, there is nothing English that he has not swallowed whole.

That has made me believe in race. Before I thought that all racial generalisations were as crude as the libels that those of Leeds spread concerning the men from Pudsey, and the talk of grossness with which natives of Edinburgh repel Glasgow's accusations of mean living. But I feel that here is a race weakly and unfastidiously given to mimicry. A blight has nipped their creative passion. This little lacquered man speaks with pride of the old discipline of the land, when the governing order of Samurai purchased their power of government by pure living and the culture of clean strength. But he speaks with equal pride of the nation's adoption of our industrialism in its crudest and least conceited form: of how the Japanese have picked up the trick, played to such perfection by the Lancashire manufacturers who were the makers of modern liberalism, of making money by the sweated factory work of women and children. Remember they were not tempted to it by the slow betrayal of the poor into the hands of the rich by undirected economic forces, as we were; they read of it in books and liked the savour of the sin. If they had been men of good heart they would have thought of Manchester and bridled themselves from this abomination. It may be argued that it would be impossible for a man in Japan to imagine Manchester; but now they have their own little Manchesters of pain and poverty, and they have no conviction of sin. On the contrary. With terror I see a gleam in my Jap's eye, a hard gleam that promises hard and enjoyed action: he is foreseeing the construction of ingenious puzzles like the Insurance Act; elaborate systems of prohibitions and permissions, like the Licensing Acts, that click neatly without making the indiscreet clash of a conclusion; tidy classifications, like the Mental Deficiency Bill. And it is better for a man to lust after scarlet sins than to lust after red-tape sins. There is no hope that he will die of delirium tremens, only the fear that he will live to eighty on total abstinence and nut-cutlets. So I see in my dreams a world that will be when I have long been dead, a world become almost divine, yet clogged in its wheels by a certain pretty little country of clean-cut rocks and almond blossoms and blue lakes starred with lily-blooms. There will be some complicated and damnably successful system of the Service State to hold back humanity in its dizzy and reckless race towards salvation by freedom. Our wisdom will be so much more difficult to imitate than our folly: they will hang at our skirts, begging us to travel no further than the Holy City of Social Reform. They will cry out to us who desire perfection that none can see God and live.

So for the past week politics have seemed to me a monster that we English have brought forth to our own destruction. If my eye fell on a Blue-Book it seemed a brick in an edifice that might be added unto by busy little yellow people until it blotted out the sun. The shortest table of statistics I saw amplified by little yellow hands till it nearly covered the page of life. And I remembered that the goddess of solid contours and architectural features, who represents the State in conventional statuary, had always reminded me of a vicar's wife in her appearance of vitality uncontrolled by intelligence; and I could see her the mother of a family, vast and plain and active as are the families of vicars, of sub-State authorities. After an interview with an officer of the Inland Revenue Office, who insisted that I was making an income of some hundreds a year (evidently having heard that journalists double their income by burglary in their evenings), and a horrible struggle between the desire to point out his characteristically masculine inaccuracy and refuse to give any information to the agent of an accursed Government, I became panic-stricken. I was a vicious syndicalist for a week. If anybody had handed me a vote I would have snarled at it.

So, purged of political passion, I went out and enjoyed London unregenerated. All sorts of things amused me. That little canal in Maida Vale which made a shabby Venice of the villa garden's stucco balustrades; that cliff of houses in the Harrow Road that looks down on the red and green lights burning on a wide barren space mossy with darkness where trains run screaming like the wind all night; mean streets in Somers Town that lead to a gasometer rising out of the thick November sunshine like a castle. Unaccountably we have made beauty where we built without plan and in meanness. The world has an odd bias towards seemliness. I looked round at it and said to myself, 'All would be well if everyone had enough to eat.'

At the weekend I went down to the country. I walked along a deep lane between rusted autumn hedgerows and looked at a hilltop where the tree-trunks stood like spears before a flaming sunset. After supper I blundered by lantern-light down a wooded hillside crepitant with night noises and crossed a little valley in which the night lay like a silent pool. The morning discovered a world so gilded by the summer's sunshine that it needed no stronger light, and I walked through golden woods to a hillside gallantly blazoned with gorse to look down on a vast Midland plain of pale pastureland chequered with black elms. Again I said to myself, 'All would be well if everyone had enough to eat.'

That night I went home having cast politics overboard with the Pentateuch and the Iron Wages Law, and had visions of England populated by thick-waisted and moral young men and women, such as Walter Crane used to draw, produced solely by economic freedom. Let them form efficient trade unions and forget the State. God forgive me! I thought of England populated by packs . . .

Distrust the pack system. The only good thing I know about packs is that they are usually led by lady animals of experience. It is a method of organisation that appeals only to the animals who do not know what the other animals look like and how kin to them they are. One sees it in a most blatant form in Spain. There the people think of humanity as the pack that has for the moment gained mastery over the other packs of wild beasts. So, though they are revolted by the idea of cruelty to their children, they are hostile to their animals, and every injury to a mule in the road or gore to a horse in the bull-ring is a pleasant and easy victory over a potential enemy. They do not know that their human intelligence makes them kings who fear no subject. Nearly as beastly a result of the pack system is the attitude of some very self-absorbed trade unions, such as the Miners', who fight any attempt of women to work freely and who mock at the suffragist movement. If they had the leisure and education to study the wider issues of politics they might have shed these barbarities.

The fact is that the consolidation of men into packs is an unnatural thing at the present stage of civilisation. Men who are bricklayers are bound together only in those things that concern bricklaying. In other things bricklayers scatter asunder like the chaff and join the two packs into which humanity divides itself – the aimless animals that paw the dust obediently and the Hounds of Heaven that urge them on to achievements of the intelligence. If they are forced to submit wholly to the occupational tie they will become more brick-layers than men, and will bare their teeth at the world because it does not lay bricks. When I have seen the more prosperous trade-unionists express disapproval of the indecorous revolt of the casual labourers, I have thought that that development of the pack system which Jack London prophesied in *The Iron Heel* might come about. He imagined that capitalists might break the back of the socialist movement by creating a labour oligarchy out of the workers who are most necessary for the smooth running of the capitalist machine: such as railway-men and miners. Well-paid, well-housed, socially regarded, they might be sufficiently grateful to their kind masters to help them in their job of keeping down the more utterly depressed workers.

It might be even so. We must fight for economic freedom, but lest the desired half-sovereign a week more should weigh down our hands to helplessness, we must ardently desire freedom that the State alone can give us. How, hunting in packs, could we solve the problem of making the educational system something more than a circus in which all the tricks are clumsily performed? How could we devise some way by which men and women can give their lives to the apparently profitless studies of art and science? Deprived of wider interests we would turn to snobbery. Out of our trade unions would spring a caste system. And it was from a caste system, with its self-satisfied pigeon-holes and prohibition of free conflict among all sorts of men, that came my mimetic little Japanese. Our last State will be worse than our first. Because we hunted in packs.

The Clarion, 5 December 1913

The Sin of Self-Sacrifice

The basis of the anti-feminist position is the idea that women ought to sacrifice the development of their own personalities for the sake of men and children: that even if they are fit to vote and to fulfil other activities of men they should not do so, because all their energies should be spent in the service of their families. Such is the view of the governing classes in this country today, and its passionate advocacy by Ellen Key has changed the continental woman's movement from a march towards freedom to a romp towards voluptuous servitude. According to these folk a woman should from her childhood be guarded from the disturbance of intellectual effort and should pass automatically through a serenely sentimental adolescence to a home. There the tranquil flame of her unspoiled soul should radiate purity and nobility upon an indefinitely extended family, exposed to the world's winds only when she goes wisely marketing. Inconceivably incandescent, inconceivably economical, like the advertisement of a motor-lamp come true.

This amounts to a claim to halos for women: for a halo is the only thing I have ever heard of that gives out light yet needs no fuel. Unless a human being is being inspired with wisdom by some supernatural power he can only gain wisdom by an experience compounded of his sensations: that is, the vibration caused by collision between his nerves and external things. We are dependent for the value of this basis of wisdom on the extent to which we lean out of ourselves and adventure among alien things. The only times when a woman's physical feelings are concentrated within herself are when she has indigestion and appendicitis; when she is well she is thinking how warmly the sunlight lies on her face or how sweet the wet loaves smell. Similarly, when a woman's mental feelings are concentrated within herself she must have inflammation of the brain. Only the mad wonder continually whether they are men or poached eggs, and discuss whether the world uses them well or ill. The sane look round on their fellow-men and delight to see who will help them in their work of making the world less madly governed: they walk the earth to choose their battlefields, and touch all it contains to find the substance most fit for the forging of weapons. Then they glow with the exhilaration of wisdom and radiate glory. So might many women were they given freedom; but they must remain tinged with no clearer light than the reflection of the kitchen range so long as they are made to ape the self-sufficiency of the maniac. As they are ignorant how can they hope to inspire those who are not ignorant? What influence can a wife who has passed from playing with dolls in her father's house to playing with saucepans and babies in her husband's house hope to have over a man who has been disciplined by years of responsible enterprise among all sorts of men? Her courage has been tried by childbirth, but her character has stood no other test.

It may be said that this is underestimating the value of home-keeping as an occupation. Of course it is. But it is a wild generalisation to say that the majority of wives in Great Britain are home-keepers in the sense of being essential to the existence of the home as was the wife in medieval agricultural England. If she were there would be no need to discuss feminism, for where a woman pays her way by performing labour she usually forces the community (if it be not too corrupt with capitalism) into recognising her equality. While the silk industry made the Burmese women economically independent, they were not submissive to men; but now that this is taken out of their hands they are threatened with that humiliation. And I was recently told by 'A. E.' that there is no need for the preaching of feminism in modern agricultural Ireland, for the farmer and the farmer's wife depend so much on each other's labour that it never occurs to them to imagine that they are different and unequal sorts. The rough home-keeping of the past, and the present in remote districts, presented difficulties which had to be met by skill and determination. Where the cow had to be milked and the churn persuaded, one simply waits for the coming of a milkman who, perhaps, has rarely seen a cow; where jelly had to be forced to jell one buys small packets from some unknown controller of jellies; where one sheared the sheep and spun its wool and wove the cloth and cut out the dress one goes to a shop and buys the finished thing easily, though probably at three times its real cost. It is all very simple and quite artificial. The woman who does these things may fill up her day with them, but the practice of them is hardly a craft. For they are tricks that a performing dog who could count his change might pull off just as well. That there is no interest in the occupation to counterbalance the solitude it entails, in these days of small homes unconnected by any local corporate life, is shown by the numbers of domestic servants who fly from its monotony to the life of the streets. And evidently their mistresses found the home no more educative, for they have not prevented their husbands and sons from preying on these women till, in their misery, they have revenged themselves on society by their disease and drunkenness. Here, in a rather important matter, the home-keeping woman has failed to radiate purity and nobility.

It may be said that the failure of women to create or influence morality does not matter: that their business lies simply with the physical nurture of the race. This is like saying that a doctor has no right to concern himself with the study of poisons because his business is with the preservation of the human body. When the body evolved the mind it evolved a queer, treacherous governor, who never knows what he does with his subject. Just as the African mind, by turning to commerce, has betrayed the African body, because sleeping-sickness travelled along the trade routes as safely as the goods, so the Western mind has betrayed the Western body by inventing the ingenious and in many ways convenient system of capitalism. So long as it persists no wealthy mother can look at her child without remembering that:

> The strongest poison ever known
> Came from Caesar's laurel crown.

No poor mother can hold her healthy child (life is such an indestructible and generous thing that nearly every baby is born healthy) without seeing him the bent extension of a machine. Men have not been able to fight the forces we have in an honest quest for civilisation called up from hell: all the energy of the world is needed to battle with them. The woman who cares merely for the physical nurture of her children is by her softness encouraging the famine that may some day starve them.

The fact is that this idea of sacrificing the individual to the race never works. It hints at a philosophical heresy, such as the belief disproved by Berkeley that matter has a substance apart from its attributes. 'There is nothing behind the facts,' said Chauncey Depew, when offered an idealist system that would 'harmonise' and 'explain' the facts of life. There is nothing behind the race but the individuals. If half the individuals agree to remain weak and undeveloped half the race is weak and undeveloped. And if every alternate link of a chain is weak it matters not how strong the others are: the chain will break all the same. Every nation that has contained a slave class has fallen to dust and ashes in spite of all its military glories and its pride of brains. And I cannot remember that any individual has ever benefited the race by self-sacrifice. I can well believe that St Simon Stylites did not like perching and that Savonarola's heart bled at his own denunciation of beauty and jollity; but these men saved no race. The people who draw down salvation to earth are the people who insist on self-realisation whether it leads to death or gaiety. Florence Nightingale saved war from its worse disgrace and helped the sick because she hated disorder, not because she thought she ought to do something toilsome. Marx set humanity on its feet because he was interested in economics. Darwin uncovered the significant eyes of truth because he enjoyed zoology.

And truly these are among the saviours of men.

And the recognition of this is the real virtue of the militant suffrage movement. Its later manifestations have seemed to some of us not immoral but pointless and extravagant. Desirable residences are more common than desirable Cabinet Ministers, yet they are sufficiently rare to be preserved. No house is wholly built with hands: it has taken many mental triumphs of the organisation of civilisation to secure that bricklayers shall unmolested lay their bricks and quarrymen convey their stone unrobbed. A house is an achievement not to be burned in a night. And these sporadic attacks on the voter are ineffective, for they create no widespread terror that would cry out to the Government for immediate pacification of the terrorists. They merely make England into a patchwork of irritations. But how admirable is the spirit of the militants! How splendidly selfish they are! There is no doubt that now Mrs Pankhurst is out of gaol again they will keep her out. All over the country we can help her. There is nothing like sympathetic reference to a lawbreaker for turning the heart of the law to water. We got Jim Larkin out of Mountjoy because we said we liked him. We can keep Mrs Pankhurst out of Holloway if, remembering what her movement really means, and how it has brought the supreme virtue of selfishness to thousands of English women, we speak well of her.

The Clarion, 12 December 1913

Part III

A Reed of Steel

Essay on Mrs Pankhurst
from *The Post-Victorians*, 1933

Editor's Introduction

It seems appropriate to print here, after some of Rebecca West's essays on the struggle for women's suffrage, her account of Mrs Pankhurst with some decades' distance and the emotions and analysis recollected in tranquillity.

Mrs Pankhurst's part in the militant campaign is well documented, as is her reputation as a brilliant speaker, publicist, organiser and propagandist – as well as her arrests, trials and her subjection to forcible feeding. Rebecca West recalls the vivid presence of Emmeline Pankhurst as a speaker, most impressed by her 'fineness', the 'French' flavour of her intellectual power, her manner, her dress and her speech. She found Mrs Pankhurst a very respectable, 'not very sharply sexed mother-type'. 'Certainly I remember that as a flapper dogsbody at the WSPU offices one was told never to put Mrs P or Christabel P in the position of being alone in a room with a man. I have no doubt Keir Hardie made a pass at her; he was a great one for the girls, but I am sure Mrs P would not have responded. Mrs Pankhurst and Christabel Pankhurst lived at home and in their offices with continual surveillance; John Kennedy could not have been active in such circumstances.' (This was in response to our discussion of a recent biographer of Keir Hardie, who, unable to accept feminism as either an ideology or a social movement comparable to socialism, could only conceive of a source for Hardie's feminism in sexual attraction for Mrs Pankhurst or her daughter.)

In this brilliant essay, Rebecca West truly analysed the character of the leader and the 'masculinist and capitalist social system' which she opposed, describing the sublimation of sex antagonism, by one who recognised the suffering caused by patriarchy, into a brilliant championship of women's causes. She praised Mrs Pankhurst's 'thunder and lightning' threats to the government and compared her physical courage to the glory of Ellen Terry and Sarah Bernhardt, the sight of her body bearing the blows of policemen and Liberal stewards as an inspiration for the development of physical courage in thousands of women.

Yet this essay was written by a member of the Left but loyal opposition to Mrs Pankhurst. Rebecca West, like some of her great European literary feminist forebears, was a champion of sexual as well as political freedom for women. Although when the WSPU launched a social purity campaign, she and her colleagues and friends on *The Freewoman* and *The Clarion* were more concerned to campaign for free love, divorce laws, women's trade unions and equal pay for equal work. Looking back from the thirties, she gives credit where it is due, praising the Pankhursts for publicising the evils of prostitution and bringing about changes long overdue in medical and legal attitudes towards syphilis and gonorrhoea. And as a propagandist and speaker she says that Mrs Pankhurst was quite simply brilliant. 'Trembling like a reed, she lifted up her hoarse, sweet voice on the platform, but the reed was of steel, and it was tremendous.'

A Reed of Steel

There has been no other woman like Emmeline Pankhurst. She was beautiful. Her pale face, with its delicate square jaw and rounded temples, recalled the pansy by its shape and a kind of velvety bloom on the expression. She dressed her taut little body with a cross between the elegance of a Frenchwoman and the neatness of a nun. She was courageous; small and fragile and no longer young, she put herself in the way of horses' hooves, she stood up on platforms under a rain of missiles, she sat in the darkness of underground jails and hunger-struck, and when they let her out because she had starved herself within touching distance of death, she rested for only a day or two and then clambered back on to the platforms, she staggered back under the horses' hooves. She did this against the grain. What she would have preferred, could her social conscience have been quieted, was to live in a pleasant suburban house and give her cronies tea with very thin bread-and-butter, and sit about in the garden in a deckchair.

Mrs Pankhurst came to these cruel and prodigious events not as some who have attained fame in middle life. She had not lived in ease all her youth and had dammed up her forces, so that there was a flood to rush forth when the dam was broken. She had borne five children, she had been distracted by the loss of a beloved husband, she had laboured long at earning a livelihood and at public work. Enough had happened to her to draw off all her natural forces. That she was not so depleted can be partly explained by the passion for the oppressed which burned in her as a form of genius; and she drew, no doubt, refreshment from the effect she had on her fellow creatures, the response they made to her peculiar quality, which was, apart from her beauty, her courage, her pity. She was vibrant. One felt, as she lifted up her hoarse, sweet voice on the platform, that she was trembling like a reed. Only the reed was of steel, and it was tremendous.

On an Atlantic liner during a great storm passengers will feel in their bones the quiver that runs through the ship's backbone as her stern rests on a wave and her prow hangs in mid-air over the trough till she finds the next wave to carry her. Something of the same sort was the disturbance, the perturbation, the suspense at the core of Mrs Pankhurst's being. She was not a particularly clever woman. One could name scores of women who were intellectually her superior. She was constitutionally naïve, she could swallow fairy-stories, she had only an imperfect grasp of the map of the universe man has drawn with his thought. She was one of those people who appear now and then in history against whom it would be frivolous to lay a complaint on these grounds, since they are part of that map. She was the embodiment of an idea. Her personality was possessed by one of man's chief theories about life, which it put to the test, and which it worked out in terms of material fact. She went forward, precariously balanced on what there was of old certainty, hanging in mid-air till she could attain a new certainty, her strength vibrating as if it were going to shatter into pieces like glass, maintaining itself because it was steel.

She was born in Manchester on 14 July 1858, of north-country stock with character. Her grandfather, a master cotton-spinner, had in his youth been cruelly used by the State. One day he was carried off to sea by the press-gang, and did not manage to make his return for many years, by which time his family had completely disappeared. Later he fled before the soldiers at the Battle of Peterloo, and with his wife, a fustian cutter of sturdy disposition, took part in the Cobdenite agitations of the Hungry Forties. His son, Robert Goulden, was brilliant and versatile. He began as an errand boy and ended as a manufacturer; he was an amateur actor who made a great impression in the heavier Shakespearean parts; he ran a theatre in Salford as a hobby and he was a romantic Liberal. He took a leading part in that altruistic movement by which Lancashire, brought to beggary by the American Civil War and constrained by every economic reason to side with the South, solidly upheld Lincoln and the North. He had by that time married a Manxwoman, who bore him five sons and five daughters. His eldest girl, little Emmeline, rattled a collecting box for the poor Negroes and learned to weep over *Uncle Tom's Cabin*, though, with an entirely characteristic refusal to restrict herself to logical categories, she gave the most fervent loyalty of her imagination to Charles I.

When she was thirteen Robert Goulden took her to school in Paris. He left her at the Ecole Normale at Neuilly, a green and spacious suburb which must have been a pleasing contrast to Manchester. In any case, Emmeline's love of beauty would have made her a friend to France; but owing to an accident, Neuilly offered a seduction even more specially appealing to her temperament. Because Mr Goulden had to make the expedition fit in with business engagements, he left her at the school during the holidays, when there was but one other pupil. This was a fascinating little girl called Noémie, who had no home to go to because her mother was dead and her father, Henri de Rochefort, was in prison in New Caledonia for the part he had played in the Commune. The two girls became instantly welded in a friendship that lasted till the end of their lives, and Emmeline learned to adore Henri de Rochefort in his daughter's talk, as later she was to adore him in his own person. He was something for a romantic little radical to adore: a splendid, spitting cat of a man, who spoke his mind in the face of any danger, who, though Napoleon III sat on the throne, began his leader on the shooting of Victor Noir by Prince Pierre-Napoleon Bonaparte with the words, '*J'ai eu la faiblesse de croire qu'un Bonaparte pouvait être autre chose qu'un assassin. J'ai osé m'imaginer qu'un duel loyal était possible dans cette famille où le meurtre et le guet-apens sont de tradition et de l'usage . . . ;*' who fought duel after duel, suffered arrest again and again, and endured exile and imprisonment with like fiery fortitude.

Emmeline was, owing to a real or maldiagnosed weakness of health, forbidden to take part seriously in the school work; she never then or later knew any form of study stricter than desultory reading, or appreciated its uses. But she was receiving, from Noémie and her absent father and her guardian, Edmond Adam, a thorough education in a certain department of French life, in the passionate and pictur-esque conduct of politics. There the prizes went to the daring. There it was no shame to act violently and fight one's enemies as if they were enemies. And in this atmosphere she spent those very formative years between thirteen and twenty; for she loved Paris so much that, when her own schooldays were over, she coaxed her father to let her stay on as companion to a younger sister.

She tried her best to stay in France for ever; and that, alas, led to her smarting and tearful removal back to Lancashire. There was a curious event which, for the first time, revealed that Emmeline was an odd fish who was not going to take life as she found it. Noémie married, and thought it would be delightful if Emmeline found a French husband and settled down as her neighbour. Such a husband could be obtained, of course, only by a bride with a *dot*. But Emmeline knew that her father was well-to-do, and she found nothing abhorrent in the *dot* system. She had disliked the scenes that her father had made when her mother brought him bills, and had seen with her clear eyes that, in a masculinist and capitalist social system where women have not economic freedom and wives are not paid, the dowry is the only way by which a woman can be given self-respecting security and independence. Romantic liberalism could go and hang itself. She was a realist. But unfortunately her father was still a romantic Liberal. When Emmeline found a pleasing suitor and asked for her *dot*, Robert Goulden stormed the house down at the idea of buying a husband for his daughter, and immediately made her leave Paris and come home. She obeyed with the worst possible grace; and suddenly looked up through her sulks and saw someone as spectacular as Rochefort, Dr Richard Marsden Pankhurst, and fell in love with him.

It was, on the surface, an astounding match. He was twice her age, a scholar with many academic honours, a distinguished jurist, whose studies filled all his leisure hours. He was dedicated to public work, of a laborious and unrewarded sort; he achieved great things in the promotion of popular education, he was a republican and an indefatigable enemy of Disraeli's imperialism. He had a great position in the North. When he arrived at a meeting thousands waited cheering and waving their handkerchiefs. Though he had what would have been a crushing handicap for most politicians, an extremely unpleasant, shrill, edgy voice, the force of his mind and the transparent beauty of his nature was such that an audience never remained conscious of this defect for more than the first few minutes. He was a saint who had put all weaknesses behind him and wore himself out in acts of benevolence. Such works of art were these private good deeds that they had something of that immortality: a visitor to Manchester more than a decade after his death thought that he must have been dead only a month or so, so vividly had some whom he had helped spoken of him.

But Emmeline was just a wicked little thing, fond of pretty clothes and French novels. It happened, however, to be a perfectly right and wise marriage. Emmeline committed herself gravely and honestly to her love for him. Her mother was deeply shocked, and tried to inspire her to the proper female monkey-tricks by telling her of the coldness with which she herself had received her prospective husband's wooings, and was shocked still more when her daughter suggested to her betrothed as a protest against the then legal disabilities of married women, that they should form a free union. (Noémie's mother had married Henri de Rochefort only on her deathbed to give her children a legal protector.) Dr Pankhurst would not consent, however, partly because he feared to expose her to disrespect, partly because he knew that those who challenged the marriage laws were usually prevented from challenging any other abuses. So they married, and were happy ever after. Not the bitterest critic of Mrs Pankhurst ever suggested that her husband did not find her, from beginning to end of the nineteen years of their marriage, a perfect wife.

They had five children: Christabel, who was born when her mother was twenty-two, Sylvia, born two years later, Frank, born two years later, Adela, born a year later and Harry, born four years later. Theirs was not a home in which parents exerted themselves to keep their children's lives a thing apart, a pool of quietness in which they could develop until they were mature. Mrs Pankhurst was a young woman, full of appetite for life, and wildly in love with her husband, so that she was delighted to stand by him in his public work. She did not neglect her children, but the stream of affairs flowed through her home and the children bobbed like corks on the tide of adult life. One of them hated it. Sylvia Pankhurst's *The Suffragette Movement* stands beside Gordon Craig's *Memories of My Mother* as an expression of the burning resentment that the child of a brilliant mother may feel at having to share her brilliance with the world. But the other children liked it, and revelled in the dramas that followed one after another. First there was the famous Manchester by-election, at which Dr Pankhurst stood as an Independent candidate on a platform including adult suffrage, republicanism, secular education, the payment of members of Parliament, Disestablishment, Home Rule, disarmament and a kind of League of Nations. The year was 1883. He was not elected; but a quarter of the electorate supported him – an incredible proportion at that time – and his expenses were £500 as against his opponent's £5,000. It was a triumphant piece of propaganda work; but it ended in personal bitterness, in the first display by Mrs Pankhurst of that ruthlessness which she shared with the armed prophets. Till then she and her family had lived in her father's home, a patriarchal dwelling where the Manx mistress of the house carried on all the domestic arts, even to bread-baking and butter-making. But though Robert Goulden had stood by Dr Pank-hurst during the by-election, he rebuked him afterwards for his socialist extremism, and to mark a dissociation of political interests Dr Pankhurst and his family left the Goulden home, accompanied by Mrs Pankhurst's sister Mary. On this separation Mrs Pankhurst re-minded her father that he had promised her some property on her marriage. He denied ever having made such a promise. They never spoke to each other again.

This deep feeling over a matter of property was odd to find in a woman who all her life long regarded money chiefly as something to give away. But it was a consequence of the simple, surgical directness of her mind. If Robert Goulden wanted to accept the masculinist and capitalist world, then he ought to be logical about it, and protect her in the only way that a woman can be protected in a masculinist and capitalist world. The only reason he could have for failing to do so must be that he did not love her. But it must also be remembered that her childhood hero had been Charles I, the King who lost his crown and his head, and that she attached an importance to Henri de Rochefort's refusal to use his marquisate which was, since the renunciation had actually been made by a previous generation of the family, historically undue. The men she specially admired were those who had power and renounced it. It is an indication that in her there was an element of sex-antagonism, that neurosis which revolts against the difference of the sexes, which calls on the one to which the neurotic does not belong to sacrifice its special advantage so that the one to which the neurotic does belong may show superior. But neuroses often engender the dynamic power by which the sane part of the mind carries on its business. Mrs Pankhurst sublimated her sex-antagonism. She was in no way a man-hater, loving her sons as deeply as her daughters, and she completely converted her desire to offend the other sex into a desire to defend her own.

Dr Pankhurst stood for Parliament again at Rotherhithe, and was again defeated. There followed a painful libel action. A Conservative speaker had told a lying story which put into Dr Pankhurst's mouth a coarse declaration of atheism. He was in fact an agnostic of the gentlest type, full of reverence and love for the person of Christ. He brought action, not so much for his own sake as to bring a test case which would show how far socialist candidates could find remedy in the new libel law for the flood of slanderous abuse that was turned on them at every election. There were aspects of this libel action which were calculated to remove certain comfortable illusions about human nature from the minds of the least critical. Dr Pankhurst, never worldly-wise, appealed to Mr A. J. Balfour as a brother agnostic, on the undisputable evidence of certain passages in *A Defence of Philosophic Doubt*. Mr Balfour received the appeal without brotherly enthusiasm, and practised the arts of evasion to avoid associating himself with this crude imbroglio. The trial itself was conducted with what might have seemed shameless prejudice to those who did not know that British justice is above suspicion. Mrs Pankhurst ran the risk of prosecution for contempt of court by sending a cutting letter to the judge who tried the case.

The Pankhursts went to live in London. There Mrs Pankhurst was extremely happy. It is true that shortly after she settled there her son

Frank died and her grief was terrible. But she had a gay time establishing herself as a political hostess with tea-urns in Russell Square
for the socialist London that was humbly proliferating in the Fabian
Society, the Social Democratic Federation, the Independent Labour
Party and half a dozen other obscure organisations; a naïve and
ludicrous parody, it must have seemed to those who really knew the
world, of the real social functions of power, where great ladies shining with diamonds received at the head of wide staircases under
magnificent chandeliers. She worked hard for all feminist causes,
for all issues which promised man more liberty, although always
she regarded herself not as an independent worker, but as her husband's helpmate. She had much amusement, too, trying to support
herself by running Emerson's, a kind of amateurish Liberty's. The
French influence came back into her life at full strength, for Henri
de Rochefort was an exile living in London and he constantly
visited her.

It had to come to an end soon. Both Mrs Pankhurst and her husband
were children about money. They spent it, not like drunken sailors
but like drunken saints. They gave it away with both hands. Emerson's,
owing to bad costing, was an expensive toy. They had taken the
Russell Square house on the fag-end of a lease without reflecting that
at the end they would have to pay dilapidations. In bad order they
retreated to Lancashire, first to Southport, and then to Manchester,
where they got on a sounder financial footing and Mrs Pankhurst
came to her proper form as a social worker. She helped to organise the
unemployed in the slump of 1894, and did much to popularise her
husband's views on productive public works as a means of relieving
unemployment. She was elected to the Chorlton Board of Guardians,
and blazed with rage because she found the little girls in the workhouse still wearing eighteenth-century dress, with low necks and no
sleeves. For some obscure reason they had no nightdresses, and they
had no drawers or knickers, even in winter-time – a fact which
infuriated her beyond bearing -- because the matron and a couple of
refined female guardians had been too modest to mention such garments to the male members of the Board. This was the kind of
tomfoolery which Mrs Pankhurst could not stand, and which her
movement did much to end. These, and many other abuses, she
reformed.

There was a fight, too, against an attempt by the City Council to
deny the I L P, now newly become formidable, the right of meeting in
the public places of Manchester. Mrs Pankhurst acted as chairman to
the speakers at the test meeting, sticking the ferrule of her open

umbrella in the ground so that the faithful could throw their pennies into it. With eight others she was arrested, and stood calmly in the dock, dressed her prettiest, wearing a little pink straw bonnet. The case against her was dismissed, though she announced that she would repeat the offence so long as she was at liberty. This she did, although she was summoned again and again. She always wore her pink straw bonnet, and it became the signal round which the rebels gathered. This was a real fight, and it took a long time to win. She lived therefore for many months under the expectation of prison. She was willing then, had the need arisen, to prove the point she proved later.

There was an election, too, at Gorton, Lancashire, where Dr Pankhurst stood as ILP candidate. The ILP had the scantiest funds, and had to use cheap methods of campaign, such as chalking announcements of meetings on the pavements. For £343 of election expenses against the Conservative candidate's £1,375, Dr Pankhurst gained 4,261 votes against the Conservative's 5,865. The Pankhurst children helped in the campaign, and it was no minor part of their education, which was indeed unconventional.

Mrs Pankhurst as a mother offers certain surprises to those who would expect her to have the same views as the kind of woman who has followed in her steps regarding feminism. She was thoroughly of her time. She believed in corporal punishment for children as mothers did in the eighties, and in making them finish their porridge even if their stomachs revolted against it. She had some of the prejudices of her Manx country-bred mother. She had no such great opinion of fresh air as a nursery remedy, and she strongly disapproved of spectacles, causing her younger son, who had weak eyes, great inconvenience thereby. And in one respect she was almost behind her times. She attached no importance to ordinary education for her daughters. They were often put in the care of governesses who gave them no lessons whatsoever, but trained them in such unusual subjects as the appreciation of Egyptian art; and when they did attend schools she connived shamelessly at their truancy. This was due in part, perhaps, to her knowledge that schools were so much part of the capitalist system that her family could have no comfortable welcome there, and it is true that at least one headmistress persecuted and humiliated the children because their father was a socialist. In those days political rancours went deeper than we care to imagine today. When Mrs Pankhurst was on the Manchester Education Committee she had to intervene to protect a woman teacher who had been dismissed by the owner of a school because it had leaked out that she was the daughter of Ernest Jones, the Chartist, who had been dead for over thirty years.

But there was also a deeper reason for Mrs Pankhurst's unconcern about education. It is said that the only occasion on which she showed overwhelming grief about a personal matter other than over the death of her husband and her sons and her final alienation from one of her family, was when her daughter Christabel decided that she would not become a professional dancer. The child had shown great promise at her dancing classes, and it had been her mother's dream that she should become a great ballerina, who should practise her art all over the world. This anecdote has been repeated querulously, as if it were proof of Mrs Pankhurst's lightmindedness. But it surely gives a clue to the secret of her greatness as a leader. She knew that no culture can evolve values which wholly negate primitive ones. She would have understood that Sir Walter Scott's boy spoke better sense than the learned when, brought up in ignorance of *Waverley* and its fame, he accounted for the fuss people made of his father by saying, 'It's commonly him that sees the hare sitting.' She had not lost touch with primitive wisdom; she knew that man's first necessity is to be a good animal, that rhythm can prove as much as many arguments, that the mind is only one of the instruments of human power.

Dr Pankhurst died. His widow was heartbroken. For a time she was too distracted to attend to any public work. But she could not be idle, for she was without means. Her husband had been splendidly careless about money. His last months had been spent in successfully organising opposition to a dirty and dangerous scheme by which the Manchester Corporation intended to pollute the Mersey with the town sewage by diverting it through a new culvert, designed to dump it in a part of the river outside the scope of sanitary jurisdiction. Had he not opposed the construction of the culvert he would have been instructed to act as Counsel for the scheme, and might have made over £8,000 by it. With poverty earned thus his family were well content, but Mrs Pankhurst had to work. She became Registrar of Births and Deaths in Chorlton and opened another Emerson's, which lingered on for some time and then had to be abandoned. She came back to public life for a little in 1900, in the pro-Boer agitation. Then she began to feel a special interest in woman suffrage, perhaps because her daughter Christabel had suddenly, and for the first time, become keenly interested in feminism, and was studying for a law degree at Victoria University. It also happened that about this time she was stung to fury by an incident connected with a memorial to her dead husband. Though she had accepted some funds raised by his wealthier friends, she had refused to touch the subscriptions gathered from the predominantly working-class readers of Robert Blatchford's *The Clarion*, on the grounds that she did not wish them to give her children an education which they could not have afforded for their own; and she suggested that the money should be spent on building a Pankhurst Memorial Hall for the use of socialist societies. When it was finished she found that the branch of the Independent Labour Party which was to use it as headquarters refused to admit women. This led her to review the attitude of the ILP and the socialist movement generally towards feminism. She found that it was no more than lukewarm; and therefore on 10 October 1903, in her drawing-room at 62 Nelson Street, she held the inaugural meeting of a society called the Women's Social and Political Union.

For the first two years the proceedings of this society were limited to humdrum harrying of the socialist societies. But the result of this routine was to force up to explosion point Mrs Pankhurst's realisation of the wrongs inflicted on women by their status, and the indifference on this subject which was felt by even the most progressive societies dominated by men. It was becoming every day more clear, too, that a certain condition she found necessary if she was to act effectively was about to be abundantly fulfilled. Oddly enough, she never did anything important alone. She had to work with an ally. For that purpose Dr Pankhurst had been perfect; but the development of her daughter Christabel made her see that he might not be irreplaceable. Though Christabel had never studied anything but dancing at all seriously until her middle teens, she was taking her law studies well, and when she went up to London to apply for admission to the Benchers of Lincoln's Inn she conducted the proceedings with a strange, cool, high-handed mastery that was remarkable in a girl in her early twenties.

In 1905 Mrs Pankhurst came to London to find a private member who would give his place in the ballot to a measure giving votes for women. There was then, as for many years before, a majority of members in the House pledged to support woman suffrage, but this meant nothing more than a polite bow and smile to their more earnest female helpers in their constituencies. Hardly any of them meant to lift a little finger to make woman suffrage an accomplished fact.

Mrs Pankhurst had the greatest difficulty in finding a sincere suffragist among the small number of members who had been fortunate in the ballot that gave them the right to introduce a Bill on one or other of the Friday afternoons of the session; but on 12 May, Mr Bamford Slack brought in a Suffrage Bill. Mrs Pankhurst brought with her to the House of Commons an immense number of women, which was swelled by members of the more old-fashioned and conservative suffrage societies, who had been excited by the agitation of the new movement. There were so many that they filled the lobby, the passages and the terrace. When it became obvious that the Bill was, as usual, going to be obstructed and talked out, Mrs Pankhurst looked round her at the great crowd of women. Much more than the future of the feminist movement was decided in that second. Then she scribbled a note to be taken in to the Prime Minister in which, with the arrogance of a leader writing to a leader, she told him that unless he gave facilities for the further discussion of this Bill her Union would work against his Government. She was a little woman in her late forties, without a penny, without a powerful friend. The threat was comic. As soon as the Bill was talked out, there was an impromptu meeting outside the House which would have been stopped had not Keir Hardie intervened.

Mrs Pankhurst went home. There were some new recruits in the North: a mill-girl called Annie Kenney, an Irish schoolteacher called Teresa Billington. All that summer Mrs Pankhurst with these girls and Christabel and Sylvia went from wake to wake in the Lancashire and Yorkshire mill-towns, and stood on I L P and trade-union platforms. In the autumn Sir Edward Grey came to speak at Manchester, and failed to reply to a letter from the Women's Social and Political Union asking him to receive a deputation. They attended his meeting and asked questions regarding the attitude of the coming Liberal Government. But these were not answered, so they interrupted the subsequent proceedings and were ejected. Outside the hall they addressed a meeting and were arrested on a charge of having assaulted the police, and were sent to prison for seven and three days in the third division. It is hardly necessary to say that the balance of the assaults committed on this occasion were committed by the stewards and policemen on the suffragists; but the suffragists would themselves hardly have troubled to raise that point. They candidly admitted they had meant to be arrested. For it was their intention to maintain that in a democratic State government rests on the consent of the governed, and that until they were granted the franchise on the same terms as men they were going to withhold that consent; and that they were going to mark the withholding of their consent by disturbing the peace, to the precise degree which the resistance of the Government made necessary; and that they would not take it that the Government had yielded unless whatever party was in power itself passed an Act for the enfranchisement of women.

For nine years this policy was carried into effect by innumerable women under the leadership of Mrs Pankhurst. For nine years no politician of any importance could address a meeting without fear of interruption. There was never any lack of women volunteers for this purpose, even though the stewards nearly always ejected them with great physical violence, sometimes of a sort that led to grave internal injuries. One of the most brilliant suffragists, or suffragettes, as the *Daily Mail* started people calling them, Mary Gawthorpe, was an invalid for many years as a result of a blow received in this way. When the harried political organisers tried to solve the problem by excluding all women from the meetings, interruptions were made through windows and skylights, even if this involved perilous climbing over roofs and gutters, and evading police search by concealment in neighbouring attics for two or three days. There were also constant disturbances at the House of Commons. When a Private Member's Bill for woman suffrage was being talked out in 1906, Mrs Pankhurst and some friends created a riot in the ladies' gallery. From that time repeated raids were made on the House of Commons by women seeking interviews with Cabinet Ministers, and these became in time vast riots which it taxed the power of Scotland Yard to keep within bounds. All the area round Whitehall and St Stephen's Square was packed with people, watching while women threw themselves against a cordon of police and withstood massed charges of mounted men. The spectators divided themselves as the night went on into supporters and opponents, and there would be dashes made to rescue individual women or to manhandle them. The police were ordered to make as few arrests as possible, so some of the women would find themselves thrown about like so many footballs.

Participation in these interruptions and in these riots meant imprisonment. Very soon the women were getting sentences of six weeks' imprisonment. They rose soon to three months, to nine months, to two years. To put the Government in an impossible position they hunger-struck, abstaining from food, and sometimes even from water. At first they were released. Then the Government employed surgical methods of forcible feeding. The prisoners resisted that, but this meant that their gums were hacked to pieces with steel gags, and the tubes were apt to injure the internal organs, and the food was often vomited, so they frequently had to be released all the same.

Then the Government passed the Cat-and-Mouse Act, which enabled
them to release the hunger-striking prisoners when they were within
touching distance of death, wait till they had recovered their health,
and then arrest them again and bring them back to death once more,
and so on. It was one of the most unlovely expedients that the English
legislature has ever invented, and it is ironical that it should have
been the work of a Liberal government. And it had the further disgrace of being ineffectual, for it entirely failed to quench the movement. That spread like wild-fire over the country. It had hundreds of
thousands of supporters, its income rose to nearly £38,000 a year, its
weekly newspaper had a circulation of 40,000. It held enthusiastic
meetings all over the country, though its militancy evoked attack,
and suffragist speakers were not protected as were Cabinet Ministers.
Many suffered grave physical injury. But for the most part these
meetings were passionate acclamations of the rightness of the cause
and its leaders. London saw long, long processions, longer than it had
ever known follow any other than Mrs Pankhurst.

The Press was overwhelmingly against them; which was one of the
first proofs that the modern sensational newspaper has no real influence, that its readers buy it for its news and not for its opinions.
There were, of course, certain noble supporters among journalists,
such as Mr Nevinson, Mr Brailsford and the late Mr H. W.
Massingham; but for the rest the Press loved to represent the movement with contempt and derision. Mrs Pankhurst and her daughters
were crazy hooligans, their followers were shrieking hysterics, their
policy was wild delirium. Nothing could be further from the truth.
The movement contained some of the *détraqués* who follow any
drum that is beaten, but these were weeded out, for the Cat and
Mouse Act was something of a test for the solider qualities.

But the movement was neither crazy nor hysterical nor delirious. It
was stone-cold in its realism. Mrs Pankhurst was not a clever
woman, but when she experienced something she incorporated it in
her mind and used it as a basis for action. When she started the
Women's Social and Political Union she was sure of two things: that
the ideas of freedom and justice which had been slowly developing in
England during the eighteenth and nineteenth centuries had grown to
such maturity that there existed an army of women resentful of being
handicapped by artificial disadvantages imposed simply on the
grounds of their sex, and that sex-antagonism was so strong among
men that it produced an attitude which, if it were provoked to candid
expression, would make every self-respecting woman want to fight it.
In both of these suppositions she was entirely correct. The real force

that made the suffrage movement was the quality of the opposition. Women, listening to anti-suffrage speeches, for the first time knew what many men really thought of them. One such speech that brought many into the movement had for its climax a jocular description of a future female Lord Chancellor being seized with labour pains on the woolsack, and left no doubt that the speaker considered labour pains themselves, apart from the setting, a funny subject. The allegation, constantly made, that all women became insane at the age of forty-five also roused much resentment. But apart from general principles, the wicked frivolity of the attitude adopted towards the women by the Liberal Government was the real recruiting-sergeant for the movement.

It must be remembered that the majority of the Liberal members of parliament, and indeed the majority of the Cabinet, were pledged to support woman suffrage. There was therefore every logical and every moral reason why they should have granted it; and they did not need to fear the ignominy of seeming to yield to force, for Christabel, with her fine political mind, frequently declared truces and gave them every opportunity to save their bacon. The explanation commonly accepted – and it is the only one that appears possible – was that the opposition to votes for women was insisted on by one important member of the Cabinet, influenced by the views of his wife who has since published book after book of almost incredible silliness. That the protection women can expect from men is highly limited and personal in its scope many suffragists learned, as they noticed that the stewards of Liberal meetings not only ejected them, but thoroughly enjoyed inflicting as much physical injury on them as possible. They were to learn that even more poignantly in the next few years, as they hid in cellars from bombs dropped by the protective sex; but the previous lesson was even more disgusting, because it was completely gratuitous. The matter could have been settled in ten minutes. But it was not, and the Cabinet Ministers who might have settled it saw nothing to limit their stewards to the task of ejection and often even encouraged them to exceed it; and outside the halls they showed even less adherence to the standards to which, one had believed, our governors adhered.

Was justice, even British justice, blind? The case of Lady Constance Lytton suggested it was not. She, chivalrous soul, suspected that some of the suffrage prisoners were roughly treated because they were persons of no social importance. She herself had been sentenced to six weeks' imprisonment, and had been instantly dismissed as medically unfit. She went to jail again, not as Lord Lytton's sister but as Jane Warton, a seamstress, and although on the second occasion as on the first she had mitral disease of the heart, she was forcibly fed within an inch of her life.

Mrs Pankhurst had said that she would go on applying pressure to the Government till it yielded. She continued to do so. She seemed made of steel, although she had suffered a most crushing bereavement in the death of her son Harry in distressing circumstances. He had contracted infantile paralysis, and to pay for his nursing-home expenses, which seemed likely to continue indefinitely, she had to leave him to go on a lecture tour in America, since for all the tens of thousands of pounds that were coming into the Union she drew no more than £200 a year. Shortly after her return he died, and this inflicted a blow from which she never recovered. But she went on inflexibly along the road she had planned. She thought of new ways of making the Government's existence intolerable every day. The plate-glass windows in the West End of London went down one night in a few minutes to answer the challenge of a member of the Government who had reproached the suffragists for having committed no act of violence comparable to the pulling up of Hyde Park railings by the Reform rioters of 1867. Christabel fled to France so that the movement could be sure of one leader to dictate the policy. Mrs Pankhurst and the two other chief officials of the Union, Frederick and Emmeline Pethick Lawrence, were tried for conspiracy and sentenced to nine months' imprisonment, in spite of the jury's plea that they should be treated with the utmost leniency. They hunger-struck and were released.

But a new side of her implacability then showed itself. Her policy had meant a ruthless renunciation of old ties. She had cut herself off entirely from the Labour Party; she was even prepared, in these later years, to attack it as a component part of the Liberal Party's majority. She had silenced her youngest daughter, Adela, as a speaker because of her frank socialist bias, and her second daughter Sylvia afterwards left the Union to form societies that were as much Labour as suffragist in the East End. She had been merciless in her preservation of party discipline. There was no nonsense about democracy in the Women's Social and Political Union. Teresa Billington had long been driven out for raising the topic. Mrs Pankhurst, Christabel and the Lawrences exercised an absolute dictatorship. But now the Lawrences had to go. They opposed further prosecution of militancy, and Christabel and Mrs Pankhurst quietly told them to relinquish their positions in the Union. There was more than appears to be said for the Pankhursts' position from their point of view. They knew that the Government intended to strip the Pethick Lawrences of their fortune by recovering from them (as the only moneyed officials of the Union) the cost of all the damage done by the militants; and as they knew that in actual fact Christabel settled the policy of the Union, they saw no reason why the Pethick Lawrences should stay on to the embarrassment of all persons concerned. But the Pethick Lawrences were heartbroken. Not for a moment did the crisis appal Mrs Pankhurst. Letters were burned in pillar-boxes; houses – but only empty ones – went up in flames; riot was everywhere. Mrs Pankhurst was again tried for conspiracy, and this time received a sentence of three years' imprisonment, though again the jury fervently recommended her to mercy. She was then dragged in and out of prison under the Cat-and-Mouse Act, while militancy rose to a pitch that had never been imagined by its most fervent supporters, and acquired a strange, new character of ultimate desperation. Emily Wilding Davison tried to stop the Derby by throwing herself under the horses' hooves and, as she had anticipated, was killed. A vast silent cortège of women followed her coffin through the streets. Mrs Pankhurst, rising from her bed in a nursing home to attend the funeral, was re-arrested. But they were careful never quite to break her body. Both the Government and the suffragettes knew what was bound to happen if Mrs Pankhurst should be killed.

Suddenly war came, and in the sight of the world her star darkened. Immediately the pacifism she had learned from Dr Pankhurst vanished and left no trace. In an instant she stopped all militancy, all suffrage work; with perfect discipline her army disbanded. She then declared herself a jingo, her paper the *Suffragette* became *Britannia*, and Christabel wrote leaders that grew into more crudely chauvinist attacks on certain members of the Government such as Lord Grey of Fallodon, for insufficiently vigorous prosecution of the war. But this did not represent nearly such a fundamental reversal as might be supposed. She had, after all, been brought up in France just after the Franco-Prussian War, and she had then conceived a lifelong hatred of Germany; and there was nothing surprising if *Britannia* translated it into French. '*J'ai eu la faiblesse de croire qu'un Bonaparte pouvait être autre chose qu'un assassin . . .*' Rochefort would have thought himself failing in an obvious duty if he had let a day pass without announcing that somebody, somewhere, was betraying France. This astonishing trace of the influence of French politics on Mrs Pankhurst, so little modified by time, makes us realise that the suffrage movement had been the copy of a French model executed with north-country persistence. We had been watching a female General Boulanger with nous.

Besides these patriotic successes and some propaganda for women's war service, Mrs Pankhurst and her daughter did little, and they did not undertake any important administrative duties. They were both of them trained and temperamentally adapted for political organisation, for which there was now no place; and the older woman, who was now fifty-six and had been leading a campaign life in and out of prison for eleven years, was too exhausted for any first-rate work. It is said that Christabel Pankhurst did much good work, much better than her writings would suggest, in an advisory capacity to a certain politician. But this was not ostentatiously done, and it must have seemed to many of their followers that Mrs Pankhurst and her daughter had passed into obscurity. Yet it was then that she did perhaps the most decisive suffrage work of her life. She persuaded a certain important politician that when peace came again she could reassemble her party and begin militancy where it had left off. There were many other causes which united to contribute to the triumph of the suffrage cause at that time. Parallel to the militant movement had developed a non-militant movement, also immensely powerful, which had caused a dangerous discontent among the older political parties. But if the threat of Mrs Pankhurst's existence had not been there women might not have been given the vote on the same terms as men in 1917, ostensibly as a reward for their war services.

After that victory, Mrs Pankhurst wellnigh vanished from the eyes of her followers. The rebellious glory was departed. She repudiated utterly now everything she had fought for in her youth beside her husband, and came out of the war a high Tory. She seemed a little puzzled what to do, for her ally had left her. Christabel, the quality of whose mind remains a profound mystery, had taken one look at the map of Europe, spread out in the sunshine of peace, and had grown pale with horror. Her gift for foreseeing political events had often amounted to clairvoyance, and there is reason to suppose that it did not desert her then. Her realisation had the effect, curious in Dr Pankhurst's daughter, bred in agnosticism, of making her announce that here were the signs and portents that herald the second coming of the Lord Jesus Christ. She went to America and led a frugal life as an evangelist of a sober and unsensational kind, devoting her leisure to the care of an adopted daughter. For a time Mrs Pankhurst lived in Canada, delivering lectures to women's societies on such subjects as the legal protection of women and children, public health, the blessings of the British Empire, and the contempt for liberty she had seen during a visit to Russia. But finally she returned to England and accepted the post of nursing the unpromising constituency of Whitechapel as a Tory candidate, a duty which she fulfilled conscientiously. She secured no financial advantage by this conservatism, for she was paid only a pittance and lived over a baker's shop; she could have attained a much higher standard of living by remaining an unattached feminist writer and lecturer. Now she enjoyed life in little, gentle, old-ladyish ways. She loved window-shopping, and sometimes bought a dress at the sales and remodelled it herself. She liked dropping in on her old friends, the Marshalls, where 'she had her own chair', and talking about the old days in France, about her husband, about her dead boys. There were letters from Christabel and Adela who, though long alienated from her mother by her communist views, was ultimately reconciled to her. But Mrs Pankhurst had never wanted to be old, and her body had been hideously maltreated. As a result of injuries received in forcible feedings, she still suffered from a recurrent form of jaundice. In 1928, shortly after women had received full adult suffrage, she went to church on Easter Monday in the country, was driven home to Whitechapel, took to her bed and, for no particular medical reason, died. She left £72.

It is all forgotten. We forget everything now. We have forgotten what came before the war. We have forgotten the war. There are so many newspapers so full of so much news, so many motor-cars, so many films, that image is superimposed on image and nothing is clearly seen. In an emptier age, which left more room for the essential, it would be remembered that Emmeline Pankhurst with all her limitations was glorious. Somehow, in her terse, austere way she was as physically glorious as Ellen Terry or Sarah Bernhardt. She was glorious in her physical courage, in her obstinacy, in her integrity. Her achievements have suffered in repute owing to the fashion of jeering at the parliamentary system. Women novelists who want to strike out a line as being specially broadminded declare they think we are no better for the vote; if they spent half an hour turning over pre-war newspapers and looking out references to women's employment and legal and social status, they might come to a different opinion. Women who do not like working in offices and cannot get married write letters to the papers ascribing their plight to feminism. But even before women got the vote they had to work in offices, with the only difference that they received less money and worked under worse conditions; and then as now there existed no machinery to compel men to marry women they did not want. Few intelligent women in a position to compare the past with the present will deny that the vote brought with it substantial benefits of both a material and spiritual kind.

There were also incidental benefits arising out of the movement. The suffragettes' indignant denunciation of the insanitary conditions in the jails meant an immense advance of public opinion regarding penal reform. In 1913 it suddenly came into Christabel Pankhurst's head to write a series of articles regarding the prevalence of venereal disease. These were ill-informed and badly written, but they scattered like wind an age-long conspiracy of prudishness, and enabled society to own the existence of these diseases and set about exterminating them as had never been possible before. But Mrs Pankhurst's most valuable indirect contribution to her time was made in May 1905; a dusty and obscure provincial, she sent in a threatening note to the Prime Minister, and spent the next years proving that the threat had thunder and lightning behind it. She thereby broke down the assumption of English politicians, which till then no legislative actions, no extensions of the franchise had been able to touch, that the only people who were politically important were those who were socially important; and all the democratic movements of her day shared in the benefits. It would be absurd to deny that the ultimate reason for the rise of the Labour Party was the devoted work of its adherents, but it would be equally absurd to deny that between 1905 and 1914 it found its path smoothed by an increasingly respectful attitude on the part of St Stephen's, the Press and the public.

But Mrs Pankhurst's chief and most poignant value to the historian will be her demonstration of what happens to a great human being of action in a transition period. She was the last popular leader to act on inspiration derived from the principles of the French Revolution; she put her body and soul at the service of Liberty, Equality and Fraternity, and earned a triumph for them. Then doubt seized her, as it was to seize a generation. In the midst of her battle for democracy she was obliged, lest that battle should be lost, to become a dictator. Later we were all to debate whether the sacrifice of principle could be justified in the case of Russia. She trembled under the strain of conflict, and perhaps she trembled also because she foresaw that she was to gain a victory, and then confront a mystery. She had always said and felt she wanted the vote to feed the hungry. Enfranchised, she found herself aware that economic revolution was infinitely more difficult and drastic than the fiercest political revolution. With her childlike honesty, her hate of pretentiousness, she failed to put up a good show to cover her perplexity. She spoke the truth – she owned she saw it better to camp among the ruins of capitalism than to push out into the uncharted desert. With her whole personality she enacted our perplexity, as earlier she had enacted our revolt, a priestess of the people.

This account is founded chiefly on my own recollections, and on the writings of Sylvia Pankhurst, in conversations with Mrs Marshall, and from notes supplied by Mr Arthur Marshall, to whom I would like to express my gratitude.

1933

Part IV

A Blast from
the Female Vortex

'Indissoluble Matrimony',
a short story from *Blast 1*, 20 June 1914

Editor's Introduction

'Indissoluble Matrimony' was published in the first number of Wyndham Lewis's *Blast*, on 20 June 1914. The first version of Ford Madox Ford's *The Good Soldier*, herein titled 'The Saddest Story' was also in this issue, as well as work by Ezra Pound and Wyndham Lewis himself. *Blast* appeared 'just before the fog of war came down. It was of a bright puce colour, in general appearance not unlike a telephone book. It contained manifestos, poems, plays, stories, and outbursts of one sort or another.' It also contained visual material, and was the main organ of the Vorticist Movement in Britain of which Wyndham Lewis was a prominent member, both as writer and painter (see his fine portrait of Rebecca West).

Vorticism, as Malcolm Bradbury says, was 'one of the very few British modern-form movements in the arts'. It was compounded of various new sources of energy and form, and, unusually in Britain, it brought together both painters and writers in 'The Great English Vortex'. Wyndham Lewis, the editor of *Blast*, described the movement in writing as 'a hard, unromantic external presentation of kinetic forces, an arrangement of surfaces'.

One of *Blast*'s first blasts was at the suffragettes, who were exhorted in the boldest type to behave themselves where art was concerned (both the Rokeby 'Venus' and a portrait of Henry James had been damaged by suffragettes). 'In destruction, as in other things, stick to what you understand. We make you a present of our votes. Only leave works of art alone. You might some day destroy a good picture by accident . . . We admire your energy. You and artists are the only things (you don't mind being called things?) left in England with a little life in them . . . leave art alone, brave comrades.'

The experience of the world of political action had been invaluable for Rebecca West the artist. It was another group of 'cranks' from whom she learned at *Blast*. Among the ranks of the artistic rebels who wrote for it, Rebecca West met Ford Madox Ford, one of the stylists of the age. Their influence worked both ways. Ford's major contribution to the English novel was, with Conrad, the invention of the unreliable narrator, personally involved with the events of his story, and alternately confusing and exciting the reader, who must attempt to get at the truth. Ford's *The Good Soldier* was considered one of the finest examples of this technique. Rebecca West's *The Return of the Soldier*, like Ford's Tietjens novel *No More Parades*, is a study of shell shock and the effects of the First World War on the relations between the sexes. It is this novel of Rebecca West's written in 1919 ('this was the saddest spring' says its narrator), which reflects the Vorticist aesthetic most strongly. It succeeds aesthetically in modernist narrative technique, as a novel of social protest, a Freudian study of shell shock and a feminist comment on the male impotence which is the product of war.

The story that follows, brilliant in its own right, foreshadows the later fiction to come from Rebecca West's pen. An early champion of Ford and Lawrence, she is in 'Indissoluble Matrimony' writing in the psychological tradition of Lawrence and the Brontës. The story is a nightmare, hallucinatory in that it imagines with the greatest force the plight of the highly sexed intellectual socialist woman. It is a psychological study of impotent male rage in the battle of the sexes, and can be seen as a dramatisation of the title of one of her later essays, 'I Regard Marriage With Fear and Horror'. Part of its power is perhaps derived from the projection of her own fears. But that a 22-year-old girl could body forth those fears is a considerable feat, and it anticipates the depths of emotion of the second part of her much later novel *The Judge*. Unlike Ibsen's Rebecca West, *her* heroine does not drown in the mill race. George may not be able to dissolve their marriage ties but it is Evadne's spirit which is 'indissoluble'.

Indissoluble Matrimony

When George Silverton opened the front door he found that the house was not empty for all its darkness. The spitting noise of the striking of damp matches and mild, growling exclamations of annoyance told him that his wife was trying to light the dining-room gas. He went in and with some short, hostile sound of greeting lit a match and brought brightness into the little room. Then, irritated by his own folly in bringing private papers into his wife's presence, he stuffed the letters he had brought from the office deep into the pockets of his overcoat. He looked at her suspiciously, but she had not seen them, being busy in unwinding her orange motor-veil. His eyes remained on her face to brood a little sourly on her moving loveliness, which he had not been sure of finding: for she was one of those women who create an illusion alternately of extreme beauty and extreme ugliness. Under her curious dress, designed in some pitifully cheap and worthless stuff by a successful mood of her indiscreet taste – she had black blood in her – her long body seemed pulsing with some exaltation. The blood was coursing violently under her luminous yellow skin, and her lids, dusky with fatigue, drooped contentedly over her great humid black eyes. Perpetually she raised her hand to the mass of black hair that was coiled on her thick golden neck and stroked it with secretive enjoyment, as a cat licks its fur. And her large mouth smiled frankly, but abstractedly, at some digested pleasure.

There was a time when George would have looked on this riot of excited loveliness with suspicion. But now he knew it was almost certainly caused by some trifle – a long walk through stinging weather, the report of a socialist victory at a by-election, or the intoxication of a waltz refrain floating from the municipal bandstand across the flats of the local recreation ground. And even if it had been caused by some amorous interlude he would not have greatly cared. In the ten years since their marriage he had lost the quality which would have made him resentful. He now believed that quality to be purely physical. Unless one was in good condition and responsive to the messages sent out by the flesh Evadne could hardly concern one. He turned the bitter thought over in his heart and stung himself by deliberately gazing unmoved upon her beautiful joyful body.

'Let's have supper now!' she said rather greedily.

He looked at the table and saw she had set it before she went out. As usual she had been in an improvident hurry: it was carelessly done. Besides what an absurd supper to set before a hungry solicitor's clerk! In the centre, obviously intended as the principal dish, was a bowl of plums, softly red, soaked with the sun, glowing like jewels in the downward stream of the incandescent light. Beside them was a great yellow melon, its sleek sides fluted with rich growth, and a honeycomb glistening on a willow-pattern dish. The only sensible food to be seen was a plate of tongue laid at his place.

'I can't sit down to supper without washing my hands!'

While he splashed in the bathroom upstairs he heard her pull a chair to the table and sit down to her supper. It annoyed him. There was no ritual about it. While he was eating the tongue she would be crushing honey on new bread, or stripping a plum of its purple skin and holding the golden globe up to the gas to see the light filter through. The meal would pass in silence. She would innocently take his dumbness for a sign of abstraction and forbear to babble. He would find the words choked on his lips by the weight of dullness that always oppressed him in her presence. Then, just about the time when he was beginning to feel able to formulate his obscure grievances against her, she would rise from the table without a word and run upstairs to her work, humming in that uncanny, Negro way of hers.

And so it was. She ate with an appalling catholicity of taste, with a nice child's love of sweet foods, and occasionally she broke into that hoarse, beautiful croon. Every now and then she looked at him with too obvious speculations as to whether his silence was due to weariness or uncertain temper. Timidly she cut him an enormous slice of the melon, which he did not want. Then she rose abruptly and flung herself into the rocking-chair on the hearth. She clasped her hands behind her head and strained backwards so that the muslin stretched over her strong breasts. She sang softly to the ceiling.

There was something about the fantastic figure that made him feel as though they were not properly married.

'Evadne?'

''S?'

'What have you been up to this evening?'

'I was at Milly Stafordale's.'

He was silent again. That name brought up the memory of his courting days. It was under the benign eyes of blonde, plebeian Milly that he had wooed the distracting creature in the rocking-chair.

Ten years before, when he was twenty-five, his firm had been reduced to hysteria over the estates of an extraordinarily stupid old woman, named Mrs Mary Ellerker. Her stupidity, grappling with the complexity of the sources of the vast income which rushed in spate from the properties of four deceased husbands, demanded oceans of explanations even over her weekly rents. Silverton alone in the office, by reason of a certain natural incapacity for excitement, could deal calmly with this marvel of imbecility. He alone could endure to sit with patience in the black-panelled drawing-room amidst the jungle of shiny mahogany furniture and talk to a mass of darkness, who rested heavily in the window-seat and now and then made an idiotic remark in a bright, hearty voice. But it shook even him. Mrs Mary Ellerker was obscene. Yet she was perfectly sane and although of that remarkable plainness noticeable in most oft-married women, in good enough physical condition. She merely presented the loathsome spectacle of an ignorant mind, contorted by the artificial idiocy of coquetry, lack of responsibility and hatred of discipline, stripped naked by old age. That was the real horror of her. One feared to think how many women were really like Mrs Ellerker under their armour of physical perfection or social grace. For this reason he turned eyes of hate on Mrs Ellerker's pretty little companion, Milly Stafordale, who smiled at him over her embroidery with wintry northern brightness. When she was old she too would be obscene.

This horror obsessed him. Never before had he feared anything. He had never lived more than half an hour from a police station and, as he had by some chance missed the melancholy clairvoyance of adolescence, he had never conceived of any horror with which the police could not deal. This disgust of women revealed to him that the world is a place of subtle perils. He began to fear marriage as he feared death. The thought of intimacy with some lovely, desirable and necessary wife turned him sick as he sat at his lunch. The secret obscenity of women! He talked darkly of it to his friends. He wondered why the Church did not provide a service for the absolution of men after marriage. Wife desertion seemed to him a beautiful return of the tainted body to cleanliness.

On his fifth visit to Mrs Ellerker he could not begin his business at once. One of Milly Stafordale's friends had come in to sing to the old lady. She stood by the piano against the light, so that he saw her washed with darkness. And before he had time to apprehend the sleepy wonder of her beauty, she had begun to sing. Now he knew that her voice was a purely physical attribute, built in her as she lay in her mother's womb, and no index of her spiritual values. But then, as it welled up from the thick golden throat and clung to her lips, it seemed a sublime achievement of the soul. It was smouldering contralto such as only those of black blood can possess. As she sang her great black eyes lay on him with the innocent shamelessness of a young animal, and he remembered hopefully that he was good-looking. Suddenly she stood in silence, playing with her heavy black plait. Mrs Ellerker broke into silly thanks. The girl's mother, who had been playing the accompaniment, rose and stood rolling up her music. Silverton, sick with excitement, was introduced to them. He noticed that the mother was a little darker than the conventions permit. Their name was Hannan – Mrs Arthur Hannan and Evadne. They moved lithely and quietly out of the room, the girl's eyes still lingering on his face.

The thought of her splendour and the rolling echoes of her voice disturbed him all night. Next day, going to his office, he travelled with her on the horse-car that bound his suburb to Petrick. One of the horses fell lame, and she had time to tell him that she was studying at a commercial college. He quivered with distress. All the time he had a dizzy illusion that she was nestling up against him. They parted shyly. During the next few days they met constantly. He began to go and see them in the evening at their home – a mean flat crowded with cheap glories of bead curtains and Oriental hangings that set off the women's alien beauty. Mrs Hannan was a widow and they lived alone, in a wonderful silence. He talked more than he had ever done in his whole life before. He took a dislike to the widow, she was consumed with fiery passions, no fit guardian for the tender girl.

Now he could imagine with what silent rapture Evadne had watched his agitation. Almost from the first she had meant to marry him. He was physically attractive, though not strong. His intellect was gently stimulating like a mild white wine. And it was time she married. She was ripe for adult things. This was the real wound in his soul. He had tasted of a divine thing created in his time for dreams out of her rich beauty, her loneliness, her romantic poverty, her immaculate youth. He had known love. And Evadne had never known anything more than a magnificent physical adventure which she had secured at the right time as she would have engaged a cab to take her to the station in time for the cheapest excursion train. It was a quick way to light-hearted living. With loathing he remembered how in the days of their engagement she used to gaze purely into his blinking eyes and with her unashamed kisses incite him to extravagant embraces. Now he cursed her for having obtained his spiritual revolution on false pretences. Only for a little time had he had his illusion, for their marriage was hastened by Mrs Hannan's sudden death. After three months of savage mourning Evadne flung herself into marriage, and her excited candour had enlightened him very soon.

That marriage had lasted ten years. And to Evadne their relationship was just the same as ever. Her vitality needed him as it needed the fruit on the table before him. He shook with wrath and a sense of outraged decency.

'Oh George!' She was yawning widely.

'What's the matter?' he said without interest.

'It's so beastly dull.'

'I can't help that, can I?'

'No.' She smiled placidly at him. 'We're a couple of dull dogs, aren't we? I wish we had children.'

After a minute she suggested, apparently as an alternative amusement, 'Perhaps the post hasn't passed.'

As she spoke there was a rat-tat and the slither of a letter under the door. Evadne picked herself up and ran out of the lobby. After a second or two, during which she made irritating inarticulate exclamations, she came in reading the letter and stroking her bust with a gesture of satisfaction.

'They want me to speak at Longton's meeting on the nineteenth,' she purred.

'Longton? What's he up to?'

Stephen Longton was the owner of the biggest iron-works in Petrick, a man whose refusal to adopt the livery of busy oafishness thought proper to commercial men aroused the gravest suspicions.

'He's standing as socialist candidate for the town council.'

'. . . Socialist!' he muttered.

He set his jaw. That was a side of Evadne he considered as little as possible. He had never been able to assimilate the fact that Evadne had, two years after their marriage, passed through his own orthodox radicalism to a passionate socialism, and that after reading enormously of economics she had begun to write for the socialist Press and to speak successfully at meetings. In the jaundiced recesses of his mind he took it for granted that her work would have the lax fibre of her character: that it would be infected with her Oriental crudities. Although once or twice he had been congratulated on her brilliance, he mistrusted this phase in her activity as a caper of the sensualist.

His eyes blazed on her and found the depraved, over-sexed creature, looking milder than a gazelle, holding out a handbill to him.

'They've taken it for granted!'

He saw her name – his name – MRS EVADNE SILVERTON. It was at first the blaze of stout scarlet letters on the dazzling white ground that made him blink. Then he was convulsed with rage.

'Georgie dear!'

She stepped forward and caught his weak body to her bosom. He wrenched himself away. Spiritual nausea made him determined to be a better man than her.

'A pair of you! You and Longton!' he snarled scornfully. Then seeing her startled face, he controlled himself.

'I thought it would please you,' said Evadne, a little waspishly.

'You mustn't have anything to do with Longton,' he stormed.

A change passed over her. She became ugly. Her face was heavy with intellect, her lips coarse with power. He was at arms with a socialist lead. Much would he have preferred the bland sensualist again.

'Why?'

'Because,' his lips stuck together like blotting paper 'he's not the sort of man my wife should – should –'

With movements which terrified him by their rough energy, she folded up the bills and put them back in the envelope.

'George. I suppose you mean that he's a bad man.' He nodded. 'I know quite well that the girl who used to be his typist is his mistress.' She spoke it sweetly, as if reasoning with an old fool. 'But she's got consumption. She'll be dead in six months. In fact, I think it's rather nice of him. To look after her and all that.'

'My God!' He leapt to his feet, extending a shaking forefinger. As she turned to him, the smile dying on her lips, his excited weakness wrapped him in a paramnesic illusion: it seemed to him that he had been through all this before – a long, long time ago. 'My God, you talk like a woman off the streets!'

Evadne's lips lifted over her strong teeth. With clever cruelty she fixed his eyes with hers, well knowing that he longed to fall forward and bury his head on the table in a transport of hysterical sobs. After a moment of this torture she turned away, herself distressed by a desire to cry.

'How can you say such dreadful, dreadful things!' she protested, chokingly.

He sat down again. His eyes looked little and red, but they blazed on her. 'I wonder if you are,' he said softly.

'Are what?' she asked petulantly, a tear rolling down her nose.

'You know,' he answered, nodding.

'George, George, George!' she cried.

'You've always been keen on kissing and making love, haven't you, my precious. At first you startled me, you did! I didn't know women were like that.' From that morass he suddenly stepped on to a high peak of terror. Amazed to find himself sincere, he cried, 'I don't believe good women are!'

'Georgie, how can you be so silly!' exclaimed Evadne shrilly. 'You know quite well I've been as true to you as any woman could be.' She sought his eyes with a liquid glance of reproach. He averted his gaze, sickened at having put himself in the wrong. For even while he degraded his tongue his pure soul fainted with loathing of her fleshliness.

'I . . . I'm sorry.'

Too wily to forgive him at once, she showed him a lowering profile with downcast lids. Of course, he knew it was a fraud. An imputation against her chastity was no more poignant than a reflection on the cleanliness of her nails – rude and spiteful, but that was all. But for a time they kept up the deception, while she cleared the table in steely silence.

'Evadne, I'm sorry. I'm tired.' His throat was dry. He could not bear the discord of a row added to the horror of their companionship. 'Evadne, do forgive me – I don't know what I meant by . . .'

'That's all right, silly!' she said suddenly and bent over the table to kiss him. Her brow was smooth. It was evident from her splendid expression that she was preoccupied. Then she finished clearing up the dishes and took them into the kitchen. While she was out of the room he rose from his seat and sat down in the armchair by the fire, setting his bulldog pipe alight. For a very short time he was free of her voluptuous presence. But she ran back soon, having put the kettle on and changed her blouse for a loose dressing-jacket, and sat down on the arm of his chair. Once or twice she bent and kissed his brow, but for the most part she lay back with his head drawn to her bosom, rocking herself rhythmically. Silverton, a little disgusted by their contact, sat quite motionless and passed into a doze. He revolved in his mind the incidents of his day's routine and remembered a snub from a superior. So he opened his eyes and tried to think of something else. It was then that he became conscious that the rhythm of Evadne's movement was not regular. It was broken as though she rocked in time to music. Music? His sense of hearing crept up to hear if there was any sound of music in the breaths she was emitting rather heavily every now and then. At first he could hear nothing. Then it struck him that each breath was a muttered phrase. He stiffened, and hatred flamed through his veins. The words came clearly through her lips . . . 'The present system of wage-slavery . . .'

'Evadne!' He sprang to his feet. 'You're preparing your speech!'

She did not move. 'I am,' she said.

'Damn it, you shan't speak!'

'Damn it, I will!'

'Evadne, you shan't speak! If you do I swear to God above I'll turn you out into the streets.' She rose and came towards him. She looked black and dangerous. She trod softly like a cat with her head down. In spite of himself, his tongue licked his lips in fear and he cowered a moment before he picked up a knife from the table. For a space she looked down on him and the sharp blade.

'You idiot, can't you hear the kettle's boiling over?'

He shrank back, letting the knife fall on the floor. For three minutes he stood there controlling his breath and trying to still his heart. Then he followed her into the kitchen. She was making a noise with a basinful of dishes.

'Stop that row.'

She turned round with a dripping dishcloth in her hand and pondered whether to throw it at him. But she was tired and wanted peace; so that she could finish the rough draft of her speech. So she stood waiting.

'Did you understand what I said then? If you don't promise me here and now . . .'

She flung her arms upwards with a cry and dashed past him. He made to run after her upstairs, but stumbled on the threshold of the lobby and sat with his ankle twisted under him, shaking with rage. In a second she ran downstairs again, clothed in a big cloak with a black bundle clutched to her breast. For the first time in their married life she was seized with a convulsion of sobs. She dashed out the front door and banged it with such passion that a glass pane shivered to fragments behind her.

'What's this? What's this?' he cried stupidly, standing up. He perceived with an insane certainty that she was going to meet some unknown lover. 'I'll come and tell him what a slut you are!' he shouted after her and stumbled to the door. It was jammed now and he had to drag at it.

The night was flooded with the yellow moonshine of midsummer; it seemed to drip from the lacquered leaves of the shrubs in the front garden. In its soft clarity he could see her plainly, although she was now two hundred yards away. She was hastening to the north end of Sumatra Crescent, an end that curled up the hill like a silly kitten's tail and stopped abruptly in green fields. So he knew that she was going to the young man who had just bought the Georgian manor, whose elm trees crowned the hill. Oh, how he hated her! Yet he must follow her, or else she would cover up her adulteries so that he could not take his legal revenge. So he began to run – silently, for he wore his carpet-slippers. He was only a hundred yards behind her when she slipped through a gap in the hedge to tread a field-path. She still walked with pride, for though she was town-bred, night in the open seemed not at all fearful to her. As he shuffled in pursuit his carpet-slippers were engulfed in a shining pool of mud. He raised one with a squelch, the other was left. This seemed the last humiliation. He kicked the other one off his foot and padded on in his socks, snuffling in anticipation of a cold. Then physical pain sent him back to the puddle to pluck out the slippers. It was a dirty job. His heart battered his breast as he saw that Evadne had gained the furthest hedge and was crossing the stile into the lane that ran up to the manor gates.

'Go on, you beast!' he muttered. 'Go on, go on!' After a scamper he climbed the stile and thrust his lean neck beyond a mass of wilted hawthorn bloom that crumbled into vagrant petals at his touch.

The lane mounted yellow as cheese to where the moon lay on the iron tracery of the manor gates. Evadne was not there. Hardly believing his eyes he hobbled over into the lane and looked in the other direction. There he saw her disappearing round the bend of the road. Gathering himself up to a run, he tried to think out his bearings. He had seldom passed this way, and like most people without strong primitive instincts he had no sense of orientation. With difficulty he remembered that after a mile's mazy wanderings between high hedges this lane sloped suddenly to the bowl of heather overhung by the moorlands, in which lay the Petrick reservoirs, two untamed lakes.

'Eh! She's going to meet him by the water!' he cursed to himself. He remembered the withered ash tree, seared by lightning to its root, that stood by the road at the bare frontier of the moor. 'May God strike her like that,' he prayed, 'as she fouls the other man's lips with her kisses. Oh God! Let me strangle her. Or bury a knife deep in her breast.' Suddenly he broke into a lolloping run. 'Oh my Lord, I'll be able to divorce her. I'll be free. Free to live alone. To do my day's work and sleep my night's sleep without her. I'll get a job somewhere else and forget her. I'll bring her to the dogs. No clean man or woman in Petrick will look at her now. They won't have her to speak at that meeting now!' His throat swelled with joy, he leapt high in the air. 'I'll lie about her. If I can prove that she's wrong with this man they'll believe me if I say she's a bad woman and drinks. I'll make her name a joke. And then . . .'

He flung wide his arms in ecstasy: the left struck against stone. More pain than he had thought his body could hold convulsed him, so that he sank on the ground hugging his aching arm. He looked backwards as he writhed and saw that the hedge had stopped; above him was the great stone wall of the county asylum. The question broke on him – was there any lunatic in its confines so slavered with madness as he himself? Nothing but madness could have accounted for the torrent of ugly words, the sea of uglier thoughts that was now a part of him. 'Oh God, for me to turn like this!' he cried, rolling over full-length on the grassy bank by the roadside. That the infidelity of his wife, a thing that should have brought out the stern manliness of his true nature, should have discovered him as lecherous-lipped as any pot-house lounger, was the most infamous accident of his married life. The sense of sin descended on him so that his tears flowed hot and bitterly. 'Have I gone to the Unitarian chapel every Sunday morning and to the Ethical Society every evening for nothing?' his spirit asked itself in its travail. 'All those Browning lectures for nothing . . .' He said the Lord's Prayer several times and lay for a minute quietly crying. The relaxation of his muscles brought him a sense of rest which seemed forgiveness falling from God. The tears dried on his cheeks. His calmer consciousness heard the sound of rushing waters mingled with the beating of blood in his ears. He got up and scrambled round the turn of the road that brought him to the withered ash tree.

He walked forward on the parched heatherland to the mound whose scarred sides, heaped with boulders, tufted with mountain grasses, shone before him in the moonlight. He scrambled up to it hurriedly and hoisted himself from ledge to ledge till he fell on his knees with a squeal of pain. His ankle was caught in a crevice of the rock. Gulping down his agony at this final physical humiliation he heaved himself upright and raced on to the summit, and found himself before the Devil's Cauldron, filled to the brim with yellow moonshine and the fiery play of summer lightning. The rugged crags opposite him were a low barricade against the stars to which the mound where he stood shot forward like a bridge. To the left of this the long Lisbech pond lay like a trailing serpent; its silver scales glittered as the wind swept down from the vaster moorlands to the east. To the right under a steep drop of twenty feet was the Whimsey pond, more sinister, shaped in an unnatural oval, sheltered from the wind by the high ridge so that the undisturbed moonlight lay across it like a sharp-edged sword.

He looked about for some sign of Evadne. She could not be on the land by the margin of the lakes, for the light blazed so strongly that each reed could be clearly seen like a black dagger stabbing the silver. He looked down Lisbech and saw far east a knot of red and green and orange lights. Perhaps for some devilish purpose Evadne had sought Lisbech railway station. But his volcanic mind had preserved one grain of sense that assured him that, subtle as Evadne's villainy might be, it would not lead her to walk five miles out of her way to a terminus which she could have reached in fifteen minutes by taking a train from the station down the road. She must be under cover somewhere here. He went down the gentle slope that fell from the top of the ridge to Lisbech pond in a disorder of rough heather, unhappy patches of cultivated grass and coppices of silver birch, fringed with flaming broom that seemed faintly tarnished in the moonlight. At the bottom was a roughly hewn path which he followed in hot aimless hurry. In a little he approached a riot of falling waters. There was a slice ten feet broad carved out of the ridge, and to this narrow channel of black shining rock the floods of Lisbech leapt some feet and raced through to Whimsey. The noise beat him back. The gap was spanned by a gaunt thing of paint-blistered iron, on which he stood dizzily and noticed how the wide step that ran on each side of the channel through to the other pond was smeared with sinister green slime. Now his physical distress reminded him of Evadne, whom he had almost forgotten in contemplation of these lonely waters. The idea of her had been present but obscured, as sometimes toothache may cease active torture. His blood-lust set him on and he staggered forward with covered ears. Even as he went something caught his eye in a thicket high up on the slope near the crags. Against the slender pride of some silver birches stood a gnarled hawthorn tree, its branches flattened under the stern moorland winds so that it grew squat like an opened umbrella. In its dark shadows, faintly illumined by a few boughs of withered blossom, there moved a strange bluish light. Even while he did not know what it was it made his flesh stir.

The light emerged. It was the moonlight reflected from Evadne's body. She was clad in a black bathing-dress, and her arms and legs and the broad streak of flesh laid bare by a rent down the back shone brilliantly white, so that she seemed like a grotesquely patterned wild animal as she ran down to the lake. Whirling her arms above her head she trampled down into the water and struck out strongly. Her movements were full of brisk delight and she swam quickly. The moonlight made her the centre of a little feathery blur of black and silver, with a comet's tail trailing in her wake.

Nothing in all his married life had ever staggered Silverton so much as this. He had imagined his wife's adultery so strongly that it had come to be. It was now as real as their marriage; more real than their courtship. So this seemed to be the last crime of the adulteress. She had dragged him over those squelching fields and these rough moors and changed him from a man of irritations, but no passions, into a cold designer of murderous treacheries, so that he might witness a swimming exhibition! For a minute he was stunned. Then he sprang down to the rushy edge and ran along in the direction of her course, crying, 'Evadne! Evadne!' She did not hear him. At last he achieved a chest-note and shouted, 'Evadne! Come here!' The black-and-silver feather shivered in mid-water. She turned immediately and swam back to shore. He suspected sullenness in her slowness, but was glad of it, for after the shock of this extraordinary incident he wanted to go to sleep. Drowsiness lay on him like lead. He shook himself like a dog and wrenched off his linen collar, winking at the bright moon to keep himself awake. As she came quite near he was exasperated by the happy, snorting breaths she drew, and strolled a pace or two up the bank. To his enragement the face she lifted as she waded to dry land was placid, and she scrambled gaily up the bank to his side.

'Oh George, why did you come!' she exclaimed quite affectionately, laying a damp hand on his shoulder.

'Oh damn it, what does this mean?' he cried, committing a horrid tenor squeak. 'What are you doing?'

'Why, George,' she said, 'I came here for a bathe.'

He stared into her face and could make nothing of it. It was only sweet surfaces of flesh, soft radiances of eye and lip, a lovely lie of comeliness. He forgot this present grievance in a cold search for the source of her peculiar hatefulness. Under this sick gaze she pouted and turned away with a peevish gesture. He made no sign and stood silent, watching her saunter to that gaunt iron bridge. The roar of the little waterfall did not disturb her splendid nerves and she drooped sensuously over the hand-rail, sniffing up the sweet night smell; too evidently trying to abase him to another apology.

A mosquito whirred into his face. He killed it viciously and strode off towards his wife, who showed by a common little toss of the head that she was conscious of his coming.

'Look here, Evadne!' he panted. 'What did you come here for? Tell me the truth and I promise I'll not . . . I'll not . . .'

'Not *what*, George?'

'Oh please, please tell me the truth, do Evadne!' he cried pitifully.

'But, dear, what is there to carry on about so? You went on so queerly about my meeting that my head felt fit to split, and I thought the long walk and the dip would do me good.' She broke off, amazed at the wave of horror that passed over his face.

His heart sank. From the loose-lipped hurry in the telling of her story, from the bigness of her eyes and the lack of subtlety in her voice, he knew that this was the truth. Here was no adulteress whom he could accuse in the law courts and condemn into the street, no resourceful sinner whose merry crimes he could discover. Here was merely his good wife, the faithful attendant of his hearth, relentless wrecker of his soul.

She came towards him as a cat approaches a displeased master, and hovered about him on the stone coping of the noisy sluice.

'Indeed!' he found himself saying sarcastically. 'Indeed!'

'Yes, George Silverton, indeed!' she burst out, a little frightened. 'And why shouldn't I? I used to come here often enough on summer nights with poor Mamma.'

'Yes!' he shouted. It was exactly the sort of thing that would appeal to that weird half-black woman from the back of beyond. 'Mamma!' he cried tauntingly, 'Mamma!'

There was a flash of silence between them before Evadne, clutching her breast and balancing herself dangerously on her heels on the stone coping, broke into gentle shrieks. 'You dare talk of my Mamma, my poor Mamma, and she cold in her grave! I haven't been happy since she died and I married you, you silly little misery, you!' Then the rage was suddenly wiped off her brain by the perception of a crisis.

The trickle of silence overflowed into a lake, over which their spirits flew, looking at each other's reflection in the calm waters: in the hurry of their flight they had never before seen each other. They stood facing one another with dropped heads, quietly thinking.

The strong passion which filled them threatened to disintegrate their souls as a magnetic current decomposes the electrolyte, so they fought to organise their sensations. They tried to arrange themselves and their lives for comprehension, but beyond sudden lyric visions of old incidents of hatefulness – such as a smarting quarrel of six years ago as to whether Evadne had or had not cheated the railway company out of one-and-eightpence on an excursion ticket – the past was intangible. It trailed behind this intense event as the pale hair trails behind the burning comet. They were preoccupied with the moment. Quite often George had found a mean pleasure in the thought that by never giving Evadne a child he had cheated her out of one form of experience, and now he paid the price for this unnatural pride of sterility. For now the spiritual offspring of their intercourse came to birth. A sublime loathing was between them. For a little time it was a huge perilous horror, but afterwards, like men aboard a ship whose masts seek the sky through steep waves, they found a drunken pride in the adventure. This was the very absolute of hatred. It cheapened the memory of the fantasias of irritation and ill-will they had performed in the less boring moments of their marriage, and they felt dazed, as amateurs who had found themselves creating a masterpiece. For the first time they were possessed by a supreme emotion and they felt a glad desire to strip away restraint and express it nakedly. It was ecstasy; they felt tall and full of blood.

Like people who, bewitched by Christ, see the whole earth as the breathing body of God, so they saw the universe as the substance and the symbol of their hatred. The stars trembled overhead with wrath. A wind from behind the angry crags set the moonlight on Lisbech quivering with rage, and the squat hawthorn tree creaked slowly like the irritation of a dull little man. The dry moors, parched with harsh anger, waited thirstily and, sending out the murmur of rustling mountain grass and the cry of wakening fowl, seemed to huddle closer to the lake. But this sense of the earth's sympathy slipped away from them and they loathed all matter as the dull wrapping of their flame-like passion. At their wishing matter fell away and they saw sarcastic visions. He saw her as a toad squatting on the clean earth, obscuring the stars and pressing down its hot moist body on the cheerful fields. She felt his long boneless body coiled round the roots of the lovely tree of life. They shivered fastidiously. With an uplifting sense of responsibility they realised that they must kill each other.

A bird rose over their heads with a leaping flight that made it seem as though its black body was bouncing against the bright sky. The foolish noise and motion precipitated their thoughts. They were broken into a new conception of life. They perceived that God is war and his creatures are meant to fight. When dogs walk through the world cats must climb trees. The virgin must snare the wanton, the fine lover must put the prude to the sword. The gross man of action walks, spurred on by the bloodless bodies of the men of thought, who lie quiet and cunningly do not tell him where his grossness leads him. The flesh must smother the spirit, the spirit must set the flesh on fire and watch it burn. And those who were gentle by nature and shrank from the ordained brutality were betrayers of their kind, surrendering the earth to the seed of their enemies. In this war there is no dis-

charge. If they succumbed to peace now, the rest of their lives would
be dishonourable, like the exile of a rebel who has begged his life as
the reward of cowardice. It was their first experience of religious
passion, and they abandoned themselves to it so that their immediate
personal qualities fell away from them. Neither his weakness nor her
prudence stood in the way of the event.

They measured each other with the eye. To her he was a spidery
thing against the velvet blackness and hard silver surfaces of the
pond. The light soaked her bathing-dress so that she seemed, against
the jagged shadows of the rock cutting, as though she were clad in a
garment of dark polished mail. Her knees were bent so clearly, her
toes gripped the coping so strongly. He understood very clearly that if
he did not kill her instantly she would drop him easily into the deep
riot of waters. Yet for a space he could not move, but stood expecting
a degrading death. Indeed, he gave her time to kill him. But she was
without power too, and struggled weakly with a hallucination. The
quarrel in Sumatra Crescent with its suggestion of vast and unmen-
tionable antagonisms; her swift race through the moon-drenched
countryside, all crepitant with night noises; the swimming in the
wine-like lake; their isolation on the moor, which was expressedly
hostile to them, as nature always is to lonely man; and this stark
contest face to face, with their resentments heaped between them
like a pile of naked swords – these things were so strange that her
civilised self shrank back appalled. There entered into her the primitive woman who is the curse of all women: a creature of the most
utter femaleness, useless, save for childbirth, with no strong brain to
make her physical weakness a light accident, abjectly and corruptingly afraid of man. A squaw, she dared not strike her lord.

The illusion passed like a moment of faintness and left her enraged
at having forgotten her superiority even for an instant. In the material
world she had a thousand times been defeated into making prudent
reservations and practising unnatural docilities. But in the world of
thought she had maintained unfalteringly her masterfulness in spite
of the strong yearning of her temperament towards voluptuous surrenders. That was her virtue. Its violation whipped her to action and
she would have killed him at once, had not his moment come a
second before hers. Sweating horribly, he had dropped his head forward on his chest; his eyes fell on her feet and marked the plebeian
moulding of her ankle, which rose thickly over a crease of flesh from
the heel to the calf. The woman was coarse in grain and pattern.

He had no instinct for honourable attack, so he found himself
striking her in the stomach. She reeled from pain, not because his

strength overcame hers. For the first time her eyes looked into his candidly open, unveiled by languor or lust; their hard brightness told him how she despised him for that unwarlike blow. He cried out as he realised that this was another of her despicable victories and that the whole burden of the crime now lay on him, for he had begun it. But the rage was stopped on his lips as her arms, flung wildly out as she fell backwards, caught him about the waist with abominable justness of eye and evil intention. So they fell body to body into the quarrelling waters.

The feathery confusion had looked so soft, yet it seemed the solid rock they stuck. The breath shot out of him and suffocation warmly stuffed his ears and nose. Then the rock cleft and he was swallowed by a brawling blackness in which whirled a vortex that flung him again and again on a sharp thing that burned his shoulder. All about him fought the waters, and they cut his flesh like knives. His pain was past belief. Though God might be war, he desired peace in his time, and he yearned for another God – a child's God, an immense arm coming down from the hills and lifting him to a kindly bosom. Soon his body would burst for breath, his agony would smash in his breast-bone. So great was his pain that his consciousness was strained to apprehend it, as a too tightly stretched canvas splits and rips.

Suddenly the air was sweet on his mouth. The starlight seemed as hearty as a cheer. The world was still there, the world in which he had lived, so he must be safe. His own weakness and lovableness induced enjoyable tears, and there was a delicious moment of abandonment to comfortable whining before he realised that the water would not kindly buoy him up for long, and that even now a hostile current clasped his waist. He braced his flaccid body against the sucking blackness and flung his head back so that the water should not bubble so hungrily against the cords of his throat. Above him the slime of the rock was sticky with moonbeams, and the leprous light brought to his mind a newspaper paragraph, read years ago, which told him that the dawn had discovered floating in some oily Mersey dock, under walls as infected with wet growth as this, a corpse whose blood-encrusted finger-tips were deeply cleft. On the instant his own fingertips seemed hot with blood and deeply cleft from clawing at the impregnable rock. He screamed gaspingly, and beat his hands through the strangling flood. Action, which he had always loathed and dreaded, had broken the hard mould of his self-possession, and the dry dust of his character was blown hither and thither by fear. But one sharp fragment of intelligence which survived this detrition of his personality perceived that a certain gleam on the rock about a foot above the water was not the cold putrescence of the slime, but certainly the hard and merry light of a moon-ray striking on solid metal. His left hand clutched upwards at it, and he swung from a rounded projection. It was, his touch told him, a leaden ring hanging obliquely from the rock, to which his memory could visualise precisely in some past drier time when Lisbech sent no flood to Whimsey, a waterman mooring a boat strewn with pale-bellied perch. And behind the stooping waterman he remembered a flight of narrow steps that led up a buttress to a stone shelf that ran through the cutting. Unquestionably he was safe. He swung in a happy rhythm from the ring, his limp body trailing like a caterpillar through the stream to the foot of the steps, while he gasped in strength. A part of him was in agony, for his arm was nearly dragged out of its socket, and a part of him was embarrassed because his hysteria shook him with a deep rumbling chuckle that sounded as though he meditated on some unseemly joke; the whole was pervaded by a twilight atmosphere of unenthusiastic gratitude for his rescue, like the quietly cheerful tone of a Sunday evening sacred concert. After a minute's deep breathing he hauled himself up by the other hand and prepared to swing himself on to the steps.

But first, to shake off the wet worsted rags, once his socks, that now stuck uncomfortably between his toes, he splashed his feet outwards to midstream. A certain porpoise-like surface met his left foot. Fear dappled his face with goose-flesh. Without turning his head he knew what it was. It was Evadne's fat flesh rising on each side of her deep-furrowed spine through the rent in her bathing-dress.

Once more hatred marched through his soul like a king: a compelling service by his godhead and, like all gods, a little hated for his harsh lien on his worshipper. He saw his wife as the curtain of flesh between him and celibacy, and solitude and all those delicate abstentions from life which his soul desired. He saw her as the invisible worm destroying the rose of the world with her dark secret love. Now he knelt on the lowest stone step watching her wet seal-smooth head bobbing nearer on the waters. As her strong arms, covered with little dark points where her thick hairs were clotted with moisture, stretched out towards safety he bent forward and laid his hands on her head. He held her face under water. Scornfully he noticed the bubbles that rose to the surface from her protesting mouth and nostrils, and the foam raised by her arms and her thick ankles. To the end the creature persisted in turmoil, in movement, in action . . .

She dropped like a stone. His hands, with nothing to resist them, slapped the water foolishly and he nearly overbalanced forward into the stream. He rose to his feet very stiffly. 'I must be a very strong man,' he said, as he slowly climbed the steps. 'I must be a very strong man,' he repeated, a little louder, as with hot and painful rigidity of the joints he stretched himself out at full length along the stone shelf. Weakness closed him in like a lead coffin. For a little time the wetness of his clothes persisted in being felt; then the sensation oozed out of him and his body fell out of knowledge. There was neither pain nor joy nor any other reckless ploughing of the brain by nerves. He knew unconsciousness, or rather the fullest consciousness he had ever known. For the world became nothingness, and nothingness which is free from the yeasty nuisance of matter and the ugliness of generation was the law of his being. He was absorbed into vacuity, the untamed substance of the universe, round which he conceived passion and thought to circle as straws caught up by the wind. He saw God and lived.

In Heaven a thousand years are a day. And this little corner of time in which he found happiness shrank to a nutshell as he opened his eyes again. This peace was hardly printed on his heart, yet the brightness of the night was blurred by the dawn. With the grunting carefulness of a man drunk with fatigue, he crawled along the stone shelf to the iron bridge, where he stood with his back to the roaring sluice and rested. All things seemed different now and happier. Like most timid people he disliked the night, and the commonplace hand which the dawn laid on the scene seemed to him a sanctification. The dimmed moon sank to her setting behind the crags. The jewel lights of Lisbech railway station were weak, cheerful twinklings. A steaming bluish milk of morning mist had been spilt on the hard silver surface of the lake, and the reeds no longer stabbed it like little daggers, but seemed a feathery fringe, like the pampas grass in the front garden in Sumatra Crescent. The black crags became brownish, and the mist disguised the sternness of the moor. This weakening of effects was exactly what he had always thought the extinction of Evadne would bring the world. He smiled happily at the moon.

Yet he was moved to sudden angry speech. 'If I had my time over again,' he said, 'I wouldn't touch her with the tongs.' For the cold he had known all along he would catch had settled in his head, and his handkerchief was wet through.

He leaned over the bridge and looked along Lisbech and thought of Evadne. For the first time for many years he saw her image without spirits, and wondered without indignation why she had so often looked like the cat about to steal the cream. What was the cream? And did she ever steal it? Now he would never know. He thought of her very generously and sighed over the perversity of fate in letting so much comeliness.

'If she had married a butcher or a veterinary surgeon she might have been happy,' he said, and shook his head at the glassy black water that slid under the bridge to that boiling sluice.

A gust of ague reminded him that wet clothes clung to his fevered body and that he ought to change as quickly as possible, or expect to be laid up for weeks. He turned along the path that led back across the moor to the withered ash tree, and was learning the torture of bare feet on gravel when he cried out to himself: 'I shall be hanged for killing my wife.' It did not come as a trumpet-call, for he was one of those people who never quite hear what is said to them, and this deafishness extended in him to emotional things. It stole on him calmly, like a fog closing on a city. When he first felt hemmed in by this certainty he looked over his shoulder to the crags, remembering tales of how Jacobite fugitives had hidden on the moors for many weeks. There lay at least another day of freedom. But he was the kind of man who always goes home. He stumbled on, not very unhappy, except for his feet. Like many people of weak temperament he did not fear death. Indeed, it had a peculiar appeal to him; for while it was important, exciting, it did not, like most important and exciting things, try to create action. He allowed his imagination the vanity of painting pictures. He saw himself standing in their bedroom, plotting this last event, with the white sheet and the high lights of the mahogany wardrobe shining ghostly at him through the darkness. He saw himself raising a thin hand to the gas bracket and turning on the tap. He saw himself staggering to their bed while death crept in at his nostrils. He saw his corpse lying in full daylight, and for the first time knew himself certainly, unquestionably dignified.

He threw back his chest in pride; but at that moment the path stopped and he found himself staggering down the mound of heatherland and boulders with bleeding feet. Always he had suffered from sore feet, which had not exactly disgusted but, worse still, disappointed Evadne. A certain wistfulness she had always evinced when she found herself the superior animal had enraged and humiliated him many times. He felt that sting him now, and flung himself down the mound cursing. When he stumbled up to the withered ash tree he hated her so much that it seemed as though she were alive again, and a sharp wind blowing down from the moor terrified him like her touch.

He rested there. Leaning against the stripped grey trunk, he smiled up at the sky, which was now so touched to ineffectiveness by the dawn that it looked like a tent of faded silk. There was the peace of weakness in him, which he took to be spiritual, because it had no apparent physical justification, but he lost it as his dripping clothes chilled his tired flesh. His discomfort reminded him that the phantasmic night was passing from him. Daylight threatened him; the daylight in which for so many years he had worked in the solicitor's office and been snubbed and ignored. '"The garish day,"' he murmured disgustedly, quoting the blasphemy of some hymn-writer. He wanted his death to happen in this phantasmic night.

So he limped his way along the road. The birds had not yet begun to sing, but the rustling noises of the night had ceased. The silent highway was consecrated to his proud progress. He staggered happily like a tired child returning from a lovely birthday walk: his death in the little bedroom, which for the first time he would have to himself, was a culminating treat to be gloated over like the promise of a favourite pudding for supper. As he walked he brooded dozingly on large and swelling thoughts. Like all people of weak passions and enterprise he loved to think of Napoleon, and in the shadow of the great asylum wall he strutted a few steps of his advance from murder to suicide, with arms crossed on his breast and thin legs trying to strut massively. He was so happy. He wished that a military band went before him, and pretended that the high hedges were solemn lines of men, stricken in awe to silence as their king rode out to some nobly self-chosen doom. Vast he seemed to himself, and magnificent like music, and solemn like the Sphinx. He had saved the earth from corruption by killing Evadne, for whom he now felt the unremorseful pity a conqueror might bestow on a devastated empire. He might have grieved that his victory brought him death, but with immense pride he found that the occasion was exactly described by a text. 'He saved others, Himself He could not save.' He had missed the stile in the field above Sumatra Crescent and had to go back and hunt for it in the hedge. So quickly had his satisfaction borne him home.

The field had the fantastic air that jerry-builders give to land poised on the knife-edge of town and country, so that he walked in romance to his very door. The unmarred grass sloped to a stone-hedge of towers of loose brick, trenches and mounds of shining clay, and the fine intentful spires of the scaffolding round the last unfinished house. And he looked down on Petrick. Though to the actual eye it was but a confusion of dark instances through the twilight, a breaking of velvety perspectives, he saw more intensely than ever before its squalid walls and squalid homes where mean men and mean women enlaced their unwholesome lives. Yet he did not shrink from entering for his great experience, as Christ did not shrink from being born in a stable. He swaggered with humility over the trodden mud of the field and the new white flags of Sumatra Crescent. Down the road before him there passed a dim figure, who paused at each lamp-post and raised a long wand to behead the yellow gas-flowers that were now wilting before the dawn; a ghostly herald preparing the world to be his deathbed. The crescent curved in quiet darkness, save for one house, where blazed a gas-lit room with undrawn blinds. The brightness had the startled quality of a scream. He looked in almost anxiously as he passed, and met the blank eyes of a man in evening clothes who stood by the window shaking a medicine bottle. His face was like a wax mask softened by heat: the features were blurred with the suffering which comes from the spectacle of suffering. His eyes lay unshiftingly on George's face as he went by and he went on shaking the bottle. It seemed as though he would never stop.

In the hour of his grandeur George was not forgetful of the griefs of the little human people, but interceded with God for the sake of this stranger. Everything was beautiful, beautiful, beautiful.

His own little house looked solemn as a temple. He leaned against the lamp-post at the gate and stared at its empty windows and neat bricks. The disorder of the shattered pane of glass could be overlooked by considering a sign that this house was a holy place, like the Passover blood on the lintel. The propriety of the evenly drawn blind pleased him enormously. He had always known that this was how the great tragic things of the world had accomplished themselves: quietly. Evadne's raging activity belonged to trivial or annoying things like spring-cleaning or thunderstorms. Well, the house belonged to him now. He opened the gate and went up the asphalt path, sourly noticing that Evadne had as usual left out the lawnmower, though it might very easily have rained, with the wind coming up as it was. A stray cat that had been sleeping in the tuft of pampas grass in the middle of the lawn was roused by his coming, and fled insolently close to his legs. He hated all wild homeless things, and bent for a stone to throw at it. But instead his fingers touched a slug, which reminded him of the feeling of Evadne's flesh through the slit in her bathing-dress. And suddenly the garden was possessed by her presence; she seemed to amble there as she had so often done, sowing seeds unwisely and tormenting the last days of an ailing geranium by insane transplantation, exclaiming absurdly over such mere weeds as morning glory. He caught the very clucking of her voice . . . The front door opened at his touch.

The little lobby with its closed doors seemed stuffed with expectant silence. He realised that he had come to the theatre of his great adventure. Then panic seized him. Because this was the home where he and she had lived together so horribly he doubted whether he could do this splendid momentous thing, for here he had always been a poor thing with the habit of failure. His heart beat in him more quickly than his raw feet could pad up the oil-clothed stairs. Behind the deal door at the end of the passage was death. Nothingness! It would escape him, even the idea of it would escape him if he did not go to it at once. When he burst at last into its presence he felt so victorious that he sank back against the door waiting for death to come to him without turning on the gas. He was so happy. His death was coming true.

But Evadne lay on his deathbed. She slept there soundly, with her head flung back on the pillows so that her eyes and brow seemed small in shadow, and her mouth and jaw huge above her thick throat in the light. Her wet hair straggled across the pillow on to a broken cane chair covered with her tumbled clothes. Her breast, silvered with sweat, shone in the ray of the street lamp that had always disturbed their nights. The counterpane rose enormously over her hips in rolls of glazed linen. Out of mere innocent sleep her sensuality was distilling a most drunken pleasure.

Not for one moment did he think this a phantasmic appearance. Evadne was not the sort of woman to have a ghost.

Still leaning against the door he tried to think it all out, but his thoughts came brokenly, because the dawnlight flowing in at the window confused him by its pale glare and that lax figure on the bed held his attention. It must have been that when he laid his murderous hands on her head she had simply dropped below the surface and swum a few strokes under water as any expert swimmer can. Probably he had never even put her into danger, for she was a great lusty creature and the weir was a little place. He had imagined the wonder and peril of the battle as he had imagined his victory. He sneezed exhaustingly, and from his physical distress realised how absurd it was ever to have thought that he had killed her. Bodies like his do not kill bodies like hers.

Now his soul was naked and lonely as though the walls of his body had fallen in at death, and the grossness of Evadne's sleep made him suffer more unlovely a destitution than any old beggarwoman squatting by the roadside in the rain. He had thought he had had what every man most desires: one night of power over a woman for the business of murder or love. But it had been a lie. Nothing beautiful had ever happened to him. He would have wept, but the hatred he had learnt on the moors obstructed all tears in his throat. At least this night had given him passion enough to put an end to it all.

Quietly he went to the window and drew down the sash. There was no fireplace, so that sealed the room. Then he crept over to the gas bracket and raised his thin hand, as he had imagined in his hour of vain glory by the lake. He had forgotten Evadne's thrifty habit of turning off the gas at the main to prevent leakage when she went to bed.

He was beaten. He undressed and got into bed; as he had done every night for ten years, and as he would do every night until he died. Still sleeping, Evadne caressed him with warm arms.

Blast 1, 20 June 1914

Part V

Fleet Street Feminist

Selected Articles from the
Daily News, March 1915 – August 1917

V Fleet Street Feminist

Editor's Introduction

Rebecca West is not mentioned in Stephen Koss's fine study of A. G. Gardiner and the *Daily News, Fleet Street Radical*. But she was there, writing articles and reviews from 1914, a time when she was also writing her book on Henry James (published in 1916, a brilliant model literary criticism, but barely noticed by contemporary journals). She had by then a small son, Anthony, born in August 1914, and was still involved with H. G. Wells, the father of her child, whom she had met in 1912. It was a full life.

Her presence at the *Daily News* must have been felt in its own way as strongly as that of Shaw, Wells and Arnold Bennett, men whom she later dubbed her 'uncles' in literature. In addition to the articles reprinted here, she wrote many other brilliant pieces – on Freud, on Edward Carson and the Irish question, on anti-semitism, pacifism, on Bertrand Russell.

Rebecca West's absence from the history of English journalism is striking. As a journalist she wrote openly and directly at this period as a feminist and socialist critic of patriarchal attitudes and imperialism in literature and in politics. Her work always excited controversy; her essays always brought hundreds of arguments in letters to the editor. These articles from the *Daily News* represent her attempt to reach a larger audience than that claimed by *The Freewoman* and *The Clarion*. She expanded her following considerably and though Fleet Street was not exactly a hotbed of feminism, the *Daily News* appreciated lively and provocative writing.

At the beginning of the twentieth century, the *Daily News* was regarded as the chief organ of the Liberal Party. Its first issue had appeared in 1846 (the first editor was Charles Dickens, but he stayed only 26 days, 17 issues, and looked back on his editorship as a brief mistake. Harriet Martineau contributed over 1,500 pieces to the paper).

The paper was dedicated to free trade and social justice and was concerned to reach the widest possible audience with its message. It championed causes such as Italian unification and anti-slavery in America, and supported campaigns against privilege and monopoly at home.

It was A. G. Gardiner, one of the most famous editors in the history of Fleet Street, who published Rebecca West's articles. During his editorship of the *Daily News* from 1902 to 1919 he attracted to his paper many of the most celebrated names in liberal journalism (Nevinson and Brailsford among them). And it was during his editorship too that the paper was attempting to forge some sort of an alliance between the political forces of liberalism and labour.

By 1909 its circulation was nearly 400,000 (with a northern edition produced in Manchester). It was making its appeal, as Stephen Koss says, 'to the suburban classes whose self regard and dedication to self improvement set the tone for the era'. Though at this period the *Daily News* was somewhat reluctant to come out officially against the government, it did allow its correspondents considerable freedom to argue against specific government policies. There were articles sympathetic to Indian demands for self-determination and to Irish Home Rule: Christabel Pankhurst was a featured contributor to the correspondence columns, and also provided Gardiner with 'documents' to support the case for women's suffrage. (It is also true that Brailsford, a staunch supporter of women's suffrage, and Nevinson both resigned in 1909 after Gardiner had refused to repudiate in the columns of the paper the government's policy of forcibly feeding women suffragette prisoners.)

Rebecca West's reviews in the *Daily News* were as ever bold. She begged no forgiveness for her boldness, and no lingering guilt for transgression colours her attacks on the most revered authorities or the reputations of writers – even Tolstoy. Much as she admired the content of Theodore Dreiser's novels, she protests about his sloppy writing. 'Unless one protects one's fastidiousness by style, the mud will get into one's matter.' She deplores Bennett's *Hilda Lessways* as 'not so much a study of a woman based on observation, but a rash deduction from a couple of hair-pins'. (Later, when it became fashionable to mock Bennett, she praised his heroine in *The Lion's Share*.) During the First World War Rebecca West reviewed Ford Madox Ford's *The Good Soldier* as 'a much better book than any of us deserve.' May Sinclair's *Belgium Journal* is praised as 'one of the few books of permanent value produced by the war'.

Though women, art and labour continued to be the loudest notes on her trumpet, she also attacked anti-semitism, irresponsible pacifism and the cult of the Earth Mother. Here is a description of feminist 'types' from before the First World War. 'The galoshes-and-velour-hat type . . . who was very well up in facts and figures, but a little unsympathetic about changes in the marriage laws, the amber-cigarette-holder type of suffragette who called stridently across the Soho restaurant for the wine list, and whose trump card was her speech on unmarried mothers; the stoutish type who effected purple djibbahs and spoke in a rich, almost greasy contralto about the Mother Soul, the white-faced type whose courage in gaol was one of the few intimations of how we would meet our enemies.'

But perhaps the greatest importance of these essays lies in their specific analysis of the issues of women and work, issues which are as alive today as they were in 1916, and still not solved. In 1912 she wrote:

Every woman who has risen from the floral stage of political activity (that is, the Primrose League), or the vegetable stage (that is, the Women's Liberal Association), must admire the Suffragettes. Yet we may wish that they had spared a little of their dear irreverence and blessed pluck to stir up the industrial woman to revolt. We have clever Miss Pankhurst trying to get the vote and earnest Miss Macarthur trying to get organised trade unions; but seemingly we have no women who have read the signs of the times, who have discovered that political power and trade unionism are pin-pricks in the hide of the capitalist monster. Where are our women Syndicalists?

Ladies of Great Britain, we are clever, we are efficient, we are trustworthy, we are twice the women that our grandmothers were, but we have not enough devil in us. We are afraid of going back to first causes. We want to earn good wages. But we try to do it by being amenable and competent wage-slaves, and thus pleasing the capitalist. We never try to do it by fighting the capitalist and turning him out of the workshop. The other day Mr Ramsay MacDonald complained that women do not make good enough Socialists for him. The whole trouble is that women make Socialists which are just good enough for Mr Ramsay MacDonald. They accept as doles from the capitalist class what they should take as rights.

Popular Novelists

The Carnival of Florence by Marjorie Bowen, *The Temple of Dawn* by
I. A. R. Wylie, *Billie's Mother* by Mary H. J. Skrine

There are two kinds of historical novel: the dietetic and the dressy. In
the first one cries 'Tush!' and calls for nut-brown ale and a pasty. In
the second one sighs 'Ah God, my lord!' and wimples, when one does
not stomacher. In both cases local colour is not the complexion of the
story but an impediment in its speech, but the latter has attracted a
higher type of intellect by the delicious opportunity it affords of
spending the afternoon in museums, looking at pretty things in glass
cases and pretending that one is doing a good day's work. For the
literary mind enjoys almost everything except its work. Chief among
the students of the upholstery of the past is Miss Marjorie Bowen,
who brings to the research enormous romping vitality and a love for
beauty of language in which one would believe more thoroughly if
she did not so frequently split her infinitives neatly down the middle.
And chief among even her works is *The Carnival of Florence*. There
never was a story more completely strangled by its own doublet and
hose. The struggle between neoplatonism and Savonarola is carried
on among the voluminous folds of the heroine's wardrobe, and as
soon as a character manages to get his feet out of the brocade he is
immediately sent off to show the reader round the sights of Florence.
Even if he babbles of green fields he babbles with a Baedeker. 'They
heard Fra Silvestro raving again in the delirium of his fever, and
singing hoarsely of the woods of the Casentino and the white and
purple anemones that grew round the shrines and crosses of San
Giovanni Gualberto near the sanctuary of Vallombrosa (open all day;
fee to sacristan 1 lira).

Miss Bowen has every qualification that a historical novelist
needs; she writes with eupeptic liveliness, and she loves a fight. And
yet the kindest thing one could say about her is that she has done for
history what Sir Herbert Tree has done for Shakespeare. There is the
same dependence for effect on confused gorgeousness and an excessive affirmation that the principal characters liked everything hand-

some about them. Apparently Miss Bowen's method of composition is to shut her eyes, think of a historical period, and double it. This magnifying of the hastily conceived picturesque is pleasing when it counts the jewelled taps in the Medicis' bathroom; but when it shows us Savonarola, looking something like a gorilla with a high moral purpose, taking in his hand a sardonyx intaglio of the Lady Venus and smashing it to bright splinters with the heavy crucifix on his girdle, we know that something more than the intaglio has been smashed. Good material has been picked up and dropped. For there was drama of the real, illuminating sort in the spectacle of Savonarola. He was the representative of thousands of honest and intelligent souls to whom it seemed, at this period of the Renaissance when the only influence that culture exerted on the current conduct of vice was to make Italian immorality 'nearer that of devils than of beasts', that beauty and wisdom were mysteriously knit to cruelty and corruption; that, in fact, life was not worth living. If one omits this one aspect which makes Savonarola relevant to the Renaissance there is left on one's hands a man of an inherent unpicturesqueness which one can hide only by throwing up a continual dust of melodrama.

Not that one objects to melodrama. *The Temple of Dawn* has a hero called Leigh Daring, who turns away from the scorn of his beloved with a bitter laugh; and the waves of whisky and soda close over his head for years until the tocsin of danger sounds and he emerges dripping, but still a gentleman. And yet one reads it with real respect because there trots among the coincidences a sturdy Yorkshire-terrier intelligence whose shrewdness salts with the horse-sense the most machine-made of her melodramatic tableaux. This intelligence has evidently been maddened, during Miss Wylie's life in India, by the contradiction between the Anglo-Indian cant of 'respect for white women' and the treatment which white women receive at the hands of white men in their own country. And she has satirised it in the angrily written, sincerely felt incident of the Indian Prince and his white wife. The English garrison is shocked beyond measure when Govind Singh brings home to Fort Akbar an English wife, and exacts a promise that he will treat her 'as she would be treated in her own land by her own people'. When, at the wedding festivities, he tears the jewels from his bride and flings them to a nautch girl, whom he bids mount the throne in her place, they indignantly remind him of this promise; to which he retorts that that is what he is doing: this degradation is the nearest India can approach to the treatment she was receiving in her own land from her own people before she married, when she was a sweated shop-girl and

prostitute. That artless, passionate episode is one of the most credi-
table literary by-products of the woman's movement.

Another book which ought to engage the attentions of suffragettes
is *Billie's Mother*. It profusely justifies every accusation that any
irritated man could ever have brought against the female sex. The
story stands knee-deep in legal inaccuracies. Neither providence nor
the Law Society does anything to the solicitor who informs Billie's
mother that by English law a child belongs solely to its mother until
it is eight years old. And Billie's father has hardly finished telling
Billie's mother that their marriage was invalid because he married
her under a false name when he remarks that as the police are after
him he had better go to Spain, where there is no extradition. There is
the amazing lack of public conscience of which women are so often
accused; the heroine is supposed to have risen to the heights of moral
grandeur when she commits perjury to save her worthless husband
from arrest for murder. And there is a quite unjustifiable assumption
that every woman who has had a child has reached thereby a nobility
unattainable by any man. Perhaps some day some man will make
things equal by writing about the heavenly wisdom in the eyes of a
young father. Really, the suffragettes ought to buy this book up.

Daily News, 25 March 1915

Mr Hueffer's New Novel

The Good Soldier by Ford Madox Hueffer [Ford]

Mr Ford Madox Hueffer is the Scholar Gipsy of English letters; he is
the author who is recognised only as he disappears round the corner.
It is impossible for anybody with any kind of sense about writing to
miss some sort of distant apprehension of the magnificence of his
work; but unfortunately this apprehension usually takes the form of
enthusiastic but belated discoveries of work that he left on the
doorstep ten years ago.

The Good Soldier will put an end to any such sequestration of Mr
Hueffer's wealth. For it is as impossible to miss the light of its
extreme beauty and wisdom as it would be to miss the full moon on a
clear night. Its first claim on the attention is the obvious loveliness of
the colour and cadence of its language, and it is also clever as the
novels of Mr Henry James are clever, with all sorts of acute discoveries about human nature; and at times it is radiantly witty. And

behind these things there is the delight of a noble and ambitious design, and behind that again, there is the thing we call inspiration – a force of passion which so sustains the story in its flight that never once does it appear as the work of a man's invention. It is because of that unison of inspiration and the finest technique that this story, this close and relentless recital of how the good soldier struggled from the mere clean innocence which was the most his class could expect of him to the knowledge of love, can bear up under the vastness of its subject. For the subject is, one realises when one has come to the end of this saddest story, much vaster than one had imagined that any story about well-bred people, who live in sunny houses with deer in the park, and play polo, and go to Nauheim for the cure, could possibly contain.

It is the record of the spiritual life of Edward Ashburnham, who was a large, fair person of the governing class, with an entirely deceptive appearance of being just the kind of person he looked. It was his misfortune that he had brought to the business of landowning a fatal touch of imagination which made him believe it his duty to be 'an overlord doing his best by his dependants, the dependants meanwhile doing their best by the overlord'; to make life splendid and noble and easier for everybody by his government. And since this ideal meant that he became in his way a creative artist, he began to feel the desire to go to some woman for 'moral support, the encouragement, the relief from the sense of loneliness, the assurance of his own worth'. And although Leonora, his wife, was fine and proud, a northern light among women, she simply could not understand that marriage meant anything but an appearance of loyalty before the world and the efficient management of one's husband's estate. She 'had a vague sort of idea that, to a man, all women are the same after three weeks of close intercourse. She thought that the kindness should no longer appeal, the soft and mournful voice no longer thrill, the tall darkness no longer give a man the illusion that he was going into the depths of an unexplored wood.' And so poor Edward walked the world starved.

His starvation leads him into any number of gentle, innocent, sentimental passions. It delivers him over as the prey of a terrible and wholly credible American, a cold and controlled egoist who reads like the real truth about an Anne Douglas Sedgwick or Edith Wharton heroine. And meanwhile his wife becomes so embittered by what she considers as an insane, and possibly rather nasty, obsession, that she loses her pride and her nobility and becomes, in that last hour when Edward has found a real passion, so darkly, subtly treacherous that he and the quite innocent young girl whom he loves are precipitated down into the blackest tragedy. All three are lost; and perhaps Leonora, robbed of her fineness, is most lost of all.

And when one has come to the end of this beautiful and moving story it is worth while reading the book over again simply to observe the wonders of its technique. Mr Hueffer has used the device, invented and used successfully by Mr Henry James and used not nearly so credibly by Mr Conrad, of presenting the story not as it appeared to a divine and omnipresent intelligence, but as it was observed by some intervener not too intimately concerned in the plot. It is a device that always breaks down at the great moment, when the revelatory detail must be given; but it has the great advantage of setting the tone of the prose from the beginning to the end. And out of the leisured colloquialism of the gentle American who tells the story Mr Hueffer has made a prose that falls on the page like sunlight. It was the supreme triumph of art, that effect of effortlessness and inevitableness, which Mengs described when he said that one of Velasquez's pictures seemed to be painted not by the hand but by pure thought. Indeed, this is a much, much better book than any of us deserve.

Daily News, 2 April 1915

A Novel of Feminism

Angela's Business by Henry Sydnor Harrison

This tale of a serious young American who tried to find out the true destiny of womanhood is the most amusing novel that has yet been written round feminism. The description of the Redmantle Club reception, 'full of people who liked to wear breakfast-gowns in the evening, people with uncombed hair and burning pop-eyes, people who had little chin, indeed, but yet far more chin than humour,' recalls very painfully the phase through which the feminist movement was passing when it was interrupted by the war. After enduring a lecture by Miss Hodger on 'The Higher Law and the Richness of Personality, of Contributions to the Race and Enhancement of the Life Stream', the unfortunate hero fell right into the net of the hearth-side anarchist, Professor Pollock, who drew him in with a hand as large and soft as a beefsteak.

Pollock was a thin, bald young man, with the conventional flowing necktie, and the new disappearing chin . . . 'How are we going to relieve this White Slave situation, Garrott? How? How? . . . What, you admit that you have no remedy to lay down? None whatever?' 'At the moment, none. It is one of the grave –' The younger and even freer Miss Hodger, who had been hovering near, exploded a mouthful of cigarette smoke, and exclaimed excitedly, 'Oh, sister, only think! Mr Garrott has no remedy for the White Slave situation!' They thought it most reprehensible of him to have no remedy, and closed in on him, bursting with theirs. 'Have you not considered the necessities of the living wage?' demanded the elder Miss Hodger's joyless voice, suddenly at his elbow. 'Living wage – bah!' said Professor Pollock, hotly. 'A mere sop – a mere feeble temporising.' 'You must get into their homes!' cried the youngest Miss Hodger, who admitted homes only as places to get into. 'You must take them very, very young.'

Not unnaturally, Mr Garrott turns very gladly from this sort of thing to the gentle Angela, who declares that 'truly it seems to me that – just making a home is sometimes all the business a woman could possibly attend to'. However, the painful discovery that the womanly woman may become a spider luring one in to bridge parties, a boa constrictor who entangles one in embraces one had not premeditated, a bird of prey who tracks one round the town in her Fordette, drives him back to the arms of the suffragette heroine, who is 'his dearest comrade, his work-fellow and his playmate, his human free and equal', who thought 'there was no competence a man had that this woman did not have . . . had tilled and kept sweet the garden of her womanhood', without resorting to the use of Fordettes.

The only pity is that this love affair is conducted with the extreme dilatoriness which characterises most amorous undertakings in American fiction. The hero and heroine are so long in approaching one another that it seems as incredible that they should arrive at any crucial meeting as that there should be a collision between two hearses. A small fund should be raised by suffering reviewers to send the works of Mrs Aphra Behn, and those other Restoration dramatists who knew how to be expeditious in these matters, to the United States for distribution among the more deliberate school of novelists.

Daily News, 4 May 1915

Mr Wells through American Eyes

The World of H. G. Wells by Van Wyck Brooks

Mr Van Wyck Brooks is one of those young American writers who would have made excellent wives and mothers. He fails from sheer excess of the housewifely qualities. He is saving: just as in happier circumstances he would have put every scrap into the stockpot, so now he refuses to throw away the very driest bone of thought, and insists on boiling it up into his mental soup. He is hospitable: the deadest idea does not get turned away from his doorstep. He is cleanly: his bleached, scentless style suggests that he hung out the English language on the line in the dry, pure breezes of Boston before he used it. He has as much religion as my William likes: while hesitating to commit himself to the crudities of Christianity he yet maintains that there must be something that these scientists leave out – something warm and kind, but not so warm as to cause inconvenient ecstasy, not so much a God indeed as a nicely covered hot-water-bottle heating the cold bed of life. He is capable of drawing a comparison between Mr H. G. Wells and Matthew Arnold without pausing to speculate whether it is decent to imagine Mr Wells as the uncle of Mrs Humphry Ward.

All these qualities which should, had the sex of the author permitted it, have been the joy of some good man's home, contribute to a vast blot-like impression of wrongness which proves once more that the senses are the gates of the soul. For if Mr Van Wyck Brooks had had that eye for print which corresponds to an ear for music, if he had been able to apprehend that prose has colour and smell and taste, he would not have become involved in the system of errors which makes this book so much more unpleasant than one could have imagined a book by a pleasant person could possibly be. 'I don't know,' he says, 'that the tales of Wells are better tales' than those by Jules Verne, and that amazed confession makes one wonder whether there are young men who insist on entering the profession of tea-tasting in spite of the disadvantage of having been born without the sense of taste.

'His range is very small,' he says elsewhere. 'The same figures reappear constantly. There is the Wells hero: Lewisham, Capes, Ponderevo, Remington, Trafford Stratton; there is the Wells heroine: Ann Veronica, Isabel, Marjorie, Lady Mary.' This is like contending the ultimate identity of the letters of the alphabet. To relish its absurdity one need only think of poor little Mr Lewisham, pathetic as a netted calf, watching with terror the advances of Ann Veronica . . . Or one may imagine Trafford, that thoroughly nice young man, blenching and wishing that Uncle Ponderevo would not lay his large moist hand on his coat-collar and talk so loudly of cornering ipecac. And, although one can imagine Mr Wells's heroines forming a War Fund Committee which would presently be banned by Scotland Yard on account of financial complexity, they have nothing in common except their persistent trait of dishonesty.

Ann Veronica was a common young woman with, as we say nowadays, push and go; Isabel was an attractive shadow who talked nervously about babies; Marjorie was torn by the soul of a pawnbroker; and the book in which Lady Mary appeared had better been called not *The Passionate Friends*, but *The New Messalina*.

And just as a character is the same as any other character to Mr Van Wyck Brooks, so a book is the same as any other book. He mentions *The Passionate Friends* as though it were not the worst book written since *Robert Elsmere*, and he talks of *The New Utopia*, with its vision of the world governed by a guild of stuffed bishops called Samurai, as though it were a settled and sober judgement instead of the last frenzied attempt of Mr Wells to set his steed at the Fabian fence. He mentions *Mr Polly* as though it were not one of the great books of the world, and a good fellow to *Don Quixote*, and has not been struck by the epic quality of *Tono-Bungay*. It is evident from his guarded references to Mr Wells's work, that for lack of a personal palate he accepts the current vulgarism that books which aim at the expression of ideas are not art. It is an entirely mystic belief that a piece of work can be deprived of beauty by its intention. One might as well allege that a girl walking along the street is more or less pretty according to whether she is going to a music-hall or a sacred concert. Swift, who wrote pamphlets like an angry angel whose tongue had got the better of its wings; Shelley, who sang not as the linnet does, but because he was a crank; Anatole France, who still produces the socialist monthly for which he wrote *Crainquebille* – all these bear witness that beauty is the fruit of any intensity, even if it be moral. As Mr Wells himself has put it, 'Beauty isn't a special inserted sort of thing . . . It is just life, pure life, life nascent, running clear and strong.'

And Mr Van Wyck Brooks is as wrong about wisdom as he is about beauty. Mr Wells it appears,

is an 'intellectual' rather than an artist, that is to say, he naturally grasps and interprets life in the light of ideas rather than in the light of experience. To Conrad [whom Mr Van Wyck Brooks has chosen as his antithesis] the spirit of unrest is a personal mood, a thing, as people used to say, between man and his Maker; whereas to Wells the spirit of unrest is not a mood but a rationally explicable frame of mind, a sense of restricted function, an issue to be fought out not between man and nature but between man and society.

The loose, pretentious phrasing of it, with its assumption that man is not a part of nature and equally venerable, is the kind of thing that happens to a nation which admits the sham psychology of Stanley Hall and Munsterberg to its universities. But the test which Mr Van Wyck Brooks adopts in umpiring between the two writers is incredibly näive for any culture. Mr Conrad must be right about life, because he has gone down to the sea in ships, and Mr Wells must be wrong because he is a 'scientist' and has made 'an overbalancing study of science at the expense of the humanities'. One realises the humour of this test in reflecting that the branch of science in which Mr Wells is learned is biology, which is the study of life stripped naked; or in imagining how pleased Mr Conrad would be at hearing that he owed his vision to the fact that he was intellectually undeveloped. But one simply despairs of any progress ever being made on earth when one finds a literate young man like Mr Van Wyck Brooks pretending, like any grocer who lays down the law on an education committee because he is a 'practical man', that those who grapple with the appearances of life are inherently superior to those who, with no less stress and mental adventure, try to unveil its reality. But Mr Van Wyck Brooks nullifies the effect of his own book by making one feel that nothing matters very much, and that English literature is a joke we play on America.

Daily News, 14 August 1915

Miss Sinclair's Genius

A Journal of Impressions in Belgium by May Sinclair

The contrast between the manner of Miss Sinclair's genius and its achievements is difficult to define. It is as though the usual literary process had been reversed and a mouse had produced a mountain. She writes about life as though she were a little girl sitting on a tin trunk at a railway station and watching the people go by; she writes as though at the most hopeful estimate she might be another Miss

Mitford; and out of this piteousness and diffidence and round-eyed observation there amazingly comes a fierce, large vision of reality. It is entirely characteristic of Miss Sinclair that this record of seventeen days spent in Belgium, which is largely a record of humiliations, and is told with the extremest timidity and a trembling meticulosity about the lightest facts, should be one of the few books of permanent value produced by the war.

Partly it is because her meticulosity makes her describe what writers more accustomed to the battlefield leave one to take for granted. 'While we were hanging about the station a shell was hurled over the side of the village from the German batteries. It careered over the roofs, with a track that was luminous in the dusk, like a curved sheet of lightning.' We have been hearing of bursting shells ever since the war began and trying to visualise them, and not till now has anyone paused to tell us what they looked like. And partly it is because she writes of such a company of heroes as never lived before: of girls of nineteen who trudge over turnip-fields among the bullets to look for the wounded, not in any sudden flame of courage, but as a daily occupation; of women who stayed in Antwerp at their posts till the red skies fell in on them.

And partly because it is very plain that the writer has written none of these things for her own profit. One does not refer to the little printed slip that tells one that the royalties of this book will go to the National Committee for Relief in Belgium, for nowadays such generosity is as common as courage. The book is pleasant with a rarer thing than that. 'I remember,' she writes,

the Sunday evening when the Commandant dropped in after he had come back from Belgium. He said, 'They are bringing up the heavy siege guns from Namur, and there is going to be a terrific bombardment of Antwerp, and I think it will be very interesting for you to see it.' I remember replying with passionate sincerity that I would rather die than see it; that if I could nurse the wounded I would face any bombardment you please to name; but to go and look on couldn't help – I couldn't and I wouldn't, and that was flat.

The book is given a solemnity by her sense that it is as indecent to intrude without cause upon the deathbed of Europe as it would be to intrude upon the deathbed of a neighbour.

Miss Sinclair has written down nothing except the sights that came under her eyes while she was secretary and reporter to a certain famous Field Ambulance Corps. She makes no attempt to state the case for Belgium, and when one comes to think of it one cannot imagine Miss Sinclair presuming to express an opinion upon international affairs. Yet by her mysterious subterranean methods she makes one ache for Belgium as one used to before the sorrows of the nations had made one numb, and remember that all our sacrifices will be little things beside that immortal sacrifice. She tells us of the Flandria Palace Hotel, 'a huge building of extravagant design, wearing its turrets, its balconies, its very roofs, like so much decoration', strange and stricken as a military hospital, its corridors reeking with the bitter-sweet smell of anaesthetics; and one moves in the nightmare atmosphere of a country living yesterday in peace and laughter and industry, with perhaps a little grossness here and there, and today utterly flooded with death.

And there is the unendurable description of the refugees asleep in the Palais des Fêtes at Ghent:

It is where the great Annual Shows were held and the vast civic entertainments given. Miles of country round Ghent are given up to market-gardening. There are whole fields of begonias out here, brilliant and vivid in the sun. They will never be sold, never gathered, never shown in the Palais des Fêtes. It is the peasants, the men and women who tilled these fields, and their children that are being shown here, in the splendid and wonderful place where they never set foot before. There are four thousand of them lying on straw in the outer hall, in a space larger than Olympia . . .

And so the passage goes on, hard and inflexible with the numbness that comes to those who look on such horror. One can imagine, in some drowsy schoolroom of two thousand years hence, the children of some future civilisation constructing it and getting a ghostly thrill of the long dead danger as the children of today construe Pliny's account of the flight from Vesuvius.

And there is the description of the smoke from the burning factory of Schoonard trailing like an enormous cloud across the southern sky:

East of it, on the sky-line, was a whole fleet of little clouds that hung low over the earth; that rose from it; rose and were never lifted, but, as they were shredded away, scattered and vanished, were perpetually renewed. This movement of their death and rebirth had a horrible sinister pulse in it. Each cloud of this fleet of clouds was the smoke from a burning village.

And against this background, which is a miracle of dreadfulness, there moves the Ambulance Corps, which is a miracle of human splendour. It is merciful that, just as one discovers that the world is capable of being infinitely more atrocious than one had imagined, one learns that it is also capable of being infinitely more noble. One perceives quite clearly that some members of this Ambulance Corps must have been intolerable as individuals: 'practical' women who use their common sense to rasp their neighbours' shins and regard suavity as a part of incompetence. And yet, united by their collective purpose of courage, they became an organisation so magnificent in its fearlessness that one accepts as a real tragedy the personal grief which makes this book muted like words spoken by one who holds back the tears. No triumph of good work that may come to Miss Sinclair will ever make up to her for the discovery that the artist is unfitted for the life of action. And yet every page of this gallant, humiliated book makes it plain that while it is glorious that England should have women who walk quietly under the rain of bullets it is glorious too that England should have women who grieve inconsolably because the face of danger has not been turned to them.

Daily News, 24 August 1915

The Woman Worker

Good Points of the Factory System

Women in Modern Industry by B. L. Hutchins

Miss B. L. Hutchins has conspicuously escaped from the Fabian tradition of conscientious bad writing. *Women in Modern Industry* is written in a straight and sexless manner which is always pleasant and a little unexpected in works that are even indirectly a part of the feminist movement. But Miss Hutchins has not escaped from the Fabian tradition of studying social problems from London. The Fabians send out forms from Tothill Street as Noah sent out doves from the ark, and the form is almost as limited in its power of expression as the dove. It can do little but bring back a statistic in its beak. And it has not supplied Miss Hutchins with anything like enough material to justify the comprehensive title of the book.

The volume consists of a historical sketch of women in industry up to the eighteenth century, a detailed study of the effect of the industrial revolution upon women, a survey of their trade unions, and a chapter on the effect of the war upon women workers. How partial a view of the position of women in industry this gives may be judged from the fact that there is no mention of the women in the ubiquitous boot-and-shoe trade except in a paragraph of an additional chapter in which Mr J. J. Mallon discusses the very incomplete Wages Census taken by the Board of Trade nearly ten years ago. Dundee and

Nottingham are towns that leap to the mind at once as affording interesting opportunities for the observation of women workers, but there is only a passing reference to the one and none at all to the other. But what Miss Hutchins does deal with is treated with excellent sense and unusual ease of presentation.

The historical sketch of women's work is necessarily slight in view of the lack of data; but it does demonstrate that 'the women of the industrial classes have always worked, and worked hard. It is only in quite modern times, so far as I can discover, that the question whether some kinds of work were not too hard for women has been raised.' In the woman's movement one has learned to fear the writers who inquire into the beginnings of things: too often they desire to remould the marriage laws in the light of the behaviour of courting octopi and regard the hut-making of the primitive Fuegians as a claim to the English parliamentary franchise.

But this research into the past has its lesson for the present. It puts in their proper place those young men who are to be found in every branch of the I L P and all other local symptoms of socialism desiring with a mixture of hostility and kindly sexual protectiveness (which is much worse to withdraw women from the labour world into which, they conceive, they were suddenly thrust by the industrial revolution.

Indeed, the whole book is a wholesome corrective to the new socialist mythology which has it that the snake crawled into the Garden of Eden with a spinning jenny held in its fangs. The industrial revolution was one of the world's growing pains. Its immediate effects were incredibly horrible. We can hardly realise the sudden beggary that it brought upon the people even when we read that the weekly income of an average Lancashire weaving family of six persons declined in six years from £2 12s to £1 13s, and in another thirteen years to a bare 12s. But in the end the industrial revolution brought the people four great benefits. 'By the use of mechanical power the need for muscular strength is diminished and greater possibilities are opened up to the weaker classes of workers;' though, when one thinks of the agonies of 'speeding-up' in the modern mill, one may doubt whether the strain has not been merely shifted from the muscles to the nerves. It has raised the status of women workers and made them freer, because they are now paid their own wages instead of sharing in a collective income of the family as they commonly did under the domestic system. It has led to State control of the conditions of work. And it has forced the workers to mix with each other and combine. They have become a new people.

There are just one or two noticeable blemishes on Miss Hutchins's excellent study of the crisis and its results. It seems strange that she should regard the influx of rural labourers to the factories as evidence on the side of the canting professions of the early manufacturers that these factories were home from home. All it meant was that the governing classes had the poor on toast both in town and country, and the poor preferred the town toast as more sociable. Like so many social students, Miss Hutchins writes as though the domestic system had disappeared and left not one vestige behind it. Yet surely, it is very common, particularly in the West Riding, for the old handlooms still to be worked by half the family while the other half goes to the mill. And while she gives the history of framework knitting up till the eighteenth century, she never mentions that sinister feature of modern rural life, the knitting-machine. Yet it is surely valuable in considering the domestic system to note how a cottager's wife who works a knitting-machine seems to get much less fresh air and exercise than the ordinary mill-girl. Nor does she mention the fact, in its way of immense significance, of the superiority of home-spun cloth to the machine-made product.

The survey of trade unionism is useful, and the story of the uprising of sweated women in 1911 reminds us of the much sweeter victories of peace. But one must protest against the constant demand that 'women' must not be allowed to carry excessive weights, that 'women' must not overstrain their constitutions. It is the fashion among certain kinds of feminist to emphasise this admission of the weakness of their sex in order to demonstrate their broadmindedness. This not only makes a false suggestion that women are infected animals in the flock, but it is also grossly unfair to men, who probably suffer much more from these things.

Surely it is common knowledge among the less-skilled labourers in the North that there is a certain famous factory where no man can work for more than a year, and where men are sometimes wrecked for life after a fortnight's work. Protection in this respect must be given not to women but to workers. Miss Hutchins' neglect of this point is due to the lack of first-hand knowledge which prevents her book from being supremely good. But it is as good as any book written on industry from a study could possibly be.

Daily News, 19 November 1915

Mr Bennett's Trilogy

These Twain by Arnold Bennett

Just as *Clayhanger* was a large and discursive account of the growth to maturity of a middle-class man, so this last volume, which completes the trilogy, is a large and discursive account of the growth to maturity of a middle-class marriage. Hilda Lessways emerged upon marriage from the discomforts of keeping a Brighton boarding-house, grim and flushed, like a young woman drawn backward through a hedge. Edwin Clayhanger stood back and gazed at the long-desired woman like a man who had long suffered from a chilly sitting-room, and had at last found the right type of gas stove. That is not the complete statement of the case, for within each there burned the pure fire of passion, but it conveys the attitudes which their peculiar temperaments adopted towards marriage in their cooler moments. And this volume is the story of their discomfiture. They had shut up shop and foresworn adventure, and when they got home they found adventure sitting on the hearth. Edwin Clayhanger found himself imprisoned in an incredibly fantastic existence. One might figure him as a man living in a large and rambling house of many rooms with a magically elusive companion. Its aspect changed from hour to hour: sometimes the rooms were infinite and flooded with sunshine, and at other times they were still numberless, but all filled with damp dreariness; and yet again it would shrink to something small and hut-like, tottering in the winds, or rear to the skies the domes of a palace. And his companion was not more stable, being today an enraged presence in a distant attic treading with the firm step of anger; and tomorrow warm in his arms, nearly himself, nearly a part of his identity. And gradually, apart from the shocks and despairs and raptures of the moment, grows up in him a conviction that out of the whole world this is the one home, this the one relationship, that suits his soul.

So far as this volume is the recital of Clayhanger's adventures in marriage it is wholly admirable. It is wonderful of Mr Bennett to have created a figure at once so drab and so charming, so appealing in its mixture of competence and timidity, of kind social conformity and gentle intellectual scepticism, and it is wonderful of him to know Clayhanger so well that he can gossip endlessly about him without ever seeming to 'make it up'. And it is also an achievement that the anecdotes by which he reveals the spiritual progress of his friend are

beautiful as well as true. There are people who turn up their noses at
Mr Bennett because he is not one of our picturesque writers, being
neither a Polish sailor in the Malay Straits or an undergraduate
discovering the underworld, but merely a kind of literary four-
wheeler that crawls up and down the Five Towns. We recommend
them to read the exquisite incident that occurs when Clayhanger
goes to Ingpen's rooms. Edwin has been called away to the hospital by
the Factory Inspector (who had been badly injured in an accident), in
the middle of a crisis when he is bitterly resenting his married loss of
liberty. Ingpen sends him to his rooms to burn his letters. There is a
line of light under the door. He finds a girl there asleep. He looks
down on her slim body, limp with the abandonment of unconsciousness, on the white ear peeping out of her hair, and sees here 'the
realisation of a dream that was to marriage what poetry is to prose'.
And then she starts up and he sees that she is old and not graceful and
undistinguished. 'I think you're gentleman enough not to say anything about me being here,' she said, rather nastily. 'It was quite an
accident. I could easily explain it, but you know what people are!'
The romance wilts on the page like a rose held in the hand, it ends in
mockery like a Heine lyric. It is Apollo who holds the reins of Mr
Bennett's dingy four-wheeler.

But when Mr Bennett changes the large, loose world to which
Clayhanger accustomed us for the smaller, neater, more eventful
world of *Hilda Lessways* the book suffers. There is too much plot in
These Twain. The French swaggerer whose bigamous marriage with
Hilda had been the cause of her early distresses reappears as a wrongly
convicted prisoner in Dartmoor, who has to be helped by the
Clayhangers to a free pardon and subsequently to escape to America
from the vindictive fidelity of his first wife. None of these things
matter, and they have a grossly accidental quality. Moreover, they
offend by bringing Hilda into action when it is plainly her duty to
float as a subjective being in Edwin's consciousness. If one considers
her as a real person one perceives that she is not so much a study of a
woman based upon observation, but a rash deduction from a couple of
hair-pins; but one can accept her as the illusory image a man might
make to himself of the woman he loves. As such she is as beautifully
powerful a creation as the mean and squalidly domestic Benbows, as
smug in the sense that they were carrying on the torch of life as
Auntie Hamps, who found a mysterious consolation on her deathbed
at the sight of their uninteresting children; or the Bigreaves seen here
scattering into homeless degeneracy; or anything, indeed, for it is
nearly all wonderful in that multitudinous background of Five

Towns' life against which we see, commonplace but mysterious, shambling but dignified, our Edwin Clayhanger.

Daily News, 14 January 1916

Mr Thomas Hardy

Thomas Hardy by Harold Child

One cannot erect any majestic tower of criticism on the narrow basis of twenty thousand words, and there is no use trying to justify one's liking for Mr Child's essay on Thomas Hardy by the pretence that it is a very momentous event in the world of letters. It compels one's affections not so much by any feats of writing or insight as by the many manifestations that its author loves Mr Hardy's genius. If he were not possessed by real passion he could not have handled so lightly one of the most tedious of all literary tasks and given such excellent working models of the plots of the novels. The only time when one doubts his understanding is when he states that Tess murdered Alec d'Urberville 'to be free to join her husband'. Surely the blow that made the red spot on the ceiling was a blind gesture of vengeance against the spoiler who had once more shut her out of the sunshine, delivered with that characteristic clumsiness which makes one feel that if one had engaged Tess as a cook she would have gone in heavily for breakages.

And though it is merely a matter of taste, one wishes Mr Child had not described Arabella as 'a gross village girl' who dragged down Jude the Obscure. Arabella, with her delightful habit of hatching birds' eggs in her bodice, was one of the world's good things of the steak-and-onions and beer-and-cheese order. Jude was much more likely to become a great man by following the instinct for vital things that he showed when he married her, than by giving way to the desire for culture which he expressed in his positively American respect for the older universities and his longing to read anything on earth so long as it was not in English.

There is one point, too, where his appreciation of the bleak beauty of Mr Hardy's poetry fails. While he gives *The Dynasts* its high pinnacle as an epic, he underrates the sensuous loveliness of it. It is not the loveliness one expects of poetry, but it leaves the authentic thrill and it lives in the memory like a real thing. It comes to one like a personal recollection of a moving moment that one evening

Napoleon and Josephine wrangled the world to war in a twilit room while the white gowns of the girls playing at ball in the garden glimmered through the dusk.

But Mr Child's slight depreciation of the beauty of *The Dynasts* is a little thing beside the fact that he loves Mr Hardy's poetry as it ought to be loved. Nature has had longer than literature to force its public to accept its different sorts of beauty and nowadays nobody dislikes the Downs because they are unsuitable for tennis-lawns and are not favourable for the growing of geraniums. But towards literature we preserve the attitude that the eighteenth century adopted towards nature when it called the Alps 'horrid and undisciplined', and turn our steps away from any poetry which rises with the sheerness of the precipice which is not clothed with the vegetation of fancy, which shows nakedly the very structure of the earth.

The sympathy which Mr Child shows for Mr Hardy's genius is so profound that it is surprising to find that he is equally distressed at Mr Hardy's discontent with love, which he condemns as an organ that plays too small a music, a lamp that gives too faint a light, an experience that does not change life enough, and at his view of woman as a weak thing that climbs up a few steps of the ladder toward free thought and unsuperstitious living, but always falls to the bottom again, and that he yet does not see the obvious connection between these two views and their common explanation. Mr Hardy was bound to find love an unsubstantial thing so long as he believed that there were none but flimsy women to love. That he believes all women flimsy is a consequence of his being a novelist of the people. Sue Bridehead, with her half-hearted renunciation of orthodoxy, that is inspired not so much by her own intellect as by obedience to the will of Jude, and her scuttling back to the rabbit-holes of convention at the time when Jude is most sorely in need of her help against society, is woman as innumerable working men have seen her.

A working man approached on the subject of woman suffrage nearly always grumbles that girls are not sufficiently independent to form trade unions; that his wife believes in what he believes, and will work out no creed of her own; that when he is not looking she runs round to the priest or reads fortunes from tea-leaves, or otherwise resumes relations with whatever seems to him to be superstitious; and it is always assumed that these are defects innate in women. A working girl never makes enough to afford substantial meals, and after her marriage she gets what is left over of the good food, which her husband must necessarily have to keep up his strength for working; and, in consequence, her brain never receives the red blood by which it must be nourished before it can find a faith or hold to it. When every woman demands that her steak shall be red inside and black outside there will be no more Sue Brideheads; but in these days, when many women have to lunch on tea and buns, a great many men do get the false impression that they are weak creatures, incapable of carrying out the bargains even of love.

When it is considered that this is the only one of all the grievances against life recorded by Mr Hardy which he does not perceive could be altered by the will of mankind working through its intellect, one perceives how right Mr Child is in insisting that Mr Hardy is fundamentally an optimist. He draws the agony of Tess to show us what beauty might flower before us if man would but surrender his lust and jealousy and passion for pelting the unhappy. His contemplation of tragedy is a profound recognition of joy, for he is enabled to look on what would revolt the sentimentalist by his consciousness that life at its worst is glorious.

> – Yet, would men look at true things,
> And unilluded view things,
> And count to bear undue things.
>
> The real might mend the seeming,
> Facts better their foredeeming,
> And Life its disesteeming.

That is the fine truth about the author whom the foolish are never tired of abusing as (to quote Mr Chesterton's malignant phrase) 'the village atheist brooding and blaspheming over the village idiot'; and one could say nothing better about Mr Child's essay than that he lovingly expounds it.

Daily News, 21 February 1916

American Women: Their Work as Reformers

Women's Work in Municipalities by Mary Ritter Beard

This is the barbaric yawp of social reform. In this country municipal advance is wrung from the hands of established persons with paunches by earnest people with spectacles. But over in America it seems to be carried out by pioneer mothers who have run out into the yard, with flour on their aprons and frying-pans in their hands, to tell the male that lounges against the gate-post that if he doesn't do that chore he has been told about there will be trouble. They are violent, they are sometimes incredibly naïve and even blatantly ignorant – they extend their blessing to that Dr Mabel McCoy Irwin who got the Post Office to suppress *Man and Superman* in the mails – but they have the strong right arm and the short, invigorating temper of the housewife.

They get things done. 'In Woonsocket, in the dry region of South Dakota, the women of a club requested the Town Fathers to supply them with pure and more abundant water.' The Fathers were unenthusiastic. 'The women, nothing daunted, organised an Improvement Association, collected money and hired an expert to drill an artesian well.' In Pasadena, California, a women's club is collecting a fund (to which, we are glad to hear, 'the Pasadena Elks have donated a lot') for the establishment of a free public market under sanitary conditions. The Women's Town Improvement Association of Westport, Connecticut, laid 2,000 feet of sidewalk. The Women's City Club of Chicago campaigned for a modern method of garbage disposal.

Those American activities may strike the ignorant as teaching no lesson to the Englishwoman; in our established country, it may seem to them, all these things have been done already. Yet innumerable Medical Officers of Health of English districts complain every year in their reports that there can be no reduction of the deaths due to pulmonary disorders until the roads have been improved. And our government reports show again and again that one of the most conspicuous causes behind a high rate of infant mortality is an antiquated system of refuse destruction, particularly when associated with bad housing conditions. These American agitations, which seem no more statesmanlike than the flapping of dust, protect the State at its roots.

And they do subtle things too. They have little methods of investigation that stab down into the heart of the present capitalist system, devices that we have just begun to think about. Here in London one very often hears it said that it is a waste of money to give elementary-schoolchildren scholarships to take them on to the secondary schools because the children never do well in the new conditions; and one out of two people who learn this fact accept it as a proof of the inherent lowerness of the lower classes. But over there they have thrown light on this social system by appointing visiting teachers who attend to the schoolchildren's intelligences as our school nurses attend to their health.

In her report on Visiting Teachers for the Public Education Association of New York, Mary Flexner records the very high ratio of 45 per cent of the cases covered by visiting teachers for the years 1911–12 as being 'cases' because home poverty retarded the development of the child. In explanation of the term poverty, Miss Flexner says: 'This term is interpreted broadly to include all cases in which "economic pressure" makes of the child an illegal wage-earner or a household drudge and forces the family to adopt such a low standard of living that there is neither proper space for the child to study nor proper food to give it the stimulus to do so.' Miss Flexner further shows that 57 per cent of the cases showed lack of family appreciation of what are the needs of a normal or an abnormal child. A summary of the action taken in all the cases is a most vital part of the report.

In this country we send for a plumber when we suspect an escape of gas; why don't we then, send for a teacher when we suspect an escape of intelligence? That bright idea is just one of a constellation of bright ideas about milk depots, free dental clinics, 'follow-up' treatment of hospital patients and municipal bureaux established exclusively to deal with children's health, which make one wish that copies of this book could be sent, with insulting marginal notes, to our municipal bodies. And these reforms are administered by women almost as often as they are invented and supported by them. Mrs Mathilde Coffin Ford, for instance, examining-inspector for the Bureau of Municipal Investigation and Statistics in the City of New York, has the spending of forty million dollars a year.

There are pages in this book which will make the English suffragist blench. The Mann Act, which makes any man who travels with a woman to whom he is not married liable to five years'.imprisonment and a thousand-pound fine, no matter how old the woman may be and how willing, seems a law of intolerable harshness, when it is remembered that there are States within the Union where there is no divorce law. But then this really is the barbaric yawp of social reform. These people are not sitting round polished tables in the quiet committee-rooms of an established social system; they are shouting at each other, while a nation is being noisily run up over their heads by workmen who speak so many different tongues that they communicate chiefly by blows.

To realise how difficult is America's task of becoming a nation one must read the amazing chapter in this volume on 'The Assimilation of Races'. There it is shown how the white American corrupts himself because he believes himself to be superior to the Negro, and takes certain ways of showing it. He will not employ the Negro in any skilled occupation, no matter what talent the black man may show; 'it is not worth while to teach trades to coloured boys.' He makes the Negro live in a 'black belt' which usually includes the segregated vice district, and then charges them such high rents (from 10 to 30 per cent more than a white family would pay for similar accommodation) that they are obliged to take in lodgers, who as a rule come to be near the vice district, and are unwholesome influences in the Negro's home. The consequence is that a vast number of black men find work in drinking saloons and gambling houses, and as many black women become servants in disorderly houses; that is, it has been made the interest of the race to encourage the superior race in exactly those practices which will make it lose its superiority. How women are helping to rectify this social mistake is only one of the stories that make this book a most romantic history.

Daily News, 9 March 1916

Woman's Work

Conflicting Ideals of Woman's Work by B. L. Hutchins

It is of inestimable value that fairmindedness should be insisted upon in the feminist argument; for it was in dealing with the early feminist that the Government acquired the tact and skilfulness with which it is now handling Ireland. So one hails with gladness a popular edition of *Conflicting Ideals of Woman's Work*, that little book in which Miss Hutchins showed that both the people who want women to stay at home to create the use-values of housewifery and motherhood and to exercise influence on their husbands and children, and the other people who want women to go out into the labour market to create the exchange-values of industrial and professional efficiency and to exercise influence on public affairs, have the right on their side. It had become abundantly evident in the later phases of the suffrage movement that the woman who had not had a more or less intimate contact with a home could not be a successful feminist. For one thing it is hard to get a grasp of the economic system unless one has had the insight into it which is given by the necessity to organise the consumption of a family. For another, even the ablest women are apt to make fools of themselves if they indulge in guesswork about the fundamental relationships of life; it is not so long ago since we were being so persistently told by some of the cleverest women in England that the tenderest thought the average man could conceive for a woman was a plot to abduct her to Buenos Aires.

And on the other side the facts rush at us. It is a matter of common knowledge that a woman is apt to be a slack and listless housewife unless she has learned the pride and method of good work in some industry or profession. It is a matter of common knowledge that a large number of well-to-do wives do not create sufficient use-value to justify their support by the community. One wishes that Miss Hutchins had used her capacity to make a survey of some of our sleeker suburbs to illustrate this fact. There is a certain district half an hour from Euston that would admirably have served her purpose. There the houses, the rents of which run from £75 to £120, are on an estate owned by a great manufacturer whose aspirations towards refinement take the odd and anti-social form of prohibiting the erection of schools or shops, so the housewife has to buy thriftlessly from tradesmen at the door and send her children to a school a mile distant on a dusty high-road much used by motors. The local government of the district is bad; it is inadequately policed from a station nearly four miles distant, and of late the roads have been watered too seldom and the refuse is removed only once a fortnight. It is plainly the duty of the housewife, since her husband does his day's work in the creation of exchange-values, to organise against these attacks upon the well-being of her home. Yet, so little is it accepted by the current thought of England that the wife should earn her keep by use-values, that the housewife regards herself as having squared her account with society when she accomplishes the not exhausting task of supervising one or two servants and the embellishment of life by gramophones, tennis and the cultivation of geraniums, calceolarias and marguerites.

This book is pleasant and interesting throughout, although one has to complain sometimes that Miss Hutchins receives and cites the opinions of reactionaries with too much charity; it's as though she hushed her voice to let the parrot speak. When she quotes 'the biologists (e.g. Dr Lionel Tayler)', one would not be surprised if she went on to quote 'the sociologists (e.g. Horatio Bottomley)' or 'the zoologists (e.g. Lord George Sanger)'. As for Dr Saleeby's *Woman and Womanhood*, one remembers with agony the mental quality of that plea that little girls should be nurtured in an atmosphere of priggery, with Ruskin's silly remark that 'Woman was born to be Love visible' hanging instead of maps in the schoolroom, so that when they grow up they shall not marry men suffering from delirium tremens. And as for Dr Tayler's *The Nature of Woman*, the language of criticism breaks down, and one can only describe it as a fair scream. This shyness to admit the worthlessness of her opponents is detrimental to the atmosphere of calm which Miss Hutchins desires to bring to the discussion of feminism. For the reason that the feminists lost their temper was very often that they attempted to argue with what, being really the vestigial brute in humanity, was incapable of using words for argument or any other purpose but as a substitute for the single primitive bellow.

Most interesting of all in this volume is the discussion as to whether women should be economically independent or be supported by their menfolk, because our outlook upon it has been so profoundly changed by the war. Miss Hutchins's point that the patriarchal system is the easiest way of arranging in a loosely organised society for the support of the mother still holds good; and so, too, her point against it that 'the responsibility of a family may mean to its head not merely a stimulus to efficiency, but at times a terrible temptation to put gain before all else, to push his business in any way he can, say by advertising and puffery, or various more or less illicit methods which, though commercially profitable, do not exactly promote the social welfare'. But today we perceive a flimsiness in the fears, which yesterday were shared by all of us, that a woman must necessarily enter industry under such conditions of underpayment and inconsiderate treatment that she would be physically spoiled for motherhood, and that it must always be so because a woman is so sure of leaving her work for marriage that she never acquires sufficient skill to make it worth her employer's while to treat her well.

The Ministry of Munitions has not been an ideal supervisor of the employment of women in munition works; although its Welfare Department has published memoranda showing the evil effects of twelve-hour shifts, it gave permission to one firm to alter the system of three eight-hour shifts to two twelve-hour shifts within a week of receiving the application. But it has proved again and again that industry can easily meet the needs of women in high wages and decent conditions in workshops and canteens; and that in work in which there is a higher standard of perfection in output than in perhaps any other industry, women can easily and quickly acquire industrial skill enough to make them valued employees. And it has been borne in on many who have visited these works that there are a vast number of industrial processes which, too tedious for anybody's life work, are suitable for the episodic employment of the young girl or middle-aged woman. That out of the war there should have emerged so clear an indication that the problem of women in industry can be solved ought to suggest to Miss Hutchins that there is a peculiarly suitable field for her patience and efficiency in a survey of the employment of women on munition work. One hopes it will.

Daily News, 7 August 1916

Literary Pulp

A Comment on Strindberg

Plays: Fourth Series by August Strindberg

The Government should prohibit the import of literary pulp as well as wood pulp from Sweden. From that country comes the eroto-priggery of Miss Ellen Key, which exhorts women to abandon all personality and creative effort and be but the damp towel to bind round the heated temples of intellectual man. And from that country comes August Strindberg, that unattractive person who was never at his ease except when he was suffering from persecution mania, and who regarded three wives and a few delusions as adequate material for hundreds of plays. And from that country Strindberg constantly comes, and continues to come. What with *The Confession of a Fool, Married, Comrades, The Father* and the rest of them, one feels one knows the Strindberg family as though one had lived next door and had woken up with a start every time the police were called in. However, the publication of a fourth volume of his plays has been felt by somebody to be necessary. This selection certainly shows a gain in technical suavity; in none of the four plays has he found it necessary to introduce an epileptic fit. But in all other respects this volume confirms one's suspicion that, unless one pays the bookseller with a Jubilee sixpence, gilt to look like a half-sovereign, and waits for the change, it is an act of folly to buy any work by Strindberg.

These plays are all of a different type, and have no link beyond the fact that all the characters are moral imbeciles. The first, *The Bridal Crown,* is one of those confused boilings of supernatural and human characters which seem so delicious to the Scandinavian and Teutonic fancy, which offends one in much the same way as Hauptmann's *The Sunken Bell* or *Hannele* offends. The plot is an indescribably painful story of how a young girl and a young man belonging to the chief families of a Dabearlian village meet on a hill pasture and, since they cannot marry because there is a feud between the families, become secret lovers and have a child, whom they cradle up in the forest. When accident makes the old people forget their quarrel and withdraw their objection to the match, the man's family is so insistent that the marriage can only be permitted if the girl can wear the crown of a vestal bride, that in desperation she kills the child. Before the wedding day the wretched girl betrays her secret by her visible anguish, and is led away to gaol by the sheriff, is sentenced to death, and reprieved and sentenced to imprisonment for life.

To any sensitive author it must immediately have become apparent that such an agonising story could only be treated in a realistic method; it is indecent to let blood flow across the rainbow texture of a fairy-tale. But the whole play is peppered with supernatural beings who make unnecessary remarks and in no way seem to add to the beauty of creation. The murdered child keeps on popping up through the floor; and there is a 'Child in White' in the worst possible Victorian mode, who constantly appears and prays quite unhelpfully round the principal characters to the accompaniment of the 'bell-like notes of the harmonica'. In the end, Strindberg becomes conscious that the play is inchoate and fantastic, for even the least apt artist sometimes perceives the difference between fancy and imagination, and adds a last act. In this the villagers, when crossing the lake on Easter Sunday, are threatened with death because a gap opens in the ice, but are saved when Kersti is drowned on her way from prison to perform her annual penance at the church. For then a supernatural power closes up the ice, content with the blood offering. Since the only conceivable happy ending of this play would have been the drowning of all the characters, this act is a mistake, and one recoils at the view it gives of Strindberg's universe: that black, blood-stained pit, ruled over by the Mumbo-Jumbo who was perpetually exacting useless sacrifices and, as we learn from other works, showed his divinity chiefly by siding against the Mrs Strindberg of the moment.

But *The Bridal Crown* is a better play than *The Spook Sonata*, over which one can do nothing but wring one's hands in wonder. It is odd enough that the old lady should sit in a cupboard for twenty years saying 'Pretty Polly', and that the footman should address her as 'The Mummy'. But one is unable to understand the situation when the valet comes in during the tea-party and says of the guest of the afternoon, 'Oh, yes, I know him, and he knows me . . . For two years he came regularly into our kitchen to be fed by our cook. Because he had to be at work at a certain hour, she made the dinner far ahead of time, and we had to be satisfied with the warmed-up leavings of that beast. He drank the soup-stock, so that we got nothing but water,' and the guest of the afternoon goes into the cupboard and hangs himself with a rope kindly indicated by the hostess, while the other guests contribute a cursory 'Amen'. And then, when the student is proposing to the daughter of this strange household, she remarks that the cook 'boils the life out of the beef and drinks the stock herself, while we get nothing but fibres and water. In the same way, when we have roast, she squeezes it dry. Then she eats the gravy and drinks the juice,' and then asks the footman to 'bring the death screen', and dies behind it. Mr Borkman, the translator, whose beautiful faith in Strindberg is a matter for tears, suggests tentatively that *The Spook Sonata* should be taken as an allegory. But there is a distinct difference between an allegory and a silly story, and it appears improbable that *The Spook Sonata*, or any play in this or any other volume of Strindberg's works, has any other message to the intellect than that it is wiser to be sane than mad.

Daily News, 25 August 1916

The Girl Who Left Home

Mr Bennett's New Novel

The Lion's Share by Arnold Bennett

Sir Walter Scott, it may be remembered, divided his works into those in which he used the big bow-wow, and his lesser works. Well, in *The Lion's Share*, which is published today, Mr Arnold Bennett has not exercised his big bow-wow; that large, sombre, Five-Towns animal has lain curled up at his feet while he has drowsily recalled the odd and jolly and dangerous things one used to do before the war, and put them at the disposal of Audrey, the discontented, snub-nosed girl who was imprisoned by an exacting father in a beautiful but dreary Essex home. It is now the fashion in many intellectual circles to despise Mr Bennett, as it is the fashion to despise all authors who have performed the crude act of publishing anything. But it is interesting to notice that because he has worked so hard at the craft of writing, at the art of inventing the dreams of a not wild imagination with beauty, he cannot help but achieve good writing and beauty even in a book written without much devotion and with a light intention. For there is very great beauty in those early chapters which show Audrey, the lovely vessel of the lovely draught of youth, at once unhappy and radiant, against the background of the shallow estuary of Mozewater and its many wonders:

Red barges beating miraculously up the shallow puddles to Moze Quay, equinoctial spring-tides when the estuary was a tremendous ocean covered with foam and the sea wall felt the light lash of spray; thunderstorms in autumn gathering over the yellow melancholy of death-like sunsets, wild birds crying across miles of uncovered mud at early morning and duck-hunters crouching in punts behind a waving screen of delicate grasses to wing them, and the mysterious shapes of steamers and warships in the offing beyond the Sand . . .

Audrey's father, Mr Moze, was not a nice man. The only occasion on which he had been known to laugh was when the cat fell out of the bathroom window on to the lawn roller. Yet in her relations with him Audrey, like so many of the figures erected lately by novelists to prove the fine rebellious quality of the Younger Generation, like Ann Veronica or any of the disgruntled families that inhabit the gloom of the Repertory Theatre, leaves us unconvinced of her splendour. Since in real life clever people can usually get the upper hand of stupid people, it seems a little odd that the only victory Audrey and Ann Veronica could score over their respectively demented and imbecile parents was to run away. One will never really believe in the alleged magnificence of the Younger Generation till one reads a book about the Daughter who Stayed at Home and the father who, in consequence, started at the sound of her voice as at the crack of a whip.

But Audrey never really runs away, for on the day of her flight her father is killed in a motor accident when on his way to a meeting of an anti-Romanist society:

His connection with the society had originated in a quarrel between himself and a Catholic priest from Ipswich, who had instituted a boys' summer camp on the banks of the Mozewater near the village of Moze. Until that quarrel, the exceeding noxiousness of the Papal doctrine had not clearly presented itself to Mr Moze. In such strange ways may an ideal come to birth.

And thereafter the book is, as has been said, just a drowsy evocation of all the odd and jolly and dangerous things that could be done before the war. Innocently assuming the name and dress of a widow, so that she can have more freedom, she goes to France. Driving through Paris by night, she thrills at the sight of the Boulevards, where 'throngs of promenaders moved under theatrical trees that waved their pale emerald against the velvet sky'. She dances at the ball in the studio of the magnificent M. Dauphin, who tells her with the solemnity of the perfect snob that he counts among his friends 'more than two-thirds of the subscribers to Covent Garden Opera'. She falls in with Rosamund, the calm tyrant at the head of that 'family trio whose Christian names were three sweet symphonies', and is introduced to the suffrage movement; its sweet and steadfast, though schoolgirlish, comradeship, its delicious adventures all over the country, at the centre of the whirling joy-wheel in the exhibition, while the pursuing policemen were for ever cast off from the run by centrifugal force, at the home of the Spatts (perhaps the most cultured family in Frinton-on-Sea); and its appalling discoveries, such as the punishment cells in Holloway. And there appears, to try to lure her away from feminism, Madame Piriac, who is a vast and cruel satire of that type of woman whom one was always afraid Mr Bennett really liked: an elegant Frenchwoman, who pretends to know all sorts of tremendous secrets about life, but who has probably no profounder secret than that she uses Hinde's curlers. 'Unless you use your youth and your freedom and your money for some individual you will never be content,' she tells Audrey.

It is the whole point of the book that Audrey proves them both wrong. She picks up a violinist of genius, with large timorous eyes, and in spite of the fact that so far as one can learn from Mr Bennett's description he was, to use the American phrase, nothing to write home about, she falls in love with him. She makes a way for him through the brutally absurd musical world; she sees to it that he has a concert in the Salle Xavier. ('Wagner, at Venice, had once threatened Xavier with a stick, and also Xavier had twice run away with great exponents of the role of Isolde. His competence as a connoisseur of Wagner's music, and of the proper methods of rendering Wagner's music, could therefore not be questioned, and it was not questioned.') She marries him tempestuously, and leads him off to tour those German cities whose approval is necessary before he can have a London success. But that is not all she does. 'I want,' she cries to Rosamund,

to have a husband and a house and a family, and a cause too. That'll be just about everything, won't it? And if you imagine I can't look after all of them at once, all I can say is I don't agree with you . . . Supposing I had all these things, I fancy I could have a tiff with my husband and make it up, play with my children, alter a dress, change the furniture, tackle the servants, and go out to a meeting and perhaps have a difficulty with the police all in one day. Only if I did get into trouble with the police I should pay the fine – you see. The police aren't going to have me altogether. Nobody. Nobody, man or woman, is going to be able to boast that he's got me altogether.

She wants, in fact, the lion's share of life. One greatly admires Mr Bennett for making his small but spirited contribution to the theory of feminism so excellent and rich a story of adventure.

Daily News, 14 September 1916

Mr Hewlett's Serenade

Love and Lucy by Maurice Hewlett

Mr Meredith must look down from above on the spate of quips and epigrams and fancies his style has let loose on Mr Hewlett's pages with such emotions as those with which the man who introduced rabbits into Australia surveyed his handiwork. The cadenzas of brilliant phrases, the thin, twinkling, flirtatious tone, the disparity between the skill of the execution and the cheap, easy picturesqueness of the conception, make a Hewlett novel like an accomplished solo on the guitar. Heaven knows why any person of Mr Hewlett's industry should choose perpetually to celebrate the rococo adventures of heroines that are but richly embroidered bits of skirt, heroes that are but bragging biceps. But he has so chosen and of his choice makes something that while not fine art is always an amusing assault on the attention, and in the instance of *Love and Lucy* is a serenade to which every woman can listen with pleasure.

Every woman should slip her intelligence into her workbag, turn down the harsh electric light, and steal to the window to hear Mr Hewlett's song; and presently she will forget she has a body and a brain and such tiresome aspirations as belong to these, and will think of herself as a tureen full of cheering, nourishing soup that ladles itself out to strings of needy males. For this is a book about 'the sex': the sex that exists to come out on the balcony when the male happens to be starting on a crusade and give one melting look that keeps him all the way to Jerusalem; who inspires men not by helpful suggestion, but by the unaided power of the human eye; who is the sole spiritual occupation of all her male intimates, and who does all this not by the exercise of any rare personal quality, but simply by being 'the sex'. For his present heroine has no virtues but 'the tender dragging smile of a Luini Madonna' and a preference for clothes that cling about her knees.

The girl was careless. Mr Hewlett has so often made his heroines inadvertently marry unpleasing husbands that he does not realise that this stumbling into wedding-dresses implies a considerable degree of negligence, and that if Lucy married her cold husband with the repelling eye-glass, James Adolphus Macartney, the solicitor who specialised in ecclesiastical business and wore trousers that 'had an edge and must have been kept in order like razors; but the legend that they were stropped after every day's use is absurd,' it must have been because she loved him, or because she was a dolt. The girl had no emotional power; living with him twelve years, and being the mother of his son, she could not constrain him to the kindness she desired. The girl was incredibly weak in her tactile sensations. When a travelled man with blue eyes set in a beef-red face slips into her boudoir one evening, switches off the light and kisses her in the darkness, she (not having read *Rest Harrow*, for this was Senhouse with the biceps but without the botany) assumes it is James Adolphus, and thinks it a romantic whim of his to love like Eros in the darkness. She continues in this assumption when she is kissed again in her opera box in the darkness of the first act of *Die Walküre* and later in the dewy dusk of a New Forest thicket, and turns to James Adolphus a face so glowing with gratitude for this fantastic love-making that he is melted out of his conceited coldness and becomes a suitably sentimental lover to his Lucy. So by luck that situation came to a fortunate end; though what may have happened to the poor girl since the new Lighting Regulations one hardly likes to think . . .

But, Mr Hewlett would probably object, the girl had charm. Yet can anybody who cannot grasp that the angles at the base of an isosceles triangle are equal have charm? Can anybody who cannot – to take a simple and revealing test of intelligence – fold up a deck-chair, have charm? Lucy, one feels, could not have passed either of these tests. Isn't it a sign of commonness, like buying a watch with a handsome exterior and cheap works, to be able to regard such a person as charming? Isn't intelligence not a separate inserted quality but a necessary condition of beauty, at once a manifestation of a subtle and healthy nervous system and a power which organises mere physical perfection into beauty that stirs the soul? Mr Hewlett's novel, though it painfully recalls the time when Meredith's style spread through literature like horseradish through a garden, does some service by reminding us that at the present time the English public answers these questions in the negative. One gets some idea of what we have to pay for this idea that charm and intelligence are dissociated particularly on the stage, which is the unhappy position of being very largely governed by contemporary ideas of feminine charm, by two perform-ances that were to be seen in London a week or two ago. There was the return to the stage of Mary Anderson; so lovely, so entirely unsuggestive of any sort of mental power, whose personality seemed not fully innervated. The pleasure of her performance was exactly the same as the pleasure of eating an ice; and that is the type of pleasure ordinarily given by the English theatre. And, at the same time, there was being shown in the West End, under the unpromising title

Should a Man Forgive?, a very beautiful Italian film in which there appeared the singer, Lena Cavalini. There there was great physical beauty organised by a strong intelligence to a greater beauty that stirs the soul. In the movements of this slim Neapolitan street-child one perceived the energy that has made the Italian cut with his pick the path for the railways of nearly all the world; the splendid mental structure that gives Italy such fine engineers and such fine scientists, the large wisdom that has given her noble painters and persons capable of building noble cities. That is the kind of beauty we desire to make. From easy picturesqueness, from beauty clouded and made plump with stupidity, from the tedious decking with garlands of the dull doings of dull people, may English art be some day delivered.

Daily News, 3 November 1916

Woman

Towards a Sane Feminism by Wilma Meikle

We all know the customary progression of a book on feminism. First there is the biological prelude with its deductions on the position of women drawn from notes on the courtship of the octopus. Then there comes the historical section, which leaps hastily from a period of alleged matriarchy, the surrender of which (if it ever existed) argues such weakness on the part of women that feminists really ought to keep quiet about it, to an enumeration of the privileges enjoyed by abbesses in the Middle Ages. And the rest consists of allusions to the sweated women in the East End (a district which largely owes its depressed appearance to the number of times it has figured in inferior rhetoric), an unsympathetic treatment of the deformities wrought by the capitalist system on the sexual life of our times, passionate assertions on all sorts of grounds that women are not worms, ending in the demand, as sharp, as lacking in restraint and self-control as the cry of a man with an assassin's knife in his breast, that women should have the vote. The ordinary suffragist was a woman too enraged by contempt to think calmly on a philosophic level. And so there were very few books on feminism which kindled more than a passing admiration for their properly fierce spirit and gained a permanent dwelling in the readers' mind by their ideas or the craft of their writing.

But Miss Meikle's book is quite different. She appears in her time to have been educated at one of the older universities, which seems to have had a different effect upon her than it had upon Mr Compton Mackenzie; it is certain that if she wrote a novel about it she would not call it *Dreaming Spires*. Having passed the necessary examinations and acquired a habit of making mental interruptions, she went out from this seat of learning to serve as organiser to a non-militant suffrage society. And this book is the result of the contact between her sceptical mind, deeply impatient of dull people and prejudices, and the manifold material about human nature that came the way of anybody engaged in that kind of work. Turning over its pages is to look into the suffrage world as it was before August 1914. One sees passing before one the goloshes-and-velour-hat type of suffragist who was very well up in facts and figures, but a little unsympathetic about changes in the marriage laws; the amber-cigarette-holder type of suffragette who called stridently across the Soho restaurant for the wine-list, and whose trump card was her speech on unmarried mothers; the stoutish type who affected purple djibbahs and spoke in a rich, almost greasy, contralto about the Mother Soul; the white-faced type whose courage in gaol was one of the few intimations of how we would meet our enemies. With a brilliant literary personality – the Meikle epigram ought to be as famous as the Robey wink – she offers us an amazingly complete and intelligent summary of modern opinions.

It is not a book, perhaps, for the specialist. The chapter on 'The Break-up of the Lady' is a rough sketch of material more fully and more fairly treated by Mrs Emily Putnam in *The Lady*. But nevertheless that chapter gives one a clear impression of the realisation that although Mother did her shopping in Dover Street and frequently had the dear Bishop to tea, she was miles away from the heart of life which drove numbers of well-known young women into the movement. And always, although Miss Meikle may seem too easily satisfied with the solutions she finds for the questions she raises, it proves that by the mere fact of raising them she has put us in her debt. Her main thesis, that the pioneers of the women's movement were wrong in concentrating upon the higher education of women and that they should have tried to gain a share in the control of industry, is unsupported by any suggestions as to how this was to be done by a sex almost entirely innocent of capital. And when she brings forward the analogy of Booker T. Washington, who concentrated upon a system of industrial education for Negroes because of his conviction that economic progress is the only road to political and social equality, she seems to ignore a very interesting chapter in Mrs Mary Ritter Beard's

Women's Work in Municipalities – although it is a book to which she often refers in her excellent chapter on municipal work for women – which shows how this industrial education is for the most part wasted by the white man's refusal to employ the black man save in menial and degrading capacities. It is almost certain that the same thing would have happened to women had they followed the path Miss Meikle thinks they should have in the middle of the last century. Yet all the same, her suggestions on this point are valuable because they throw light on the poor thing that is woman's education today. For that indictment alone this book ought to be widely read.

Over the question of whether married women should depend on themselves or on their husbands, a subject that has barked the shins of innumerable feminists, Miss Meikle goes honourably wrong. It is, according to her, degrading for a woman to be kept by her husband, and she is to earn a good income in some industrial or professional occupation for which she has undergone a thorough technical training. Now it is desirable that a woman should have three or four children. That means that she will be debarred from performing unembarrassed work of the highest grade by her physical and mental condition and the need of her attention at home for a period extending from the beginning of her first pregnancy till her youngest child has finished teething, which would probably amount to from eight to twelve years. During such a long period the technical knowledge which she acquired in the years preceding her marriage would fall into disuse and decay. But, Miss Meikle argues, she need not stay at home all that time; we will have crèches in which the children will be looked after by expert nurses. A trained woman can easily look after three or four children. Yes, but if all fit women are going to have three or four children . . that feminist dream breaks down under an arithmetical consideration. But the wildness of the dream is merely due to the noble discontent with which Miss Meikle regards the follies with which the sexual life of woman is hemmed in; the lack of any arrangement by which a woman can use her life before and after her period of childbearing and rearing in useful industrial employment not rendered degrading and dangerous by her employer's greed; the fixed persuasions of servile women that once they are wives they can have brains the size of a rabbit's, provided that they have faces like Madonnas and keep up a cant of self-sacrifice; the tiresome inchoate system of one house one kitchen, and the indifference of housewives to any attempt at co-operative housekeeping; the lack of recognition which is given to talent when it rashly takes up its abode in a woman. And it is the rare quality of this book that its discontent is neither shrill nor frenzied, but musical as a little river of wit leaping from rock to rock of solid argument. This is one of the few feminist books that have a style.

Daily News, 17 November 1916

The Matter with Women's Work

Feminists and the Future

Woman on Her Own, False Gods and *The Red Robe* by Brieux

The first volume of English translations of M. Brieux's plays made one put him down as a French version of the Blue-Book supplement of the *New Statesman*. He said the necessary things about subjects which required to be discussed in a simple, strong, washable style, and if the results were not beautiful it is because he had the type of mind which believes that the exercise of artistic craft takes the edge off one's earnestness. Remembering the humour of *Les Hannetons* one took the shameless mechanical devices of *Les trois filles de M. Dupont* as being a voluntary abstinence from art. But the first play in this new volume, *Woman on Her Own*, betrays the fact that Brieux is nothing more than a Pinero who has swallowed an Ethical Church hymn-book. His heart can sing with the best of us, 'Humanity, thy name is fair,' but his hands are busy with every sort of low theatrical trick. His thesis is the entirely admirable one that a woman finds it difficult to earn her own living on account of the hostility of her male competitors and the disposition of male employers to exact sexual submission as a price of employment or promotion. But his heroine, Thérèse, although she is unimpeded by a child wrapped in her shawl and there is no snowstorm, has the hard, hard luck of a heroine of melodrama. It is credible enough that she should lose her money; most of us do nothing else. It is credible enough that her fiancé's family should have broken off the engagement and that her fiancé should do nothing but weep; capable women of her type very often do select dainty rogues in porcelain as mates. But the world into which she is driven by these catastrophies is upholstered with improbabilities.

When she goes into the office of a French feminist paper the silence is broken every few seconds by the sickening thud of the discarded virtue of one or other member of the staff; even the household-hints editor, whom one would have trusted to maintain a healthy tone, retorts to a reduction in her salary by flight with a lover. And Thérèse cries out as the proprietor's husband makes love to her (how hopelessly lacking in the wild rhythm of life is M. Brieux! This gentleman advances on his victim as though he were performing an evolution in Swedish drill), 'Wherever we want to make our way, to have the right to work and to live, we find the door barred by a man who says, "Give yourself or starve."' Now this may be true of the underpaid factory-girl, the servant, the uneducated typist, the fatigued shop-assistant; but the feminist case seems to break down if the best-equipped women, like Thérèse, who had taken a degree and could write and act, could really be prevented from earning their living by the worst men. And, in point of fact, they aren't. The performance of any kind of skilled labour so greatly increases a woman's commercial value that it confers an immunity from attempts to reward her according to her sexual value. The lift-girl in a certain government office who recently called a passenger to order by threatening to lock him in the lift and walk downstairs was a symbolic figure of the modern woman who is going to end this sort of thing. Where M. Brieux goes wrong is in presenting a highly trained woman who plainly held the key of the lift and pretending she could not use it.

But things go from bad to worse when Thérèse tries to get a footing in the industrial world. Instead of taking her place in some factory where women were already employed, she goes down to a book-bindery owned by some of her relatives, and with the air of the Honourable Emily opening a sale of work organises a union of bare-faced blacklegs. 'We need our wages,' she tells the delegate of the men's union, 'and to get hold of the jobs that we're able to do we offer our work at a cheaper rate than you do,' and has the brazen priggery to boast that the women are able to do it because they drink less. This makes one suspect that M. Brieux has lost that accuracy which a Blue-Book supplement ought to guard as its bloom. For there can never have been any need for even 'the girls, the widowed, the abandoned', to start such a villainous campaign either in France or England, since it is not underemployment but underpayment, which in spite of the older economists are two different things, that is the matter with woman's work. In consequence the action of the men unionists in driving her out of the bindery does not strike us as brutal (since Thérèse would certainly have come off much worse if she had encountered Mrs Webb), nor of any importance as regards the position of women. It would not strike us of importance even as regards the fate of Thérèse had not M. Brieux resorted to a preposterous device to disappoint our natural expectation that a woman who has been such a failure in the industrial and professional worlds would turn to the dry dock of a good man's home. Her fiancé René, who had dried his tears and risen on his dead self to a good thing in superphosphates, returns to Thérèse and tells her that he is now independent of his family and in a position to marry her, and she refuses on the ground that she retorted to an accusation of mercenary motives by his father by an oath that she would never marry his son without his consent. So when Thérèse, after the men unionists, with amazing moderation, have fired their pistols into the air, and the terrified employer has discharged her, exclaims: 'I leave by train, this evening, for Paris,' we are supposed to be appalled at the thought of this proud girl driven into sin. We are not. We are wondering why M. Brieux omitted to give us a missing will, and thinking how richly he deserves to be elected an honorary member of the British Dramatists' Club.

The other two plays, *False Gods* and *The Red Robe*, are of greater merit. *False Gods*, which tells how an Egyptian priest comes back after two years of study abroad (apparently at South Place) and tries to replace the superstitious national religion by a broad humanitarianism in a way that makes one think of him as Mr J. A. Hobson embarrassed by Egyptian costume, has the interest which attaches to any sincere discussion of religion. But one objects to his conventional assumption that it is the unhappy who believe in the grosser forms of a future life; surely that belongs more to the faith of the happy who trust that their luck will not fail them even after death. *The Red Robe* is a fine example of M. Brieux's extraordinary gift for making legal procedure comprehensible and dramatic. It is a curious proof of the colourlessness of M. Brieux's art that these plays read exactly the same in English as they do in French; there is no volatile essence in the prose to escape in translation.

Daily News, 30 November 1916

War and Women

Essays in Wartime by Havelock Ellis

In spite of a leakage of Ellen Key into the footnotes, and what the dictionary scathingly calls the common but improper use 'of avocations as a synonym for vocations', Mr Havelock Ellis's *Essays in Wartime* give a delightful further disclosure of one of the finest

English minds, remarkable for his exquisite literary manners and his inveterate appearance which he can sustain in the most difficult circumstances of being a character out of *Cranford*.

Most doctors, when they turn from their work to the world, seem to search it for some abnormality which has struck them in their clinical observations and to detect it everywhere; they see a world crawling with hysterical women and causes of cancer. But the thing that Mr Havelock Ellis seems to have noticed in his medical work is that beauty is inherent in the process of living substance, and he too searches for it everywhere and always detects it. And so there has been produced that marvellous travel book, *The Soul of Spain*, and the literary criticisms of *Affirmations* and *Impressions and Opinions*, which are so like the sympathetic diagnoses of a great doctor, which reveal to us the health and modesty of Nietzsche, the sources of Swift's tears and rage. And now it has sent out this volume of essays, in which Mr Havelock Ellis gravely but kindly turns the hose on the *Morning Post*, which (along with the tiger and the ape) lives in the heart of most of us.

It is not that he disapproves of the war, not that he is one of those pacifists who believes that the Belgium atrocities were really committed by Viscount Grey disguised as a Uhlan in a false nose and a secret understanding. He perceives clearly that 'this war, from our present point of view, is a war of States which use military methods for special ends (often, indeed, ends that have been thoroughly evil) against a State which still cherishes the primitive ideal of warfare as an end in itself'; and that the only way to sicken that State of her ideal is to give her as much war as she asks for. But he destroys every kind of argument by which people pretend that warfare is anything but an offence against humanity, that it is anything more dignified than the frog-marching of an intoxicated Power to the police station. To those who maintain that war is a biological necessity and a manifestation of the 'struggle for life', an application to mankind of the Darwinian 'law' of natural selection, he points out that Darwin

was careful to state that he used the term 'struggle for existence' in a 'metaphorical sense', and the dominant factors in the struggle for existence, as Darwin understood it, were natural suitability to the organic and inorganic environment and the capacity for adaptation to circumstances; one species flourishes while a less efficient species living alongside it languishes. Yet they may never come in actual contact, and there is nothing in the least approaching human warfare. Mr Chalmers Mitchell . . . has lately shown that even the most widely current notions of the extermination of one species by another have no foundation in fact.

One has often read – there is even a children's story on the subject – of how the Tasmanian wolf was driven out of Australia and its place taken by the dingo, but one never realised the dingo did it by sheer womanliness; 'by superior intelligence in finding food and rearing young'.

By such evidence he settles the claim that warfare is as fundamental a part of organic life as reproduction or death, and goes on to show that though warfare has played its part among primitive peoples as a developmental force, training man in virility and intelligence, it could only be so long as

the hardness of their life and the obtuseness of their sensibility reduced to a minimum the bad results of wounds and shocks, while their warfare, being free from the awful devices due to the devilry of modern man, was comparatively innocuous; even if very destructive was necessarily limited by the fact that those accumulated treasures of the past which largely make civilisation had not come into existence.

This essay on 'Evolution and Warfare' is followed by one on 'War and Eugenics', which attempts to find out the measurable effect of war on the human breed, and which does good service by recalling 'Nietzsche's pacifist writings, and quoting that fine sentence from *Human, All-Too-Human*: "In our day greater and higher tasks are assigned to men than patria and honour, and the rough old Roman patriotism has become dishonourable, at best a survival." ' These two essays run over the militarist case like a heavy dray.

Other of his essays give interesting information on matters more or less related to the war. There is an abstract of a pamphlet by the brilliant Viennese socialist, Rudolf Goldsheid, urging an after-war *entente* with England in the interests of democracy, which must make the most ardent advocate of the isolation of Germany hesitate. It appears that Dr Helene Stöcker, a German feminist of a type so revolutionary in its ideas that English suffragists hesitated to claim kinship with it, has been protesting against the treatment of the prisoners-of-war in Germany. There is also a paper on 'Masculinism and Feminism' and 'The Mental Differences of Men and Women', in which Mr Ellis scatters those suffragists who assert that these mental differences are due entirely to the confined domestic life of women by handing them the female giraffe, who, though she darns no socks, is just such a precocious, light-brained thing as we. But here Mr Ellis rather misreads the grievance of the feminist. She is not really disposed to dispute that the balance of her ductless glands is not the same as a man's; one so rarely meets them that it hardly matters. But she does feel angry when an employer (presumably on account of the different balance of her ductless glands) pays a woman sixpence an hour for skilled work in an aeroplane factory for which a man working at the same speed was paid a shilling an hour. We will be as different as Mr Ellis likes, but we are not going to lose money over it.

There are also some essays on eugenics, and the production of ability, in which the examination of a vast number of figures as to the age of the parents of geniuses leads him to the conclusion that you never can tell. Then there are some essays on the fall of the birth-rate; the agriculturist who rejoiced when he saw two blades of grass growing where one grew before knew no such joy as Mr Ellis feels when he sees one baby growing where two grew before. And always, whether he is demonstrating the inseparable connection between a high birth-rate and a high death-rate, or deploring the fertility of the herring, he keeps to the high level of his delicate, grave, rectory English.

Daily News, 20 December 1916

The Art of Making Books

Their Lives by Violet Hunt, *Hatchways* by E. Sidgwick,
The Rising Tide by Margaret Deland

These three novels prove that life is unjust all through, and that the power to create a work of art, like a good complexion, is frequently bestowed on the undeserving. Miss Sidgwick, who certainly never retires to rest without first doing exercises to develop her subtlety, is certainly an example to all of us; and Mrs Deland is so like a New England town that one might easily try to find her on the map. And yet they have had no luck with books, which remain the results of hours of contact between their fountain-pens and their writing-pads, instead of becoming living organisms. It would be useless to pretend that Miss Violet Hunt has their high claim to seriousness. She is evidently extraordinarily subject to that deep fatigue of the soul and the body which the artist experiences at the sight of his proofs; all through this book she has let her typist and her printer rip, and she drops commas as a dressmaker drops pins. The occasion seems as trivial as though a pretty woman should say a word to one over her shoulder while she was dancing. And yet somehow or other *Their*

Lives is a work of art. It gives a cold, white vision of reality that recalls Maupassant; it is a valuable historical document; it is a study of adolescence; it is a record in little of the eternal conflict between the stable and the unstable types in the community. Turning from the unsalted food of Miss Sidgwick and Mrs Deland, it almost breaks one's heart to see how easily and carelessly Miss Violet Hunt does it, simply because art is her fortuitous possession.

It is an extremely unpleasant book. Most great books are. Fernando de Rojas's *Celestina, Don Quixote, The Brothers Karamazov, The Wings of the Dove,* all agree in their profound and resigned conviction that sweetness and reason are not predominant in human affairs. The phase of grimness which has led Miss Violet Hunt to her effort in pessimism is the Victorian materialism of the eighties, as it was seen and practised by the three daughters of a pre-Raphaelite painter. Meticulously, with the controlled garrulity of Jane Austen, she describes the horsehair texture of their home life. Their lovable father was so deeply absorbed in his painting that he was of no more use to them than a gentle dove fluttering above their roof; for the rest, they were abandoned to the Victorian order of things. Their mother, a hard, noble Yorkshire woman, was afflicted with a bleak inability to live suavely and gracefully; she was as unable to conceal from her children that she disliked two of them, as later, owing to 'her dense mental purity', she was unable to help them with their love affairs. She was characteristic of an age when people neither lived according to the deep wisdom of strong instincts, nor elaborated a system of beautiful manners to compensate for the weakness of their instincts. There was no escape from this inadequate society into intellectual activities, for the pre-Raphaelite and the aesthetic movements described here with such gentle malice had nothing more to do with a woman than put her on a brocade settee with a sunflower. So all a girl could do was to sit up in the 'Trust' position till a husband was given one, and one could drop into the happy relaxation of 'Paid For'.

That was, as one had always suspected from novels of the time, such as the early books of Henry James, humiliating to sensitive and passionate women. They were at once fevered and made insensible about sex by their concentration upon it. That is the tragedy of Christina Radmall, whose character is a remarkable proof of how the artist, even one with so marked an absence of the didactic and speculative turn of mind, can always beat the professional psychologist on his own ground. It is a study of girlhood which is worth the entire two volumes compiled by Professor Stanley Hall on *Adolescence,* and which is worthy to stand beside Dostoevsky's *A*

Raw Youth. It is the account of an adolescent of genius, who is so consumed by the will to power that immaturity and exclusion from adult experience is a torment. Childhood is like a deformity, girlhood is impatiently endured as the last traces of a lingering disease. She was true to her type in forming a passion for an elderly married man of distinction, for it was her unconscious desire to love a man as richly loaded with experience as possible. It is his prudent resistance that sends her back to the marriage-market, where, since she has to deal publicly and commercially with something that should have been her secret passion, she blunders horribly. And always the disastrous contact between her experimental mind and a world inexorably opposed to the experimental method are derisively watched by her sister Virgilia, who 'had a label on her umbrella and her name inside her shoes, on her racquet, on anything that it was possible or useful to put a name on', and had the furniture-dealing mind. The account of her marriage to the exquisite Marmaduke Hall, 'when once they were married they did not mean to submit any more than was necessary to the taint of the outside world. They would take in no daily-paper at all . . . She was going to be in to tea every day at five o'clock . . . He thought, and she agreed with him, that the streets were no place for a young married woman . . .', is an indictment of Victorian respectability, which is perhaps the best part of a book that, in spite of the printer's determined effort to make it ephemeral, is of permanent value.

With the possible exception of Angela Carranza (condemned by the Inquisition of Lima in 1684), who claimed to have written her revelations with a quill from the wing of the Holy Ghost, Miss E. Sidgwick is the most pretentious woman writer who ever lived. There is, as one knows when one sees a puppy trying to scratch his right ear with his left hind-leg, an instinct for complexity in all living creatures, and it is lawful to gratify it within limits. But when, with a confused belief that any prose is delicate provided it does not appeal to the visual sense, one teases a *Family Herald* story about a duke's brother who falls in love with a humble art student into such a Bradshaw of subtleties, one puts oneself as definitely outside art as Mrs Deland when she ends a chapter in *The Rising Tide* with, 'So, in her fashion, by a back door, so to speak, Frederica Payton entered into the old idea of Duty.' Not that we object to duty – personally we always drink a large tumblerful before breakfast – but art is art. For the rest, it is an amusing (though not too amusing; one feels that it is lawful to enjoy Mrs Deland's humour in Lent) story about the cruder kind of young suffragist. Though if one designs to write a story to prove that women ought not to propose, it would be more effective to select an instance in which the man accepted rather than one in which he refused.

Daily News, 2 March 1917

Woman Worship

War, Peace and the Future by Ellen Key

Miss Ellen Key is a woman and a neutral, and she contrives to be equally offensive in both capacities. She has written a book to tell us that all the belligerent nations are sunk in a deep pit of militant passion, and that we are as bad as the rest. We learn with surprise that England – a nation which entered into the war so sadly and soberly that it had not the heart to cheer its soldiers in the streets – is demented with war frenzy, save for one exception, 'the English scientist, C. W. Saleeby' (laughter suppressed in court), who has courageously published a pamphlet about the effects of war on the race. We learn with surprise that the militant suffragettes have been banded into an army corps that 'looks forward to being sent to the front', where they will be able to use their 'cold-blooded training to kill'. We learn with surprise that we and our Allies are Bernhardeting even at those moments when we thought we were being merely agreeable.

On facts such as these, mere nightmares following heavy meals of press-cuttings, she bases her opinion that only to neutrals has it been vouchsafed to perceive the truth that war is a nasty thing, and that men get killed in it. It is impossible to record without bitterness that we also had noted it.

As a woman Miss Key is hardly more lovable. The book is, to begin with, a performance which the feminist would rather see signed by a man. The only nice thing about it is that one can put any chapter in the place of any other chapter, or any paragraph in the place of any other paragraph, or any sentence in the place of any other sentence, and the most attentive reader will not notice any difference. The chapter headings also are interchangeable without discomfort.

But more discreditable to womanhood than its individual incompetence is the brand of pacifism which it presents as a part of feminism. Miss Key's feminism has always been peculiar. It has not been a form of the worship of life, it has not been an aspiration that women should contribute more largely than they have done to the development of humanity by the exercise of intelligence and genius; it has been woman-worship. Women need not trouble to develop any human qualities. They are merely to sit still and be as female as they can, taking as their ideal not the untiring St Teresa, but the Sacred Cow of the Universe. There is a magic about mere femaleness which will enable them so to regenerate the world.

And now mere femaleness is going to end the war. It appears that men have failed to notice that war is unpleasant. This news is going to be broken to them by women, and then there will be eternal peace. Now it is obviously true that there is a large number of men who are unable to form any judgement on the moral aspect of war because of the appeal it makes to their virtuosic and adventurous impulses. The airman remembers his insolent dance above the guns, the private who was once a ploughboy knows that no crisis of peace could have changed him into a conqueror of Baghdad; and because of these things they forgive war. There is also a large number of men who regard anything they have experienced as being thereby eternally established in the order of things; they accept war as supinely as in peacetime they accepted the inefficiency of the railway system that took them up to town. There is also a number, it is to be hoped small, but certainly largely responsible for the origin and continuance of the war, of people who are the unhappy instruments of that tendency which biologists tell us is natural to the living organism, and which yet should not be allowed free play in human affairs, the tendency of the old to be jealous of the young. It is obvious that this jealousy will be felt most strongly by the elderly for the youth of their own sex, and that the war affords opportunities for gratifying this acute form of it. It is significant that the Kaiser fought only with his mouth till he had reached middle-age, and among ourselves the activities of such as the Jingo peer who spoke of himself as having 'given a nephew' to the country, and the small demented clique that still rejoices over the ennobling moral effects of war, spring from the same sinister root. In all these ways men are distracted from the business of forming a clear judgement of the moral aspect of war. So it is probable that the emotional driving force of any peace movement will come from women. One must add that this is not to be used as an argument for woman-worship, since women are as little to be trusted as men to discover the ultimate wisdom about their own essential business.

But surely anybody not possessed by the most stubborn determination not to sit silent when she had nothing to say, must see that emotion by itself can never end the war. Had that been possible the war would never have reached the end of its first year. This book is amazingly and shamelessly characteristic of its brand of pacifism in the way it contains not the smallest intimation of how this emotional revolt against war is to be turned into an intellectual attack on it. It is true that Miss Key undertakes a championship of the political enfranchisement of women which is now so belated that it has the effect of impudence, but that carries us little further. Even if her vision of a 'mass-rising of motherliness' were realised, and an army of women did march to the polling-booths to record their detestation of war, that would not help matters much. A single nation cannot establish peace upon earth any more than an individual can establish socialism by private enterprise. If every Englishwoman had recorded an anti-militarist vote in the summer of 1914 it would not have altered the situation of August in the smallest degree. We should still have been faced with the fact that Belgium had been laid waste, and that all the decency in the world must work for her restoration. Mere platitudinous assertions as to the niceness of peace and the nastiness of war are useless in such crises, and the 'motherly' advice of Miss Key that the belligerent nations should refrain from denouncing the sins of others and should turn their attention to their own defects, is actively mischievous.

If we refrain from regarding the invasion of Belgium as a crime, we foment a state of public opinion which would tolerate England's commission of a similar crime if the occasion arose. It is alert and vigorous thinking about specific points, it is the very quality of intelligence which Miss Key persistently belittles, which brings an end to war. The intellect is the sword in the hand of humanity, without which its tears and laughter are impotent as the tears and laughter of children. That is why Miss Key's feminism, this woman-worship that would have women cultivate laxness of mental tissue so that they shall dissolve into a hot emotional vapour that shall act as a Turkish bath to the Superman, is an offence not only against women but against the race.

Daily News, 13 April 1917

The Softer Sex

The Intelligence of Woman by W. L. George

The wrapper of this book, on which Mr Herbert Jenkins informs us that Mr George supports woman without flattering her, and that Mr George's love for her is perhaps the greatest tribute she has ever received, is worth the money by itself. The style is not unengaging; Mr George 'works hard', as the dramatic critics say of Mr Seymour Hicks, and there is an epigram on every page, usually about the middle. But it loses something in effectiveness because it is based on Mr George's observation of 150 women. He expects us to be surprised that he knows so many, and explains that he does not know them all really well.

They belong to that smart set in Kensington to which Mr George has already introduced us in his novels, and the accounts of their conversation, which is such as one overhears on the pier, and their domesticity, which is such as is described in the older type of comic song, adds little to the feminist discussion. One must make an exception of Case Two. 'With the object of entertaining an elderly lady, who is an invalid, a man explains, in response to her own request, the case that Germany makes for having declared war. She asks one or two questions, and then suddenly interrupts him to ask what he has been doing with himself lately in the evenings.' Mr George cites this as an example of interest in the particular as opposed to the general; but how well one knows the amateur war lecture on which that question is the perfect comment.

But the real defect of the book is that Mr George appears never to have read anything in his life. On the very first page he repeats – and alludes to it again later in the volume – that legend about the bishop who denied at the medieval church council that women have souls. Since the sole foundation for this myth that any conscientious searcher has ever been able to find is a passage in the history by Gregory of Tours, in which he relates that at the Council of Mâcon in 585 a bishop was in doubt as to whether *homo* meant women as well as men, but was ultimately persuaded by the other members that it did, it is exactly as true as it is that the Houses of Parliament have denied that women have souls. Inaccuracies like that do no particular harm, except in so far as they irritate the neat-minded reader, but unfortunately they are signs of a looseness of word and thought which occasionally makes one howl like a dog and wish one was a don. There are, for instance, several quite acceptable definitions of intellect; one may take it as the higher thinking powers as opposed to the memory and senses, or as the faculty for understanding sense-perceptions, recognising or interpreting their sensational elements, and objects known by reasoning processes. But this is what Mr George gives us:

Intellect is the ideal skeleton of man's mental power. It may be defined as an aspiration toward material advantage, absolute truth or achievement, combined with a capacity for taking steps toward successful achievement or attaining truth. From this point of view such men as Napoleon, Machiavelli, Epictetus, Leo III, Bismarck, Voltaire, Anatole France, are typical intellectuals. They are not perfect; all so far as we can tell are tainted with moral feeling or emotion – a frailty which probably explains why there has never been a British or American intellectual of the first rank. Huxley, Spencer, Darwin, Cromwell, all alike suffered grievously from good intentions. The British and American mind has long been honeycombed with moral impulse, at any rate since the Reformation; it is very much what the German mind was up to the middle of the nineteenth century. Intellect, as I conceive it, is seeing life sanely and seeing it whole, without much pity, without love; seeing life as separate from man, whose pains and delights are only phenomena; seeing love as a reaction to certain stimuli.

One wishes that those first two sentences could be read by William James, who did so love a laugh. Drooping for a moment over the mess of famous names in the next sentence, and wondering why Mr George did not add milk and sugar and make a pudding out of it, one passes on to wonder over the syntax of the next sentence, and deny the allegation in its last clause: have we not our Sir —— ? One pauses to speculate what Mr George thinks happened to the British mind at the Reformation, and how the German modern mind – whose fine flower is Rudolf Eucken! – can be said to have lost its moral impulse. And at the last sentence one's knees turn to water, for one perceives that one is in the presence of a real man of the world, like Mr Henry Arthur Jones or Mr Austin Harrison. That paragraph explains why, although ordinarily one would like to be supported without being flattered, and would enjoy hearing about the private lives of the shadowy, though florid, dramatic persons of the songs of George Robey and Miss Marie Lloyd, one does not really care what Mr George thinks about women.

This carelessness about words mates with a carelessness about facts to produce an effect of utter confusion. In the final chapter, 'After the War', which is a consideration of the economic position of women, he commits sentences like this: 'The wage-earning woman came in in the forties with the factory system, and every year she has increased in numbers.' Surely he must know that women of the labouring classes have always worked, although their wages may have been paid to their husbands and fathers; that the number of women who work has certainly not increased to any extent during the last twenty years, and has probably not increased in relation to the whole population since the forties, for the number of middle-class women who have come into the labour market is balanced by the number of married women who have withdrawn from the labour market, because modern artisans can (as their forefathers at the beginning of the industrial revolution certainly could not) afford to keep their wives at home. He is similarly in error about the number of women munition workers who have made their first appearance in industry; if he goes to any munition works he will find that practically every adult employed has previous industrial experience. The best essay in the book is 'Uniforms for Women', which makes an attempt to calculate the amount of the world's wealth which is spent on women's clothes. But Mr George forgets that the real person for women's love of finery is not feminine vanity, but feminine modesty. A dull woman is conscious she is dull, and wears orange velvet lest she should depress us too much; a dull man, unvexed by this consciousness, sticks to his broadcloth. But the whole book is condemned to tedium because Mr George has not realised that before Anatole France or Remy de Gourmont permitted themselves to write long and charming essays which consist of leisured strolls in pleached alleys of generalisations they had disciplined themselves, by years of profound scholarship, to the most exquisite apprehension of fact.

Daily News, 31 May 1917

Femininity

The Life of a Famous Frenchwoman

Madame Adam: la grande française by Winifred Stephens

It depends entirely on how far one can tolerate the thing known as femininity, whether one will whole-heartedly enjoy the life of Madame Adam which Miss Winifred Stephens, who shares with Mr William Archer the honour of being one of the real internationalising forces in English letters, has compiled partly from her own researches and partly from the seven incomparable volumes of Madame Adam's *Souvenirs*. For Madame Adam, although she had wit as well as beauty and fortitude enough to carry her through an unhappy marriage and the Franco-German War, although she had a constant energetic movement of the mind and a sense of relationships which made her a political and social power, although she is a feminist, is devastatingly feminine. She is illogical. It is like trying to make a steady friend out of an escalator to attempt to understand her attitude to republicanism and democracy; having become a republican because monarchy does not express the will of the people she then became hostile to democratic rule by parliamentary franchise because the manhood suffrage of 1851 had brought about the Empire.

She had a most unreasonable way of dipping her husband into a philosophy, as one dips litmus paper into a solution to see if it is acid or alkaline, and rejecting it if he liked it; when she met Littré, the Skeat of his time, 'she could not tolerate his positivism. Positivism suggested Comte, and Comte suggested the husband whose conduct was rendering her domestic life unbearable.'

And there is something very 'feminine', too, about her attitude to her first book; although it was a feminist counterblast to the ideas at once pompous and puppyish on the position of women which were held by Proudhon, and although she put up a good fight against the masculine insolence of publishers. When she took this extremely able volume to M. Lévy, the publisher of Victor Hugo, Renan and Dumas, he refused even to read it, remarking pleasantly: 'I can see perfectly what your . . . work is like merely by looking at you,' to which M. Aurélien Scholl kindly added: 'It would be a pity for madame to become a commonplace bluestocking. You are quite right to discourage her, my dear Lévy. She has something better to do.' And Hetzel wrote: 'Either your book is very bad or you use a coloured handkerchief, and possibly you take snuff. I can't believe a woman, who is probably ugly and certainly middle-aged, can have any right to defend against Proudhon the youth of George Sand and Daniel Stern' (a letter which suggests that, bad as it is to be 'feminine', it is almost worse to be masculine). Yet when her father exclaims over her book: 'My dear child, this means your success, your salvation, influential friendships, your grandmother's wishes realised,' and it appears that the book had been planned not only for its intellectual mission but also as the first step in a campaign for the social conquest of Paris, one remembers disagreeably the accusation that women are never great artists because they never do work for its own sake but only to serve their personal ends. And so throughout her life one feels that, spirited and successful as she was, and solid as her achievements in helping Gambetta and founding *La nouvelle revue* undoubtedly were, she still is not the creative woman whom feminists desire to see. It is not so much that she is not good enough as that the times would not permit her to be any better.

In England it is tiresome for women to find their sex regarded by men as a reason for underpaying them and treating them contemptuously, and that undoubtedly acts as a brake on the development of their capacity. But the worship that women get in Latin countries – it is impossible to believe, for instance, that in England a woman of neither birth nor wealth could have risen to a position of such social power – is almost as bad for them, since to possess a prestige for which one has not worked tends, as the proceedings of the House of Lords prove, to produce slackness in the duty of cultivating one's gifts.

The historical part of the volume is absorbingly interesting. It is a little melancholy to read the account of the Revolution of 1848 and realise that it resembles the Russian Revolution not only in the spirit of orgiastic loquacity, but also in its mental furniture; for over there in Russia they are talking today about the phalansterian movement of Fourier, the humanitarian *papisme industriel* of Saint-Simon. Madame Adam's account of the years before 1870 are not so interesting, for they deal largely with the literary world, and the lady who disposed of Manet's 'Olympia' without reference to its artistic merits because it reminded her of 'Germinie Lacerteux' is not at her best in dealing with art. Her journal of her sufferings in the Siege of Paris is of interest to those pacifists who maintain that our blockade of Germany was an unprecedented interference with the food of our civil population. And it is a lesson for our times that the ugly failure of the Commune was caused by the Government's insolent conviction that the country was so dependent on it that it could afford to be shamelessly reactionary. Important, too, is the story of the decay of La Revanche, which illustrates the contention recently made by Mr Trotter in *The Herd Instinct*, and quoted by Miss Stephens, that 'when we examine a man's behaviour objectively we find that revenge, however deathless of passion it is vowed to be at emotional moments, is in actual life constantly having to give way to more urgent and more recent needs and feelings'. The account of these later days reminds us what a debt we owe to France for refusing to be coerced by the menaces of Germany into becoming a militarist nation; at any rate, she gave humanity forty years of civilisation.

Daily News, 9 August 1917

Novelist and Dramatist

The Widowing of Mrs Holroyd by D. H. Lawrence

The discovery of Mr Lawrence is a very recent thing, being one of the good works of Mr Ford Madox Hueffer when he edited the first

English Review. And of the three novels he has published since then, one, *The Trespasser,* was two-thirds a mistake. Yet though his performance has just begun, and although he has wasted some of his time in emotional squirmings, one cannot doubt that, solitary among the younger novelists, he is a genius. He is supreme among them on technical grounds alone. While they are unanimously unaware of the existence of style (in all the works of Mr Hugh Walpole, for instance, one could find hardly one sensitive or distinguished phrase), Mr Lawrence has the gift of phrase-making. And he borrowed no man's formula: he was too inflamed with the desire to speak out the matter that was in him to waste time hunting in books for a manner. In the formula which he has found for himself he reconciles several things that have been regarded as beyond a writer's power to undertake at one and the same time. He describes the external life with as much detail as Mr Arnold Bennett at the same time that he describes the internal life with as much detail as Mr Henry James, and is as opinionative about it all as Mr Wells. One does not mean to suggest that he is a winged literary omnibus with these three illustrious 'insides', but unquestionably he has acquired their several methods of attack on material.

Possessed of these immense advantages as a novelist, Mr Lawrence has elected to become a dramatist. He has chosen for the subject of his play a relationship between a woman and her husband exactly similar to that between Paul Morel's father and mother which formed the chief interest of the early part of *Sons and Lovers.* Here again a woman of fine quality, whose dignity projects like a sharp, shining rock from a dark mass of half-divined tenderness and passions, maddens her coarse, handsome husband by her contempt for his loutish geniality and his lack of high aims. 'She could not be content with the little he might be: she would have him the much that he ought to be. So, in seeking to make him nobler than he could be, she destroyed him.'

Like Morel, Holroyd is a miner given to drinking. In the first act we see his wife as she sits in her fire-lit kitchen, wondering where her husband is spending the night, and despising herself because she is wondering about him, because she cannot feel unconcerned with this pot-house lounger. Then the children run in and bring her disgraceful news of him:

There's some women at New Inn, what's come from Nottingham . . . An' they've got paper bonnets on . . . An' my dad's dancing with her – with the pink-bonnet one, mam. Up in the club-room over the bar . . . An' you can see 'em go past the window, 'cause there isn't no curtains up, an' my father's got the pink-bonnet one – an' there's a piano, mam – and lots of folk outside watchin' lookin' at my dad! He can dance, can't he, mam?

Her quiet rage fills the kitchen like a suffocating smoke.

In the next scene he brings two of the paper-bonneted hussies home; half because they insist on coming and he is soft with beery good-fellowship; partly because he wants to madden his wife to some surrender of her dignity, to force her to speak the scorn she always looked. The hussies push their way in against her tragic silence; they giggle and drink, they squeal at rats, one of them has a disgusting, obese heart-attack, they bring the children down from their beds with their clatter, and sentimentalise greasily over the 'duckies', they whimper over their involved family histories. And Holroyd and his wife face each other in misery and defiance, hostile, brutal people, yet at the same time hurt people protesting against the mauling of their deep affection. At last he drives the hussies out and tries to get near this adored, hateful wife; but she is too numb with pain even to appreciate that he wants to make peace, so he lurches out to a night of drunkenness.

He returns so low and brawling a thing that she turns away from him and gives herself up to hating him. The next evening he does not come back for his dinner, and she contemptuously thinks him at his pot-house. But presently one of his mates comes in and asks for him uneasily; nobody has seen him, and he does not seem to have come up from the pit. All day, his mates say, Holroyd has seemed sullen and desperate, and in the evening lingered behind to avoid walking to the bottom with the other men. Slowly Mrs Holroyd begins to understand that in the loneliness to which her contempt has driven him some dreadful thing has happened to him. And so in a little while, his dead body tells her. A fall of rock had imprisoned him, and he was suffocated by the gas. She kneels beside him and weeps bitterly, not because he is dead and she had loved him – that would be a simple grief – but because he is dead and she had never succeeded in loving him.

All this is very beautifully and subtly written, so beautifully and subtly that at first one cannot understand why *The Widowing of Mrs Holroyd* is so much less a thing than *Sons and Lovers*. There is an immense difference in their importance. One keeps and reads the novel: if one lost the play in the train one would not only not buy another copy, but might even neglect to inquire at the Lost Property Office. And this failure to make an important work of art out of fine writing and an impressive subject is due to the peculiar unsuitability of the realistic drama to Mr Lawrence's special gift of drawing the development of an emotional situation. The realistic drama can do almost anything but that. It is the chosen vehicle of the spirit of comedy, and as *The Cherry Orchard* showed it can paint the soul of a people. But it has produced nothing which disproves the belief of the great ones of the past that the development of an emotional situation must be explained by something beyond the speech and action of the persons involved. The Greeks had their Chorus, the Elizabethans their convention that men speak soliloquies and long speeches of unnaturally intelligent introspection, and Mr Shaw his preposterous pretence (in the plays where he deals with emotional situations) that people talk a lot and talk wittily. Ibsen seems the exceptional realist who succeeded in making matters clear in spite of the fact that humanity does not shine in conversation. But in reality he rearranged life more than any of the conventionalists. For, instead of pulling about speech, he pulled about events and cultivated symbolism instead of soliloquies. Neither conventionalism nor symbolism would come easily to Mr Lawrence's rather dour genius, and it seems strange that he should turn to an art-form which requires them when he is a master of the gloriously untrammelled form of the novel. And so, although *The Widowing of Mrs Holroyd* is a fine play, and would probably act as well as it reads, one hopes that Mr Lawrence will not do it again.

Daily News, no date;
from Rebecca West's Clipping Book

Part VI

Miscellaneous Slings and Arrows

Articles from the *Daily Herald, Everyman,*
Manchester Daily Dispatch, Daily Chronicle,
June 1912 – November 1916

Editor's Introduction

In her early years (1911–17) as a journalist, it sometimes seemed as if there was hardly a left-wing paper in England or America to which Rebecca West did not contribute. Bennett, Chesterton, Shaw and Wells, appeared too in many of these journals and papers, mellow and avuncular, while she practised 'the duty of harsh criticism'. She was perhaps more fortunate in some of her other colleagues, the political journalists. Robert Blatchford, Nevinson and Brailsford her fellow journalists on the *Daily News*, and George Lansbury of the *Daily Herald* were real feminists. George Lansbury, indeed, ruined his career as an MP by supporting the suffragettes and socialism.

For a brief period in 1912 Rebecca West edited the women's page of Lansbury's *Daily Herald*. Besides the articles here reprinted, she also produced some vegetarian recipes, though readers of her *Clarion* articles will recognise her belief that good red meat would make revolutionary feminists out of working women. Self-denial, celibacy and vegetables were all very well, she felt, but women workers would change the world far faster on the meals their capitalist masters ate, with free and happy sex lives with their male comrades and leisure spent not in prayer and fasting, dressed in rags and sandals, but dancing in good shoes and pretty clothes. She denounced the rich and profligate always, but never joined the reformers who felt that heaven was to be gained by wearing a hair shirt.

She wrote another review of H. G. Wells's *Marriage*. It appeared in Hugh Dent's *Everyman*, for 8 November 1912, but in her clippings book she noted that he had cut down and emasculated it because he considered it 'incompatible with revealed religion, authority and ethics'. I have also included some articles from the *Manchester Daily Dispatch* in 1912 and 1913, and three essays from the *Daily Chronicle* on women's work during the war, together with a final essay from her clippings book dated 6 November 1916, in which she reaffirmed her feminism and her antagonism to capitalism.

In these articles, Rebecca West spoke for thousands of women. The recovery of her words and her renewed reputation as artist and thinker is another step in the recovery of the history of feminist and socialist traditions in British politics. Rebecca West kept the words of an early critic in her scrapbook '. . . if there ever is an English revolution there will come a point when the Reds and the Whites will sink their differences for ten minutes while they guillotine Miss West for making remarks that both sides have found intolerably wounding.' The young Rebecca West stood for revolution, free love, equal pay, the working class, votes for women and the most advanced ideas in literature. 'Justicia' has been Rebecca West's muse, judgement her method, righteous indignation her tone. She has moved with confidence from fiction and literary criticism, where women before her have worked with genius, to paths where few female feet have left their mark – moral philosophy, psychobiography, political history. Boldness is Rebecca West's strength. She polished the weapons of invective and denunciation into the tools of a fine art. She was never afraid of her own anger; it was justifiable. She turned its force against the enemy, not against herself. The deepest difference between Rebecca West and most women writers lies in her ability to express anger directly, the power to shout curses and laugh at folly and persecution, with no damage to her own ego.

Hungering and thirsting after righteousness, Rebecca West's appetite for justice has not diminished over the decades. Nor has she the slightest hesitation in expressing unpopular views. 'I'm dead to Dante,' she told me. 'Beatrice is the great boring female of all time.' She is not interested in woman as object or woman as subject, but in woman as she acts and thinks in history. 'For certainly we need rebellion. Unless woman is going to make trouble she had better not seek her emancipation.'

Domestics

The peeresses are going to prison! One of these days you will see Bow Street choked with motor-cars, and the severe simplicity of the dock will set off the creations of Paquin and Worth. Or, perhaps, they will wear their peeresses' robes and coronets. I hope so. Those of us who were not invited to the Abbey at last year's Coronation would like a chance of looking upon the great ones of the earth.

And why are they going to prison? Because they don't like the Insurance Act. Neither do socialists. So it was in the hope that the peerage had turned socialist, and that the House of Lords would open with the singing of 'The Red Flag' that sent me to the offices of the Servants' Tax Resisters' Defence Association, at South Molton Street. What I learned there sent my hopes flying high.

Many such ladies as Ellen, Countess of Desart, the Viscountess Dupplin, the Lady Louisa Fielding, Lady Massie Blomfield (I don't know why she isn't *the* Lady Massie Blomfield, but there seems to be some occult thought about these things), are going to resist the Servants' Tax. They say they don't mind paying their threepences. But they won't deduct threepence from the servants' wages.

That is a sign of grace. They are getting on. But alas! they are still members of the Anti-Socialist Union. The mind of man cannot devise an alternative scheme to this objectionable method of tax-collecting under a compulsory and contributory system of insurance. Therefore what we must have is a non-contributory scheme. But these ladies won't have that. They want to go on 'being kind' to their servants. And the milk of human kindness, as we know, is rather a dangerous drug. It makes the employer arrogant. It turns the worker into a contented slave.

They say, therefore, that sick benefit is unnecessary – that, in the few cases where a servant is turned out of the house by her mistress, she must go to a hospital where she does not 'need' her seven-and-sixpence. What servants want, the secretary, Miss Margaret Douglas, declared, is an early pension; for men and women who have reached middle age find it difficult to get situations. And where is that to come from? Miss Douglas could not suggest. It won't come from the employers. Mr Galsworthy, himself a member of the governing classes, has written a pathetic description of the old butler who, after years of trusted service with noble families, has to earn a few crusts by paper-selling. It will have to come from the State. Poor peeresses! Turn where they will to escape Lloyd George, they find themselves entering the fold of socialism.

With real pity I left this abode of sheep without a shepherd, struggling so bravely from the obscurity of the Primrose League or the Women's Liberal Association. I went to look for Miss Grace Neal, the organiser of the Domestic Workers' Union. I found her at her offices at 211 Belsize Road, Kilburn. Miss Neal has been a domestic worker since the age of ten. She has – I fancy this phrase would make the duchesses smile, but it is an honourable truth – reached a considerable degree of eminence in her profession. And she has been the moving spirit of her Union since it started. Certainly she was one of those who speak with authority.

'Do you approve of the Insurance Act as it applies to servants?'

'I disapprove of the Act altogether,' said Miss Neal emphatically. 'I am a socialist. How could I approve of a contributory scheme?'

'Do you approve of tax resistance?' I asked.

'No, I do not,' answered Miss Neal, still more emphatically. 'If there is going to be an Insurance Act we domestic workers must be included. Our industry must be recognised like any other. It is true that last year I spoke on the platform of the Servants' Tax Resisters. But that was because the servants were originally defrauded under the Act. They had to pay their threepences, yet when they were ill they received no sick benefit if their mistresses continued to give them board and lodging, or if they were taken into a hospital. That is remedied now. We get our seven-and-sixpence a week like any other worker.'

'Then you do not agree with the contention, that if a servant goes into hospital, the seven-and-sixpence is superfluous?' I asked, quoting from the Tax Resistance leaflet.

'Is seven-and-sixpence ever superfluous?' inquired Miss Neal. 'That is nonsense. Nearly all domestic workers help to support some relative. Most of the girls I know send a good part of their wages home. It is a popular delusion that women work for themselves alone, and have no dependants.'

'And the other contention that the "subsidy is inadequate" if she goes into lodgings?'

'A servant doesn't go into lodgings when she's ill. She can't. From my own experience, I can tell you that it is hard enough for a servant to get lodgings when she is well. Very few landladies would take in a girl who was ill. They know they wouldn't get their money.'

'And what about the grievance that a servant will have to pay sixpence a week – her own and the employer's contribution – when she is out of work?'

'Of course, that is a necessary evil of a contributory scheme,' said Miss Neal. 'And you must remember that servants are in a unique position concerning unemployment. Unemployment is not our difficulty. There is work for all; but it is so often under bad conditions. A servant can nearly always get work unless her mistress has refused her a character. She can rarely get into work again after that. That, by the way, is a reform our Union is fighting for. We wish to make an open character compulsory.'

'Is there any part of the Act that specially appeals to you?'

'The maternity benefit. It is a very sad and very difficult subject to talk about, but to be quite frank, our occupation is one of great temptation. For one thing, girls often have to take situations in homes they know nothing about. And for another thing, wherever you go you are exposed to advances from your employers. If it isn't the husband, it's the sons or the visitors. And the better the place the worse the temptation. Considering the state of ignorance in which most of these girls go out into service, it is a wonder more tragedies do not occur. At present, when such a misfortune befalls a girl her employers almost always turn her out into the streets. The maternity benefit may just prove the trifle that decides whether she permanently adopts an evil life or atones for her mistake by living a decent life while keeping her child.'

'And there remains the great plank in the resisters' platform – the objection of the servants to the compulsory deduction from their wages.'

'That is quite true. But you know the remedy, and so do I!' Miss Neal became fiercely socialist. 'They say the expense prevents them having a non-contributory scheme of National Insurance. Expense! Let them start by saving a few pence of those thousands they are spending on the machinery of this stupid Act. Those offices at Buckingham Gate, the hundreds of lecturers trotting round the country, the thousands of officials, the postage and printing of all those explanatory leaflets – that would give them a little pocket-money to begin with!'

'But you are not going to resist the Act, imperfect as it is?'

'No. We are going to take the half-loaf first, and get the whole afterwards.'

That is the right spirit. Let the peeresses go to prison. Let them stay there until they become 'whole hoggers' in socialism. But Miss Grace Neal and the members of the Union are the sort of people who ought to be at large, if only to give the governing classes trouble.

Daily Herald, 18 June 1912

Homeless Women

When a woman comes to London to earn her living it is fairly certain she will not make much of a living. Henceforward she must hunt for cheapness – cheap food, cheap clothes, cheap lodgings. And the last is her greatest need.

It may be said at once that most boarding-houses which give a woman anything like the comforts of a home are too expensive for the average woman worker. The girl who earns from a pound to two pounds a week must go to one of those gloomy boarding-houses which may be found at their grimmest in Bloomsbury and Bayswater, which never pretend to comfort, where the smell from the kitchen is ironically disproportionate to the amount of food consumed in the dining-room, where the landlady prizes godliness far above cleanliness. Or she may go into a bed-sitting-room in some mean street, where she will have loneliness to endure as well as squalor.

So probably, after a few months of wandering from one uncomfortable room to another, she will take refuge in one of the boarding-houses of the Young Women's Christian Association. In the matter of material comfort these vary. In some there is cleanliness and good cooking; in others a duster has never been seen and the diet consists chiefly of rice pudding and bread-and-butter. They do not cater for the worst-paid class of workers, and are only suitable for girls earning from about 23s to 30s a week. There is no doubt that the arrangements in some of these houses are most comfortable. But they have one serious drawback. The inmates have to submit to moral mollycoddling.

A girl who has suffered in these establishments once remarked bitterly that the management at least was neither young nor Christian. But that is not quite true. Putting aside the question of

Christian meekness – which is notoriously but rarely found in those having authority – the place is overwhelmed with Christianity as interpreted by elderly ladies who would certainly make excellent Christian martyrs – they would face a lion without winking – but are hardly suitable to be the managers of a girls' residential club.

There are various vexatious effects of this. Texts are excellent things in their proper place, which is in the Bible, but they are not artistic ornaments for bedroom walls. The inmates were made to pray whether they would or no, at certain regular hours. And they must not come in later than 10.30 p.m. This last is a particularly irritating infringement of personal liberty.

An inmate of one of these houses wrote defending this early closing system in *The Freewoman*, declaring that 'a girl who thinks she can come in and out of a house at any time of the night soon loses her character, and character is the most precious thing in the world to a girl – if she once loses that, she has lost all'. This is the pernicious fag-end of the harem system. A woman may go out at night to do a hundred necessary and honourable things. She will, if she is an intelligent being, go out once a week to a suffrage or a socialist meeting. And I hope that she will sometimes be able to spend a shilling going to see Pavlova. Moreover, there are times when, after a long day's work, one's nerves are rubbed up the wrong way, and nothing but a long walk through the darkness to the heights of Hampstead or Highgate will quiet them down.

What is wanted is, of course, the erection of blocks of model flats such as are now built for workmen. This form of housing has never appealed to the greedy capitalist with his eye on ten per cent, so in the case of men it has been undertaken by the LCC. Why will it not undertake this for women? It is not because it does not know of the need for them. In 1909 a petition, signed by five hundred women of the working classes, was presented to the Housing Department of the LCC, asking for some provision for their need for a roof over their heads. The LCC blandly replied that their housing powers enabled them to deal with the working classes alone. Apparently it had never heard of a working woman, although it employs Heaven knows how many thousand teachers and nurses itself.

Probably the reason why it is pretending to be both stupid and ignorant is that it fears that these flats might be used by disreputable women. The fact that disreputable women are usually better paid than respectable ones, and thus are not in the same desperate straits, has not occurred to them. In any case, surely it would be better for the LCC to stain its angel's robes by harbouring a few women of a class that are certain in any case to find shelter than to condemn thousands of working women to a life of discomfort!

But there is a poorer class than these: the women who have to live in the common lodging-houses. There is no moral mollycoddling in her case. However honestly she may be struggling to earn her living, she must live in the constant companionship of women whom the economic struggle has ground down into the mud, whose very presence is a contamination. One woman, Julia Varley, well known in the socialist movement, went down into these depths and lived there for many months. She found the conditions so appalling that the capitalist newspaper who had commissioned her to report on them refused to publish her articles, pleading that they were not suitable for family reading. The filth, the atmosphere of vice, the lack of opportunities for cleanliness, were so appalling that a woman who gets down there will find it hard to rise again.

This is another job the LCC must take on. At present it excuses itself from building Rowton Houses for women on the ground that immoral women may take shelter. I am not aware how the gentlemen using Rowton House furnish guarantees of their moral perfection.

There are many urgent reasons why the LCC and no other body should take over the building of decent common lodging-houses for women. Only the municipality is likely to manage them in a perfectly disinterested way, and not put on the screw for a larger dividend. Only the municipality can insist on a uniform standard of cleanliness, sanitation and charges. They would be able to suppress undesirable houses from a more judicious standpoint than that of philanthropic old maids. And perhaps they will allow working women to live their own lives without any impertinent 'supervision'.

But of course, the LCC will maintain its present deafness for the next few centuries unless some vigorous agitation is started. The women on the Council ought to take the initiative. Otherwise we working women may pray that Lady St Helier and her other lady colleagues may spend their time in the next world eating cold rice pudding flavoured with evangelical doctrines, and sleeping in cubicles under the disapproving eye of texts.

Daily Herald, 20 June 1912

The Noble Art

Politics is such a noble art. It requires such genius, such intellect, such greatness of mind and heart, that women can never, never take part in it. So Mr F. E. Smith says. So Sir Frederick Banbury says. So Lord Curzon says. All of them are undisputed authorities on genius and intellect and greatness. So they must be right. All you can expect of a woman is that she will lift her baby the right way up, take the chair at a Primrose League meeting, and do the dirty work of the world.

One example of the precious dignity of politics has just been given by the *Daily Express*. Thousands of men have come out to bear starvation in order to free themselves and their children from the yoke of the capitalist. But this counts for naught. Have not Labour leaders feasted on chicken and champagne?

The mind of man could not design anything more futile than this dietetic method of argument. Of late women have known in the suffrage agitation the exasperating influence of active political propaganda. They have used horsewhips; they have thrown stones; they have made injudicious and sometimes remarkably dull speeches. But they have never proved themselves so hopelessly un-fitted for politics and all forms of mental activity as certain organs of the Tory Press.

For instance, in the most acrimonious moments of the suffrage agitation, Miss Christabel Pankhurst has never taunted Mrs Humphry Ward for eating six ices in rapid succession at Rumpel-mayer's. Nor has Mrs Fawcett ever rebuked her militant sisters for lunching at Gatti's rather than Lockhart's.

The truth is politics are too childish for women. They often say women have no sense of humour. But they have a sense of decency, which might prevent them mocking the bravery of hungry men and women with chatter about chicken and champagne.

The fact is, we want a new distribution of labour. There must be some place in the scheme of existence for such people as the editor of the *Daily Express*, Sir Frederick Banbury and Mr F. E. Smith. For the last few years we have been wearied by pictures of the rich men's small daughters, romping on rugs in socks, performing in fairy plays, and many other intimate poses. This suggests a solution to the problem. Perhaps gentlemen have a way with the children.

That would be a real militant movement. The textile workers of Lancashire, the chain-makers of Cradley Heath, and the pit-brow lasses, ought to march down on London, storm the House of Commons and the offices of certain Tory journals. They would then lead their captives home in irons to look after the children.

Then the children would get a chance. The Conservatives and Liberals are always cursing the working women for leaving their homes to go out and work. They might be satisfied.

And then there would be a little less nonsense talked in politics. As it is, parliamentary news is too puerile for any woman to read without tears.

Daily Herald, 20 June 1912

Servant Slaves

One Founder's Day at Dr Barnardo's Village Home I was struck by the fact that when the former pupils walked across the platform all the women were servants. And when I came to inquire I found that all the girls who were able to go out into the world to earn their living were designed for domestic service. This seemed to me rather a strange and disquieting thing. For I could hardly believe that all these girls had a natural taste for domestic service. Certainly, one would hardly expect to find any artistic genius from those comfortable but pictureless and hideously furnished cottages. But some of the girls might have had a taste for an open-air life and wanted to take up agriculture, or have shown signs of manual dexterity that might have been made use of in the factory.

And a month or two later I learned that the Borstal system institution for girls sends all its reformed prisoners out to domestic service. That, again, seemed disquieting. One finds it hard to believe that domestic service can appeal with equal force to the girls brought up amid the unwinking piety of the Barnardo homes and the girls just rescued from a life of crime.

I am rather afraid that this wholesale consignment of human beings to a convenient sphere comes of the conception of woman as a large and perhaps more capable jellyfish whose flabbiness allows for her to be packed into any odd corner. The destruction of women is their 'damned wantlessness', as Ibsen put it. And the forcing of girls into domestic service is, of course, partly their own fault. The Laban College for women, for instance, is not getting the support it deserves.

Just at present we are in the midst of a renaissance of domestic service. At King's College the home science course has been started with an endowment of £100,000 to teach middle-class women how to scrub floors and feel perfect ladies while doing it. Anti-suffragist doctors write to the papers explaining that women are ignorant devils, who murder their children by feeding them on skim-milk once a day instead of fresh milk whenever they want it. They never explain how a woman is to buy milk for three children with eighteen shillings a week. They nag at her for buying unsavoury and mysterious trifles at fried-fish and ham-and-beef shops instead of giving the children porridge. They neglect, again, to explain how she is to afford the gas that is necessary for cooking porridge properly or how she is to spare the milk and sugar that alone make it palatable for children. One half of the movement is satisfaction of the upper- and middle-class desire to despise the poor for their poverty.

The other half is satisfaction of the vanity of women who like to stay in their homes and think themselves peculiarly precious for that reason. There is no special virtue in domestic work. Up to the beginning of the factory system the housewife produced half the wealth of the country. She had to grind her corn and bake her bread, to weave her cloth, to wash it, to make it into apparel, to be doctor, cobbler, mother and cook, to rear her pigs, salt her bacon and cure her hams. Bearing and educating her children were, of course, duties hardly needing mention.

But now man has invaded woman's sphere. He makes her bread, he weaves her cloth, he is the doctor and the cobbler, and sometimes the cook. He has snatched woman's work away from the home. What is known as domestic service is now the merest tucking in of the untidy edges of an incomplete civilisation. Keeping a house clean and doing the cooking is necessary labour. But it is not interesting, and it is not done under happy conditions.

What is wanted is surely some system of communal kitchens. When one goes along the drab streets of some middle-class suburb and thinks how miserable and tame-spirited the people who live in these monotonous kennels must be, one must remember that there is always one person more miserable than anybody else in each house. And that is the servant. Very often she has bad sleeping accommodation, very often she has no exercise, and almost certainly she lives a life barren of intellectual opportunity. She has no chance of associating with her fellow servants. She very often, by force of circumstances, works in a district remote from her family.

Surely, if in a street of twelve houses one was set aside as a house of domestic service that would make things better. One open and airy kitchen would be a better thing than a dozen mean and stuffy ones. And perhaps it might also be a sort of home for the servants. It would be a great thing to turn servants into a class-conscious guild rather than a collection of isolated drudges.

Communal kitchens, of course, are disapproved of by those who preach the beauty of home science. They say that it would break up the home. They never explain how it would do so more than the habit of sending the washing out to a laundry.

It is curious to note that this worship of domesticity never takes one form – the form of raising servants' wages. £100,000 has been sent to the home science course at King's College, but the average wages for servants in England remains at little over £17 [per annum].

Daily Herald, 22 June 1912

The Tax Resisters

I have received a letter from Miss Margaret Douglas, honorary secretary of the Servants' Tax Resisters' Defence Association, in which she protests against my version of her interview with me, which appeared in our issue of 18 June. She states that I did not ask her to suggest where money could be found for a satisfactory scheme of National Insurance. The first object of her Association is to make unworkable this present Act, which applies compulsion to the poor through the richer classes of the community. The Association, as she told me, is primarily one of servants who, rightly, resent compulsion applied in this way, which is an infringement of their rights. If they can obtain the backing of their mistresses by making them pledge themselves not to act as the instrument of compulsion, that is to the credit of the mistresses.

It is rather pathetic (Miss Douglas continues) to find in an organ which professes to be intelligent a repetition of the cry invented by politicians that the only alternative to a stamp-and-card contributory scheme was a non-contributory scheme. By repeating this they have terrified the Conservative Party and drawn the workers into their net.

It is not beyond the intellect of man to devise, for instance, a scheme which should impose a compulsory tax on the rich and give State aid for voluntary insurance on the part of the worker. Besides this, Miss Douglas does not admit that there is such a thing as a non-contributory scheme; the money has to come out of the people's pocket in any case, and any hardships inflicted by the tax inevitably fall on the worker.

My reply to all this is, of course, that I cannot make out why Miss Douglas is protesting. I certainly did not ask her to suggest where money could be found for a satisfactory scheme of National Insurance. What I asked was where she was going to get the funds for the middle-age pensions for servants, which was the only alternative she then presented to the Insurance Act.

That the only alternative to a stamp-and-card contributory scheme is a non-contributory scheme is one of the few truthful remarks made by professional politicians in our time. I agree with Miss Douglas that it is not beyond the intellect of man to devise, for instance, 'a scheme which should impose a compulsory tax on the rich and give State aid for voluntary insurance on the part of the workers'. Voluntary insurance becomes a luxury of the well-paid worker. The badly paid worker cannot be expected to give up part of his pittance by his own free will. Just as under the present scheme the poorest class of all – the casual labourers – are insurable. These things happen in all contributory schemes.

Of course, there is no such thing as a scheme that is non-contributory in the sense that the money comes from nowhere. But there is such a thing, as Miss Douglas herself suggests, as 'a compulsory tax on the rich'.

Daily Herald, 22 June 1912

Pastoral Plays for Policemen

A Happy Day in the Woodlands for Scotland Yard

On the other side of the Northern Heights, where Hampstead Heath slopes down from the Spaniards to the vales of Middlesex, lies a garden suburb. One of its most cherished possessions is a large wood that stretches over to the green fields of Finchley. The powers-that-be in the suburb have mercifully left it in its wild state.

Just now it is a very pleasant place. The larks and blackbirds sing the more sweetly now that the insistent cuckoo is quiet, and the wild roses are at their best. It was to gather some of these that a woman resident of the suburb went into these woodlands on Thursday afternoon. It was a warm day and the sky was blue, and there was pervading all things a sense of holy peace. Therefore she was shocked and surprised, on entering a green glade, to find herself surrounded by policemen.

She turned and fled along the leafy path by which she came, and ran into the arms of a police-sergeant. In her furious homeward course she passed many a blue helmet nodding 'under the blossom, under the bough'. Robert's round blue eyes and expression of exaltation while listening to a lark gave a fresh insight into the character of the Metropolitan Police.

The true explanation burst upon her later. The suburb possesses, set high on the hill, an imposing Free Church. Needless to say, this is heavily in debt. It almost makes me wish one were a church, to see how kindly and forgivingly they are treated when they emulate the Jubilee Juggins. So the congregation has arranged to clear off the debt by organising an Eisteddfod. An Eisteddfod is a bazaar with an element of strife in the shape of musical competitions.

Mr Reginald McKenna was due to open it on Thursday afternoon. The policemen were there to protect him from suffragists that might, like the bears Elisha called out to punish the ribald infants, run out from the wood in search of prey.

Is the suffrage agitation fomented by *agents provocateurs* from Scotland Yard? Think of the good times Scotland Yard has had from it! Formerly there was no form of activity possible on the political side of the Criminal Investigation Department except tracking harmless organ-grinders round Saffron Hill and denouncing them as anarchists. Now they can spend the afternoon in sylvan surroundings preserving the peace among imaginary ladies. This is a clumsy way of amusing them. It would be much cheaper to give them a free pass to cinematograph theatres twice a week.

It is impossible to live happily while the suffragists are carrying on the hunger-strike in gaol. Their window-smashing may have been tactically unwise, but that hardly affects the fact that they are enduring pain. Life is so full of inevitable tragedy, which not the wisest laws could cure, that we ought gladly to take the opportunity to wipe out this that a stroke of Mr McKenna's pen could annihilate.

Mr McKenna ought to transfer the suffragist prisoners to the first division (like their more influential leaders), not only for their sake but for ours. Lest, growing accustomed to the thought of suffering, we become as cruel as he himself.

Daily Herald, 22 June 1912

Feminism

The attitude of the public towards the woman's movement is too horrible to be unimportant. Feminism has been accepted by the sentient part of the nation, and its triumph can be judged by the names of its enemies.

Lord Curzon, Austen Chamberlain, Lord Rothschild, Fred Maddison and Sir Edward Clarke are gentlemen whom any cause would be pleased to find among its opponents. Yet the great mass of the British public, which talks little but overthrows governments, is standing by quite unmoved while the woman's movement is being frustrated and its advocates imprisoned. One can understand it tolerating the condition of affairs in which men are tortured to madness and women (such as Cecilia Haig and Mary Clarke) murdered by police brutality. Ours is such an ungentlemanly social system that few of us have any gentlemanly feelings left: we tolerate the sufferings of the suffragist under the heel of the Government just as we tolerated the suffering of the dockers under the heel of Lord Devonport. What is surprising is that the public should support the Government in its whimsical and expensive opposition to an inoffensive principle.

There must be some reason for this. We might look for it in the statesman behind the policy, remembering that the popularity of Mr Lloyd George led England to take an interest in the most uninteresting subject of Welsh Disestablishment. But Mr Asquith is the statesman behind the anti-suffragist policy, and Mr Asquith is one of the Great Unloved. Tears do not rise to strong men's eyes, women do not wave their handkerchiefs when he passes through the streets. The idea of Mr Asquith turning the public into sin cannot be held for a moment. The secret of the defeat of the woman's movement may be sought not among its opponents but among its supporters.

The fact is that the British public, being busy earning its living all day and interested in gardening in the evening, has a short memory. At the present moment it has forgotten what the woman's movement is about. It knows that the women are discontented and, deafened by the crash of breaking glass, is inclined to ascribe it to sheer cussedness. When the suffragist leaves her window and talks to the public, all it learns is that Mr Asquith has lied to the women and that Mr Winston Churchill is a sneak. But the public is accustomed to that. This has ever been the way of the English gentleman in politics, whether he was engaged in cheating the people out of the land through Enclosures Acts, forcing opium into China at bayonet-point, or cynically handing over Persia to the executioner. It hardly explains the unrest among women.

If the public perseveres and goes to the meetings held by the leaders, it will still be at a loss. If Mrs Pethick Lawrence speaks it will learn that the Race Spirit and the Mother Soul have been injured or offended in some way. If Mrs Pankhurst speaks, it will hear the bitter truth that men despise women for their wifehood and motherhood rather than honour them. If Christabel Pankhurst speaks, it will look on the mangled corpse of liberalism. Out of a confusion of eloquence will come the message of the suffragist, spoken with fine sincerity and perfect truth: 'The government of women by men has been a ghastly failure, and we have come out to end it!'

The message of the suffragist is as vague as that. The fact is that the Women's Social and Political Union, which may be taken as the inspiration of the suffrage movement, is incapable of making a more definite programme of revolt than that. It has become in its latter development a soulless society.

In 1905, when it started on its great work of rebellion, to which has since been given so much blood and brain, it was a collection of teachers, mill-girls, shop-assistants and workers of all descriptions. While they were still teachers, mill-girls and shop-assistants their revolt was effective. At early by-elections their message ran like wild-fire among the working women of the constituencies. It impressed the factory-hands with a sense of the earnestness of the new movement when they saw one of themselves lay down her tools and go away to face the great men in London; and come back after many days with a tale of suffering and insult. The propaganda of that period carried conviction with it because it came from the mouth of workers who knew that it was little use complaining unless one's grievance was bitter.

But those days are past. The mill-girls have left their mills, the teachers their schools, the shop-assistants their shops; worse still, they have left their native towns, where the condition and psychology of the inhabitants were known to them. The Women's Social and Political Union is organised from London. It has exchanged the warmer, more intimate spirit of syndicalism for the cold ideal of old-fashioned socialism, which imagined an England governed by a central bureaucracy, which would leave no room for trade unionism. Syndicalism discovered that there is a natural bond between the worker and his work, and that the worker can govern the conditions of his work much better than any detached official. Thus the suffragists of earlier days who stuck to their work could voice the grievances of their position far more effectively than the new army of detached suffragist organisers.

This army of organisers has naturally found most of its recruits in the middle classes. The middle-class woman has her grievances, but these are so firmly welded on her by her own acquiescence that they are hardly a basis for a revolution. The parasitic middle-class woman is a problem that will be automatically solved as soon as the industrial position of women is improved. One cannot expect her to leave her respected slavery until independence is made more honourable. Under these unsuitable leaders the movement has relapsed into timid conservatism, urging such safe though necessary reforms as equal penalties for adultery rather than the complete economic independence of women, where it has not abandoned all constructive intention and become a mere expression of vague discontent.

Surely it would have been better if the suffragists had used their brilliant talent for unrest in their own spheres, still keeping in mind their political aim. For instance, Miss Adela Pankhurst was a teacher. She left her profession and became a WSPU organiser: a girl of delicate health, she henceforth gave herself to a life of self-denial and danger. Open-air meetings, in rain or shine, were the main occupation of her life – punctuated by ordeals such as that at Dundee, where a few supporters of Mr Churchill (perhaps erroneously stated to have been hired for the purpose from the slums) tried to strangle her. Her health has now broken down, and the vote is not won. To what end?

It would have been better if she had stayed to foment unrest in her own profession. Consider the stinging grievances under which women teachers labour. All over the country, from the earliest stages of their training to the highest positions, women receive from one-half to two-thirds of the salary given to a man for exactly similar work. And the head-teacherships of mixed schools are reserved for men.

And now consider the unique weapon which they possess. If the women teachers of Britain should strike, the authorities would be helpless. Other strikes fail because the employers have so many resources to fall back upon. There is always the surplus of manufactured goods that will enable the manufacturer to tide over the strike without starving his markets. There is always the surplus of human beings ground down by poverty into blacklegs. But that could not happen here. There is no reserve of educated schoolchildren to satisfy the parents while the rawer material goes untaught. Mr Runciman could not beat the slums of Liverpool and bring back trainloads of blackleg elementary-schoolteachers. The Government could hardly threaten to close down its elementary schools and open rival institutions in more docile Belgium or Germany. Something would have to be done. The women would gain their economic advantage, and probably their political rights in a week or two, if someone would only breathe some devilry into the scholastic mind.

Teachers are perhaps alone in having the weapon of their emancipation ready to their hand. But revolt in other professions, while more difficult to organise, must be just as effective, and much more so than the ordinary militant outbreaks of today. The window-smashing of last March was not effective. It might have been had they been smashed from inside the drapery shop and not outside; if each stone had been a declaration that one of the wage-slaves in these bird-cages of servitude had decided to revolt. One of the women now being tortured in Mountjoy Prison, Gladys Evans, was formerly a shop-assistant. Surely it would have been better for this brave woman to have fanned some such rebellion among her fellow-workers, rather than to be condemned to five years' penal servitude for failing to set alight a theatre in which Mr Asquith did not happen to be?

For certainly we need rebellion. Unless woman is going to make trouble she had better not seek her emancipation. Men are reaping the reward of docility in their slavery. The increasingly dangerous temper of the oppressing classes and the smouldering hatred among the oppressed call for a last decisive battle. The beginnings of militancy made us hope that woman would lead the workers to this Armageddon of labour. Is she really too busy holding drawing-room meetings?

Daily Herald, 5 September 1912

The WSPU

Letter to the Editor of the *Daily Herald*

Sir,

I do not think I am unpractical when I deprecate 'the work of rebellion started by Christabel Pankhurst in 1905 being carried on largely by "middle-class" women instead of entirely by armies of workers from the mills, from the shops, from the schools'.

I can think of an instance in which the conduct of the Union by professional political organisers made a most disastrous hash of a great opportunity. In 1909 Winston Churchill visited Lancashire. Obviously, if Mr Churchill had been unpleasantly received by Lancashire the cause of the unpleasantness would have received instant attention. To that end the WSPU [Women's Social and Political Union] started a vigorous campaign led by the most brilliant organiser they ever had, Miss Mary Gawthorpe. It was miserably ineffective. Mr Churchill had a triumphant passage through Lancashire, at what time his supporters, in the ecstasies of political hysteria, mauled the suffragists in the street or sentenced them to stiff terms of imprisonment from the Bench.

For the WSPU organisers and Mr Churchill appeared before the public on the same footing – as professional politicians, with no true relation to the life of the people. All men are snobs. On the one side there was Winston Churchill, blazing with meretricious oratory and studied charm, a Cabinet Minister and escaped prisoner-of-war, with a beautiful young wife at his side and half the businessmen of Lancashire, hungry for knighthoods, crawling round his feet. On the other side were women who had nothing but the Right on their side. Need one ask which conquered?

If in every mill half the women workers had been ramming the truths of feminism into the heads of the men workers, then there might have been a public in the right frame of mind to put the fear of death into Mr Churchill. But not even Miss Gawthorpe's genius could avail against the fact that she was creating revolt from without and not from within.

It may be true that 'to carry on a great organisation you need constant and trained workers'; but I cannot see why the WSPU should need so many times more the number of professional political organisers than the trade unions of Great Britain do. During a long membership of the WSPU I have often been infuriated by the spectacle of 'constant and trained workers' superintending the sale of purple, white and green articles of absolutely no feminist interest, such as pincushions and doyleys. The professional political worker, like all non-productive workers, is a luxury to be indulged in as little as possible. If Miss Wylie wants to know why let her look at the aridity of the Labour Party and its alienation from the workers. Moreover, the political organisation of women and workers ought to spring from the conditions of their life, and should not need to be artificially imposed on them from without.

The real objection to the control of the woman's movement by the middle classes is the extreme danger of any disassociation between the emancipation of women and the emancipation of workers. Otherwise the emancipation of women may only mean their exploitation.

How easily these two may be confused may be seen from Miss Wylie's claim that Lord Curzon's stipulation that his daughters may inherit his peerage is a proof of his unconscious sympathy with feminism. Lord Curzon's stipulation is simply an expression of his vanity thirsting that his renown may go down to posterity. When the British Empire has comfortably forgotten Lord Curzon, some child will lisp, 'Papa got his title from great-grandfather Nathaniel.' Thus is he insured against his own insignificance. And Austen Chamberlain's solicitations of the females of Great Britain in the interests of Tariff Reform simply shows that he despises them sufficiently to believe that they will work for a principle abandoned in disgust by men. It is obvious that unless women who desire economic independence secure themselves the protection of a socialist State, they will be hunted down by capitalism and forced to become the most under of all underdogs.

As for Miss Cutten's contention that the great majority of the members of her local WSPU are working women (teachers, civil servants, dressmakers, nurses, etc.), I should be amazed to hear that the WSPU had ever lavished its money or its moral support on any attempt among any class of these workers to destroy the sex oppression in their professions. I should be amazed to the point of incredulity if I heard that any of these workers were consulted as to the policy of the WSPU.

In this connection it may be noted that the committee of the WSPU (which has gradually shrunk to the number of eight persons) numbers only one woman of the working classes and two of the professional classes.

I am not a teacher, and have never had any official position on the WSPU. Yours faithfully,

Rebecca West
Daily Herald, 11 September 1912

Mr Wells on Marriage

Marriage by H. G. Wells

'I'm a spiritual guttersnipe in love with unimaginable goddesses,' said that child of the age, George Ponderevo, in *Tono-Bungay*. That is the answer to those who, touching life with the coarseness of the sentimentalist, cry out that this is the age of materialism, and that men are turning from things of the spirit. The moral unrest of the day is the result of the conviction of modern men and women that, tested by some mystic, absolute standard outside themselves, life is not fine enough. *Marriage*, Mr Wells's last book, represents this spiritual dissatisfaction brooding over the dinginess that has come between us and the reality of love. With the exception of the more brutal ascetics, people have always realised the value of love. To avoid its profanation they adopted the rough-and-ready test of marriage; outside the circle of the wedding-ring all relationships were evil, within it all were sacred. It was a good working hypothesis. But now, when we have developed a more determined thirst for beauty, it seems too brutal and mechanical a law. It is not only because it falls so heavily on so many delicate flowers of the spirit that men such as Mr Wells rebel against it, though of that aspect he spoke in *The New Machiavelli*. It is also the licence, which is the necessary corollary of law, which disgusts him. With a sharp sense of the values of life, he cannot bear the artificial sanction given to gross, destructive, mutual raids on personality which often form marriages.

The blame for the ignobility of marriage he places primarily on the modern woman. He finds her guilty, first of all, of a carelessness of destiny, even as regards her motherhood. As old Sir Roderick Dover says: 'If there was one thing in which you might think woman would show a sense of some divine purpose in life it is in the matter of children, and they show about as much care in the matter – oh, as rabbits! Yes, rabbits. I stick to it. Look at the things a nice girl will marry; look at the men's children she'll consent to bring into the world. Cheerfully! Proudly! For the sake of the home and the clothes . . .' That was the crime Marjorie Pope was about to commit when the book opens. She was a creature compact of gallantry and sweetness, with a vigorous, beautiful body, and a quick mind stimulated by university discipline. Yet, simply because she was afflicted with an intolerable father, who could not be allowed to carve the chicken because he 'splashed too much and bones upset him and made him want to show up chicken in *The Times*'; and because she had got into debt at Oxbridge, she was on the verge of marriage with Will Magnet, the humorist, 'a fairish man of forty, pale, with a large, protuberant, observant grey eye – I speak particularly of the left – and a face of quiet animation, warily alert for the wit's opportunity.'

Then Professor Trafford appears, and his coming is symbolic of the promise of beauty and dignity he brings to Marjorie's life. While she is playing croquet to an obligato of facetiousness from Mr Magnet, Trafford plunges down from the skies in an aeroplane. Overcome by the clear magic of this man, who has taken great risks, who is disciplined by mental work to athleticism of character, she elopes with him.

At first sight it seems like a fine sacrifice of this girl, with her warm, purring love of ease, to marry the scientist whose long-inspired days in the laboratory brought him only a few hundreds a year. But Marjorie was one of those who make the best of both worlds. By her quiet, graceful pursuit of her own tastes, she robbed from him all peace that made his brain smooth and quick to work; then she drove him into breaking up his laborious day by desperate money-making excursions into lecturing and journalism; and finally she took him from his work altogether, and turned him into a busy commercial prostitute, perverting his splendid, fearless research to a reticent and hidden investigation of synthetic rubber for a Jewish syndicate. For she sucked him dry of money. She begins by furnishing her house too richly, and goes on to lead him into preposterous social obligations. She uses the love that brought them together as a barrier behind which to level this relentless attack on his genius. She dangles her babies at him and preens herself on the majesty of her motherhood to avert discussion. And though she knows that her latter prosperity has been brought by the joy of his life, she does not relent.

In the end he rebels, and takes her away from this 'busy death' in London to the quiet snows of Labrador, to think out the hopeless riddle of their irritating existence. He finds the secret of the shabby haste of the modern world in the victory of the grabbing spirit over the spirit of pure research into life. And he attributes – as did that vulgar and vital genius of America, David Graham Phillips – the unseemly scramble of latter-day human activity to the efforts of men to satisfy the spendthrift passion of women. It seems to him typical that Marjorie should have killed his passion for the remoter beauty for truth by her thirst for the trivial immediate beauty of a well-ordered house. And her triumph was so petty: it was like the work of the *Yellow Book* school, who sacrificed the difficult beauty of issues of the soul to the trivial loneliness of phrases and episodes.

The Traffords' marriage was what that Chatterton of philosophy, young Otto Weininger, said the relationship of men and women in the world must always be, 'the binding of eternal life in a perishable being, of the innocent in the guilty'.

Everyman, 8 November 1912

The Woman as Workmate

Her Claim to Equal Rates of Pay for Equal Quality of Work

Every man likes to think of himself as a kind of Whiteley's – a universal provider. The patriarchal system is the ideal for which he longs. He likes to dream of himself sitting on the verandah after dinner, with his wife beside him and the children in the garden, while his unmarried sisters play duets in the drawing-room and his maiden aunts hand round the coffee. This maintenance of helpless, penniless, subservient womanhood is the nearest he can get in England to the spiritual delights of the harem.

So when womanhood declares that she is no longer helpless, dislikes being penniless and refuses to be subservient the men become indignant and inarticulate. An example of this was to be seen in Mr George Edgar's recent article, 'Why Men Do Not Marry', in the *Daily Dispatch*. Mr Edgar's thesis is difficult to criticise because it consists of two mutually destructive conclusions. He stated, first, that it is absurd for women to ask for equal wages with men because they are inferior workers and have no dependants; and then he vehemently denounces women for ousting men from their work by accepting lower wages. This is the kind of argument one rarely hears except from cross-talk comedians on the halls. What makes it still more elusive is that both his conclusions are incorrect.

Mr Edgar takes the usual masculinist standpoint of regarding women as incompetent weaklings except for their maternal functions which God bestowed on them, and for which, therefore, they deserve no credit.

It is not necessary for me to discuss the question whether a woman is the equal of a man in the performance of a day's work. In the past our practice has assumed that she is not. . . . In actual terms of wages, where in the past women have elected to work in competition with men, commerce has decided that her day's work is less valuable than a man's, and has given her less wages.

This engaging contempt for the value of the women's work is an error which comes of considering only the economic conditions of England since the industrial revolution. It is as though a Chinese mandarin were to spend a short weekend in Whitechapel and then return to Peking proclaiming that all Englishmen got drunk every night and beat their wives. This degradation of women is simply the accident of a new social order that has not yet righted itself.

Why does a man support his wife? It is not only because the mother needs to be relieved from the stress of earning her own livelihood. That is a principle that has never been universally adopted even in our own country in our own time: the Lancashire cotton-operative continues to work after she has children. The maintenance of wives is a survival of the time when England was an agricultural country. It was then recognised that the work of women in the home was so valuable that the husband and wife were regarded as equal partners of a firm, and shared the profits. The wife had then to grind the corn, bake the bread, brew, do all the dairy work and tend much of the livestock, doctor her household, spin the wool and weave the cloth, make her family's clothes and cobble their shoes, and prepare all the food stuffs, such as hams and preserves. And she did it very well indeed. On the rare occasions when she did go out to work beside men she seems – so far as we can judge from documents such as the paysheets of agricultural labourers in the fifteenth century – to have been paid the same wages.

And England went very well then. It was certainly a happier and – many economists agree – a more prosperous country than it is today. Then came the industrial revolution which snatched these occupations out of the women's hands and gave them to men, leaving women only the dish-washing and floor-scrubbing, which is now regarded as peculiarly feminine work, but which had previously been done mainly by boys. The ugliness and economic embarrassment of England since then ought to cause searchings of heart among masculinists such as Mr Edgar.

So much for Mr Edgar's historical researches. Now for his theory that women have no dependants. It is true that the wife does not contribute directly to the family income (men having left her no work to do) and that her maintenance and that of her children has to be borne entirely by her husband. But there are the old as well as the young. It is the woman's place to support the old. Many working-class parents will tell one that a daughter is a better investment than a son, for the son marries and keeps a family, while the daughter will probably remain single so that she can work and provide for her parents. So one cannot advocate the restriction of a woman's wage to the sum sufficient for the support of herself alone, unless one upholds the Tierra del Fuego theory that the aged are useless, dangerous, and ought to be abolished, by exposure if possible, by a club if necessary.

Moreover, I grant that men are efficient and godlike, but they sometimes die. They then leave widows and orphans, who have to be supported. And it also happens occasionally that husbands prove more ornamental than useful, 'dainty rogues in porcelain', unable to wrestle with the rough world, and then their wives have to work for them and the children.

Mr Edgar's fear that if wages were equalised they would tend to drop to the women's level is unsupported by logical proof, and is contradicted by fact. The England of the fifteenth century, which paid its women agricultural labourers as it paid its men, was the paradise of the worker. Never since have they enjoyed similar prosperity. The Lancashire cotton-operatives, who are paid without distinction of sex, are the most well-to-do workers of today. The women are not merely asking for prestige, they are fighting for hard cash. It is not the equality, but the increase in wages they want. Of course, if men insist on women getting lower wages they may create an army of blacklegs to their own undoing.

The second conclusion, that women are ousting men out of the labour world, is a popular and curiously persistent error. In the investigations made twenty years ago by Beatrice and Sidney Webb it was stated that it was very rare for men and women to compete in the same occupation, and Mary Macarthur agrees with them today. When it appears that some industry has shifted from men to women it will usually be found that some new mechanical process has been introduced which demands the manual dexterity and attention to detail characteristic of women. In the few occupations where men and women compete equal wages will benefit men by ridding employers of the temptation to employ women as blacklegs. But, as a rule, the cry for 'equal pay for equal work' does not mean equal pay for the *same* work, but equal pay for work which exacts the same time, skill and energy.

Or, to put it differently, it is a declaration on the woman's part that she is not going to live by bread alone. She wants butter, and cake if possible; pocket money for an occasional theatre and holiday; and the ability to obey the Fifth Commandment and keep her parents out of the workhouse.

The effect on the marriage-rate of the competition between men and women must be quite insignificant. There are much more forcible reasons which prevent marriage. Important among these is the isolation of modern city life. It is possible for men and women to come up to London and live there for years without making a friend. How different from the small communities of our forefathers, when every child was born 'into society' and grew up among a circle of young men and women of the same class! And another deterrent to marriage is the raising of the standard of comfort. Few men and women are prepared to risk bringing up a family on the small means that would have sufficed for their grandparents. And this disinclination to bring children into a poverty-stricken home is not altogether contemptible. City life, with the accompanying miseries of dear food and rent, holds cruel torments for child life.

And if there is to be any romance in marriage women must be given every chance to earn a decent living at other occupations. Otherwise no man can be sure that he is loved for himself alone, and that his wife did not come to the Registry Office because she had had no luck at the Labour Exchange. Only the materialist can fear that a fair day's wage for a fair day's work will kill the wife and mother in women. The trinity of the man, the woman and the child is as indestructible as the trinity of the sun, the moon and the stars.

But one admires the humility of men who think otherwise, and hold that only by the fear of starvation are women coerced into having husbands.

Manchester Daily Dispatch, 26 November 1912

Cause of Women's Restlessness

Suffragist's Spirited Reply to Male Critics

It is just as much a sign of madness to hate all women because they are women as it is to hate black-bearded men or blue-eyed women.

And I am not a doctor. For that reason I am hardly the right person to comment on the views of Mr Berlyn and Mr Titterton. Not being a sex antagonist myself, I cannot meet them on their own ground. I would never attempt to prove that all women are angels and all men devils. By force of habit I hunt for arguments.

And for the life of me I cannot find any arguments in Mr Berlyn's article. I find that vast and loquacious contempt for women popular at the coffee stall and cabmen's shelter and two assertions.

The first assertion is the parrot cry that the suffrage movement is a middle-class movement. Well, so it is, to a great extent. But I want to clear up this mystery about the middle-class woman. What has she done, and when did she do it? Like the long-haired Magdalen in medieval art, the middle-class woman is dragged through politics by angry anti-suffragists as a creature of shame and degradation.

The only offence I can trace to the middle-class woman is the middle-class man. It is strange that when the middle-class man – according to Mr Berlyn – had been edified until the nineties by the companionship of properly supine and uneducated women, his attitude to working women was commonly so brutal. Very often he underpaid and overworked his women employees, sometimes made love to them, and always treating them as inferiors, debarred them from positions of responsibility and opportunity. Yet, strange to say, now that the hussies of Surbiton have taken to becoming suffragists the middle-class man is becoming a better employer of the working women.

That raises an important point in favour of woman suffrage – a doormat race of women does not produce a good race of men. When no encounters of wits and moral passions arise out of his human relationships, when he only meets with surrenders and indulgences, he is apt to become both tyrannous and flaccid. The abnormally submissive Scottish women of the late eighteenth and nineteenth centuries tended to develop a type of man chiefly remarkable for alcoholism.

Therefore the middle-class man who hears that the suffrage movement is discreditable because of its connection with the middle-class woman ought to be moved to support it, both from unwillingness to hear his wife and daughters insulted and from a sporting desire for self-improvement.

Mr Berlyn's other assertion is that the suffrage movement is due to the moral degeneracy of middle-class women consequent on the study of Ibsen. One wonders why this moral degeneracy (the existence of which is unproved by criminal statistics or by the visible increase of gambling halls in Surbiton) should lead women to become suffragists. The more prominent part a woman plays in the suffrage movement the more burdensome her life becomes.

Addressing open-air meetings twice or thrice a day in all weathers and spending half one's life in railway trains is not a happy life. Constant meals of eggs and bacon at commercial hotels tend to melancholia. Prison is not a nice place; and forcible feeding is a hideous thing. Surely it is obvious that if the good-looking young women who, for the most part, constitute the organising staff of the suffrage societies were really actuated by a mad craving for pleasure they had better have gone into the Gaiety chorus. Woman may have got joy out of the suffrage societies, but not pleasure: inspiration but not comfort.

And as for dragging poor Ibsen into the fight, publishers and those in charge of circulating libraries will tell you that very few middle-class women have ever read Ibsen. Neither, I think, has Mr Berlyn. For he imagines that Nora Helmer left home because she despised motherhood: whereas Ibsen states that she left home because she became conscious that playing lap-dog to a trivial husband had un-fitted her for wise motherhood. That is, her feeling of responsibility to her children was not lost, but intensified.

Certainly this revival of moral scrupulousness (temporarily lost to us in the pagan days of early Victorianism) has permeated literature. But a gospel is accepted by sympathy and not by conviction. Women read and encourage such literature because for long the soiled fabric of life had made them feel that the old idea that the suppression of women was good for the race was wrong. They began to suspect that the race can only progress by the development of its individuals: that one cannot build up the whole by destroying the part.

Biology confirms their suspicion. It is as much the duty of women to be fine individuals as it is the duty of men. Hence the acceptance of such literature. A gospel must fall on sympathetic soil, or it dies. There will never be – except among the perverse – any enthusiasm in England for the works of August Strindberg, the foremost European masculinist and hater of women.

Mr Titterton understands the situation a little better. He sincerely represents the solid, prosaic businessman who wants to keep women chained down to material things, for otherwise he fears confusing complexities of emotion, fastidiousness, possibly only to the free, may arise out of what used to be comfortable enough relations.

Of course, it is true that the suffrage movement arises from the ebullition of forces that were in the Middle Ages exhausted by the domestic activities of women. In economics we learn that, normally, every enterprise earns a surplus over the total cost of production. At different times this surplus is expended in different ways. In the Middle Ages it was used in the endowment of art, religion and charity. In this industrial period it is used to capitalise new enterprises; though there is discernible a reaction towards the endowment of art and science.

There is a similar surplus of spiritual and mental energy over and above the mere demands of earning a living in every normal human being. This surplus, too, is spent in different ways at different times.

There was little unspent in that busy time of the Middle Ages. To begin with, there was the bearing and rearing of large families; in that we must include the tragic expenditure of emotion entailed by the corresponding heavy infant mortality and, as Mr Titterton has said, there were the many activities of women – dairying, gardening, brewing, baking and so on – which she carried on with such enormous success.

Then the home was broken up, not, as Mr Titterton states with such sweet seriousness, through a lack of faith in the value of the home as a social unit, but because the woman was beaten, not by man, but by the specialised worker and the machine. They were much more competent than she was.

Brewing, for instance, was done more expensively and with less nutritive results in the home. The Irish Agricultural Organisation Society will not let the small farmers do their own dairying, but collects the milk and makes far better butter by the use of expensive machinery and specialised skill. Machinery may be ugly – indeed, it need not be so if we were wise – but it means the enrichment of life.

But Mr Titterton would have us throw overboard all the wonderful product of man's mechanistic genius in order to save himself from the emancipated woman. We lose time, we lose equality, if we go back to the old order. We give ourselves into the hands of material necessity. Dropping our ideas and our researches into wisdom, we shall go back and try to make our own furniture. There is no use pretending that it will be interesting. Mr Titterton will be horridly bored at having to make or, at least, wear home-made shoes.

Thus the use of the surplus energy of women, instead of enriching life as it did in the past, will positively impoverish it.

In any case, even if men are so afraid of women that they will risk even that, what are women to do in the long period while men are wiping out the industrialism they created but could not manage?

'Rocking her child asleep, she thinks how the flowers and the furniture should be arranged, what pattern of wallpaper would best become the room.' This would be very nice if it were not that it is bad for children to be rocked asleep, that flowers take anybody but an idiot ten minutes to arrange, and that one neither changes the furniture nor re-papers a room every day, or every week, or even every month. As a programme for the occupation of all adult women it lacks depth.

All this talk is unnecessary when women have so often, and so vehemently, told us the exact way in which they want to use their surplus energy. They wish to use it in the social service of the State. And this they think they can best perform by political action.

There is no doubt whatever that the long continued endeavour that is characteristic of women's work would be valuable in matters of government. Men are given to sudden, spasmodic bursts of energy preceded and succeeded by periods of inertia; and that explains the queer twists between reaction and revolution shown by Parliament. That steady labour that made England of the fifteenth century, her wealth produced by the domestic system, may yet build the splendid State, built of deliberate wisdom and the steady pursuit of ideas and ideals which we all see in our dreams.

Manchester Daily Dispatch, 23 January 1913

Hands That War

The Cordite Makers

The world was polished to brightness by an east wind when I visited the cordite factory, and shone with hard colours like a German toy-landscape. The marshes were very green and the scattered waters very blue, and little white clouds roamed one by one across the sky like grazing sheep on a meadow. On the hills around stood elms, and grey churches and red farms and yellow ricks, painted bright by the sharp sunshine. And very distinct on the marshes there lay the village which is always full of people, and yet is the home of nothing except death.

In the glare it showed that like so many institutions of the war it has the disordered and fantastic quality of a dream. It consists of a number of huts, some like the government-built cottages for Irish labourers, and some like the open-air shelters in a sanatorium, scattered over five hundred acres; they are connected by raised wooden gangways and interspersed with green mounds and rush ponds. It is of such vital importance to the State that it is ringed with barbed-wire entanglements and patrolled by sentries, and its products must have sent tens of thousands of our enemies to their death. And it is inhabited chiefly by pretty young girls clad in a Red-Riding-Hood fancy dress of khaki and scarlet.

Every morning at six, when the night mist still hangs over the marshes, 250 of these girls are fetched by a light railway from their barracks on a hill two miles away. When I visited the works they had already been at work for nine hours, and would work for three more. This twelve-hour shift is longer than one would wish, but it is not possible to introduce three shifts, since the girls would find an eight-hour day too light and would complain of being debarred from the opportunity of making more money; and it is not so bad as it sounds, for in these airy and isolated huts there is neither the orchestra of rattling machines nor the sense of a confined area crowded with tired people which make the ordinary factory such a fatiguing place. Indeed, these girls, working in teams of six or seven in those clean and tidy rooms, look as if they were practising a neat domestic craft rather than a deadly domestic process.

When one is made to put on rubber over-shoes before entering a hut it might be the precaution of a pernickety housewife concerned about her floors, although actually it is to prevent the grit on one's outdoor shoes igniting a stray scrap of cordite and sending oneself and the hut up to the skies in a column of flame. And there is something distinctly domestic in the character of almost every process. The girls who stand round the great drums in the hut with walls and floor awash look like millers in their caps and dresses of white waterproof, and the bags containing a white substance that lie in the dry ante-room might be sacks of flour. But, in fact, they are filling the drum with gun-cotton to be dried by hot air. And the next hut, where girls stand round great vats in which steel hands mix the gun-cotton with mineral jelly, might be part of a steam-bakery. The brown cordite paste itself looks as if it might turn into very pleasant honey-cakes; an inviting appearance that has brought gastritis to more than one unwise worker.

But how deceptive this semblance of normal life is; what extraordinary work this is for women and how extraordinarily they are doing it, is made manifest in a certain row of huts where the cordite is being pressed through wire mesh. This, in all the world, must be the place where war and grace are closest linked. Without, a strip of garden runs beside the huts, gay with shrubs and formal with a sundial. Within there is a group of girls that composes into so beautiful a picture that one remembers that the most glorious painting in the world, Velasquez's 'The Weavers', shows women working just like this.

One girl stands high on a platform against the wall, filling the cordite paste into one of the two great iron presses, and when she has finished with that she swings round the other one on a swivel with a fine free gesture. The other girls stand round the table laying out the golden cords in graduated sizes from the thickness of rope to the thinness of macaroni, the clear khaki and scarlet of their dresses shining back from the wet floor in a perpetually changing pattern as they move quickly about their work. They look very young in their pretty, childish dresses, and one thinks them good children for working so diligently. And it occurs to one as something incredible that they are now doing the last three hours of a twelve-hour shift.

If one asks the manager whether this zeal can possibly be normal, whether it is not perhaps the result of his presence, one is confronted by the awful phenomenon, beside which a waterspout or a volcano in eruption would be a little thing, of a manager talking about his employees with reverence. It seems that the girls work all day with a fury which mounts to a climax in the last three hours before the other 250 girls step into their places for the twelve-hour night shift. In these hours spies are sent out to walk along the verandah to see how the teams in the other huts are getting on, and their reports set the girls on to an orgy of competitive industry. Here again it was said that for attention, enthusiasm and discipline, there could not be better workmen than these girls.

There is matter connected with these huts, too, that showed the khaki and scarlet hoods to be no fancy dress, but a military uniform. They are a sign, for they have been dipped in a solution that makes them fireproof, that the girls are ready to face an emergency, which had arisen in those huts only a few days ago. There had been one of those incalculable happenings of which high explosives are so liable, an inflammatory mixture of air with acetone, and the cordite was ignited. Two huts were instantly gutted, and the girls had to walk out through the flame. In spite of the uniform one girl lost a hand. These, of course, are the everyday dangers of the high-explosives factory. There is very little to be feared from our enemies by land, and it is the sentries' grief and despair that their total bag for the eighteen months of their patrol of the marshes consists of one cow.

Surely, never before in modern history can women have lived a life so completely parallel to that of the regular Army. The girls who take up this work sacrifice almost as much as men who enlist; for although they make on an average 30s a week they are working much harder than most of them, particularly the large number who were formerly domestic servants, would ever have dreamed of working in peacetime. And, although their colony of wooden huts has been well planned by their employers, and is pleasantly administered by the Young Women's Christian Association, it is, so far as severance of home-ties goes, barrack life. For although they are allowed to go home for Sunday, travelling is difficult from this remote village, and the girls are so tired that most of them spend the day in bed.

And there are two things about the cordite village which the State ought never to forget, and which ought to be impressed upon the public mind by the bestowal of military rank upon the girls. First of all there is the cold fact that they face more danger every day than any soldier on home defence has seen since the beginning of the war. And secondly, there is the fact – and one wishes it could be expressed in terms of the saving of English and the losing of German life – that it is because of this army of cheerful and disciplined workers that this cordite factory has been able to increase its output since the beginning of the war by something over 1,500 per cent. It was all very well for the Army to demand high explosives, and for Mr Lloyd George to transmit the demand to industry; in the last resort the matter lay in the hands of the girls in the khaki and scarlet hoods, and the State owes them a very great debt for the way in which they have handled it.

Daily Chronicle, 1916

Hands That War

Welfare Work

Last week I went down to a munition works and found the manager uneasily digesting a leaflet which he had been sent by a certain government department. It was a production entirely characteristic of its signatory, a doctor who used to busy himself in peacetime at another government office trying to eliminate the infant mortality due to poverty by restricting the education of girls in elementary schools to instruction in baby-washing. But the manager was much too tired to see the fun of its request that he should build swimming-baths for his workers:

Swimming-baths! When I can hardly get the timber and the labour to run up new workshops! When we have to spend every penny on extensions of our business! And when my girls are so tired at the end of their twelve-hour shift that I can hardly get the lyddite workers to take their compulsory baths! And, anyway, how could I take on the organisation of anything more than I'm doing? If only people understood!

People certainly do not understand. To our generation, hypnotised by an interest in trade unionism into minimising the importance of the employer, any glimpse of the life of an armament manufacturer in wartime is a revelation. This manager was one of many who think themselves well off when they get five hours' sleep, and there is a certain man in England who saved a British Army by exertions which for eighteen months necessitated going to bed at two in the morning and getting up at six. And every minute of this long working-day is eaten up by hard mental work. The manager has all sorts of jobs to do: he has to organise the work so that all hands are kept busy, which is not an easy matter in such as the shell-making department, where the processes occupy different lengths of time; he has to alter his whole scheme when a cargo of American shells comes in and has to be filled up with explosives; since the routine of the buyer has completely broken down under war conditions he has to keep the factory fed with such diverse materials as coal and cambric, beeswax and Japanese silk; he has to search the country for carpenters and glaziers and builders, and set them to design; and he has to settle labour disputes.

'Well,' I said to the manager, 'you don't have much of that to do with the girls.'

'No,' he answered. 'My girls are as good as gold. I'm not saying that because they are cheap, for there isn't a girl here who gets less than 35s a week; nor because they're submissive, for they are as independent as the devil, but because they're patriotic, and turn out the stuff as fast as they can. But still, you know, they can't help being a lot of trouble.

'You see, there's getting them in the first place. It all takes time, hunting them out from the Labour Exchange, and looking them over to see which of them are the type that sticks. And then, when they are here, there's the question of their housing. I employed five hundred girls before the War, and now I employ two thousand; the extra fifteen hundred girls can't live in the treetops. Most of them have to lodge three miles away, in houses belonging to the foremen of —— Works, and they have to pay through the nose for the accommodation. It's shameful how these poor girls are swindled; sometimes they have to pay a guinea a week for a bedroom. So a hostel has to be built, and there's that to worry about. Then, there's putting up cloakrooms and lavatories, and getting charwomen to look after them. And there's the general difficulty of dealing with them. No man can understand the way a girl's mind works; one racks one's brains to select a thoroughly nice overlooker, and the minute the choice is announced they all go on strike for some absurd little reason that a man could never have foretold if he had thought until doomsday.

'But, thank Heaven,' he said, as he went into a building where 500 girls were having a midnight dinner of mutton and cabbage, 'these canteens are very largely off our hands. These ladies whom you see at the counter, making themselves unpopular at the moment by refusing to give the girls their tea absolutely black and to drench the pickles in crude vinegar, they run the whole show. Isn't it fine of them to come down here, an hour's journey from any decent lodgings, and stick at this deadly work? It means giving up all their normal social life and hanging about here either all day long or all night long, with dreary hours between the meals when there is nothing to do except paste labels on the glasses of home-made potted meat. I think they are splendid.'

'But are they,' I asked, 'entirely satisfactory? As satisfactory as you would expect one of your department heads to be?'

'Oh, no,' he said, 'for they are ladies, after all. And ladies don't understand how to handle subordinates. I get them lots of cooks, but they are always quarrelling with them and dismissing them for impertinence. I have to come over here nearly every day and smooth them down.' He sighed, and went on staunchly, 'But they are splendid.'

The Ministry of Munitions has grasped these difficulties, and has perceived that this work done by voluntary associations breaks down not because incompetence is a graceful feminine characteristic like smooth skin or the hairless lip, but because it is largely performed by women who have never known the discipline of wage-earning, who have never been obliged to study the psychology of their subordinates. So it has created its Welfare Supervision Department, and called in at its head Mr Seebohm Rowntree who, long ago, began to use the rich profits of the most popular luxury trades to lift from industry the guilt of devouring the lives of its workers. He works now with a staff of four inspectors who are all university women with relevant experience; one, for instance, who took a Moral Science Tripos from Newnham, has for six years held appointments on factory staffs in England and Scotland; and where they find that the employers have been unable to organise comfortable conditions for their women workers they advise the appointment of a woman supervisor. Here and there they find employers that have strayed out of the Stone Age, whose offices are like damp caves, where the light does not come, who govern by the club. But for the most part the employers gladly comply: 'Things are supposed to be all right in my shop, and the unions say they are quite satisfied,' said one employer. 'But that man over there is turning out eleven shells a day and the woman beside him is turning out thirty. I'll do anything for my women workers.'

So there is a new form of national service for women: the Welfare Supervisor, to accept full responsibility for the entire life of the women workers, except when they are actually at their machines. She engages them and learns to reject the type with kiss-curls and pink suede slippers, that would otherwise come only to leave in the evening of the third day. She has to be consulted before a girl is dismissed. She interviews any girl who wishes to leave, and finds out her reasons; so the firm that has been steadily losing its best workers comes to discover the secret drinking-club or the organised 'rag' that is at the root of the mischief. She investigates complaints; and so finds out, perhaps, that such-and-such a girl is being cheated over piecework or being annoyed by a foreman, and the firm consequently in danger of losing a steady worker. She helps the girls to get lodgings, and sees that they are not cheated. She assists in the selection of overlookers, which is a very delicate matter, owing to certain standards which cannot be laid down to mere female contrariness, since it is a matter of fact that a certain Welsh colliery went on strike because the manager's typist, a girl of flawless virtue, wore openwork stockings; she is careful not to choose anybody who has made herself unpopular by 'pinching another girl's "bloke"'. And she supervises the canteens; and since it has been found that the health of the workers depends hardly at all on whether they work eight or twelve hours a day, but very much on the quality and quantity of the food they eat, this work is of the greatest importance.

These women are among the comfortingly significant features that emerge from the purposeless welter of war. They are assets to England, they introduce reason and sympathy into the snarling colloquy of labour and capital; and they mark that industry has at last recognised that women have brains as well as hands.

Daily Chronicle, 1916

Hands That War
The Night Shift

The American woman journalist with whom I travelled down to the munition works looked out of the window of the car at one of the new beauties, stranger than starlight, which wartime has given the night; a mild beam lay athwart the western sky, with little misty moons running hither and thither beneath it. She exclaimed at the calm beauty of it, and went on to wonder at the serenity with which London lay under these perilous skies. She, who had lived on the edge of an Indian reservation, when fights were more frequent than showers, had felt her first moment of panic when she had seen a Zeppelin overhead and thought it the most miraculous thing in the world that we could bear up under this menace night after night. 'But I suppose,' she said, 'that one gets used to living on one's head.'

That, indeed, is the chief duty of the civil population in wartime; to get used to living on one's head. There were two thousand people in the factory which was the end of our journey who were practising that difficult art. It had been carried to a high pitch by the manager and his son, who assured us that it did not matter at all that they had expected us the previous night and had waited up till three in the morning, because they often stayed up as late as that although they had to be down at the works again at eight. Indeed, they sometimes stayed up the whole night and did thirty-six hours at a stretch. Such things have to be done when one is increasing one's output by five hundred per cent, and trying to force it up still further, employing four times as much labour, and putting up new shops as fast as one can get the necessary timber and labour. One has to spend one's physical capital as recklessly as one has to spend one's financial capital on these extensions of business. And the chief consolation of this unquiet life is that in the square mile of works behind the offices there is an army of workers who, although they come of a sex and a class who owe England little for benefits received, are ready to match sacrifice for sacrifice with their employers.

They cannot be beaten at the art of living on their heads. These girls work with a passionate diligence which one can only realise when one hears that in a certain shop four of them, who have been at work for only a few months, produce a larger output than four men who have been trained to this process for six years. And they stick to their work, each girl doing day shift one week and night shift the next, with a discipline to which their splendid timekeeping records bear witness. Here one had come to holy ground, where patriotism was not an excuse for grumbling at the Government, but an inspiration for hard thinking and hard working.

When we stepped out of the office into the discreetly darkened factory field, it presented, like so many high explosive works, a delusive appearance of rusticity. The wooden gangway went between trees and over running water; there was a sweet night smell coming up from the long, wet meadow grass, and as one passed the sheds one expected to hear from within the stir and heavy breath of sleeping cattle. But the trees had been planted to check the course of explosions; the water ran yellow from the lyddite shops; the sweet night smell was dispersed by puffs of thick-scented steam; and when the manager turned on the switch at the door of the shed, one looked in on stacks of bright shells, waiting there till they might be sent off to deliver in some far country their message of death. And as one went on there appeared more and more manifestations that the darkness was full of many people placidly busy about the world's present purpose of self-destruction.

Here an arch shot out light and fumes into the blackness, as though it were the door of a brightly lit chapel where incense was burning. But within there was a little room where two girls passed slowly along rows of empty shells ranged on the floor, one pouring in the orange fluid lyddite, the other thrusting in a rod and bidding her stop when the lyddite solidified round it for an inch from the bottom; and who filled the shell up to the top, when the lyddite had set into a jelly, with a mixture of beeswax, resin and tallow, called 'kitty'. In another shop one found women taking long hanks of cordite, the fine golden strands tied together with thread, so that they looked like switches of false hair, and winding them into charges on bright brass wheels cut in the shape of a wild rose. In yet another there was a great circle of women sitting at sewing-machines, making covers for these charges out of the fine cambric that is used for expensive baby-frocks, and turning gleaming sheets of Japanese silk into sachets, for gun-cotton. Further we came to the point where two long corridors partitioned into cells met at right angles; from two long perspectives came the constant hammering of the filling of cartridges with cordite, which was fed into the cells from a great spool kept for safety's sake outside the building in corrugated-iron sheds. And through that noise there floated, until the presence of the 'boss' was noticed, the strains of 'All Dressed Up and Nowhere to Go'.

That song was one sign of the magnificent levity of the girls, and their splendid indifference to the fact that they were not quite half through the twelve-hour night shift, and that when they were done they would have to sleep through the sunshine in dingy lodgings for which they were grossly overcharged. But it was in the room where they fill the detonators with fulminate of mercury that one fully realised the gallant quality of these human beings that wave their hair-ribbons over high explosives; the grey dust that lay on the bench in one of these huts was enough to raze great towns to the ground. It ignites for quite frivolous reasons; the windows of these rooms are hooded with wire netting, because one day a similar shop in Scotland went up in flames the moment after a robin flew in and pecked at the dust. It stands to reason that, although the women in these works are guarded by every possible device, even in some processes shutting a door between themselves and their machine while it is at work, this stuff, which is more savage than any animal, breaks out. The manager, very sadly, for he regarded his factory with the passion of an artist for his created work, and felt an injury to his workers as a personal disgrace, gave a melancholy list. Two hands, two feet, two eyes and minor injuries. This way of living on one's head means not only sweating the energy out of one's body and turning night into day, but also the risk of mutilation and death.

As the midnight hooter sounded and the workers rushed out to the canteen, dispersing the stillness of the night with the high, delighted yawn of the released factory girl, one perceived that these were not picked women, but just the common stuff of humanity rising to the occasion. And as the night wore on to morning, and the manager still led us through hut after hut, where women sat very still, their whole life concentrated in their leaping hands, until the lights danced before our eyes, he told us many stories, showing just how ordinary these girls were.

'A few days ago,' he told us, 'I came in and found a girl sitting with a grumpy face, and I said to her, "Now what's the matter with you?" She said to me, "It's those girls over there keep plaguing me so." So I said, "That's too bad. But what are they doing to you?" "Why," she said, "they keep on throwing the detonators at me!"'

He laughed, and shuddered at the thought of what might have happened, and went on to enunciate the great truth that girls are queer. 'There's a shop where they keep on dropping cartridge-caps on the floor, and it was so dark you couldn't help treading on them. So I had windows put in all along the dado, so that you could see where you were going. Now what do you think they say I did that for? So that the foreman and I can see their ankles!' Of such queer Cockney stuff is the army of women, who with a royal lavishness give up the night to industry for the sake of far-off men; who sometimes give in the darkness much more than that. Two hands, two feet, two eyes . . .

Daily Chronicle, 1916

Socialism in the Searchlight

Since I am a socialist, the war has brought but few surprises to me except its vastness and its cruelty. No one knew better than English socialists that in the German Empire was a people rotten with militarism and ripe for war, so frequently had German socialists announced at socialist and trade union congresses that they had not the slightest intention of lifting their little fingers to avert any war declared by their Fatherland. And that Englishmen have formed themselves into an army that lives gallantly through the worst horrors that have yet vexed this earth and triumphs over death by magnificent dying, is no surprise to socialists. For it has always been our faith that the people are capable of every sort of splendid living, and that in consequence not one of them should be allowed to be thwarted and maimed by poverty. Nor is it a surprise to socialists that when the State was in a tight place it had immediately to resort to socialism and take over the railways and many of the important means of production.

And not at all is it a surprise that this resort to socialism has been so foolishly negotiated in a great many cases; as it has been, for instance, in the case of the railway companies who, since they have had their normal profits guaranteed by the Government, find it to their interest to make travelling as uncomfortable as possible for the civil passenger. We expected it to be so, for by the capitalist system England has squandered half the brains of which it has such need in this crisis.

If we had a socialist State guaranteeing every baby the food and clothing necessary for its healthy development and every child an education suited to its natural gifts, England would have a much larger number of people of proven ability from whom to select her administrators. As it is we have to choose our governors from conspicuous members of the small upper and middle classes with the uneasy consciousness that under the capitalist system conspicuousness can be purchased.

So far the war has confirmed me in socialism.

But there have been moments since the beginning of the war which have made me doubt whether the socialist campaign, particularly as it was manifested in trade unionism, had not developed prematurely. The trade unions showed that they did not understand that it might be as necessary to protect themselves from aggressive persons of another nation as well as of another class. They revealed themselves devoid of chivalry; there was an utter lack of concern for the plight of Belgium. They appeared to think that the working class could justify its existence by being as tiresomely obstructive as possible to all national business. They did not counter the folly of their rulers by being wiser but by being more foolish.

When Mr Lloyd George made the disastrous error of going up to Scotland with Lord Murray of Elibank as his 'labour adviser', the Clyde workers proved themselves almost deserving of such tactless treatment by 'ragging' him at his meetings like silly schoolboys.

But these are merely the inevitable disharmonies of any great constructive movement.

At the building of the most beautiful bridge in the world there has to be a lot of harsh scaffolding, unsightly huts run up for the navvies, noise of hammers and cranes. And trade unionism is one of the bridges by which Britain is passing over the turmoil of war into peace. If trade unionism had not fought for higher wages and better conditions you would not have your British Army today.

Wellington had to fight with men who had joined the Army because the poverty of the English proletariat was a worse horror than war, and he complained bitterly that their courage was frequently cancelled by their vices. They broke and scattered, as may be read in *The Dynasts*, in the Peninsular War, and it is certain they could hardly have withstood the heavier strain of this war. For the life in the trenches, and for the grinding work of our munition works, we require the men the trade unions have made for us; disciplined and made bright-witted by the free education the individualists fought against, physically nourished and made confident that England is worth fighting for by the high wages and better conditions that trade unionism had obtained.

That is one opinion which remains unchanged.

Another matter on which no sane person has had to change his or her opinion is feminism. It is enough to make any feminist dance with rage to hear the continual exclamations of surprise at the fact that women can do practically everything. We told you so again and again, and you would not believe it. When England's Worst Woman

Novelist and a bevy of peeresses signed manifestos to say they were not conscious of having any capacity, you wagged your heads and said that of course woman's place was the home.

But are you conscious of what you owe to the suffragettes?

I admit that the silly campaign of arson and violence which was in full swing at the beginning of the war, must have contributed to the effect of lawlessness which made Germany think it a propitious moment for the outbreak of hostilities. I admit that one bows one's head with shame when one hears of former officials of the Women's Social and Political Union mobbing Lord Haldane with idiot cries of treachery. But if the suffragettes and suffragists had not conducted their campaign there would not have been the vast and willing army of women which is taking men's places all over the country.

The very rough-and-tumble of the movement had its merits; in Palace Yard or at the street corners they acquired a courage which now they use in the service of their country.

The story of the work of the Scottish Suffrage Societies' hospital in Serbia and Rumania is immortal. The biggest factory in France which supplies an article most necessary to our armies is under the sole charge of a woman under thirty, who was formerly a suffrage organiser. One could cite many such cases. And one doubts that women would have gone into the dangerous high explosive factories, the engineering shops and the fields, and worked with quite such fidelity and enthusiasm if it had not been so vigorously affirmed by the suffragists in the last few years that women ought to be independent and courageous and capable.

The uniformity with which all socialist movements have turned to the benefit of England in her hour of crisis is the cause of the only change of opinion socialists have had any reason to know. Before the war we were sometimes vexed by faint doubts as to whether ours was a faith that could be put into practice only in peacetime. There seemed just a possibility that under the strain of war some new sanction for the capitalist system might appear.

We can now change our opinions as to the likelihood of that appearance.

Daily Chronicle, 6 November 1916

Index